Fundamentals of
Biological Anthropology

John H. Relethford
State University of New York
College at Oneonta

Mayfield Publishing Company
Mountain View, California
London • Toronto

Library of Congress Cataloging-in-Publication Data
Relethford, John.
    [Human species]
    Fundamentals of biological anthropology / John H. Relethford.
    p. cm.
    An abridgement of: The human species. 2nd ed. 1993.
    Includes bibliographical references and index.
    ISBN 1-55934-280-3
    1. Physical anthropology. I. Title.
GN60.R392 1994
573—dc20   93-28692
                                                            CIP

Manufactured in the United States of America

10 9 8 7 6 5 4 3 2

Mayfield Publishing Company
1280 Villa Street
Mountain View, California 94041

Sponsoring editor, Janet M. Beatty; production editor, Lynn Rabin Bauer;
manuscript editor, Lauren Root; text designer, Al Burkhardt; cover photograph:
Evans and Sutherland, courtesy Monica Suder and Associates Library; art editor,
Susan Breitbard; illustrators, Barbara Barnett, Susan Breitbard, Joan Carol, Marilyn
Kreiger, Leonard Morgan, and Alan Noyes; manufacturing manager, Martha Branch.
The text was set in 10/12 Galliard by Thompson Type and printed on 50# Somerset
Matte by Arcata Graphics.

Preface

This text is an abridged and slightly rewritten version of the second edition of my text *The Human Species: An Introduction to Biological Anthropology.* Why a brief version of a textbook? No single textbook can accommodate perfectly all the different ways in which an introductory course in biological/physical anthropology is taught. Instructors vary in terms of their interests, use of supplemental readings, and allotted time for their courses. This text will serve several audiences for which the larger version might not be appropriate. First, a shorter text is more useful for those teaching on a quarter system, or a summer session, as opposed to a 15-week semester. Second, some instructors like having supplemental readings, and a shorter text suits this arrangement. Third, some instructors like texts with less detail than traditional introductory books—this text fills this need. Fourth, the shorter length of the book makes it more useful in general anthropology or archaeology/physical anthropology courses. Fifth, some instructors may prefer a slightly different organizational structure. This text differs slightly in organization from the larger edition by including the material on human biology and culture in a single chapter placed with other chapters on human variation.

Organization

As its title indicates, *Fundamentals of Biological Anthropology* provides a basic introduction to the field of biological anthropology (also known as physical anthropology), which deals with the biological aspects of human origins, evolution, and variation. As such, biological anthropology is an evolutionary science. Though biological anthropology focuses on the *biological* aspects of the human species, it also deals extensively with the *cultural* dimensions of humanity, emphasizing the interrelationship between biology and culture.

The first three chapters of the book provide some essential evolutionary background. Chapter 1 introduces the field of anthropology in general, and biological anthropology specifically, and also looks at the nature of evolutionary theory. Chapter 2 covers the basic principles of human genetics. Chapter 3, which examines evolutionary theory in more detail, discusses microevolution (population genetics) and macroevolution (especially the origin of species).

The next three chapters explore the nature of human biological variation. Chapter 4 furnishes case studies of human microevolution, particularly gene flow, genetic drift, and natural selection. Chapter 5 contrasts the microevolutionary approach to human variation with the dated, but still popular, racial approach to variation, using skin color and IQ test scores as examples. The importance of the relationship of human biology and culture is emphasized in Chapter 6, which presents brief reviews and case studies from the fields of human growth, human adaptation, human health and disease (biomedical anthropology), and demography.

In comparing humans to other living creatures, the next two chapters focus on variation in a wider perspective. Chapter 7 examines the taxonomy and behavior of mammals and primates, with particular emphasis on comparison with humans. Chapter 8 focuses on apes and humans, specifically on their biological and behavioral similarities and differences.

The final three chapters deal with the fossil record of human evolution. Chapter 9 reviews some basic methods of paleontology, surveys the history of life prior to the emergence of primates, and concludes with evidence and discussion of the origin and evolution of the primates. Chapter 10 deals with the first hominids—*Australopithecus* and *Homo habilis*—and explains major evolutionary trends. Chapter 11, which concludes the review of human evolution, examines the evolution of *Homo erectus,* archaic *Homo sapiens,* and anatomically modern *Homo sapiens.*

Features

• *All areas of contemporary biological anthropology are covered.* Many traditional texts in this field cover the basics of evolution and genetics, primate studies, the fossil record for human evolution, and selected studies of human variation. This text provides a more balanced treatment of the field of biological anthropology, including material on subjects often neglected. Topics of special concern are human growth, health and disease, and demography.

• *The relationship of human biology and culture is a major focus.* The biocultural framework is introduced in the first chapter and integrated throughout the text. Chapter 6 is entirely devoted to biocultural issues—growth, adaptation, health and disease, and demography—that are often omitted from many introductory texts.

• *A review of cell biology occurs early in the text.* For many, the basic genetics they learned in a high school biology class is but a dim memory. To help underprepared students better understand the basics, I include this review at the end of Chapter 2. Full-color illustrations depict the processes of mitosis and meiosis clearly and vividly.

• *Behavior is discussed in an evolutionary context.* I have not devoted separate chapters to primate behavior or the archaeology of early humans because I believe that such material must be covered along with biological evolution. Thus, I include discussions that integrate biology and behavior, including those on genetics and IQ (Chapter 2); inbreeding (Chapter 3); migration, marriage systems, and social structure (Chapter 4), race and intelligence (Chapter 5); culture change and human biology (Chapter 6); primate behavior (Chapters 7 and 8); and the behavior of early humans (Chapters 10 and 11).

• *Hypothesis testing is emphasized.* From the first chapter, where the students are introduced to the scientific method, I emphasize *how* various hypotheses are tested. Rather than provide a dogmatic approach with all the "right" answers, this text examines evidence about human variation and evolution in the context of hypothesis testing.

Study Helps

To make this text more accessible, I have kept technical jargon to a minimum; yet every introductory text contains a number of specialized terms that students must learn. The first mention of these terms appears in **boldface** type, and accompanying short definitions appear in the text margins. A glossary is provided at the end of the book, often providing more detailed definitions.

Each chapter ends with a summary and a list of supplemental readings. The summaries put each chapter's material in more general terms and help students relate the content to other chapters. The supplemental readings are included for those who wish to look further into a given topic, either for clarification or to satisfy an awakened curiosity. A list of references appears at the end of the book, providing the complete reference for studies cited in the text.

Ancillaries

The *Instructor's Manual* includes a test bank as well as chapter overviews and outlines, topics for class discussions, and sources for laboratory equipment.

A *Computerized Test Bank* is available free of charge to qualifying adopters. It is a powerful, easy-to-use test generation system that provides all test items on computer disk for IBM-compatible and Macintosh computers. Instructors can select, add, or edit questions, randomize them, and print tests appropriate for their individual classes. The system also includes a convenient "gradebook" that enables the instructor to keep detailed performance records for individual students and for the entire class; maintain student averages; graph each student's progress; and set the desired grade distribution, maximum score, and weight for every test.

Acknowledgments

My thanks go to the dedicated and hardworking people at Mayfield, both those I have dealt with personally and the others behind the scenes. I give special thanks to Jan Beatty, sponsoring editor, for continued encouragement and support. I am also extremely grateful to Lynn Rabin Bauer, production editor, for her hard work, dedication, and patience. Pamela Trainer, permissions editor, has also been a great help.

I also thank my colleagues who reviewed part or all of the second edition of *The Human Species,* and whose ideas I have tried to carry over into this abridged version: Helen L. Ball, University of Massachusetts; Douglas E. Crews, Ohio State University; Janis Hutchinson, University of Houston; Lyle Konigsberg, University of Tennessee; Paul Sciulli, Ohio State University; Mark Stoneking, Pennsylvania State University; Alan Swedlund, University of Massachusetts; Jane Underwood, University of Arizona; and Dennis van Gerven, University of Colorado. Having been a reviewer myself, I appreciate the extensive time and effort these individuals have taken.

This one's dedicated to my in-laws, George and Terry Adler, and, as always, to my wife Hollie Jaffe and my beautiful boys—David, Benjamin, and Zane.

Contents

CHAPTER 8   # Apes and Humans   176

CHAPTER 9   # The Origin and Evolution of the Primates   207

CHAPTER **1**

The Study of Biological Anthropology

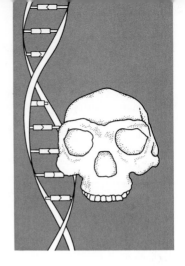

What is anthropology? To many people, it is the study of the exotic extremes of human nature. To others, it is the study of ancient ruins and lost civilizations. The study of anthropology seems strange to many, and the practitioners of this field, the anthropologists, seem even stranger. The stereotype of an anthropologist is a pith-helmeted, pipe-smoking eccentric tracking chimpanzees through the forest, digging up the bones of million-year-old ancestors, interviewing lost tribes about their sexual customs, and recording the words of the last speakers of a language. Another popular image presented in the media is Indiana Jones, the intrepid archaeologist of the film *Raiders of the Lost Ark*. Here is a man who is versed in the customs and languages of many societies past and present, feels at home anywhere in the world, and makes a living teaching, finding lost treasures, rescuing beautiful women in distress, and fighting Nazis (Figure 1.1).

Of course, Indiana Jones is a fictional character. Some real-life anthropologists are almost as well known, such as Jane Goodall, Margaret Mead, Donald Johanson, and the late Dian Fossey. These anthropologists have studied chimpanzees, Samoan culture, the fossils of human ancestors, and gorillas. Their research conjures up images of anthropology every bit as varied as the imaginary adventures of Indiana Jones. Anthropologists do study all these things, and more. The sheer diversity of topics investigated by anthropologists seems almost to defy any sort of logic. The methods of data collection and analysis are almost as diverse. What pulls these different subjects together?

1

anthropology The science that investigates human biological and cultural variation and evolution.

culture Behavior that is learned and socially transmitted.

In one obvious sense, they all share an interest in the same subject—human beings. In fact, the traditional textbook definition of anthropology is the "study of humans." Though this definition is easy to remember, it is not terribly useful. After all, scientists in other fields, such as researchers in anatomy and biochemistry, also study humans. And there are many fields within the social sciences whose sole interest is humans. History, geography, political science, economics, sociology, and psychology are all devoted to the study of human beings, and no one would argue that these fields are merely branches of anthropology.

What Is Anthropology?

What, then, is a suitable definition of anthropology? **Anthropology** could be described as the science of human cultural and biological variation and evolution. The first part of this definition includes both human culture and biology. **Culture** is learned behavior. Culture includes social and economic systems, marriage customs, religion, philosophy, and all other behaviors that are acquired through the process of learning rather than being instinctual. The joint emphasis on culture and biology is an important feature of anthropology, and one that sets it apart from many other fields.

Biology and Culture

To the anthropologist, humans must be understood in terms of learned behavior as well as biology. We rely extensively on learned behaviors in virtually all aspects of our life. Even the expression of our sexual drives must be understood in light of human cultural systems. Although the actual basis of our sex drive is biological, the ways in which we express it are shaped by behaviors we have learned. The very inventiveness of humans, with our vast technology, is testimony to the powerful effect of learning. On the other hand, however, we are not purely cultural creatures. We are also biological organisms. We need to eat and breathe, and we are affected by our external environment. In addition, our biology sets certain limits on our potential behaviors. For example, all human cultures have some type of social structure that provides for the care of children until they are old enough to fend for themselves. This is not simply kindness to children; our biological position as mammals requires such attentiveness to children for survival. In contrast with other animal species, whose infants need little or no care, human infants are physically incapable of taking care of themselves.

Anthropology is concerned not only with culture and biology, but also with their interaction. Just as humans are not solely cultural or solely biological, we are not simply the sum of these two, either. Humans are

Figure 1.1

Indiana Jones, the fictional archaeologist who serves as many people's model for an anthropologist.   (Eva Sereny, © Lucasfilm Ltd. [LFL] 1984. All Rights Reserved)

biocultural organisms, which means that our culture and biology influence each other. The **biocultural approach** to studying human beings is the main theme of this book, and you will examine many examples of biocultural interaction.

The biocultural perspective of anthropology points to one of the unique strengths of anthropology as a science: it is **holistic,** meaning that it takes into consideration all aspects of human existence. Population growth provides an example. Where the sociologist may be concerned with effects of population growth on social structure and the psychologist may be concerned with effects of population growth on psychological stress, the anthropologist is interested potentially in all aspects of population growth. In a given study, this analysis may include the relationship among diet, fertility, religion, disease, social systems, nutrition, and political systems, to name but a few factors.

Variation

A major characteristic of anthropology is its concern with **variation.** In a general sense, variation refers to differences among individuals or populations. The anthropologist is interested in differences and similarities among human groups, in terms of both biology and culture. Anthropologists use the **comparative approach** to attempt to generalize about those aspects of human behavior and biology that are similar in all populations and those that are unique to specific environments and cultures. How do groups of people differ from one another? *Why* do they differ? These are questions about variation, and they apply equally to cultural and biological traits (Figure 1.2).

Evolution

Evolution is change in living organisms over generations. Both cultural and biological evolution interest anthropologists. How and why do human culture and biology change? For example, anthropologists may be interested in the origin of marriage systems. When, how, and why did certain marriage systems evolve? For that matter, when did the custom of marriage first originate, and why? Another example is skin color. An anthropologist would be interested in what skin color the first humans may have had, and where, when, how, and why other skin colors may have evolved.

Adaptation

In addition to the concepts of variation and evolution, the anthropologist is interested in the process of **adaptation.** At the broadest level, adaptations are advantageous changes. Any aspect of biology or behavior that confers some advantage on an individual or population can be considered an adaptation. Cultural adaptations include technological devices

biocultural approach Studying humans in terms of the interaction between biology and culture in evolutionary adaptation.

holistic Integrating all aspects of existence in understanding human variation and evolution.

variation The differences that exist between individuals or populations.

comparative approach Comparing human populations to determine common and unique behaviors or biological traits.

evolution Change in populations of organisms from one generation to the next.

adaptation The process of successful interaction between a population and an environment.

Figure 1.2

Biological variation in a group of children.   (© Peter Menzel/Stock Boston)

such as clothing, shelter, and methods of food production. Such technologies can improve the well-being of humans. Cultural adaptations also include social systems and rules for behaviors. For example, the belief in certain societies that sexual relations with a woman must be avoided for some time after she gives birth can be adaptive in the sense that these behaviors influence the rate of population growth.

Adaptations can also be biological. Some biological adaptations are physiological in nature and involve metabolic changes. For example, when you are too hot, you will sweat. Sweating is a short-term physiological response that removes excess heat through the process of evaporation. Within limits, it aids in maintaining a constant body temperature. Likewise, shivering is an adaptive response to cold. The act of shivering increases metabolic rate and provides more heat.

Biological adaptations can also be genetic in nature. Here, changes in genes over many generations produce variation in biological traits. The darker skin color of many humans native to regions near the equator is one example of a long-term genetic adaptation. The darker skin provides protection from the harmful effects of ultraviolet radiation (see Chapter 5 for more information on skin color and variation).

The Subfields of Anthropology

In a general sense, anthropology is concerned with determining what humans are, how they evolved, and how they differ from one another. Where other disciplines focus on specific issues of humanity, anthropology is unique in dealing simultaneously with questions of origins, evolution, variation, and adaptation.

Even though anthropology has a wide scope that appears to encompass anything and everything pertaining to humans, the study of anthropology in the United States is often characterized by four separate subfields, each with a specific focus. These four subfields are cultural anthropology, anthropological archaeology, linguistic anthropology, and biological anthropology.

Cultural anthropology. **Cultural anthropology** deals primarily with variation in the cultures of populations in the present or recent past. Its subjects include social, political, economic, and ideological aspects of human cultures. Cultural anthropologists look at all aspects of behavior within a society. Even when they are interested in a specific aspect of a culture, such as marriage systems, they look at how these behaviors relate to all other aspects of culture. Marriage systems, for example, may have an effect on the system of inheritance and may also be closely related to religious views. Comparison of cultures is used to determine common and unique features among different cultures. Information from this subfield will be presented later in the book to aid in the interpretation of the relationship between human culture and biology.

Anthropological archaeology. Archaeology is the study of cultural behaviors in the historic and prehistoric past. **Anthropological archaeology** uses the methods of archaeology to infer the behaviors of past societies. The archaeologist deals with such remains of past societies as tools, shelters, remains of animals eaten for food, and other objects that have survived. These remains, termed *artifacts,* are used to reconstruct past behavior. To help fill in the gaps, the archaeologist makes use of the findings of cultural anthropologists who have studied similar societies.

cultural anthropology Focuses on variations in cultural behaviors among human populations.

anthropological archaeology Focuses on cultural variation in prehistoric (and some historic) populations by analyzing the culture's remains.

linguistic anthropology
Focuses on the nature of human language, the relationship of language to culture, and the languages of nonliterate peoples.

biological anthropology
Focuses on the biological evolution of humans and human ancestors, the relationship of humans to other organisms, and patterns of biological variation within and among human populations. Also referred to as physical anthropology.

Archaeological findings are critical in understanding the behavior of early humans and their evolution. Some of these findings for the earliest humans are presented later in this text.

Linguistic anthropology. **Linguistic anthropology** is the study of language. Spoken language is a behavior that appears to be uniquely human. This subfield of anthropology deals with the analysis of languages usually in nonliterate societies and with general trends in the evolution of languages. A major question raised by linguistic anthropology concerns the extent to which language shapes culture. Is language necessary for the transmission of culture? Does a language provide information about the beliefs and practices of a human culture?

Biological anthropology must consider many of the findings of linguistic anthropology in the analysis of human variation and evolution. When comparing humans and apes, we must ask whether language is a unique human characteristic. If it is, then what biological and behavioral differences exist between apes and humans that lead to the fact that one species has language and the other lacks it? Linguistics is also important in considering human evolution. When did language begin? Why?

Biological anthropology. The subject of this book is the subfield of **biological anthropology,** which is concerned with the biological evolution and variation of the human species, past and present. Biological anthropology is often referred to by another name—*physical anthropology.* The course you are currently enrolled in might be known by either name. Actually, the two names refer to the same field. Early in the twentieth century the field was first known as physical anthropology, reflecting its then primary interest in the *physical* variation of past and present humans and our primate relatives. Much of the research in the field focused on descriptive studies of physical variations with little theoretical background. Starting in the 1950s, physical anthropologists became more familiar with the rapidly growing fields of genetics and evolutionary science. As a result, the field of physical anthropology became more concerned with biological processes, particularly with genetics. After a while, many in the field began using the term *biological anthropology* to emphasize the new focus on biological processes. In most circles today, the two terms are used more or less interchangeably.

There are several traditionally defined areas within biological anthropology, such as primate studies, paleoanthropology, and human variation. Primate studies are concerned with defining humans in the natural world, specifically in terms of the primates (a group of mammals that includes prosimians, monkeys, apes, and humans). Primate studies look at the anatomy, behavior, and evolution of the primates as a standard of comparison with those aspects of humans. In this way, we can learn something about what it is to be human.

Paleoanthropology is the study of the fossil remains of human evolution. Researchers in this field are interested in determining who our ancestors were, and when, how, and why they evolved. Paleoanthropologists work closely with archaeologists to reconstruct the behaviors of our ancestors.

The study of human variation is concerned with how and why humans differ from each other in their biological makeup. This subfield considers the ways in which culture and biology interact in the modern world, including such topics as the genetics of populations, demography (the study of population size and composition), physical growth and development, and human health and disease. Several decades ago, human variation was the concern of only a few biological anthropologists. Today it is perhaps the largest research area within biological anthropology.

Figure 1.3 shows three biological anthropologists in the midst of their research. Barbara Smuts is an associate professor of anthropology and psychology at the University of Michigan. Much of her research has focused on the behavior of baboons, particularly the social relationships between mothers and daughters. She is currently involved in two new projects, one of which is a study of olive baboons in Africa that will examine social relationships among adults. She plans to study these groups for periods of 4 to 5 months repeatedly over several years. Dr. Smuts is also investigating infant development and mother-infant relationships among wild bottlenose dolphins in Australia. This work is interdisciplinary, involving collaboration with biologists and psychologists.

Henry McHenry is a professor of anthropology at the University of California at Davis whose primary research interest is in the field of paleoanthropology. Figure 1.3 shows him measuring and comparing skulls of early *Homo sapiens* from Africa, dated more than 200,000 years ago. Dr. McHenry's research focuses specifically on estimating body size of early humans from their skeletal remains. By comparing these estimates with living humans and other primates, he is able to make inferences on a wide variety of topics, including sex differences in body size, variations in relative brain size, and many other aspects of ecology and social behavior.

An associate professor of anthropology at Emory University in Atlanta, Georgia, Carol Worthman is also director of the Laboratory for Comparative Human Biology at Emory. At present, the laboratory is conducting research on human populations in Papua New Guinea, South America, Tibet, Outer Mongolia, and the United States. Using a variety of hormone measures obtained from blood, urine, and saliva, Dr. Worthman explores a wide range of interrelationships between biology and culture. Her current research includes looking at causes of late maturation in traditional societies, the effects of social practices (such as nursing) on reproductive function and fertility, and reasons for sex differences in rates of depression and conduct disorder.

This book examines the range of fields within modern biological anthropology. It is not, however, organized around these fields but rather

Figure 1.3

Barbara Smuts (University of Michigan) sits among the olive baboons she studies in Kenya; Henry McHenry (University of California, Davis) compares archaic and modern African *Homo sapiens* skulls; Carol Worthman (Emory University) analyzes data in the university laboratory. (Courtesy of Barbara Smuts; Henry McHenry, photo by Dr. C. K. Brain; and Carol Worthman)

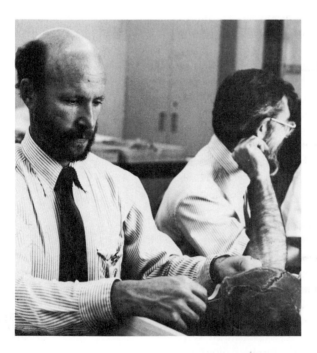

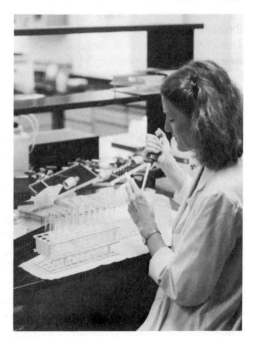

around a set of basic questions that biological anthropology seeks to answer. The first question, on which the other questions rest, is: *What is evolution?* How do populations change over time? What is the relationship between genetics and evolution? How does evolution produce variation within species and differences among species? And what is the evidence for evolution? We take up these basic questions later in this chapter and in the following two chapters.

The second question relates to the similarities and differences among living human beings: *How and why do humans vary?* With the exception of identical twins, each of us is biologically unique. We also all have basic similarities, however. Some of our differences are clearly visible; some people are dark and some are light, some are tall and some are short, some have long noses and some have short noses. In spite of these differences, all forms of living humans share a great many traits. We all have the same basic anatomy, the same number of limbs, and so on. Other similarities and differences are less apparent but nonetheless important. Some people have certain blood types, some have resistance to certain diseases, and so on. In looking at human variation, we must focus on how and why we vary. We can answer these questions by examining the ongoing evolution of human populations, discussed in Chapters 4–6. Besides providing background in human variation, these chapters expand on the mechanisms of evolution by providing many examples of recent or present-day evolutionary changes in human populations.

The third question is: *What are humans?* Specifically, what is unique about the biology of humans, and what do we share with other animals? That is, what is our place in the natural world? Where do we fit in? Who are our closest living relatives? It is obvious that we share certain traits with many different creatures. Humans and other mammals, along with birds, fish, and reptiles, all have an internal spinal column. Both humans and dogs have four limbs. There are also many differences. Humans have much larger brains than dogs or cats or tropical fish. Humans have small canine teeth. Why do these similarities and differences exist, and what do they mean? These basic questions all make up the scientific study of the larger question, "What are humans?" Chapters 7 and 8 deal with the classification of living organisms and our relationship to other animals, mammals, and primates.

The fourth question is: *How have humans evolved?* We are interested in determining who our ancestors were, where they came from, and why they evolved. We look at the differences between humans and other creatures to try to determine what has changed. By analyzing the fossil record we attempt to determine how and why these changes have occurred. The study of human evolution seeks to answer questions such as: When and why did humans evolve their large brains? When and why did humans start walking on two legs? When was fire first used to cook food? What did the first stone tools look like, and how were they used? We address these questions in Chapters 9–11.

hypothesis An explanation of observed facts.

Science and Evolution

Biological anthropology is an evolutionary science. All the major questions just presented may be addressed using modern evolutionary theory. Biological evolution simply refers to change in the genetic makeup of populations over time.

Characteristics of Science

Before we consider how evolution works, it is important to understand exactly what a science is.

Facts. At one time or another, you have probably heard someone make the statement that evolution is a theory, not a fact. Or you might have heard that it is a fact, not a theory. Which is it, theory or fact? The truth of the matter is that someone who makes either of these statements does not understand what a theory or a fact is. Evolution is both fact and theory. A fact is simply a verifiable truth. It is a fact that the earth is round. It is a fact that when you drop something, it falls to the ground. Evolution is a fact. Living organisms have changed in the past and they continue to change today. There are forms of life living today that did not exist millions of years ago. There are also forms of life that did live in the past but are not around today, such as our ancestors (Figure 1.4). Certain organisms have shown definite changes in their biological makeup. Horses, for example, used to have five toes, then three, and today they have one. Human beings have larger brains and smaller teeth today than they did a million years ago. All of these statements and many others are verifiable truths. They are facts.

Hypotheses. What is a hypothesis? A **hypothesis** is simply an explanation of observed facts. For example, consider gravity. Gravity is a fact. It is observable. Many hypotheses could be generated to explain gravity. You could hypothesize that gravity is caused by a giant living in the core of our planet drawing in air, thus causing a pull on all objects on the earth's surface. Bizarre as it sounds, this is a scientific hypothesis because it can be tested. It is, however, easily shown to be incorrect (air movement can be measured and it does not flow in the postulated direction).

Testability. To be scientific, a hypothesis must be testable. The potential must exist for a hypothesis to be rejected. Not all hypotheses can be tested, however, and for this reason they are not scientific hypotheses. That doesn't necessarily mean they are true or false, but only that they cannot be tested. For example, you might come up with a hypothesis that all the fossils we have ever found were put in the ground by God to confuse us.

Figure 1.4

A skull of *Australopithecus africanus,* a hominid that lived two to three million years ago.   (© K. Cannon-Bonaventre/Anthro-Photo)

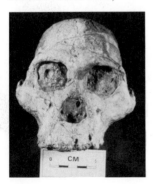

This is not a scientific hypothesis because we have no objective way of testing the statement.

Many evolutionary hypotheses, however, are testable. For example, specific predictions about the fossil record can be made based on our knowledge of evolution. One such prediction is that humans evolved after the extinction of the dinosaurs. The potential exists for this statement to be rejected; all we need is evidence that humans existed before, or at the same time as, the dinosaurs. Since we have found no such evidence, we cannot reject the hypothesis. We can, however, imagine a situation in which the hypothesis could be rejected. If we cannot imagine such a situation, then the hypothesis cannot be tested. For example, imagine that someone tells you that all the people on the earth were created 5 minutes ago, complete with memories! Any evidence you muster against this idea could be explained away. Therefore, this hypothesis is not scientific since there is no possible way to reject it.

Theories. What is the difference between a theory and a hypothesis? In some disciplines the two terms are sometimes used to mean the same thing. In the natural and physical sciences, however, theory means something different than hypothesis. A **theory** is a set of hypotheses that have been tested repeatedly and that have not been rejected. Evolution falls into this category. Evidence from many sources has confirmed the basic hypotheses making up evolutionary theory (discussed later in the chapter).

The Development of Evolutionary Theory

As with all general theories, modern evolutionary theory is not static. Scientific research is a dynamic process, with new evidence being used to support, clarify, and, most important, reject previous ideas. There will always be continual refinements in specific aspects of the theory and its applications. Because science is a dynamic process, evolutionary theory did not come about overnight. Charles Darwin (1809–1882) is most often credited as the "father of evolutionary thought" (Figure 1.5). It is true that Darwin provided a powerful idea that forms the center of modern evolutionary thought. He did not work in an intellectual vacuum, however, but rather built on the ideas of earlier scholars. Darwin's model was not the first evolutionary theory; it forms, rather, the basis of the one that has stood the test of time.

Pre-Darwinian thought. To understand Darwin's contribution and evolution in general, it is necessary to take a look at earlier ideas. For many centuries the concept of change, biological or otherwise, was rather unusual in Western thought. Much of Greek philosophy, for example, posits a static, unchanging view of the world. In later Western thought, the universe, earth, and all living creatures were regarded as having been created by God in their present form, showing little if any change over many

theory A set of hypotheses that have been tested repeatedly and that have not been rejected. This term is sometimes used in a different sense in social science literature.

Figure 1.5

Charles Darwin. (Neg. no. 326697. Courtesy Department of Library Sciences, American Museum of Natural History)

taxonomy A formal classification of organisms.

species A group of populations whose members can interbreed naturally and produce fertile offspring.

genus Groups of species with similar adaptations.

catastrophism The hypothesis that explains evolutionary change in terms of repeated natural catastrophes.

acquired characteristics Lamarck's hypothesis that traits change in response to environmental demands and are passed on to offspring.

generations. Many biologists (then called natural historians) shared this view, and their science consisted mainly of description and categorization. A good example is Carolus Linneaus (1707–1778), a Swedish naturalist who compiled the first formal classification of all known living creatures. A classification is called a **taxonomy** and it serves to help organize information. Linnaeus's taxonomy organized all known living creatures into meaningful groups. For example, humans, dogs, cats, and many other animals are mammals, characterized primarily by the presence of mammary glands to feed offspring. Linneas used a variety of traits to place all then known creatures into various categories. Such a taxonomy helps in clarifying relationships between different organisms. For example, bats are classified as mammals because they possess mammary glands, and not as birds simply because they have wings.

Linnaeus also gave organisms a name reflecting their genus and species. A **species** is a group of populations whose members can interbreed and produce fertile offspring. A **genus** is a group of similar species, often sharing certain common forms of adaptation. Modern humans, for example, are known by the name *Homo sapiens*. The first word is the genus and the second word is the species.

The reason for the relationships among organisms, however, was not often addressed by early natural historians. The living world was felt to be the product of God's work, and the task of the natural historian was description and classification. This static view of the world began to change in the eighteenth and nineteenth centuries. One important reason for this change was that excavations began to produce many fossils that did not fit neatly into the classification system. Discovery of the fossil record began to chip away at the view that the world is as it always had been, and the concept of change began to be incorporated into explanations of the origin of life. Not all scholars, however, came up with the same hypotheses.

One French anatomist, Cuvier (1769–1832), analyzed many of the fossil remains found in quarries. He showed that many of these belonged to animals that no longer existed; that is, they had become extinct. Cuvier used a hypothesis called **catastrophism** to explain these extinctions. The hypothesis posited a series of catastrophes in the planet's past, during which many living creatures were destroyed. Following these catastrophes, organisms from unaffected areas moved in. The changes over time observed in the fossil record could therefore be explained as a continual process of catastrophes followed by repopulation from other regions (Mayr 1982).

Another hypothesis was put forth by the French scientist Lamarck (1744–1829). He believed that evolution occurred through a natural process of organisms adjusting to their environment. One of his ideas was that an organism could change during its lifetime and then pass these changes on to its offspring. According to Lamarck's idea of **acquired characteristics,** a jungle cat that developed stronger leg muscles through constant running and jumping would pass along stronger muscles to its offspring.

Of course, it is easy now to reject the concept of acquired characteristics. For example, someone who loses a finger in an accident will still have children with the correct number of fingers. Instead of looking back and ridiculing Lamarck for his ideas, we must realize that he was actually quite astute in noting the intimate relationship among organisms, their environments, and evolution.

Charles Darwin and natural selection. Cuvier and Lamarck are perhaps the best-known examples of what many have called "pre-Darwinian" theorists. Evolution was well accepted, and various models were being developed to explain this fact, before Darwin. Charles Darwin developed the theory of natural selection that has since been supported by testing. His major contribution was to combine information from a variety of different fields, such as geology and economics, to form his theory.

Charles Darwin had been interested in biology and geology since he was a small child. Born to well-to-do parents, Darwin attended college and had planned to enter the ministry, although he was not as enthusiastic about this career as he was about his studies of natural history. Because of his scientific and social connections, Darwin was able to accompany the scientific survey ship *Beagle* as an unpaid naturalist. The *Beagle* conducted a five-year journey around the world collecting plant and animal specimens in South America and the Galapagos Islands (in the Pacific Ocean near Ecuador), among other places (Figure 1.6).

During these travels, Darwin came to several basic conclusions about variation in living organisms. First, he found a tremendous amount of observable variation in most living species. Instead of looking at the world in terms of fixed, rigid categories (as did mainstream biology in his time), Darwin saw that individuals within species varied considerably from place to place.

Darwin also noted that the variations he saw made sense in terms of the environment (Figure 1.7). Creatures in cold climates often have fur for protection. Birds in areas where insects live deep inside tree branches have long beaks to allow them to extract these insects and eat them. In other words, organisms appear well adapted to specific environments. Darwin believed that the environment acted to change organisms over time. But how?

To help answer this question, Darwin turned to the writings of the economist Thomas Malthus (1766–1834), who had noted that more individuals are born in most species than can possibly survive. In other words, many organisms die before reaching maturity and reproducing. If it were not for this mortality, populations would grow too large for their environments to support them.

To Charles Darwin, the ideas of Malthus provided the needed information to solve the problem of adaptation and evolution. Not all individuals in a species survive and reproduce. Some failure to reproduce may be random, but some is related to specific characteristics of an individual. If

Figure 1.6

Darwin's observations of variation in the different regions he visited aboard the H.M.S. *Beagle* shaped his theory of natural selection.

there are two birds, one with a short beak and one with a long beak, in an environment that requires reaching inside branches to feed, it stands to reason that the bird with the longer beak is more likely to feed itself, survive, and reproduce. In certain environments, some individuals possess traits that enhance their probability of survival and reproduction. If these traits are due, in part or whole, to inherited characteristics, then they will be passed on to the next generation.

In some ways, Darwin's idea was not new. Animal and plant breeders had used this principle for centuries. Controlled breeding and artificial selection had resulted in many traits in domesticated plants and animals, such as livestock size, milk production in cows, and a variety of other traits. The same principle is used in producing pedigreed dogs and many forms of tropical fish. The difference is that Darwin saw that nature (the environment) could select those individuals that survived and reproduced. Hence, he called his concept **natural selection.**

Although the theory of evolution by natural selection is most often associated with Charles Darwin, another English natural historian, Alfred Russel Wallace (1823–1913), came up with essentially the same idea. In fact, Darwin and Wallace communicated their ideas to each other and first presented the theory of natural selection in a joint paper in 1858. Many scholars feel that Wallace's independent work urged Darwin finally to put forward the ideas he had developed years earlier but had not published (Gould 1977a). To ensure timely publication, Darwin condensed his many years of work into a 490-page "abstract" entitled *On the Origin of Species by Means of Natural Selection,* published in 1859 (Futuyma 1983).

An example of natural selection. One excellent example of how natural selection works is the story of populations of the peppered moth in England over the last few centuries (Figure 1.8). These moths come in two distinct colors, dark and light. Early observations found that most of these moths were light-colored, thus allowing them to camouflage themselves on tree trunks. By blending in, they had a better chance of avoiding the birds that tried to eat them. Roughly 1 percent of the moths, however, were dark-colored and thus at an obvious disadvantage. Naturalists noted that the frequency of dark-colored moths increased to almost 90 percent in the century following the beginning of the Industrial Revolution in England (Grant 1985). The reason for this change was the fact that industrialization brought about massive pollution in the surrounding countryside. The trees became darker in color after being covered with soot. The light moths were at a disadvantage, and the dark moths, now better camouflaged, were better-off. Proportionately, more dark moths survived and passed their dark color to the next generation. In evolutionary terminology, the dark moths were *selected for* and the light moths were *selected against.* After antipollution laws were passed and the environment began to recover, the situation reversed: once again light moths survived better, and were selected for, whereas dark moths were selected against.

This well-known study shows us more than just the workings of natural selection. It also illustrates several important principles of evolution. First, we cannot always state with absolute certainty which traits are "good" and which are "bad." It depends on the specific environment. When the trees were light in color, the light-colored moths were at an advantage, but when the situation changed, the dark-colored moths gained the advantage. Second, evolution does not proceed unopposed in one direction. Under certain situations, biological traits can change in a different direction. In the case of the moths, evolution produced a change from light to dark to light again. Third, evolution does not occur in a vacuum. It is affected by changes in the environment and by changes in other species. In this example, changes in the cultural evolution of humans led to a change in the environment, which further affected the evolution of

natural selection A mechanism for evolutionary change favoring the survival and reproduction of some organisms over others because of their biological characteristics.

Figure 1.7

The sizes, beak shapes, and diets of this sample of Darwin's finches show differences in adaptation among closely related species.   (From E. Peter Volpe, *Understanding Evolution,* 5th ed. Copyright ©1985 Wm. C. Brown Communication, Inc., Dubuque, Iowa. All Rights Reserved. Reprinted by permission)

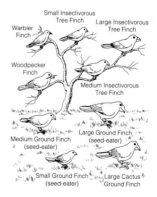

Figure 1.8

Adaptation in the peppered moth. The dark-colored moth is more visible on light-colored tree trunks and therefore at greater risk of being seen and eaten by a bird (*top*). The light-colored moth is at greater risk of being eaten on dark-colored tree trunks (*bottom*).   (©Michael Tweedie/ Photo Researchers)

the moths. Finally, the moth study shows us the critical importance of variation to the evolutionary process. If the original population of moths did not possess the dark-colored variation, they might have been wiped out after the trees turned darker in color. Variation must exist for natural selection to operate effectively.

Modern evolutionary thought. Darwin provided part of the answer of how evolution worked, but he did not have all the answers. Many early critics of Darwin's work focused on certain questions that Darwin could not answer. One important question concerns the origins of variation: Given that natural selection operates on existing variation, then where do those variations come from? Why, at the outset, were some moths light and others dark? Natural selection can only act on preexisting variation; it cannot create new variations. Another question is: How are traits inherited? The theory of natural selection states that certain traits are selected for and passed on to future generations. How are these traits passed on? Darwin knew that traits were inherited, but he did not know the mechanism. Still another question involves how new forms and structures come into being.

Darwin is to be remembered and praised for his work in providing the critical base from which evolutionary science developed. He did not, however, have all the answers, as no scientist does. Modern evolutionary theory relies not only on the work of Darwin and Wallace but also on developments in genetics, zoology, embryology, physiology, and mathematics, to name but a few fields. The basic concept of natural selection as stated by Darwin has been tested and found to be valid. Refinements have been added, and some aspects of the original idea have been changed. We now have answers to many of Darwin's questions. Modern evolutionary theory will be discussed in greater detail in the next two chapters.

Evidence for Evolution

Because this book is concerned with human variation and evolution, you will be provided with numerous examples of how evolution works in past and present human populations. It is important to understand from the start that biological evolution is a documented fact and that the modern theory of evolution has stood up under many scientific tests.

The fossil record provides evidence of evolution. The story the fossils tell is one of change. Creatures existed in the past that are no longer with us. Sequential changes are found in many fossils showing the change of certain features over time from a common ancestor, as in the case of the horse. Apart from demonstrating that evolution did occur, the fossil record also provides tests of the predictions made from evolutionary theory. For example, the theory predicts that single-celled organisms evolved before multicelled organisms. The fossil record supports this prediction—multicelled organisms are found in layers of earth millions of years after the first appearance of single-celled organisms. Note that the possibility always remains that the opposite could be found! If multicelled organisms were indeed found to have evolved before single-celled organisms, then the theory of evolution would be rejected. A good scientific theory always allows for the possibility that it may be rejected. The fact that we have not found such a case in countless examinations of the fossil record strengthens the case for evolutionary theory. Remember, in science you do not prove a theory; rather, you fail to reject it.

The fossil record is not the only evidence we have that evolution has occurred. Comparison of living organisms provides further confirmation. For example, the African apes are the closest living relatives of humans. We see this in a number of characteristics. African apes and humans share the same type of dental pattern, have a similar shoulder structure, and have DNA (the genetic code) that is over 98 percent identical. Even though any one of these traits, or others, could be explained as coincidental, why do so many independent traits show the same pattern? One possibility, of course, is that they were designed that way by an ultimate Creator. The problem with this idea is that it cannot be tested. It is a matter of faith and not of science. Another problem is that we must then ask ourselves why a Creator would use the same basic pattern for so many traits in different creatures. Evolution, on the other hand, offers an explanation. Apes and humans share many characteristics because they evolved from a common ancestor (Figure 1.9).

Another example of shared characteristics is the python, a large snake. Like many vertebrates, the python has a pelvis, the skeletal structure that connects the lower legs to the upper body (Futuyma 1983). From a structural standpoint, of what possible use is a pelvis to a creature that has no legs? If the python was created, then what purpose would there have been to give it a pelvis? We can of course argue that no one can understand the motivations of a Creator, but that is hardly a scientific explanation. Evolutionary reasoning provides an answer: the python has retained the pelvis from an earlier ancestor that did have legs.

Another line of evidence supporting evolution is the laboratory and field studies of living organisms. Ongoing evolutionary change has been documented in many organisms, including humans. Specific predictions of the effect of evolutionary mechanisms have been tested and verified in controlled experiments and observational studies. The study of moth color is but one of many examples of this kind of analysis.

Science and Religion

The subject of evolution has always been controversial, and the implications of evolution have sometimes frightened people. For example, the fact that humans and apes evolved from a common ancestor has always upset some people who feel that their humanity is somehow degraded by having ancestors supposedly less worthy than ourselves. Another conflict

Figure 1.9

The percentage of genetic distance between humans and the great apes (chimpanzee, gorilla, and orangutan). Combined with other biological evidence, genetic data show us how closely related we are to the apes, especially the chimpanzee.   (From *Human Evolution: An Illustrated Introduction* by Roger Lewin, © 1984 by Blackwell Scientific Publications. Reprinted with permission by W. H. Freeman and Company)

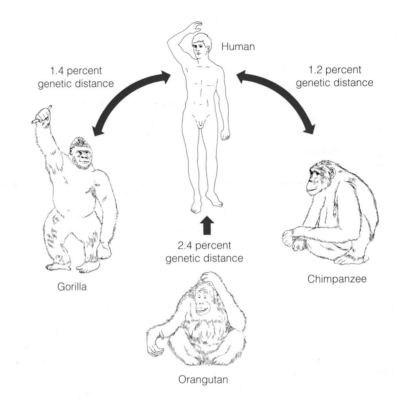

Figure 1.10

The Scopes Trial. William Jennings Bryan (*right*) represented the state of Tennessee and Clarence Darrow (*left*) represented John Scopes.   (© AP/Wide World Photos)

lies in the implications evolution has for religious views. In the United States a number of laws have prohibited the teaching of evolution in public schools. Many of these laws stayed on the books until the late 1960s.

Numerous legal battles have been fought over these anti-evolution laws. Perhaps the most famous of these was the "Scopes Monkey Trial" in 1925. John Scopes, a high school teacher in Dayton, Tennessee, was arrested for violating the state law prohibiting the teaching of evolution. The town and trial quickly became the center of national attention, primarily because of the two celebrities in the case—William Jennings Bryan, a former U.S. Secretary of State, who represented the state of Tennessee, and Clarence Darrow, one of the most famous American trial lawyers, who represented Scopes. The battle between these two eloquent speakers captured the attention of the country (Figure 1.10). In the end, Scopes was found guilty of violating the law, and he was fined $100. The fine was later suspended on a legal technicality. The story of this trial, which has been dramatized in play and movie versions as *Inherit the Wind,* is a powerful story portraying the fight of those who feel strongly about academic freedom and freedom of speech against ignorance and oppression. In reality, the original arrest of Scopes appears to have been planned by several local people, including Scopes, to put the town on the map (Gould 1983).

In retrospect, the Scopes trial may seem amusing. We laugh at early attempts to control subject matter in classrooms and often feel that we have gone beyond such battles. Nothing could be further from the truth, however. For many people, evolution represents a threat to their beliefs in the sudden creation of all life by a creator. Attempts to legislate the teaching of the Biblical view of creation in science classes, however, violate the First Amendment of the Constitution as an establishment of religion. To circumvent this problem, opponents of evolution have devised a new strategy by calling their teachings "creation science," supposedly the scientific study of special creation. The word *God* does not always appear in definitions of creation science, but the word *creator* often does.

In March 1981, the Arkansas state legislature passed a law (Act 590) requiring that creation science be taught in public schools for equal amounts of time as evolution. The American Civil Liberties Union challenged this law, and it was overturned in a federal district court in 1982. A similar law passed in Louisiana in 1981 was later overturned. The Louisiana case has since been appealed and brought to the U.S. Supreme Court, which upheld the ruling of the lower court in 1987. Among other legal problems they raise, both the Arkansas and Louisiana laws have been found to be unconstitutional under the First Amendment.

What is "creation science"? Why shouldn't it be taught in science classes? Shouldn't science be open to new ideas? These questions all center on the issue of whether creation science is a science or not. As typically applied, creation science is not a science; at best, it is a grab bag of ideas spruced up with scientific jargon. One of the original definitions is found in Act 590 of the Arkansas law, which defines creation science as

> the scientific evidence for creation and inferences from these scientific evidences. Creation-science includes the scientific evidences and related inferences that indicate: (1) Sudden creation of the universe, energy, and life from nothing; (2) The insufficiency of mutation and natural selection in bringing about development of all living kinds from a single organism; (3) Changes only within fixed limits of originally created kinds of plants and animals; (4) Separate ancestry for man and apes; (5) Explanation of the earth's geology by catastrophism, including the occurrence of a worldwide flood; and (6) A relatively recent inception of the earth and living kinds. (Montagu 1984:376–377)

None of these statements is supported by scientific evidence, and creationist writers generally use very little actual evidence to support their views. Some have written that the Biblical Flood can be supported by the fossil record. Earth's past is essentially recorded by the order in which different levels of earth and fossils are found. In general, that is, the deeper a fossil is found the older it is. Creationists explain this order as being caused by the flight of animals from the Flood. As the waters rose, they say, birds flew and small mammals ran up mountains to escape drowning; these creatures were therefore drowned at higher elevations.

According to creationists, then, you will find fish at lower levels and birds and mammals at higher levels. The fossil record does show this phenomenon. Isn't this proof for "creation science"? No. Think about the Flood scenario for a moment and you will see that it just doesn't make sense. Why didn't the winged reptiles fly away like the birds did? Why are single-celled organisms found earlier than multicelled organisms of similar size and overall shape? Why did large, heavy creatures such as giant tortoises and hippopotami survive instead of sinking? Why didn't the small, fast dinosaurs survive? Why did certain fish die before others, when they were just as swift and just as good at swimming? Many challenges can be raised to the idea of a single gigantic flood causing the order found in the fossil record (Kitcher 1982; Futuyma 1983). The fossil record, in short, provides ample evidence to reject the Flood hypothesis.

Another example cited by creationists as "proof" of special creation is the "fact" that dinosaur and human footprints have been found at the same geological level along the Paluxy River in Texas. Closer examination has shown that the footprints were not distinguishable and that a number of tracks had been carved to attract tourists and their money (Kitcher 1982).

The main "scientific" work of the creationists consists of attempting to find fault with evolutionary theory. The reasoning is that if evolution can be rejected, then special creation must be true. This strategy actually uses an important feature of scientific research by attempting to reject a given hypothesis. The problem is that none of the creationists' attacks on evolution has been supported by scientific evidence. Certainly some predictions of evolutionary theory have been proven incorrect, but that is to be expected because science is a dynamic process. The basic findings of evolution, however, have been supported time and time again.

Another problem is that this method works only when the hypothesis and its alternative cover all possible cases. Are evolution and special creation by a single creator the only possible explanations? Perhaps the universe was created by several creators. Perhaps the universe and natural law was created by a creator, but life evolved from natural law. You might try to think up other alternatives. Remember, however, that to be scientific a hypothesis must be testable.

On an emotional level, the doctrines of "creation science" attract many people. Given the concept of free speech, why shouldn't creation science be given equal time? The problem with equal time is that it assumes that both ideas have equal merit. Consider that some people still believe the earth is flat. They are certainly entitled to their opinion, but it would be absurd to mandate "equal time" in geography and geology classes for this idea. Also, the concept of equal time is not really that fairminded after all. The specific story many creationists refer to is the Biblical story of Genesis. Many other cultures have their own creation stories. Shouldn't they receive equal time as well? In one sense, they should, though the proper forum for such discussions is probably a course in comparative religions, not a science class.

Perhaps the biggest problem advocates of "creation science" have introduced is that they appear to place religion and science at odds with each other. Religion and science both represent ways of looking at the world and, though they work on different levels, they are not contradictory. You can be religious and believe in God and still accept the fact of evolution and evolutionary theory. Only if you take the story of Genesis as a literal, historical account does a conflict exist. Most major religions in the world accept the findings of evolution. Many people, including some scientists, look to the evolutionary process as evidence of God's work.

Many creationists fear that science has eroded our faith in God and has therefore led to a decline in morals and values. They imply that science (and evolution in particular) makes statements about human morality. It does not. Science has nothing to say about right and wrong; that is the function of social ethics, philosophies, and religion. Religion and science are important to many people. To put them at odds with each other does both a disservice. It is no surprise that many ministers, priests, and rabbis have joined in the fight against the laws of "creation science."

SUMMARY

Anthropology is the study of human biological and cultural variation and evolution. Anthropology asks questions that focus on what humans are and the origins, evolution, and variation of our biology and behaviors, since humans are both biological and cultural organisms. In the United States, anthropology is characterized by four subfields with specific concerns: cultural anthropology (the study of cultural behavior), anthropological archaeology (the study of past cultures), linguistic anthropology (the study of language as a human characteristic), and biological anthropology (the study of human biological evolution and variation).

As a science, anthropology has certain requirements and characteristics. Hypotheses must be testable and verifiable. The main theoretical base of biological anthropology is the theory of evolution. A major feature of evolutionary theory is Darwin's idea of natural selection. In any environment in which resources are necessarily limited, some organisms are more likely to survive and reproduce than others because of their biological characteristics. Those who survive pass these traits on to the next generation.

A current controversy involves the efforts of certain people to pass laws requiring that "creation science" be taught in public schools. Examination of this field shows that it is not a science at all. Apart from these debates, it should be noted that today there is little conflict between religion and science in the United States. Each perspective addresses different questions in different ways.

Supplemental Readings

Edey, M. A., and D. C. Johanson. 1989. *Blueprints: Solving the Mystery of Evolution*. Boston: Little, Brown. A nontechnical, well-written book focusing on the history of evolutionary thought.

Futuyma, D. J. 1983. *Science on Trial: The Case for Evolution*. New York: Pantheon Books. An excellent review of evolution and a detailed critique of "creation science," particularly strong in its discussion of scientific method and evidence for evolution.

Godfrey, L. G., ed. 1983. *Scientists Confront Creationism*. New York: W. W. Norton. A collection of papers discussing the fallacy of "creation science."

Gould, S. J. 1977. *Ever Since Darwin*. New York: W. W. Norton.

_____. 1980. *The Panda's Thumb*. New York: W. W. Norton.

_____. 1983. *Hen's Teeth and Horse's Toes*. New York: W. W. Norton.

_____. 1985. *The Flamingo's Smile*. New York: W. W. Norton.

_____. 1991. *Bully for Brontosaurus*. New York: W. W. Norton.

_____. 1993. *Eight Little Piggies*. New York: W. W. Norton. Containing articles written by the author for *Natural History* and other popular publications, these six books provide excellent discussions of evolutionary fact and theory as well as the history of evolutionary thought.

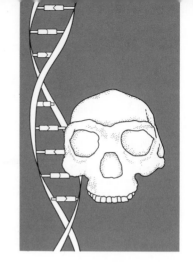

CHAPTER 2

Human Genetics

Is human behavior the result of biology *or* culture? This question has been asked countless times in human history, often with serious cultural and political consequences. To anthropologists, the question is somewhat meaningless; we recognize *both* biological and cultural factors as important and look at the relative potential contributions of both.

To understand human biological variation and evolution, we must consider the science of genetics. The study of genetics actually encompasses a number of different areas, depending on the level of analysis. Genetics can be studied on the molecular level, with the focus on what genes are and how they act to produce biological structures.

Genetics also involves the process of inheritance. To what extent are we a reflection of our parents? How are traits inherited? This branch of the field is called **Mendelian genetics,** after the scientist Gregor Mendel, who first worked out many of the principles of inheritance.

Finally, genetics can be studied at the level of a population. Here we are interested in describing the patterns of genetic variation within and among different populations. The changes that take place in the frequency of genes within a population constitute the process of **microevolution.** At the level of the population, we seek the reasons for evolutionary change from one generation to the next. Projection of these findings allows us to understand better the long-term pattern of evolution over thousands and millions of years and the origin of new species (**macroevolution**).

Mendelian genetics The branch of genetics concerned with patterns and processes of inheritance. This field was named after Gregor Mendel, the first scientist to work out many of these principles.

microevolution Short-term evolutionary change.

macroevolution Long-term evolutionary change.

23

DNA The molecule that provides the genetic code for biological structures and the means to translate this code.

base Chemical unit that makes up part of the DNA molecule whose sequence specifies genetic instructions.

Figure 2.1

The structure of the DNA molecule. DNA consists of two strands arranged in a helix joined together by chemical bases (see text).

Molecular Genetics

DNA: The Genetic Code

The study of genetics at the molecular level concerns the amazing properties of a molecule known as deoxyribonucleic acid, or **DNA** for short. The DNA molecule provides the codes for biological structures and the means to translate this code. It is perhaps best to think of DNA as a set of instructions for determining the makeup of biological organisms. Quite simply, DNA provides information for building, operating, and repairing organisms. In this context, the process of genetic inheritance is seen as the transmission of this information, or the passing on of the instructions needed for biological structures. An understanding of both the structure and function of DNA is necessary to understand the processes of genetic inheritance and evolution. The exact biochemistry of DNA is beyond the scope of this text, but its basic nature can be discussed in the context of information transfer.

The structure of DNA. The physical appearance of the DNA molecule resembles a ladder that has been twisted into the shape of a helix (Figures 2.1 and 2.2). In biochemical terms, the rungs of the ladder are of major importance. These rungs are made up of chemical units called **bases.** There are four possible types of bases, identified by the first letter of their longer chemical names: A (adenine), T (thymine), G (guanine), and C (cytosine). These bases form the "alphabet" used in specifying and carrying out genetic instructions.

All biological structures, from nerve cells to blood cells to bone cells, are made up predominantly of proteins. Proteins in turn are made up of amino acids, whose chemical properties allow them to bond together to form proteins. Each amino acid is coded for by three of the four chemical bases just discussed. There are 64 possible codes that can be specified, using some combination of three bases. This might not seem like a lot, except for the fact that only 20 amino acids need to be specified by the genetic code. The three-base code provides more than enough possibilities to code for these amino acids. A list of the different DNA sequences is shown in Table 2.1.

The ability of the DNA molecule to make use of the different amino acid codes lies in a simple property of the chemical bases. The base A bonds with the base T, and the base G bonds with the base C. This chemical property allows the DNA molecule to carry out a number of functions, including the ability to make copies of itself and to direct the synthesis of proteins.

Functions of DNA. The DNA molecule can make copies of itself (see Figure 2.3). Remember that the DNA molecule is made up of two strands that form the long arms of the ladder. Each rung of the ladder consists of two bases. If one part of the rung contains the base A, then the other part of the rung will contain the base T, since A and T bond together.

The DNA molecule can separate into two separate strands. Once separate, each strand will attract free-floating bases. When new bases have attached themselves to the original strands, the result is two identical DNA molecules. Keep in mind that this description is somewhat oversimplified—in reality, the process is biochemically much more complex.

The ability of the DNA molecule to control protein synthesis also involves the attraction of complementary bases, but with the help of another molecule—ribonucleic acid, or **RNA** for short. In simple terms, RNA serves as the messenger for the information coded by the DNA molecule. One major difference between DNA and RNA is that in RNA the base A attracts a base called U (uracil) instead of T.

Consider the DNA base sequence GGT. In protein synthesis, the DNA molecule separates into two strands, and one strand (containing CCA) becomes inactive. The active strand, GGT, attracts free-floating

> **RNA** The molecule that functions to carry out the instructions for protein synthesis specified by the DNA molecule.

T A B L E 2.1
DNA Base Sequences for Amino Acids

First base	Second base							
	A		T		C		G	
A	AAA	Phenylalanine	ATA	Tyrosine	ACA	Cysteine	AGA	Serine
	AAT	Leucine	ATT	Stop	ACT	Stop	AGT	Serine
	AAC	Leucine	ATC	Stop	ACC	Tryptophan	AGC	Serine
	AAG	Phenylalanine	ATG	Tyrosine	ACG	Cysteine	AGG	Serine
T	TAA	Isoleucine	TTA	Asparagine	TCA	Serine	TGA	Threonine
	TAT	Isoleucine	TTT	Lysine	TCT	Arginine	TGT	Threonine
	TAC	Methionine	TTC	Lysine	TCC	Arginine	TGC	Threonine
	TAG	Isoleucine	TTG	Asparagine	TCG	Serine	TGG	Threonine
C	CAA	Valine	CTA	Aspartic acid	CCA	Glycine	CGA	Alanine
	CAT	Valine	CTT	Glutamic acid	CCT	Glycine	CGT	Alanine
	CAC	Valine	CTC	Glutamic acid	CCC	Glycine	CGC	Alanine
	CAG	Valine	CTG	Aspartic acid	CCG	Glycine	CGG	Alanine
G	GAA	Leucine	GTA	Histidine	GCA	Arginine	GGA	Proline
	GAT	Leucine	GTT	Glutamine	GCT	Arginine	GGT	Proline
	GAC	Leucine	GTC	Glutamine	GCC	Arginine	GGC	Proline
	GAG	Leucine	GTG	Histidine	GCG	Arginine	GGG	Proline

Rows refer to the first of the three bases and columns refer to the second of the three bases. These base sequences are for the DNA molecule. The 64 different combinations code for 20 amino acids and one termination sequence ("Stop"). To convert to messenger RNA, substitute U for A, A for T, G for C, and C for G. To convert to transfer RNA, substitute U for A.

Figure 2.2

Computer representation of the DNA molecule.   (© Will & Demi McIntyre/Photo Researchers, Inc.)

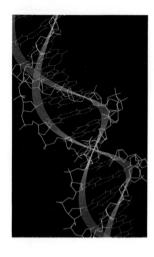

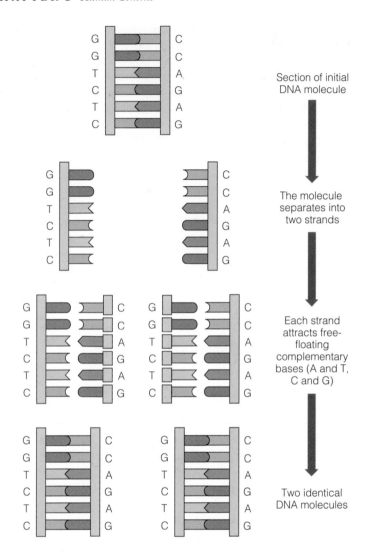

Section of initial DNA molecule

The molecule separates into two strands

Each strand attracts free-floating complementary bases (A and T, C and G)

Two identical DNA molecules

Figure 2.3

Replication of the DNA molecule.

messenger RNA The form of RNA that transports the genetic instructions from the DNA molecule to the site of protein synthesis.

transfer RNA A free-floating molecule that is attracted to a strand of messenger RNA, resulting in the synthesis of a protein chain.

bases to form a strand of **messenger RNA.** Since A bonds with T and G bonds with C, this strand consists of the sequence CCA. This strand then travels to the site of protein synthesis. Once there, the strand of messenger RNA transfers its information by attracting **transfer RNA,** which is a free-floating molecule. The sequence of messenger RNA containing the sequence CCA attracts a transfer RNA molecule with a complementary sequence—GGU. The result is that the amino acid proline (specified by the RNA sequence GGU or the DNA sequence GGT) is included in the chain of amino acids making up a particular protein. To summarize, one strand of the DNA molecule produces the complementary strand of messenger RNA, which then travels to the site of protein synthesis and attracts a complementary strand of transfer RNA, which carries the specified

Figure 2.4

Protein synthesis.

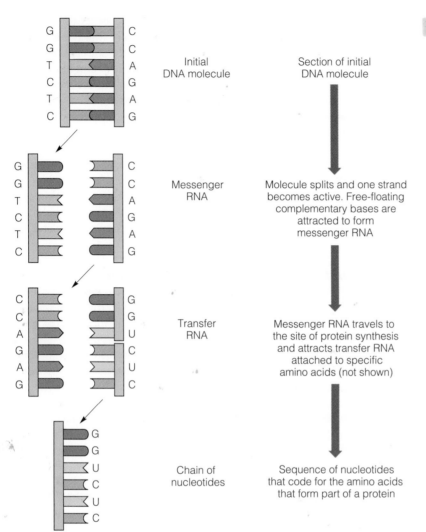

Initial DNA molecule	Section of initial DNA molecule
Messenger RNA	Molecule splits and one strand becomes active. Free-floating complementary bases are attracted to form messenger RNA
Transfer RNA	Messenger RNA travels to the site of protein synthesis and attracts transfer RNA attached to specific amino acids (not shown)
Chain of nucleotides	Sequence of nucleotides that code for the amino acids that form part of a protein

amino acid. This process is illustrated for the DNA sequence GGTCTC in Figure 2.4.

This simplified discussion shows the basic nature of the structure and functions of the DNA molecule. More advanced discussion can be found in most genetics textbooks. For our purposes, however, the broad view will suffice. If we consider DNA as a "code," we can then look at the processes of transmission and change of information without actually having to consider the exact biochemical mechanisms.

Chromosomes and Genes

The DNA is contained within the nucleus of each cell. Another form of DNA, contained in a part of the cell called the mitochondria, is dis-

chromosome Long strand of
DNA sequences.

gene The section of DNA
responsible for a given
biological function.

hemoglobin The molecule in
blood cells that transports
oxygen.

structural genes Genes that
code for the production of
proteins.

regulatory genes Genes that
code for the regulation of such
biological processes as growth
and development.

cussed later in Chapter 11. The DNA sequences are bound together by
proteins in long strands called **chromosomes** that are found within the
nucleus of each cell. With the exception of those in the sex cells (egg and
sperm), chromosomes occur in pairs. Most body cells contain both members of these pairs. Different species have different numbers of chromosomes. For example, humans have 23 pairs, chimpanzees have 24 pairs,
fruit flies have 4 pairs, and certain plant species have thousands of pairs.
There is no relationship between the number of chromosome pairs a species has and its intelligence or biological complexity.

With certain exceptions, each cell in the human body contains a
complete set of chromosomes and DNA. Nerve cells contain the DNA for
bone cells and vice versa. Some type of regulation takes place within different cells to ensure that only certain genes are expressed in the right
places, but the exact nature of this regulation is not known completely at
present.

Structural and regulatory genes. A **gene** is defined as the segment
of DNA responsible for a certain function, such as the production of a
given protein (Sutton and Wagner 1985). For example, the **hemoglobin**
molecule in your blood (which transports oxygen) is made up of four
protein chains—two identical alpha chains and two identical beta chains.
For each chain, there are sections of the human DNA containing the
genetic code for the proteins in that chain. Genes that code for the production of a protein are known as **structural genes.**

Aside from manufacture of proteins, another function of genes is the
regulation of biological processes. For example, consider the fact that in
many humans the enzyme needed to digest milk sugar stops being produced several years after birth. Or consider the fact that sexual maturation
in humans occurs during adolescence and not in infancy. Many biological
characteristics are subject to regulation in terms of when they take effect
or are expressed. Genes that are responsible for this regulation are known
as **regulatory genes,** and they act by turning other genes on or off at the
appropriate time.

Regulatory genes may have great evolutionary significance. For example, regulatory genes may help explain the great physical differences
between chimpanzees and humans even though over 98 percent of their
structural genes are identical. The major genetic difference between humans and chimpanzees may be caused by regulatory genes, which act on
timing of growth and development, and could lead to differences in brain
size, facial structures, and other physical features.

Mitosis and meiosis. The DNA molecule provides for the transmission of genetic information. Production of proteins and regulation are only
two aspects of information transfer. Since organisms start life as a single
cell that subsequently multiplies, it is essential that the genetic information
within the initial cell is transferred to all future cells. The ability of DNA

to replicate itself is involved in the process of cell replication, known as **mitosis** (Figure 2.5). When a cell divides, each chromosome duplicates and then splits. Each chromosome has replicated itself, so that when the cell finishes dividing, the result is two cells with the full set of chromosomes.

The process is different when information is passed on from one generation to the next. The genetic code is passed on from parents to offspring through the sex cells; the sperm in males and the egg in females. The sex cells, however, do not contain the full set of chromosomes but only one chromosome from each pair (i.e., only one-half of the set). If both chromosomes in each pair were passed on, your children would have 23 pairs from both you and your mate, for a total of 46 pairs. Your children's children would receive 46 pairs from each parent, for a total of 92 pairs. If this process continued, there would soon not be enough room in a cell for all of the chromosome pairs!

Sex cells contain only one of each pair of chromosomes. Whereas your other body cells have a total of 46 chromosomes (2 each for 23 pairs), your sex cells contain only 23 chromosomes (1 from each pair). When you have a child, you contribute 23 chromosomes, and your mate contributes 23 chromosomes. Your child then has the normal complement of 46 chromosomes in 23 pairs.

Sex cells are created through the process of **meiosis** (Figure 2.6). Basically, this involves the replication of chromosomes followed by cell division, followed by another cell division without an intervening round of replication. In sperm, the result is that four sex cells are produced from the initial set of 23 pairs of chromosomes. The process is similar in egg cells except that only one of the four progeny cells is functional.

The process of meiosis is extremely important in understanding genetic inheritance. Since only one of each pair of chromosomes is found in a functional sex cell, this means that a person contributes half of his or her offspring's genes. The other half comes from the other parent. Usually, each human child has a full set of 23 chromosome pairs, one of each pair from each parent (Figure 2.7).

Mendelian Genetics

Many of the facts known about genetic inheritance were discovered over a century before the structure of DNA was known. Although people knew where babies came from and noted the close resemblance of parents and children, the mechanisms of inheritance were unknown until the nineteenth century. An Austrian priest, Gregor Mendel (1822–1884), carried out an extensive series of experiments in plant breeding. His carefully tabulated results provided the basis of what we know about the mechanisms of genetic inheritance.

mitosis The process of replication of chromosomes in body cells.

meiosis The creation of sex cells by replication of chromosomes followed by two cell divisions.

Figure 2.5

The process of mitosis, the formation of body cells. Each chromosome copies itself, the attached copies line up in the cell, and the original and copy split when the cell divides. The result is two identical cells. (From *Human Antiquity: An Introduction to Physical Anthropology and Archaeology*, 2d ed., by Kenneth Feder and Michael Park, Fig 4.2. Copyright © 1993 by Mayfield Publishing Company)

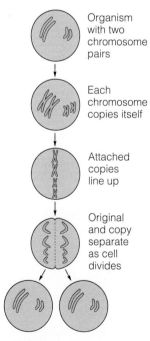

Organism with two chromosome pairs

Each chromosome copies itself

Attached copies line up

Original and copy separate as cell divides

Daughter cells are copies of parent cell

Figure 2.6

The process of meiosis, the formation of sex cells. Meiosis begins in the same way as mitosis: each chromosome makes a copy of itself. The pairs of chromosomes then segregate, forming four sex cells, each with one chromosome rather than a pair of chromosomes. (Adapted from *Human Antiquity: An Introduction to Physical Anthropology and Archaeology*, 2d ed., by Kenneth Feder and Michael Park, Fig. 4.2. Copyright © 1993 by Mayfield Publishing Company)

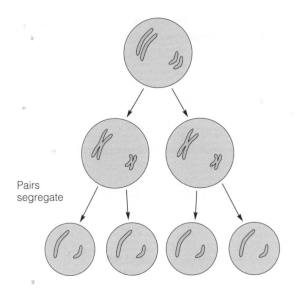

Pairs segregate

Each sex cell has half the normal number of chromosomes

Figure 2.7

All 23 pairs of chromosomes typically found in a human being. This set of chromosomes came from a man—note the 23rd pair has an X chromosome and a Y chromosome. (© CNRI/ Science Photo Library/Photo Researchers, Inc.)

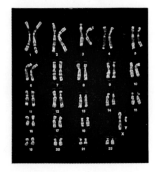

Before Mendel's research, it was commonly assumed that inheritance involved the blending together of genetic information in the egg and sperm. The genetic material was thought to mix together in the same way that different color paints mix together. Mendel's experiments showed a different pattern of inheritance—the genetic information is inherited in discrete units (genes). These genes do not blend together in an offspring.

In one experiment, Mendel crossed pea plants whose seeds were yellow with pea plants whose seeds were green (Figure 2.8). Under the idea of blending, one might expect all offspring to have mustard-colored seeds—a mixture of the yellow and green. In reality, Mendel found that all the offspring plants had yellow seeds. This discovery suggested that somehow one trait (yellow seed color) dominated in its effects.

When Mendel crossed the plants in this new generation together, he found that some of their offspring had yellow seeds and some had green seeds. Somehow the genetic information for green seeds had been hidden for a generation and then appeared again. Mendel counted how many there were of each color. The ratio of plants with yellow seeds to those with green seeds was very close to a 3:1 ratio. This finding suggested to Mendel that a regular process occurred during inheritance that could be explained in terms of simple mathematical principles. With these, and other, results, Mendel formulated several principles of inheritance. Though Mendel's work remained virtually unknown during his lifetime, his work was rediscovered in 1900. In recognition of his accomplishments, the science of genetic inheritance is called Mendelian genetics.

Genotypes and Phenotypes

The specific position of a gene on a chromosome is called a **locus** (plural **loci**). The alternative forms of a gene at a locus are called **alleles.** For example, a number of different genetic systems control the types of molecules present on the surface of red blood cells. One of these blood groups, known as the MN system, determines whether or not you have M molecules, N molecules, or both on the surface of your red blood cells. The MN system has two forms, or alleles—*M* and *N*. Another blood group system, the ABO system, has three alleles—*A*, *B*, and *O*. Even though three different forms of this gene are found in the human species, each individual only has two genes at the ABO locus. Some genetic loci have only one allele, some have two, and some have three or more.

Mendel's Law of Segregation. The genetic basis of any trait is determined by an allele from each parent. At any given locus there are two alleles, one on each member of the chromosome pair. One allele came from the mother and one allele came from the father. Alleles occur in pairs, and when sex cells are formed only one of each pair is passed on (**Mendel's Law of Segregation**).

locus The specific location of a gene on a chromosome.

allele The alternative form of a gene that occurs at a given locus. Some genes have only one allele, some have two, and some have many alternative forms. Alleles occur in pairs, one on each chromosome.

Mendel's Law of Segregation Sex cells contain one of each pair of alleles.

Figure 2.8

The seven phenotypic characteristics investigated by Gregor Mendel in his experiments on breeding in pea plants. Each of the seven traits has two distinct phenotypes.

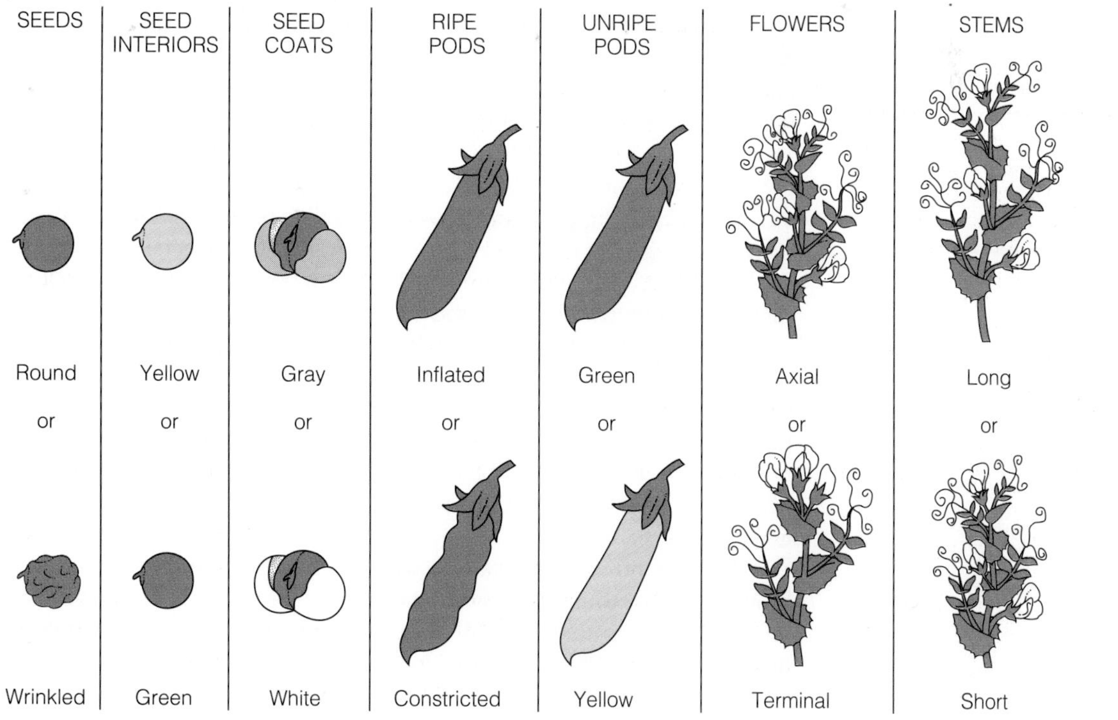

SEEDS	SEED INTERIORS	SEED COATS	RIPE PODS	UNRIPE PODS	FLOWERS	STEMS
Round	Yellow	Gray	Inflated	Green	Axial	Long
or	or	or	or	or	or	or
Wrinkled	Green	White	Constricted	Yellow	Terminal	Short

genotype The genetic endowment of an individual from the two alleles present at a given locus.

homozygous Both alleles at a given locus are identical.

heterozygous The two alleles at a given locus are different.

phenotype The observable appearance of a given genotype in the organism.

dominant allele An allele that masks the effect of the other allele (which is recessive) in a heterozygous genotype.

recessive allele An allele whose effect is masked by the other allele (which is dominant) in a heterozygous genotype.

The two alleles at a locus in an individual specify the **genotype,** the genetic endowment of an individual. The two alleles might be the same form or might be different. If the alleles from both parents are the same, the genotype is **homozygous.** If the alleles from the parents are different, the genotype is **heterozygous.**

The actual observable trait is known as the **phenotype.** The relationship between genotype and phenotype is affected by the relationship between the two alleles present at any locus. If the genotype is homozygous, both alleles contain the same genetic information. What happens in heterozygotes, where the two alleles are different?

Dominant and recessive alleles. In a heterozygote, an allele is **dominant** when it masks the effect of the other allele at a given locus. The opposite of a dominant allele is a **recessive** allele, whose effect may be masked. A simple example helps make these concepts clearer. One genetic trait in human beings is the ability to taste certain substances, including a chemical known as PTC. The ability to taste PTC appears to be controlled by a single locus and is also affected to some extent by environmental factors such as diet. There are two alleles for the PTC-tasting trait: the allele *T,* which is also called the "taster" allele, and the allele *t,* which is also called the "non-taster" allele. Given these two alleles, three combinations of alleles can be present in an individual. A person could have the *T* allele from both parents, which would give the genotype *TT.* A person could have a *t* allele from both parents, giving the genotype *tt.* Both *TT* and *tt* are homozygous genotypes because both alleles are the same. The third possible genotype occurs when the allele from one parent is *T* and the allele from the other parent is *t.* This gives the heterozygous genotype of *Tt.* It does not matter which parent provided the *T* allele and which provided the *t* allele; the genotype is the same in both cases.

What phenotype is associated with each genotype? The phenotype is affected by both the relationship of the two alleles and by the environment. For the moment, let us ignore possible environmental effects. Consider the *T* allele as providing instructions that allow tasting and the *t* allele as providing instructions for nontasting. If the genotype is *TT,* then both alleles code for tasting and the phenotype is obviously "taster." Likewise, if the genotype is *tt,* then both alleles code for nontasting and the phenotype is "nontaster." What of the heterozygote *Tt?* One allele codes for tasting and one codes for nontasting. Does this mean that both will be expressed, and a person will have the tasting ability but not as much as a person with genotype *TT?* Or does it mean that only one of the alleles is expressed? If so, which one?

There is no way you can answer this question using only the data provided so far. You must know if either the *T* or *t* allele is dominant, and this can be determined only through experimentation. For this trait, it turns out that the *T* allele is dominant and the *t* allele is recessive. When both alleles are present in a genotype, the *T* allele masks the effect of the *t* allele. Therefore, a person with the genotype *Tt* has the "taster" phenotype (Table 2.2). The relationship between genotype and phenotype does not take into consideration known environmental effects on PTC tasting. Under certain types of diet, some "tasters" will show less ability to taste weaker concentrations of the PTC chemical.

The action of dominant and recessive alleles explains why Mendel's second-generation pea plants all had yellow seeds. The allele for yellow seed color is dominant, and the allele for green seed color is recessive.

Dominance and recessiveness refers only to the effect an allele has in producing a phenotype. These terms say nothing about the frequency or value of an allele. Dominant alleles can be common or rare, harmful or helpful.

Codominant alleles. Some alleles are **codominant,** meaning that when two different alleles are present in a genotype, then both are expressed. That is, neither allele is dominant or recessive. One example of a codominant genetic system in humans is the MN blood group, mentioned before. There are two alleles—*M,* which codes for the production of M molecules, and *N,* which codes for the production of N molecules. Therefore, there are three possible genotypes: *MM, MN,* and *NN.*

The phenotypes for the homozygous genotypes are easy to determine. Individuals with genotype *MM* have two alleles coding for the production of M molecules and will have the M molecule phenotype. Likewise, individuals with the genotype *NN* will have two *N* alleles and will have the N molecule phenotype. But what of the heterozygote genotype *MN*? Experimentation has shown that the *M* and *N* alleles are codominant. When both are present (genotype *MN*), then both are expressed. Therefore, an individual with genotype *MN* will produce both M and N molecules. Their phenotype is MN, indicating the presence of both molecules (Table 2.3).

In complex genetic systems with more than two alleles some alleles may be dominant and some may be codominant. A good example of dominance and codominance in the same system is the ABO blood group. The alleles, genotypes, and phenotypes of this system are described in Table 2.4.

Predicting Offspring Distributions

When parents each contribute a sex cell, they are passing on only one allele at each locus to their offspring. The possible genotypes and phenotypes of the offspring reflect a 50 percent chance of transmittal for any given allele of a parent. This simple statement of probability allows prediction of the likely distribution of genotypes and phenotypes among the offspring.

Figure 2.9 illustrates this method using the MN blood group system for two hypothetical parents, each with the genotype *MN*. Each parent has a 50 percent chance of passing on an *M* allele and a 50 percent chance of

codominant When both alleles affect the phenotype of a heterozygous genotype and neither is dominant over the other.

**T A B L E   2.2
Genotypes and
Phenotypes for
PTC Tasting**

Genotype	Phenotype
TT	Taster
Tt	Taster
tt	Nontaster

Because *T* is dominant, the genotypes *TT* and *Tt* both produce the taster phenotype. This example is somewhat oversimplified, since in reality the phenotype can also be affected by diet.

Figure 2.9

Inheritance of MN blood group phenotypes for two parents both with *MN* genotype.

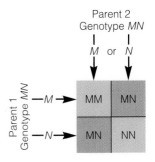

TABLE 2.3
Genotypes and Phenotypes of the
MN Blood Group System

Genotype	Phenotype
MM	M molecules
MN	M and N molecules
NN	N molecules

The *M* and *N* alleles are codominant,
so they are both expressed in the
heterozygote.

TABLE 2.4
Genotypes and Phenotypes of the ABO System

The ABO system has three alleles (*A, B, O*) that code for the
type of molecule on the surface of the red blood cells (A, B, and
O molecules). The *A* and *B* alleles are codominant, and the O
allele is recessive to both *A* and *B*.

Genotype	Phenotype
AA	A
AO	A
BB	B
BO	B
AB	AB
OO	O

Note: There are also different forms of the *A* allele not shown here (A_1,
A_2, etc.).

passing on an *N* allele. Given these probabilities, we expect one out of four
offspring (25 percent) to have genotype *MM*, and therefore phenotype M. In two out of four cases (50 percent), we expect the offspring to
have genotype *MN*, and therefore phenotype MN. Finally, in one out
of four cases (25 percent), we expect the offspring to have genotype
NN, and therefore phenotype N.

Analysis of possible offspring shows that recessive alleles can produce
an interesting effect; it is possible for children to have a different phenotype than either of the parents. For example, consider two parents both
with the genotype *Tt* for the PTC-tasting locus. Both parents have the
"taster" phenotype. What genotypes and phenotypes will their children
be likely to have? The expected genotype distribution is 25 percent *TT*,
50 percent *Tt,* and 25 percent *tt*.

Given this distribution of genotypes, what is the probable distribution of phenotypes? Genotypes *TT* and *Tt* are both "tasters," and therefore
75 percent of the children are expected to also be "tasters." Twenty-five
percent of the children, however, are expected to have the genotype *tt* and
will therefore have the "nontaster" phenotype. These children would have
a different phenotype than either parent. A recessive trait can therefore
remain hidden in one generation.

Chromosomes and Inheritance

Alleles occur in pairs. Mendel showed that when alleles are passed on
from parents to offspring, only one of each pair is contributed by each
parent. The specific chromosome at any pair that is passed on is random.

There is a 50 percent chance of either chromosome being passed on each time a sex cell is created.

Mendel's Law of Independent Assortment. Mendel's experiments revealed another aspect of probability in inheritance and the creation of sex cells. **Mendel's Law of Independent Assortment** states that the segregation of any pair of chromosomes does not influence the segregation of any other pair of chromosomes. In other words, chromosomes from separate pairs are inherited independently.

Independent assortment provides a powerful mechanism for shuffling different combinations of chromosomes and thus introduces great potential for genetic diversity. In humans, who have 23 chromosome pairs, there are $2^{23} = 8,388,608$ possible combinations of sex cells. This means that two parents could produce a maximum of 70,368,744,177,664 genetically unique offspring (= $2^{23} \times 2^{23}$)!

Linkage. A major implication of Mendel's Law of Independent Assortment is that genes are inherited independently. This is true only to the extent that genes are on different chromosomes. Remember, it is the pairs of chromosomes that separate during meiosis, not each individual pair of alleles. When alleles are on the same chromosome, they are inherited together. This is called **linkage.** Linked alleles are not inherited independently since they are, by definition, on the same chromosome.

Crossing over. An exception to the rule of linkage is **crossing over,** the switching of segments of DNA between the chromosome pairs during meiosis. Suppose, for example, that there are two genetic loci on the same chromosome, the first having alleles A or a and the second having alleles B or b. Suppose that you have the genotypes Aa and Bb with one chromosome containing the A allele and the B allele, and the other chromosome having the a allele and the b allele. Since these two loci are both on the same chromosome, you would expect linkage to cause the two systems to be inherited together. That is, your possible sex cells would have A and B, or a and b. Any offspring inheriting the A allele would also be expected to inherit the B allele. Likewise, any offspring inheriting the a allele would also inherit the b allele. During meiosis, chromosome pairs sometimes exchange pieces, a process known as crossing over. For example, the segment of DNA containing the a allele could switch with the segment of DNA containing the A allele on the other chromosome. Therefore, you could have a sex cell with a and B, or a sex cell with A and b (Figure 2.10). Crossing over does not change the genetic material. The alleles are still the same, but they can occur in different combinations. Crossing over provides yet another mechanism for increasing genetic variation by providing new combinations of alleles.

Mendel's Law of Independent Assortment The segregation of any pair of chromosomes does not affect the probability of segregation for other pairs of chromosomes.

linkage When alleles on the same chromosome are inherited together.

crossing over When segments of DNA switch between pairs of chromosomes.

Figure 2.10

Crossing over in chromosomes.

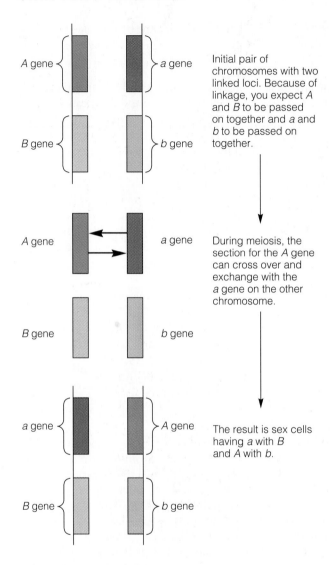

A gene — *a* gene

Initial pair of chromosomes with two linked loci. Because of linkage, you expect *A* and *B* to be passed on together and *a* and *b* to be passed on together.

B gene — *b* gene

A gene — *a* gene

During meiosis, the section for the *A* gene can cross over and exchange with the *a* gene on the other chromosome.

B gene — *b* gene

a gene — *A* gene

The result is sex cells having *a* with *B* and *A* with *b*.

B gene — *b* gene

Sex chromosomes and sex determination. One of the 23 pairs of human chromosomes is called the sex chromosome pair because these chromosomes contain the genetic information determining the individual's sex. There are two forms of sex chromosomes, X and Y. Females have two X chromosomes (XX), and males have one X and one Y chromosome (XY).

The Y chromosome is much smaller than the X chromosome. Almost all genes found on X are therefore not found on Y. This means that males possess only one allele for certain traits because their Y chromosome lacks the corresponding section of DNA. Therefore, males will manifest a trait given only one allele, whereas females require the same allele from both parents to show the trait. An example of this sex difference is hemophilia, a genetic disorder that interferes with the normal process of blood clotting. The allele for hemophilia is recessive and is found on the segment of the X chromosome that has no corresponding portion on the Y chromosome. For females to be hemophiliac, they must inherit two copies of this allele, one from each parent. This is unlikely since the hemophilia allele is rare. Males, on the other hand, need only inherit one copy on the X chromosome from the mother. As a result, hemophilia is more common in males than females.

The Genetics of Complex Physical Traits

The discussion of genetics thus far has focused on simple discrete genetic traits. Traits such as the MN blood group are genetically "simple" because they result from the action of a single locus with a clear-cut mode of inheritance. These traits are also discrete, meaning that they produce a finite number of phenotypes.

These simple discrete traits are very useful for demonstrating the basic principles of Mendelian inheritance. It is not wise, however, to think of all biological traits as resulting from a single locus, exhibiting a finite number of phenotypes, or not being affected by the environment. Many of the characteristics of interest in human evolution, such as skin color, body size, brain size, and intelligence, do not fall into this simple category. Such traits have a complex mode of inheritance in that one or more genes may contribute to the phenotype and they may be affected by the environment. The combined action of genetics and environment produces traits with a continuous distribution.

Complex traits tend to produce more individuals with average values than extreme values. It is not uncommon to find human males between 1,676 and 1,981 mm (5.5 and 6.5 feet) tall. It is much rarer to find someone taller than 2,134 mm (7 feet). A typical distribution of a complex trait such as human height is shown in Figure 2.11.

Many complex traits are **polygenic,** the result of two or more loci. When several loci act to control a trait, many different genotypes and phenotypes can result. A number of physical characteristics, such as human skin color and height, may be polygenic. A single allele can also have multiple effects on an organism. When an allele has effects on multiple traits, this is referred to as **pleiotropy.** In humans, the sickle cell allele affects the structure of the blood's hemoglobin and also leads to changes in overall body growth and health.

The concepts of polygenic traits and pleiotropy are important in considering the interrelated nature of biological systems. Analysis of simple discrete traits on a gene-by-gene basis is useful in understanding genetics, but it should not lead you to think that any organism is simply a collection of single, independent loci.

polygenic Refers to a genetic trait affected by two or more loci.

pleiotropy When a single allele can have multiple effects on an organism.

Figure 2.11

The distribution of a continuous trait. Most individuals have a value close to the average for the population. This type of curve is called a normal distribution.

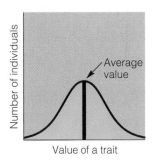

Number of individuals

Average value

Value of a trait

mutation A mechanism for evolutionary change resulting from a random change in the genetic code and the ultimate source of all genetic variation.

Mutations

As shown earlier, the process of genetic inheritance produces new combinations of genes in offspring. The independent assortment of chromosomes during meiosis and the action of crossing over both act to create new genetic combinations. They do not act to create any new genetic material. In order to explain past evolution, we need a mechanism for introducing new alleles and variation. The origin of new genetic variation was a problem to Darwin, but we now know new alleles are brought about through the process of mutation.

Evolutionary Significance of Mutations

A **mutation** is a change in the genetic code. Mutations are the ultimate source of all genetic variation. Mutations are caused by a number of environmental factors such as background radiation, which includes radiation from the earth's crust and cosmic rays. Such background radiation is all around us, in the air we breathe and the food we eat. Mutations may also be caused by heat and ingested substances such as caffeine.

Mutations can take place in any cell of the body. To have evolutionary importance, however, the mutation must occur in a sex cell. A mutation in a skin cell on the end of your finger has no evolutionary significance because it will not be passed on to your offspring. Mutations in the body cells rarely have special significance.

Mutations are random. That is, there is no way of predicting when a specific mutation will take place, or what, if any, phenotypic effect it will have. All we can do is estimate the probability of a mutation occurring at a given locus over a given amount of time. The randomness of mutations also means that mutations do not appear when they might be needed. Many mosquitoes have adapted to insecticides because a mutation was present in the population that acted to confer some resistance to the insecticide. If that mutation had not been present, the mosquitoes would have died. The mosquitoes' need for a certain genetic variant had no effect on whether or not the mutation appeared.

Mutations can have different effects depending on the specific type of mutation and the environment. The conventional view of mutations has long been that they are mostly harmful. Some mutations, however, are advantageous. They lead to change that improves the survival and reproduction of organisms. In recent decades, we have also discovered that some mutations are neutral. That is, the genetic change has no detectable effect on survival or reproduction. There is continued controversy among geneticists about the relative frequency of neutral mutations. Some claim that many mutations are neutral in their effect. Others note the difficulties in detecting the effects of many mutations.

Whether or not a mutation is neutral, advantageous, or disadvantageous depends in large part on the environment. Genetic variants that are harmful in certain environments might actually be helpful in other environments.

Types of Mutations

Mutations fall into two basic groups: point mutations and chromosomal mutations. **Point mutations** are changes in the sequence of bases in the DNA of a single gene. **Chromosomal mutations** are changes in chromosomes and involve large numbers of genes. These include deletions and additions of chromosomal segments, movement of chromosomal segments to new locations, and changes in chromosome number.

Point mutations. When a DNA base is changed, a different amino acid is sometimes specified, which changes the protein structure. Some point mutations are neutral because they do not lead to any change in the specified amino acid. Referring back to Table 2.1, note that many amino acids are specified by different DNA base sequences. For example, the amino acid glycine is specified by the sequence CCA. If a mutation occurs in which the third base changes from an A to a G, the net result is the sequence CCG, which also specifies glycine. This hypothetical mutation leads to no biochemical change and is neutral.

Other changes in base sequences can lead to biochemical changes and affect the survival and reproduction of an individual. One widely studied point mutation is in the allele for the beta chain of the hemoglobin molecule. Here the normal hemoglobin allele has mutated to a form known as the **sickle cell allele.** The red blood cells produced in individuals with two copies of this mutant allele are misshapen and do not transport oxygen efficiently. When two sickle cell alleles are present, the result is a severe form of anemia (sickle cell anemia) that leads to sickness and death. The specific cause of the sickle cell allele is a mutation in the sixth amino acid of the beta chain (out of 146 amino acids). This small change affects the entire structure of the red blood cells and in turn the well-being of the individual.

Chromosomal mutations. Chromosomal mutations occur when a segment of a chromosome carrying more than one gene is changed. Sometimes the segment will contain thousands of genes. In some cases the entire chromosome is changed. These mutations can occur when an entire section of DNA is deleted or added. Sections of DNA can also change position along the chromosome, thus changing the genetic message. The entire chromosome can also be inverted. An entire chromosome from a pair can be lost (**monosymy** = one chromosome) or can occur in duplicate, giving three chromosomes (**trisomy**).

---

point mutation A type of mutation in which the sequence of bases of DNA in a single gene are changed.

chromosomal mutation A type of mutation in which large sections of chromosomes are changed. These changes include rearrangements, deletions, additions, movements, and changes in chromosome numbers.

sickle cell allele An allele of the hemoglobin locus. Individuals homozygous for the sickle cell allele have sickle cell anemia.

monosymy When only one chromosome rather than a pair is present in body cells.

trisomy When three chromosomes rather than a pair occur in body cells.

Figure 2.12

Facial appearance of a child
with Down syndrome.
(Courtesy March of Dimes Birth
Defect Foundation)

Several chromosomal mutations in humans are associated with specific mental and physical disorders. Down syndrome is a condition characterized by certain facial features (Figure 2.12), poor physical growth, and mental retardation (usually mild). Down syndrome is most often caused by the duplication of one of the 21st chromosome pair. Affected individuals have a total of 47 chromosomes, one more than the normal 46. Down syndrome can also be caused by mutations of the 21st chromosome. In some individuals the change involves the exchange of parts of the 21st chromosome with other chromosomes.

Rates of Mutations

Specific mutations are relatively rare events, although the *exact* rate of mutations is difficult to determine in many cases. Part of the problem in determining the rate of point mutations is the fact that several different base sequences can specify the same amino acid. If there is no observable change, then the mutation will usually go unnoticed. A mutation is also more apparent if it involves a dominant allele. Another problem in identifying both point mutations and chromosomal mutations is that harmful mutations may result in spontaneous abortion (miscarriage) before pregnancy has been detected. Some researchers feel that a large number of unrecognized conceptions are expelled spontaneously during the first few weeks after conception. If so, a prediction of mutation rates based on recognized conceptions will be an underestimate.

Despite these problems, research has provided estimates of a range in the rates of mutation. For point mutations in humans, this range is from 1 to 100 mutations per million sex cells (Lerner and Libby 1976). This translates to a probability between 0.000001 and 0.0001 of a mutation occurring at a given locus for a given sex cell.

Regardless of the specific mutation rates for a given gene or chromosome, one thing is clear—mutation rates are generally low. Given these low probabilities, it may be tempting to regard mutation as so rare that it has no special evolutionary significance. The problem with this reasoning is that the estimated rates refer to a *single* specific locus. Human chromosomes have many loci. The exact number is not known, but it has been estimated at roughly 100,000 (Woodward 1992). The probability that a specific locus will show a mutation in any individual is low, but the probability of *any* locus showing a mutation is much higher.

Genetics and Behavior

Perhaps the most controversial topic in genetics is the question of the extent to which behavior is governed by genetic factors. The controversy arises not so much from academic debate but from the social implications, real and imagined, of this question. Problems arise out of a misunderstanding of the basic concepts of genetics or are produced by those seeking any "scientific" fact, regardless of truth, to support and further their own social or political agenda. Much of this controversy revolves around the concept of race, which is discussed in Chapter 5. The present section focuses on basic strategies involved in relating genes and behavior.

The Nature-Nurture Debate

Is a behavior, such as intelligence or shyness, caused by genes ("nature") or the physical and cultural environment ("nurture")? The debate of nature versus nurture has a long history in Western civilization. The prevalent view among scientists reflects not only current research but also the social and cultural climate of the times. Scientists are people, too, as susceptible to biases and prejudices as everyone else. A major lesson of the history of science is that cultural beliefs influence the methodology and interpretation of scientific results.

At the beginning of the twentieth century, the prevalent view was that "nature" was the more important determinant of many behaviors, particularly intelligence. This emphasis shifted to "nurture" during the period from the 1930s to the 1960s, when environmental factors were seen as being the most, if not the only, important factor.

Much of the debate over nature versus nurture is nonsense, however. Any attempt to relegate human behaviors to either genetics *or* environment is fruitless. Genes and environment are both important. The proper question is not which is more important, but rather how they interact.

For example, consider the nature of maternal behaviors. The studies of primate behavior discussed in Chapters 7 to 9 show clearly that maternal behaviors are in part the result of learning within a social context. Females with good mothers tend to be good mothers themselves. Chimpanzee females learn, and practice, maternal behaviors as part of socialization. Experiments with monkeys have shown that maternally deprived infants tend to grow up to be poor parents. Learning clearly has an effect on maternal behaviors. Does this mean that there is no genetic component? Of course not.

Intelligence and IQ Test Scores

Perhaps the most widely discussed behavior in the nature-nurture debate has been intelligence. This debate has not been merely academic; it has influenced events and governmental policies throughout human history. In the early twentieth century, prospective immigrants were turned away from the United States and many women underwent involuntary sterilization, both actions based on the then-prevalent views about the genetic basis of intelligence (Gould 1981).

dizygotic twins Twins who
develop from two separate
fertilized eggs (zygotes).

monozygotic twins Identical
twins who develop from a
single fertilized egg (zygote).

Intelligence is difficult to define. It encompasses a number of separate behavioral capacities such as problem-solving abilities (verbal and mathematical), spatial awareness, memory and accumulated knowledge, and the vaguely defined but important quantity we call "common sense." Some psychologists list up to 120 different components of intelligence (Bodmer and Cavalli-Sforza 1976). In spite of a long history of misguided attempts, intelligence cannot be defined as a single quantity. Nonetheless, most intelligence tests do exactly that—attempt to reduce behaviors taken to demonstrate these abilities to a single, measurable value.

The most commonly used form of intelligence assessment is the IQ test, which provides a single measure called the *intelligence quotient*. This measure was originally derived by dividing a person's "mental age" by his or her chronological age, thus providing a value that takes experience into account. The tests are designed so that the average score is 100. The IQ test was first developed in France by Alfred Binet, who sought a means by which to identify children with learning disabilities. The purpose of the test was not to measure intelligence per se but rather to identify those students who would most likely require special education. The test was designed to provide a rough cutoff point below which a student was felt to be in need of special programs; it was not designed to provide an index for comparing individuals within the "normal" range. That is, someone with an IQ score of 120 should not be considered as inherently "better" or "smarter" than someone with a score of 110.

As used in the United States today, IQ tests serve more as an index of predicted performance in school than as a general measure of intelligence. There are many problems in interpreting IQ scores. Scores vary over a person's lifetime, thus reflecting learning and differences in maturation rather than innate knowledge. The tests have also been found to be culturally biased, and there has been little success in developing a "culture-free" test.

Although IQ scores do not provide an accurate reflection of the elusive character of intelligence, they still provide basic information regarding knowledge, learning, and problem solving. What, then, of the issue of genetic versus environmental influences on IQ scores? The bottom line is that both genetics and environment have an influence on the test scores. Many studies have shown that there is a direct relationship between biological relatedness and IQ scores (Figure 2.13). Monozygotic twins show the greatest similarity in test scores, followed by dizygotic twins and other siblings, followed by unrelated individuals. This pattern is expected for a trait that is genetically influenced. (Such studies rely extensively on the comparison of twins. There are two different types of twins: **dizygotic twins,** who grow from two separate zygotes and are no more related than any two siblings, and **monozygotic twins,** who develop from the same zygote and are genetically identical.)

There is also much evidence for environmental influences on IQ test scores. Within each biologically defined category, such as identical twins,

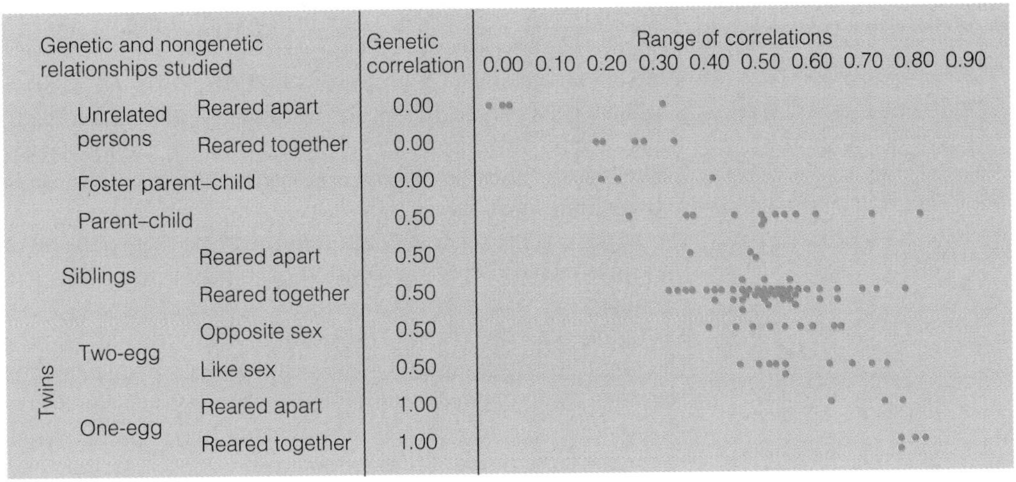

Genetic and nongenetic relationships studied		Genetic correlation	Range of correlations 0.00 0.10 0.20 0.30 0.40 0.50 0.60 0.70 0.80 0.90
Unrelated persons	Reared apart	0.00	
	Reared together	0.00	
Foster parent–child		0.00	
Parent–child		0.50	
Siblings	Reared apart	0.50	
	Reared together	0.50	
Twins — Two-egg	Opposite sex	0.50	
	Like sex	0.50	
Twins — One-egg	Reared apart	1.00	
	Reared together	1.00	

Figure 2.13

Summary of studies reporting on the correlation among individuals' IQ scores. Correlations are measures of similarity; the higher the value, the more similar two individuals' IQ scores. The dots represent the values found in various studies. The genetic correlation is the value expected under a situation of complete inheritance. Even though the correlations increase with genetic relatedness, there is still a great range within any specific class of comparison. For example, monozygotic twins raised together are expected to have a correlation of 1.0, and they have been observed to have correlations ranging from roughly 0.75 to close to 1.0. (Adapted with permission from: S. Singer, *Human Genetics*, 1978, page 79, publisher W. H. Freeman)

correlation in test scores varies from one study to the next. Also, studies comparing environmental factors show that genetic inheritance does not account for all of the variation in IQ scores. The correlation of test scores varies when we compare pairs of individuals raised together with those pairs raised apart. For example, the average correlation between identical twins raised together is higher than the average correlation between identical twins raised apart from each other. If genetics alone were responsible for IQ scores, these correlations would be the same. The fact that they are different, and that the correlation in scores is higher in twins who have been raised together, indicates that a similar environment leads to similar test scores. Findings are similar when comparing similar and different environments of dizygotic twins, siblings, and parents and children (Sutton and Wagner 1985).

A variety of environmental factors have been demonstrated to have an effect on IQ test scores. These include diet, disease, educational quality, and social class, among others (Gould 1981). Intelligence, as reflected by IQ scores, is a highly variable complex trait that reflects the interaction of both genes and environment. The question of which is more important is to a large extent meaningless in considering biocultural organisms such as human beings.

SUMMARY

The DNA molecule specifies the genetic code or set of instructions needed to produce biological structures. DNA acts along with a related molecule, RNA, to translate these instructions into proteins. The DNA is contained along structures called chromosomes within the cell. Chromosomes come in pairs. A segment of DNA that codes for a certain product is called a gene. The different forms of genes present at a locus are called alleles. The DNA molecule has the ability to make copies of itself, allowing transmission of genetic information from cell to cell, and from generation to generation.

Meiosis is the process of sex cell formation that results in one of each chromosome pair being transmitted from parent to offspring. Each individual receives half of his or her alleles from each parent. The two alleles together specify the genetic constitution of an individual—the genotype. The physical manifestation of the genotype is known as the phenotype. The relationship between genotype and phenotype depends on whether an allele is dominant, recessive, or codominant. In complex physical traits, the phenotype is the result of the combined effect of genetics and environment.

The ultimate source of all genetic variation is mutation—a random change in the genetic code. Some mutations are neutral in effect; others are helpful or harmful. The effect of any mutation often depends on the specific environmental conditions. Mutations for any given allele are relatively rare events, but given the large number of loci in many organisms, it is highly probable that each individual has at least one mutant allele.

Genetic factors have been linked to human behaviors, such as those measured by intelligence test scores. Such behaviors appear to be influenced by both genetics and environment. Given the biocultural nature of human beings, it should be no surprise that both genes and environment have an effect on both biology and behavior.

Supplemental Readings

Bodmer, W. F., and L. L. Cavalli-Sforza. 1976. *Genetics, Evolution, and Man.* San Francisco: W. H. Freeman.

Lerner, J. M., and W. J. Libby. 1976. *Heredity, Evolution and Society.* 2d ed. San Francisco: W. H. Freeman. These two texts, though out of date in some areas, contain excellent reviews of the basic principles of molecular and Mendelian genetics, with special attention to human genetics.

Woodward, V. 1992. *Human Heredity and Society.* St. Paul, Minn.: West. A recent and well-written introduction to molecular and Mendelian genetics that focuses on humans.

Cell Biology: A Review

This section, which focuses on the structure of the cell and on the processes of mitosis and meiosis, can be used as a supplement for students wishing to review the basic biology necessary for an understanding of the fundamental principles of Mendelian genetics.

The Cell

All living creatures are made up of cells. Humans, like many organisms, are multicelled. Figure 2.14 shows some of the components of a typical cell. Two major structures are the *nucleus* and the *cytoplasm;* the latter contains a number of other structures. The entire body of the cell is enclosed by a *cell membrane*.

Within the cytoplasm, *mitochondria* convert some cellular material into energy, that is then used for cellular activity. *Ribosomes* are small particles that are frequently attached to a larger structure known as the *endoplasmic reticulum*. Composed of RNA and proteins, ribosomes serve as sites for the manufacture of proteins.

As discussed earlier, the DNA sequences that make up the genetic code are bound together by proteins in long strands known as *chromosomes*. In body cells, chromosomes come in pairs and humans have 23 pairs of chromosomes. The chromosomes within the nucleus of the cell contain all of the DNA, with the exception of something called mitochondrial DNA.

Figure 2.14

Schematic diagram of a cell.

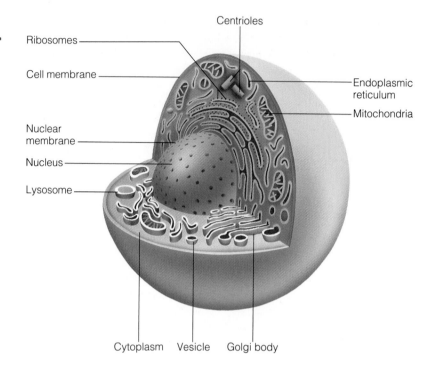

Centrioles

Ribosomes

Cell membrane

Endoplasmic reticulum

Mitochondria

Nuclear membrane

Nucleus

Lysosome

Cytoplasm   Vesicle   Golgi body

Mitosis

DNA has the ability to make copies of itself. This ability is vital for transmitting genetic information from cell to cell and for transmitting genetic information from generation to generation. The replication of DNA is part of the process of cell replication. We will examine two basic processes: mitosis, the replication of body cells, and meiosis, the replication of sex cells.

Mitosis produces two identical body cells from one original. Between cell divisions, each chromosome produces an exact copy of itself, resulting in two pairs with two chromosomes each. When a cell divides, each part contains one of each of the pairs of chromosomes. Thus, two identical body cells, each with the full number of chromosome pairs, is produced. As outlined in Figure 2.15, five stages compose the process of mitosis: interphase, prophase, metaphase, anaphase, and telophase. (Technically speaking, some people do not refer to interphase as a stage.)

During *interphase,* the chromosomes, that are dispersed throughout the nucleus, duplicate. During *prophase,* the chromosomes, each of which is attached to its copy, become tightly coiled and move toward one another in the nucleus. Each of the two copies is called a *chromatid* and their point of attachment, the *centromere*. Small structures located outside the nuclear membrane, known as *centrioles* (see Figure 2.14), move toward opposite ends of the cell and *spindle fibers* form between the centrioles. The nuclear membrane then dissolves.

During *metaphase,* the duplicated chromosomes line up along the middle of the cell and the spindle fibers attach to the centromeres. During *anaphase,* the centromere divides and the two strands of chromatids (original and duplicate) split and move toward opposite ends of the cell. During *telophase,* new nuclear membranes form around each of the two clusters of chromosomes. Finally, the cell membrane pinches in the middle, creating two identical cells.

Meiosis

Meiosis, the production of sex cells (gametes), differs from mitosis in several ways. The main difference is that sex cells contain only half of an organism's DNA—one chromosome from each pair. Thus, when a new zygote, or fertilized egg, is formed from the joining of egg and sperm, the offspring will have 23 chromosome pairs. One of each pair comes from the mother and one of each pair comes from the father.

Meiosis involves two cycles of cell division. The total sequence of events following the initial duplication of chromosomes (interphase) involves eight stages: prophase I, metaphase I, anaphase I, telophase I, prophase II, metaphase II, anaphase II, and telophase II. Figure 2.16 presents a diagram of this process for the production of sperm cells, for a hypothetical organism with two chromosome pairs. Each of the two pairs of chromosomes has replicated itself by the start of prophase I, leading to eight chromatids: the two chromosomes of each pair duplicate, giving a total of $2 \times 2 \times 2 = 8$ chromatids, each pair of which attaches to one of the centromeres through a process known as *synapsis*. At the end of prophase I the nuclear membrane dissolves. Then, during metaphase I, the paired chromosomes line up and spindle fibers form. The copies separate during anaphase I. During telophase I, the nuclear membranes reform and the cell divides. The realization of two cells, each containing eight chromatids, constitutes prophase II. During metaphase II the chromosomes line up, after which the centromeres split and the chromatids separate, completing anaphase II. The nuclear membranes reform during telophase II, and the cell divides. The net result of this sequence of two cell divisions is four sperm cells, each with two chromosomes—half of the genetic material of the father. The process is similar for the production of egg cells from the female, except that the net result is one egg cell and three structures known as *polar bodies* that do not function as sex cells.

Meiosis thus allows half of a parent's genetic material to be passed on to the next generation. When a sperm cell fertilizes an egg cell, the total

Figure 2.15

The five phases of mitosis. In this example, the original body cell contains two pairs of chromosomes. Mitosis produces two identical body cells, each containing two chromosome pairs (a total of four chromosomes each).

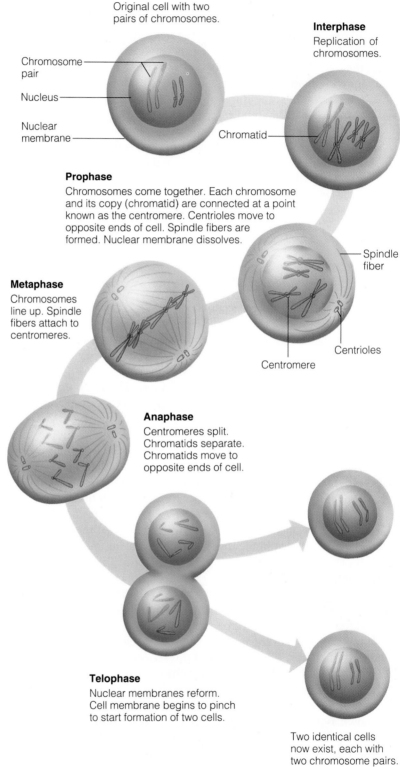

Original cell with two pairs of chromosomes.

Chromosome pair

Nucleus

Nuclear membrane

Chromatid

Interphase
Replication of chromosomes.

Prophase
Chromosomes come together. Each chromosome and its copy (chromatid) are connected at a point known as the centromere. Centrioles move to opposite ends of cell. Spindle fibers are formed. Nuclear membrane dissolves.

Spindle fiber

Metaphase
Chromosomes line up. Spindle fibers attach to centromeres.

Centromere

Centrioles

Anaphase
Centromeres split. Chromatids separate. Chromatids move to opposite ends of cell.

Telophase
Nuclear membranes reform. Cell membrane begins to pinch to start formation of two cells.

Two identical cells now exist, each with two chromosome pairs.

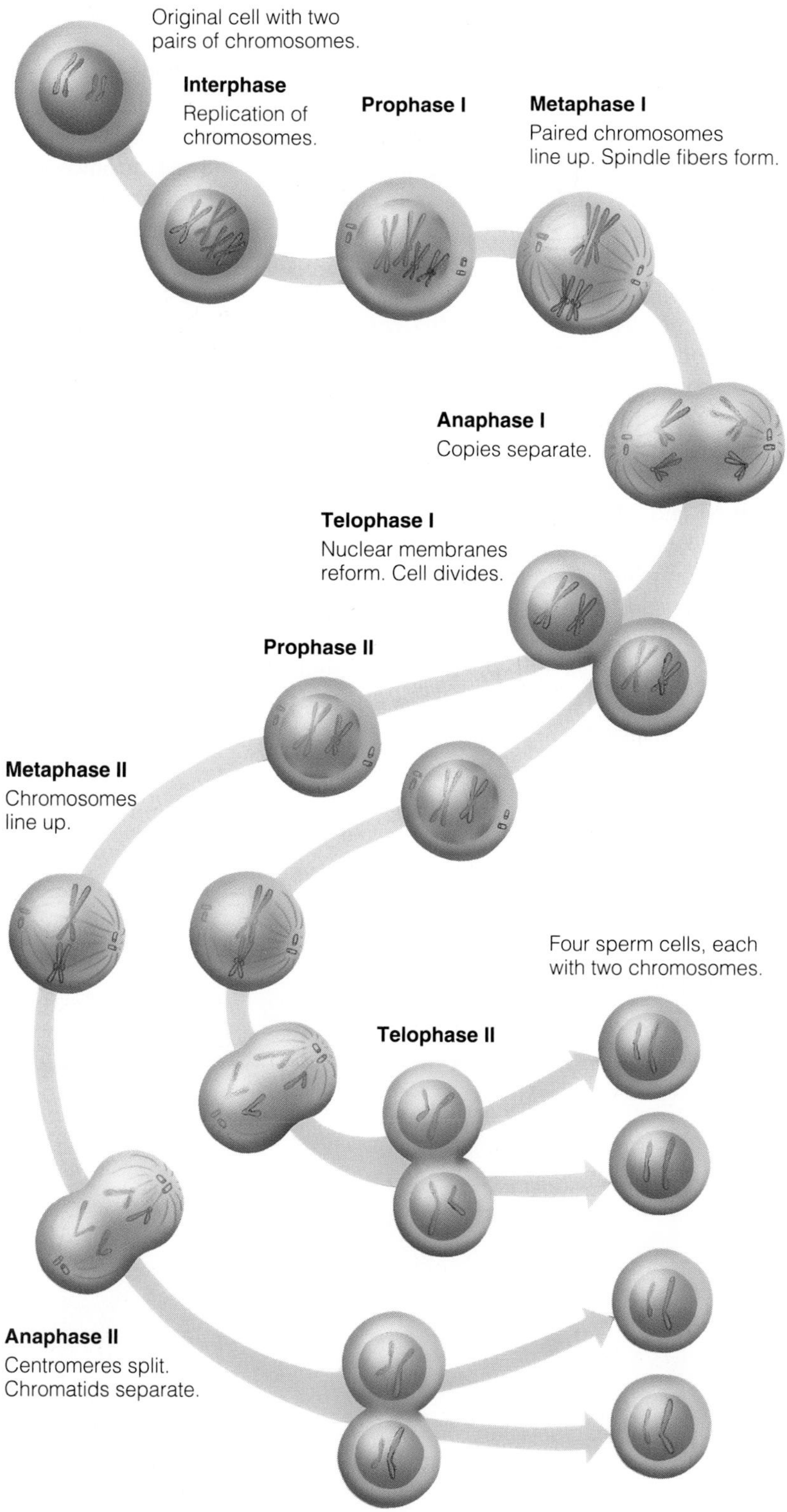

Original cell with two pairs of chromosomes.

Interphase
Replication of chromosomes.

Prophase I

Metaphase I
Paired chromosomes line up. Spindle fibers form.

Anaphase I
Copies separate.

Telophase I
Nuclear membranes reform. Cell divides.

Prophase II

Metaphase II
Chromosomes line up.

Four sperm cells, each with two chromosomes.

Telophase II

Anaphase II
Centromeres split. Chromatids separate.

Figure 2.16

The phases of meiosis for a sperm cell. In this example, the original cell contained two chromosome pairs. As a result of meiosis, four sperm cells were produced, each with two chromosomes. The process is similar for egg cells, except that one egg cell and three polar bodies are produced.

number of chromosomes is restored. For humans, the resulting zygote contains $23 + 23 = 46$ chromosomes, or 23 chromosome pairs.

Sex cells may also contain genetic combinations not present in the parent. When synapsis occurs during prophase I, and the chromosomes pair with their copies, becoming attached to one another at several places, the potential exists for genetic material to be exchanged, a process known as *crossing over*. The resulting genetic combinations allow for variation in each sex cell from its source.

Independent assortment also enhances genetic variability. As discussed earlier, according to this principle, the segregation of any pair of chromosomes does not affect the probability of segregation of any other pair of chromosomes. If you had two chromosome pairs, A and B, with two chromosomes each (A1 and A2, and B1 and B2), only one of each pair will be found in any sex cell. However, you might have one sex cell with A1 and B1 and another sex cell with A1 and B2. Whichever member of the first pair of chromosomes is found in any given sex cell has no bearing on whichever member of the second pair is also found in that sex cell. Independent assortment results from processes occurring during metaphase I. When the paired chromosomes line up, they do so at random and are not influenced by whether they originally came from the person's mother or father. This process allows for tremendous genetic variability in potential offspring.

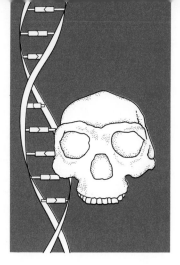

CHAPTER 3

Evolutionary Theory

Biological evolution is genetic change through time and can be studied at two different levels. Microevolution consists of changes in the frequency of alleles in a population from one generation to the next. Macroevolution comprises long-term patterns of genetic change over thousands and millions of generations as well as the process of species formation.

Microevolution

Microevolution takes into account changes in the frequency of alleles from one generation to the next. The focus is generally not on the specific genotypes or phenotypes of individuals, but rather on the total pattern of an entire biological population. We are interested in defining the relative frequencies of different alleles, genotypes, and phenotypes for the entire population being studied. We then seek to determine if any apparent change in these frequencies has occurred over time. If changes have occurred, we try to explain them.

Population Genetics

The term **breeding population** is used frequently in evolutionary theory. In an abstract sense, a breeding population is a group of organisms that tends to choose mates within the group. This definition is a bit tricky because it is not clear what proportion of mating within a group defines a breeding population.

breeding population A group of organisms that tend to choose mates from within the group.

51

For example, suppose you travel to a village in a remote mountain region. You find that 99 percent of all the people in the village are married to others who were born in the same village. In this case, the village would appear to fit our ideal definition. But, what if only 80 percent of the people choose their mates from within the village? What if the number were 50 percent? At what point do you stop referring to the population as a "breeding population"? There is no quick and ready answer to this question.

On a practical level, human populations are initially most often defined on the basis of geographic and political boundaries. A small isolated island, for example, easily fits the requirements of a defined population. In most cases, the local geographic unit (such as town or village) is used. Because many human populations have distinct geographic boundaries, this solution often provides the best approach. Care must be taken, however, to ensure that a local geographic unit, such as a town, is not composed of distinct subpopulations, such as groups belonging to different religious sects.

Another potential problem in defining populations is determining the difference between the total census population and the breeding population. Microevolutionary theory specifically concerns those individuals who contribute to the next generation. The total population refers to everybody, whether or not they are likely to breed. The breeding population is smaller than the total population because of a number of factors. First, some individuals in the total population will be too young or too old to mate. Second, cultural factors and geographic distribution may act to limit an individual's choice of mate, and as a consequence some individuals will not breed. If, for example, you live in an isolated area, there may not be enough individuals of the opposite sex from which to choose a mate.

Once a population has been defined, the next step in microevolutionary analysis is to determine the frequencies of genotypes and alleles within the population.

Genotype and allele frequencies. The genotype frequency is a measure of the relative proportions of different genotypes within a population. Likewise, an allele frequency is simply a measure of the relative proportion of alleles within a population. Genotype frequencies are obtained by dividing the number of individuals with each genotype by the total number of individuals. For example, consider a hypothetical population of 200 people for the MN blood group system where there are 98 people with genotype *MM*, 84 people with genotype *MN*, and 18 people with genotype *NN*. The genotype frequencies are therefore:

Frequency of *MM* = 98/200 = 0.49

Frequency of *MN* = 84/200 = 0.42

Frequency of *NN* = 18/200 = 0.09

Note that the total frequency of all genotypes adds up to 1 (0.49 + 0.42 + 0.09 = 1). Allele frequencies are computed by counting the

T A B L E   3.1
Example of Allele Frequency Computation

Imagine you have just collected information on *MN* blood group genotypes for 250 humans in a given population. Your data are:

Number of *MM* genotype = 40

Number of *MN* genotype = 120

Number of *NN* genotype = 90

The allele frequencies are computed as follows:

Genotype	Number of people	Total number of alleles	Number of *M* alleles	Number of *N* alleles
MM	40	80	80	0
MN	120	240	120	120
NN	90	180	0	180
Total	250	500	200	300

The relative frequency of the *M* allele is computed as the number of *M* alleles divided by the total number of alleles: 200/500 = 0.4.

The relative frequency of the *N* allele is computed as the number of *N* alleles divided by the total number of alleles: 300/500 = 0.6.

As a check, note that the relative frequencies of the alleles must add up to 1.0 (0.4 + 0.6 = 1.0).

---

number of each allele and dividing that number by the total number of alleles. An example of allele frequency computation is given in Table 3.1.

Hardy-Weinberg equilibrium. The mathematical basis of microevolutionary theory rests upon Mendel's principles and the use of a model known as **Hardy-Weinberg equilibrium.** This model provides a method of predicting genotype frequencies in future generations under the assumption that mating is at random and that no evolution takes place.

The Hardy-Weinberg equilibrium model is a mathematical statement using symbols to represent allele frequencies. Many microevolutionary models assume a single locus with two alleles (e.g., *A* and *a*). By convention, the symbols p and q are used to represent the frequencies of the *A* allele and the *a* allele, respectively. These symbols are a form of shorthand because it is easier to say p than "the frequency of the *A* allele."

The Hardy-Weinberg equilibrium model states that given allele frequencies of p and q, the expected genotype frequencies are:

Frequency of *AA* = p^2

Frequency of *Aa* = $2pq$

Frequency of *aa* = q^2

Hardy-Weinberg equilibrium In the absence of evolutionary forces, allele frequencies remain constant from one generation to the next.

evolutionary forces Four mechanisms that can cause changes in allele frequencies from one generation to the next.

nonrandom mating Patterns of mate choice that influence the distributions of genotype and phenotype frequencies.

inbreeding Mating between biologically related individuals.

assortative mating Mating between phenotypically similar or dissimilar individuals.

Assume a population with two alleles (A and a) with allele frequencies of $p = 0.6$ and $q = 0.4$. Using the Hardy-Weinberg equilibrium model, the predicted genotype frequencies are:

$$AA = (0.6)^2 = (0.6)\,(0.6) = 0.36$$
$$Aa = 2(0.6)\,(0.4) \qquad\quad = 0.48$$
$$aa = (0.4)^2 = (0.4)\,(0.4) = 0.16$$

The Hardy-Weinberg equilibrium model can also be used to show that, given certain assumptions, there will be no change in allele frequency from one generation to the next.

The Hardy-Weinberg equilibrium model makes several assumptions. It assumes random mating within the population (with respect to the locus or loci of interest). That is, every individual has an equal chance of mating with any individual of the opposite sex (both sexes are also assumed to have equal allele frequencies). The Hardy-Weinberg equilibrium model also assumes that the population is large enough that there is no variation in allele frequencies caused by sampling (no genetic drift); there is no movement into or out of the population (no gene flow); there are no new alleles (no mutation); and there is no difference in the fertility or mortality of different genotypes (no natural selection). If we compare the expected genotype frequencies with those actually observed and find no difference, then we can conclude that the population is in Hardy-Weinberg equilibrium. If the predicted and observed genotype frequencies are not the same, then the population is not in Hardy-Weinberg equilibrium, and we know that at least one of the assumptions must be incorrect. That is, we know that nonrandom mating, genetic drift, gene flow, mutation, natural selection, or some combination of these factors is present. Further analysis would then be needed to determine which of these assumptions was incorrect.

There are two basic reasons a population might not be in a state of Hardy-Weinberg equilibrium. Observed and predicted genotype frequencies may differ because of the effects of evolutionary forces and/or nonrandom mating. **Evolutionary forces** are those mechanisms that actually lead to a change in allele frequency over time. The evolutionary forces are mutation, natural selection, genetic drift, and gene flow. These four forces are the only mechanisms that can cause the frequency of an allele to change over time. Random mating is one form of mating system. **Nonrandom mating,** however, refers to the patterns of mate choice within a population and its genetic consequences. Nonrandom mating includes **inbreeding,** the mating of biologically related individuals (Figure 3.1), and **assortative mating,** mating on the basis of phenotypic similarity or dissimilarity. Mating systems do not change allele frequencies, but they do have an effect on the *rate* of allele frequency change.

Figure 3.1

Inbreeding is used with many domesticated animals to produce certain types of characteristics. (Courtesy of Kenneth Feder, Central Connecticut State University)

Evolutionary Forces

Mutation. Mutation introduces new alleles into a population. Therefore, the frequency of different alleles will change over time. For example, consider a genetic locus with a single allele, *A*, for a population of 100 people (and 200 alleles). Everyone in the population will have genotype *AA*, and the frequency of the *A* allele is 1.0 (100 percent). Now, assume that one of the *A* alleles being passed on to the next generation changes into a new form, *a*. Assuming the population stays the same size (to make the mathematics a bit easier), there will be 199 *A* alleles and 1 *a* allele in the next generation. The frequency of *A* will have changed from 1.0 to 0.995 (199/200), and the frequency of *a* will have changed from 0.0 to 0.005 (1/200).

If there is no further evolutionary change, the allele frequencies will remain the same in future generations. If this mutation continues to recur, the frequency of the *a* allele will slowly increase, assuming no other evolutionary forces are operating. For typical mutation rates, such a process would take a very long time.

Although mutations are vital to evolution because they provide new variations, mutation rates are low and do not lead, by themselves, to major changes in allele frequency. The other evolutionary forces increase or decrease the frequencies of mutant alleles.

Many discrete genetic traits are **polymorphisms** (many forms). A genetic polymorphism is a locus with two or more alleles having frequencies too large to be a result of mutation alone. The usual, somewhat arbitrary, cutoff point for these allele frequencies is 0.01. If an allele has a frequency greater than 0.01, we can safely assume this relatively high frequency is caused by factors other than mutation: natural selection, genetic drift, and/or gene flow.

Natural selection. As discussed in Chapter 1, natural selection filters genetic variation. Individuals with certain biological characteristics that allow them to survive to reproduce, pass on the alleles for such characteristics to the next generation. Natural selection does not create new genetic variation (only mutation can do that), but it does change the relative frequencies of different alleles.

The analysis of natural selection focuses on **fitness,** the probability of survival and reproduction of an organism. For any locus, fitness is measured as the relative genetic contribution of a genotype to the next generation. Imagine a locus with two alleles, *A* and *a*, and the genotypes *AA*, *Aa*, and *aa*. If all individuals with genotypes *AA* and *Aa* survive and reproduce but only half of those with genotype *aa* survive and reproduce, then the fitness of genotype *aa* is half of that of genotypes *AA* and *Aa*. Fitness refers to the proportion of individuals with a given phenotype who survive and reproduce.

polymorphism A discrete genetic trait in which there are at least two alleles at a locus having frequencies greater than 0.01.

fitness An organism's probability of survival and reproduction.

Selection against recessive alleles. Let us assume that the fitness of genotypes AA and Aa is 100 percent. That is, all individuals with these genotypes survive and reproduce in equal numbers. Further assume that the fitness of individuals with genotype aa is 0 percent. That is, no one with genotype aa will survive and reproduce. This example corresponds to a situation where a recessive allele (a) is fatal for those who have two copies (aa). Now, assume a population of 200 people before selection with the following distribution of genotypes: AA = 50, Aa = 100, aa = 50. Using the methods shown in Table 3.1, the allele frequencies can be found: the frequency of A is 0.5, and the frequency of a is 0.5.

Table 3.2 shows the process of natural selection using these hypothetical numbers. After selection, the number of individuals in each genotype is: AA = 50, Aa = 100, aa = 0. All individuals with genotypes AA and Aa survive, and none of those with genotype aa survive. After selection, there are 150 individuals, and the allele frequencies are A = 0.6667 and a = 0.3333.

This example shows the effect of selection against a recessive allele. The frequency of the a allele drops from 0.5 to 0.3333. Since a is a harmful allele, however, you might expect that the a allele would be totally eliminated. This does not occur. Since the heterozygote (Aa) is not eliminated through selection, these individuals continue to pass the a allele on to the next generation. The recessive allele a cannot be eliminated in a single generation.

A case of selection against recessive homozygotes in humans is Tay-Sachs disease. This affliction is caused by a metabolic disorder that results in blindness, mental retardation, and the destruction of the central nervous system. Children with Tay-Sachs disease generally die within the first few years of life. The disease is caused by a recessive allele and occurs in those individuals who are homozygous. Heterozygotes carry the allele but do not show any major biological impairments.

When deleterious alleles are recessive, such as with Tay-Sachs disease, the frequency is generally not zero, since heterozygotes continue to pass the allele on from generation to generation. Nonetheless, the frequency of a harmful recessive allele will still be very low. This low fequency is maintained by mutation but is kept from increasing by natural selection.

Selection against dominant alleles. What if a dominant allele is selected against? As an example, consider the same starting point, as in the previous example: AA = 50, Aa = 100, and aa = 50, giving initial allele frequencies of A = 0.5 and a = 0.5. Complete selection against the dominant allele (A) will mean a fitness of 0 percent for genotypes AA and Aa and a fitness of 100 percent for the genotype aa. After selection, there are no AA individuals, no Aa individuals, and 50 aa individuals. The allele frequencies after selection are A = 0.0 and a = 1.0. The dominant allele has been completely eliminated after one generation of selection. If the fitness values of AA and Aa were greater than zero but less than 100

T A B L E   3.2
Example of Natural Selection against a Recessive Homozygote

This example uses an initial population size before selection of 200 people. The locus has two alleles, *A* and *a*. Initially there are 50 people with genotype *AA*, 100 people with genotype *Aa,* and 50 people with genotype *aa*. The allele frequencies before selection are therefore 0.5 for *A* and 0.5 for *a*. The fitness values have been chosen to illustrate total selection against the recessive homozygote.

| | Genotype | | | |
	AA	*Aa*	*aa*	Total
Number of people before selection	50	100	50	200
Fitness (percentage that survives)	100%	100%	0%	
Number of people after selection	50	100	0	150

There are 150 people after selection. Using the method of allele frequency computation shown in Table 3.1 and in the text, the allele frequencies after selection are 200/300 = 0.667 for the *A* allele and 100/300 = 0.333 for the *a* allele.

percent, then the *A* allele would not be eliminated because some individuals with this allele would survive.

An example of a dominant allele in human beings is achondroplastic dwarfism. This type of dwarfism (small body size and abnormal body proportions) is caused by a dominant allele found in very low frequencies in human populations—roughly 0.00005. Because the achondroplastic allele is dominant, individuals with one or two of the alleles will show the disease. Virtually all achondroplastic dwarfs are heterozygotes. The condition is usually caused by a mutation occurring in the sex cells of one parent.

The low frequency of achondroplastic dwarfs is the result of natural selection acting to remove the harmful allele from the population. Although there is no major risk of mortality for a heterozygous achondroplastic dwarf, selection acts on differential reproduction. Given their physical appearance, these dwarfs have few opportunities to mate.

Selection for the heterozygote. The previous examples discussed selection against recessive and dominant homozygotes, which act to increase the frequency of one allele and decrease the frequency of another. Selection could also occur *for* recessive or dominant homozygotes, which would

balancing selection Selection for the heterozygote and against the homozygotes (the heterozygote is most fit).

genetic drift A mechanism for evolutionary change resulting from the random fluctuations of gene frequencies from one generation to the next.

act to increase the frequency of an allele. With time, the allele frequencies will approach 0 or 1, depending on which allele is selected against.

Is there a way that natural selection can produce intermediate values? The answer is a form of selection known as selection for the heterozygote (and therefore against the homozygotes). Consider fitness values of: $AA = 70$ percent, $Aa = 100$ percent, and $aa = 20$ percent. Here, only 70 percent of those with genotype AA and 20 percent of those with genotype aa survive for every 100 people with genotype Aa (the heterozygote). Selection is for the heterozygote and against the homozygotes. Let the frequency of both the A and a alleles equal 0.5. In a population of 200 people, this means we start with 50 AA people, 100 Aa people, and 50 aa people before selection. Given the fitness values above, there will be 35 people with AA, 100 with Aa, and 10 with aa after selection. The allele frequencies after selection are $A = 0.586$ and $a = 0.414$.

Why would the frequency of the A allele increase and the frequency of the a allele decrease? Selection for the heterozygote involves selection for and against both alleles. Because the fitness of AA is greater in this example than the fitness of aa (70 percent versus 20 percent), proportionately more individuals with genotype AA will survive and reproduce. Hence, proportionately more A alleles will appear in the next generation.

Figure 3.2 shows the pattern of allele frequency change over 20 generations using the initial values and fitness values in this example. There is no change in the allele frequency after approximately eight generations. This is the expected pattern when there is selection for the heterozygote. A balance is reached between selection for and against the two alleles A and a. The exact value of this balancing point will depend on the fitness values of the homozygous genotypes. Selection for the heterozygote is also called **balancing selection.**

Genetic drift.   **Genetic drift** is the random change in allele frequency from one generation to the next. These random changes are the result of the nature of probability. Think for a moment about flipping a coin in the air. What is the probability of its landing with the head facing up? It is 50 percent. Suppose you flip a coin 10 times. How many heads and how many tails do you expect to get? Since the probability of getting a head or a tail is 50 percent, you expect to get five heads and five tails. Try this experiment several times. Did you always get five tails and five heads? Sometimes you will get five heads and five tails, but sometimes you get different numbers.

What does this have to do with genetics? The reproductive process in this way is like a coin toss. During the process of sex cell replication (meiosis), only one allele out of two at a given locus is used. The probability of either allele being passed on is 50 percent, just like a coin toss. Imagine a locus with two alleles, A and a. Now imagine a man and a woman, each with genotype Aa, who have a child. The man can pass on either an A allele or an a allele. Likewise, a woman can pass on either an A

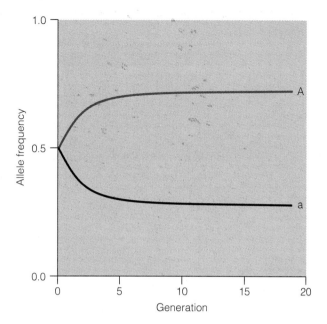

Figure 3.2

Change over time in allele frequencies when there is selection for the heterozygote (*Aa*). The initial allele frequencies are both 0.5. The fitness of each genotype (the relative frequency of survival) is: *AA* = 70%, *Aa* = 100%, and *aa* = 20%.

allele or an *a* allele. As we saw in the last chapter, the probable distribution of genotypes among the children are 25 percent *AA*, 50 percent *Aa*, and 25 percent *aa*. If the couple has four children, you would expect one with *AA*, two with *Aa*, and one with *aa*. Thanks to random chance, however, the couple may get a different distribution of genotypes.

When genetic drift occurs in populations, the same principle applies. Allele frequencies can change because of random chance. Sometimes the allele frequency will increase, and sometimes it will decrease. The direction of allele frequency change caused by genetic drift is random. The only time drift will not produce a change in allele frequency is when only one allele is present at a given locus. For example, if each parent passed on an *A* allele to each of the four children, the frequency of the *A* allele would be 1.0 among the children. The *a* allele would have been lost.

Genetic drift occurs in each generation. Figure 3.3 shows the results of three computer simulations of drift. In each case, the initial allele frequency was 0.5, and the population size was equal to 10 individuals (20 alleles) in each generation. The simulation was allowed to continue in each case for 20 generations. The graphs show the changes in allele frequency over time. Note that each of the three simulations shows a different pattern. This is expected because genetic drift is a random process. Each simulation is an independent event.

In each of these three graphs, the allele frequency fluctuates up and down. In Figure 3.3a, the allele frequency after 20 generations is 0.3. In Figure 3.3b, the allele frequency after 20 generations is 0.75. In Figure 3.3c, the allele frequency is equal to 1.0 after 10 generations, and it does

Figure 3.3

Figure 3.3

Three computer simulations of 20 generations of genetic drift for populations of 10 individuals. Each simulation started with an initial allele frequency of 0.5.

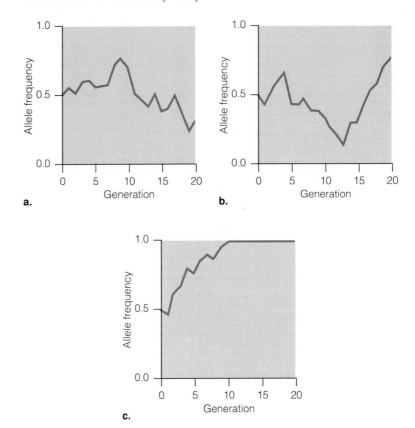

not change any more. Given enough time, and assuming no other evolutionary forces affect allele frequencies, genetic drift will ultimately lead to an allele's becoming fixed at a value of 0.0 or 1.0. Thus, genetic drift leads to the reduction of variation within a population, given enough time.

The effect of genetic drift depends on the size of the breeding population. The larger the population size, the less change will occur from one generation to the next. Thinking back to the coin toss analogy will show you that this makes sense. If you flip a coin 10 times and get three heads and seven tails, it is not that unusual. If you flip a coin 1 million times, however, it would be much less likely that you would get the same proportions—300,000 heads and 700,000 tails. This is because of a basic principle of probability: the greater the number of events, the fewer deviations from the expected frequencies (50 percent heads and 50 percent tails).

The effect of population size on genetic drift is shown in Figure 3.4. These graphs show the results of 1,000 simulations of genetic drift for four different values of breeding population size: $N = 10, 50, 100, 1,000$. In each computer run the initial allele frequency was set to 0.5, and the simulation was allowed to continue for 20 generations. The four graphs

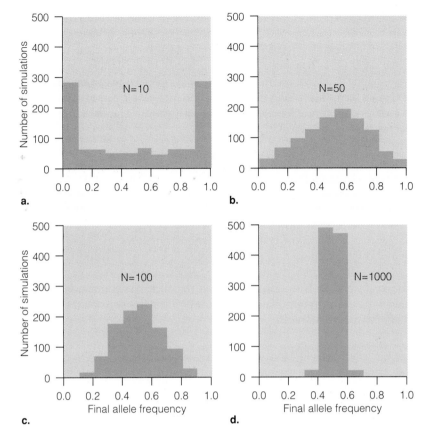

Figure 3.4

Allele frequency distributions for 1,000 computer simulations of 20 generations of genetic drift. The distributions show the number of times a given allele frequency was reached after 20 generations of drift. In all cases, the initial allele frequency was 0.5. Each graph represents a different value of population size: (a) = 10, (b) = 50, (c) = 100, (d) = 1,000.

show the distribution of allele frequency values after 20 generations of genetic drift. It is clear from these graphs that the larger the population size, the fewer deviations in allele frequency caused by genetic drift. The main point here is that genetic drift has the greatest evolutionary effect in relatively small breeding populations.

Genetic drift in human populations is shown in a case study of a group known as the Dunkers, a religious sect that emigrated from Germany to the United States in the early 1700s. Approximately 50 families composed the initial group. Glass (1953) studied the genetic characteristics of the descendants of the original founding group living in Pennsylvania. These populations have never been greater than several hundred people and thus provide a unique opportunity to study genetic drift in a small human group. Glass found that the Dunker population differed in a number of genetic traits from both the modern German and U.S. populations. Furthermore, the allele frequencies of Germany and the United States were almost identical, suggesting that other factors such as natural selection were unlikely. For example, the allele frequencies for the MN blood group were roughly $M = 0.55$ and $N = 0.45$ for both the United States and German samples. In the Dunker population, however, the allele frequencies were $M = 0.655$ and $N = 0.345$. Based on these and additional data, Glass concluded that the genetics of the Dunker population were shaped to a large extent by genetic drift over two centuries. Although 200 years seems like a long time to you and me, it is a fraction of an instant in evolutionary time. Genetic drift can clearly produce rapid changes under the proper circumstances.

Gene flow. The fourth evolutionary force is **gene flow,** the movement of alleles from one population to another. Gene flow involves the movement of alleles between at least two populations. When gene flow occurs, the two populations mix genetically and tend to become more similar. Under most conditions, the more the two populations mix, the more similar they will become genetically (assuming that the two environments are not different enough to produce different effects of natural selection).

Consider a genetic locus with two alleles, A and a. Assume two populations, 1 and 2. Now, assume that all the alleles in population 1 are A and all the alleles in population 2 are a. The allele frequencies of these two imaginary populations are:

Population 1	Population 2
Frequency of A = 1.0	Frequency of A = 0.0
Frequency of a = 0.0	Frequency of a = 1.0

Now imagine a situation where 10 percent of the people in population 1 move to population 2, and vice versa. This movement constitutes gene flow. What effect will the gene flow have? After gene flow has taken place, population 1 is made up of 90 percent A alleles and 10 percent a alleles. Population 2 is made up of 10 percent A alleles and 90 percent a alleles. The allele frequencies of the two populations, though still different, have become more similar as the consequence of gene flow. If the same rate of gene flow (10 percent) continues generation after generation, the two populations will become more and more similar genetically. After 20 generations of gene flow, the two populations will be almost identical. The accumulated effects of gene flow over time are shown for this hypothetical example in Figure 3.5.

Apart from making populations more similar, gene flow can also introduce new variation within a population. In the example, a new allele (a) was introduced into population 1 as the result of gene flow. A new mutation arising in one population can be spread throughout the rest of a species by gene flow.

Compared to many other organisms, humans are relatively mobile creatures. Human populations show a great deal of variation in degree of migration. Even today, many humans live and work within a small area

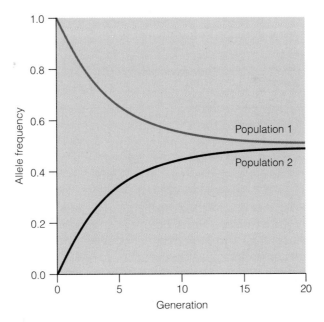

Figure 3.5

Effects of gene flow over time. Population 1 started with an allele frequency of 1.0 and population 2 started with an allele frequency of 0.0. The two populations exchange 10 percent of their genes with each generation. Over time, the continued gene flow acts to make the two populations more similar genetically.

and choose mates from nearby. Some people are more mobile than others, the extent of their mobility depending on a number of factors such as available technology, occupation, income, and other social factors.

In spite of local and regional differences, humans today all belong to the same species. Even though genetic variation exists among populations, they are in fact characterized more by their similarity. A critical factor in the cohesiveness of the human species, gene flow acts to reduce differences among groups.

The amount of gene flow between human populations depends on a variety of environmental and cultural factors. Geographic distance is a major determinant of migration and gene flow. The further two populations are apart geographically, the less likely they are to exchange mates. Even in today's modern world, with access to jet airplanes and other devices, you are still more likely to choose a spouse from nearby than from across the country. Exceptions to the rule do occur, of course, but the influence of geographic distance is still very strong.

Geographic distance is a major determinant of human migration and gene flow, but it is not the only one. Ethnic differences also act to limit them. Most large cities have distinct neighborhoods that correspond to different ethnic communities. A large proportion of marriages take place within these groups because of the common human preference for marrying within one's own social and cultural group. Likewise, religious differences also act as barriers to gene flow because many, though not all, people prefer to marry within the same religion. Further, social class and educational differences can also limit gene flow.

admixture The interbreeding of individuals from two or more initially distinct gene pools.

Throughout human history there have been many examples of large-scale migrations from different parts of the world. In many cases, new populations are formed through the process of **admixture,** the mixing of individuals from two or more initially different groups, such as African Americans. Large numbers of Africans were brought against their will to the United States as slaves and, in some cases, the women had children by their masters. Since that time some interbreeding between African Americans and European Americans has continued. Genetically, this is a situation of European gene flow into the transplanted African population of the United States.

By analyzing modern allele frequencies, the approximate amount of European admixture can be determined. Though the methods are not exact, they do provide a rough idea of the total amount of gene flow. Most of these studies suggest European admixture in African Americans that ranges from 4 to 31 percent (Chakraborty 1986). The estimate of admixture varies with social and geographic factors; African-American populations in northern states generally have higher proportions of European admixture.

Interaction of the evolutionary forces. It is convenient to discuss each of the four evolutionary forces separately, but in reality they act together to produce allele frequency change. Mutation acts to introduce new genetic variants; natural selection, genetic drift, and gene flow act to change the frequency of the mutant allele. Sometimes the evolutionary forces act together, and sometimes they act in opposition. Their exact interaction depends on a wide variety of factors, such as the biochemical and physical effects of different alleles, presence or absence of dominance, population size, population distribution, and the environment, to name but a few. Many biological anthropologists attempt to unravel some of these factors in human population studies.

In general, we look at how natural selection, genetic drift, and gene flow act to increase or decrease genetic variation within and between groups. (Mutation gets less attention because, even though it introduces new genetic variants, the change in allele frequency in one generation is low.) An increase in variation within a population means that individuals within the population will be more genetically different from one another. A decrease in variation within a population means the reverse; individuals will become more similar to one another genetically. An increase in variation among populations means that two or more populations will become more different from one another genetically, and a decrease in variation within populations means the reverse.

Let us first consider the effects of genetic drift, gene flow, and natural selection on allele frequency variation. Genetic drift tends to remove alleles from a population and therefore acts to reduce variation within a population. On the other hand, because genetic drift is a random event and occurs independently in different populations, the pattern of genetic drift will

TABLE 3.3
Summary of the Effects of Selection, Drift, and Gene Flow
on Variation within and among Populations

Evolutionary force	Variation within populations	Variation among populations
Selection	Increase or decrease	Increase or decrease
Genetic drift	Decrease	Increase
Gene flow	Increase	Decrease

A decrease in variation within a population makes individuals more similar to one another, whereas an increase in variation within a population makes individuals less similar to one another. A decrease in variation among populations makes the populations more similar to one another, whereas an increase in variation among populations makes the populations less similar to one another. Note that natural selection can either increase or decrease variation; the exact effect depends on the type of selection and differences in environment (see text).

tend to be different on average in different populations. On average, then, genetic drift will act to increase variation among populations. Gene flow acts to introduce new alleles into a population and can have the effect of increasing variation within a population. Gene flow also acts to reduce variation among populations in most cases.

Selection can either increase or decrease variation among populations, depending on environmental variation. If two populations have similar environments, then natural selection will take place in the same way in both groups and therefore will act to reduce genetic differences between them. On the other hand, if the two populations are in different enough environments that natural selection operates in different ways, then variation between the populations may be increased. Table 3.3 summarizes the effects of different evolutionary forces on variation within and among populations.

Different evolutionary forces can produce the same, or opposite, effects. Different forces can also act in opposition to one another. Genetic drift and gene flow, for example, have opposite effects on variation within and among populations. If both of these forces operate at the same time, they can counteract each other.

Nonrandom Mating

Recall that one of the assumptions of the Hardy-Weinberg equilibrium model is random mating. Everyone has the same chance of mating with everyone else (with respect to the locus or loci under consideration). In reality, populations often show deviations from random mating. From

inbreeding coefficient The increase in the probability of homozygous offspring because of inbreeding.

an evolutionary standpoint, we are interested in nonrandom mating: who mates with whom and the genetic similarities of those who mate. Deviations from random mating do not lead to changes in allele frequencies. Patterns of nonrandom mating, however, can influence the rate of allele frequency change by interacting with the evolutionary forces.

Inbreeding. Inbreeding refers to mating with a close biological relative. Actually, we are all inbred to some extent, but we generally reserve the term for close biological relatedness. Though the definition of "close" is somewhat arbitrary, we are usually interested in matings between first cousins or closer.

Inbreeding is not an evolutionary force because it does not cause any changes in allele frequencies. What, then, is the genetic effect of inbreeding? Closely related individuals are likely to have similar alleles inherited from a common ancestor, and thus the effect of inbreeding is to make homozygous offspring more likely. For example, brothers and sisters share more alleles than any two unrelated individuals. If brothers and sisters mate, there is an increased probability (25 percent) that their offspring will receive identical alleles. If two first cousins mate, there is also an increased probability (6.25 percent) that their offspring will receive identical alleles.

The increase in the probability of homozygous offspring is also termed the **inbreeding coefficient.** This coefficient can also be interpreted as the proportion of loci that are homozygous because of common ancestry. Computation of inbreeding coefficients is beyond the scope of this text, but Table 3.4 lists these coefficients for several forms of close inbreeding. Note that the increased probability of homozygous offspring in third cousins is relatively low (1.6 percent). Inbreeding coefficients for more distantly related couples, such as fourth cousins, are even lower and have little, if any, genetic impact.

Inbreeding changes the genotype proportions from those expected under Hardy-Weinberg equilibrium. Inbreeding increases the proportion of homozygotes and decreases the proportion of heterozygotes in a population. Allele frequencies are not changed, only the genotype frequencies.

Inbreeding by itself does not lead to changes in allele frequencies. Inbreeding can influence the rate of allele frequency change by interacting with natural selection. For example, if there is selection against recessive homozygotes, then inbreeding leads to a more rapid decline in the frequency of the recessive allele. This occurs because natural selection has more homozygotes to act on as compared to a state of random mating.

The genetic effects of inbreeding are often harmful. Studies have shown that the incidence of congenital birth defects and mortality during the first year of life is higher among inbred offspring than among others (Bittles et al. 1991). The risk of birth defects in offspring of first cousins has been estimated at between 1.3 and 1.8 times that of the offspring of

T A B L E   3.4
Inbreeding Coefficients for Certain Close Marriages

Marriage	Inbreeding coefficient
Parent–child	¼ = 0.250
Siblings	¼ = 0.250
Uncle–niece Aunt–nephew Half siblings	⅛ = 0.125
First cousins	¹⁄₁₆ = 0.063
Second cousins	¹⁄₃₂ = 0.031
Third cousins	¹⁄₆₄ = 0.016

The inbreeding coefficient is an estimate of the increased probability that children of these marriages will have two identical alleles because of descent from a common ancestor.

unrelated parents (Bodmer and Cavalli-Sforza 1976). Some studies have suggested that inbreeding can lead to mental retardation, but others have not confirmed this.

Assortative mating. Another form of nonrandom mating is assortative mating, which describes mating made on the basis of some observable characteristic. One of the most obvious examples of assortative mating in the United States is skin color. The frequency of marriages between European Americans and African Americans is low. Americans tend most often to marry someone with a similar skin color.

It should be no surprise that mating is not random in human populations. If you list the characteristics you prefer in a spouse, you will most often identify social and biological traits. Social characteristics may include economic status, ethnicity, religion, and/or educational level. Phenotypic characteristics are likely to include skin color, height, weight, and hair color.

When mates are chosen on the basis of similar characteristics, it is **positive assortative mating.** If there is a genetic basis for these characteristics, then the genetic effect is the same as that of inbreeding. The frequency of homozygotes is increased relative to random mating. In theory we could also expect the reverse, **negative assortative mating,** whereby mates are chosen on the basis of having different phenotypic characteristics. If it were common, for example, for short males to choose tall females for mates, then that would be a case of negative assortative mating. There is little evidence that negative assortative mating is common in human populations.

The old idea that opposites attract has few data to support it. Studies of marriage choice have shown that people tend to choose spouses with similar social and biological characteristics. In the United States, positive assortative mating has been demonstrated for skin color, height, weight, and eye color, in addition to a variety of social, religious, ethnic, and educational variables (Buss 1985).

positive assortative mating
Mates chosen on the basis of similar phenotypic characteristics.

negative assortative mating
Mates chosen on the basis of different phenotypic characteristics.

Macroevolution

To many, but not all, evolutionary biologists, macroevolution is merely the net effect of microevolutionary change over long periods of time. Some, however, believe that additional forces must be considered in explaining macroevolution.

Perhaps the single largest task of macroevolutionary theory is to explain the origin of new species. The origin of new species has been observed in historical times and in the present. Some new species have been brought about by human intervention and controlled breeding, as with many species of tropical fish. There are also examples of new species having arisen naturally in the recent past, such as certain types of fruit flies. We also have information on populations in the process of forming new species, such as certain groups of snails. Most of what we observe about new species formation comes from analysis of the fossil record.

How do new species come into being? It is ironic that even though the title of Darwin's book was *On the Origin of Species,* it did not deal very much with this question. Instead, Darwin sought to explain the basic nature of evolutionary change, believing that extension of these principles could explain the formation of new species. Indeed, even though there are different models of species formation, all essentially use the processes of microevolution for explanation.

Taxonomy and Evolution

An understanding of the origin of species begins with consideration of the definition of the term *species*. There is considerable controversy regarding its definition and how it relates to models of evolutionary change (Ereshefsky 1992). A discussion of macroevolution and the origin of species must begin with an understanding of certain principles of biological classification.

In Chapter 1, you read about Linnaeus's attempt to construct a system of classification for all living creatures. Instead of simply making up a list of all known organisms, Linnaeus developed a scheme by which creatures could be grouped together according to certain shared characteristics. The system of biological classification is called a taxonomy. Even though we now make use of Linnaeus's scheme to describe patterns of evolution, Linnaeus did not have this objective in mind. Rather, he sought to understand the nature of God's design in living organisms.

If you think for a moment, you will realize that a great deal of your daily life revolves around your use and understanding of different systems of classification. In biology, a taxonomy is a system of classification that shows relationships between different groups of organisms. This may sound simple enough but can actually be rather difficult. For example, consider the following list of organisms: flounder, bat, shark, canary, lizard, horse, and whale. How would you classify these creatures? One way might be to put certain animals together according to size: the flounder, bat, canary, and lizard in a "small" category, the shark and horse in a "medium" category, and the whale in a "large" category. Another method would be to put the animals in groups according to where they live: the flounder, shark, and whale in the water; the bat and canary in the air; and the lizard and horse on the land. Still another method would be to put the shark in a separate category from all the others because the shark's skeleton is made of cartilage instead of bone.

The problem with this example is that none of these three ways of classification agrees with the other two. There is no consistency. Biologists actually classify these animals into the following groups: fish (flounder and shark), reptiles (lizard), birds (canary), and mammals (bat, horse, whale). These groups reflect certain common characteristics, such as mammary glands for the mammals. But what makes this system of classification any better than those based on size or habitat? For our purposes, we require taxonomies that reflect evolutionary patterns. As we will see, organisms can have similar traits because they inherited these traits from a common ancestor. Thus, the presence of mammary glands in the bat, horse, and whale represents a trait that has been inherited from a common ancestral species.

Taxonomies are useful in trying to understand evolutionary relationships. In order to reflect the evolutionary process, the taxonomy must reflect evolutionary changes. The groups of mammals, birds, reptiles, and fish are based on characteristics that reflect evolutionary relationships.

Taxonomic categories. The Linnean taxonomy is a hierarchical classification. That is, each category contains a number of subcategories, which contain further subcategories, and so on. Biological classification uses a number of categories. The more commonly used categories are: kingdom, phylum (plural *phyla*), class, order, family, genus (plural *genera*), and species. In addition, prefixes are often added to distinguish further breakdowns within a particular category, such as subphylum or infraorder. The scientific name given to an organism consists of the genus and species names in Latin. The scientific name for the common house mouse is *Mus musculus*. Modern human beings are known as *Homo sapiens*, translated roughly as "wise humans."

Any given genus may contain a number of different species. The genus *Homo*, for example, contains modern humans (*Homo sapiens*) as well as extinct human species (*Homo erectus* and *Homo habilis*). These three species are placed in the same genus because of certain common characteristics, such as large brain size.

The categories of classification are often vaguely defined. Genus, for example, refers to a group of species that shares similar environments, patterns of adaptation, and physical structures. An example is the horse and the zebra, different species that are placed in the genus *Equus* (there are several species of zebra). These species are four-legged, hoofed grazers. The basis for assigning a given species to one genus or another is often unclear. This uncertainty is even more problematic when fossil remains are assigned to different categories. The only category with a precise meaning is the species, and even that has certain problems in application.

The biological species concept. Species may be defined on the basis of reproduction. If organisms from two populations are capable of breeding naturally and can produce fertile offspring, then they belong to the same

species Includes organisms from separate populations capable of breeding naturally and producing offspring.

species. Note that this definition has several parts. First, organisms from two populations must be capable of interbreeding. Second, these matings must occur in nature. Third and finally, the offspring must be *fertile*, that is, capable of producing further offspring.

Perhaps the best-known example of application of the species concept is the mule. Mules are farm animals produced as the offspring of a horse bred with a donkey. The horse and the donkey interbreed naturally, which satisfies the first and second parts of the species definition. The offspring (mules) are sterile, however, and cannot produce further offspring. The only way to get a mule is to mate a horse and a donkey. Because the offspring are not fertile, the horse and the donkey are considered separate species (see Figure 3.6). On the other hand, all human populations around the world belong to the same species because members can interbreed and produce fertile offspring.

The concept of biological species appears to provide a useful test for the purposes of classification. One of its problems, however, is that it only provides a simple yes or no answer to the question of similarity. It does not reflect any degree of similarity among organisms that belong to different species. For example, horses and donkeys are obviously more similar to each other than either is to an ant. The different species names show only that all are different species, but not which species are more similar to each other. The fact that horses and donkeys can interbreed shows us that they are closely related species.

The idea of species, moreover, flatly assumes that two organisms either belong or do not belong to the same species. It does not allow for any kind of intermediate state. Any system of classification tends to ignore variation within groups. In the real world, however, evolution and variation work to

Figure 3.6

The horse and donkey can mate and produce offspring (a mule), but two mules cannot produce offspring. Therefore, the horse and donkey belong to two separate species although they are closely related.

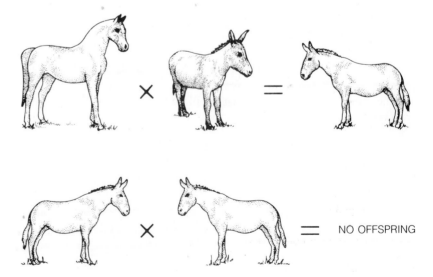

break down rigid systems of classification. Organisms become difficult to classify when they are constantly changing.

As an example of this problem, consider the populations of gypsy moths in Asia. When moths from the populations farthest apart are bred, their offspring are sterile. According to the biological species concept, these populations of moths belong to separate species. Populations that are closer together, however, are capable of producing fertile offspring, which suggests that they belong to the same species (Futuyma 1986).

Modes of species change. The biological species concept is useful when comparing two or more populations living at a single point in time. In theory, reproductive isolation can be tested to determine if these populations belong to the same species. How can the biological species concept be applied when comparing groups of organisms over a period of time? This question requires looking at two different modes of the evolutionary change of species.

First, a species can change over time. According to this mode of evolutionary change, a single species exists at any given point in time but evolves over a period of time. An example is the evolution of humans. The most likely scenario of human evolution over the past two million years (see Chapters 10 and 11) is a change from a species known as *Homo habilis* into a species known as *Homo erectus* into our own species *Homo sapiens*. While a single species exists within the genus *Homo* at any point in time, there is continued evolutionary change such that the most recent forms (ourselves) are quite different from the earliest forms.

This mode of species change is known as **anagenesis,** or straight-line evolution. It is illustrated as a straight line, as shown in Figure 3.7 where form A evolves into form B and then into form C. Although this mode of evolutionary change is fairly straightforward, complications arise when considering the naming of species. Should form A be called a different species from form B? The problem is that the traditional biological species concept doesn't really apply. Form A and form B are by necessity isolated from each other reproductively since they lived at different times.

Many researchers modify the species concept to deal with this type of situation. Different physical forms along a single lineage (an evolutionary line such as that shown in Figure 3.7) are given different species names out of convenience, and as a label to represent the types of physical change shown over time. Such forms are referred to as **paleospecies** and are used more as labels than as units representing the species concept.

Anagenesis is not the only mode of species change. If you think about it, anagenesis is not completely sufficient as an explanation of macroevolution. Where do new species come from? The other mode of species change is **cladogenesis,** or branching evolution. Cladogenesis involves the formation of new species (speciation) whereby one or more new species branch off from an original species. In Figure 3.8, a portion of species A first branches off to produce species B (living at the same time), then a portion of species B branches to produce species C. This example starts

anagenesis The transformation of a single species over time.

paleospecies Species identified from fossil remains based on their physical similarities and differences to other species.

cladogenesis The formation of one or more new species from another over time.

Figure 3.7

Anagenesis, the linear evolution of a species over time. Form A changes over time into form B and then further changes into form C.

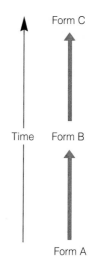

Figure 3.8

Cladogenesis, the origin of
new species. Species A splits
and forms a new species B,
which later splits to form
species C. The process begins
with a single species (A) and
ends with three species
(A, B, C).

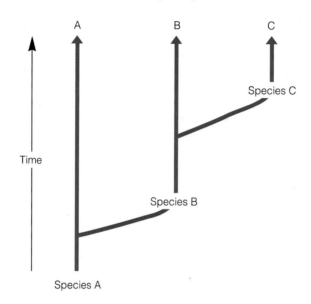

reproductive isolation The
genetic isolation of populations that may render
them incapable of producing
offspring.

speciation The origin of a
new species.

with one species and ends up with three. The factors responsible for speciation will be discussed later in this chapter.

Patterns of Macroevolution

Evolutionary forces interact to change populations over time (anagenesis) and lead to the formation of new species (cladogenesis). In addition
to these processes, the study of macroevolution is concerned with the rate
of evolutionary change and the failure of species to adapt over time.

Speciation. The fossil record shows many examples of new species
arising. How? You know that genetic differences between populations
come about as a result of evolutionary forces. For a population to become
a new species, these genetic differences must be great enough to prevent
successful interbreeding with the original parent species. For this to occur,
the population must become reproductively isolated from the original
parent species. **Reproductive isolation** is genetic change that can lead to
an inability to produce fertile offspring. How does this happen? The
evolutionary forces can produce such a situation. The first step in **speciation** (the formation of a new species from a parent species) is the elimination or reduction of gene flow between populations. Because gene flow
acts to reduce differences between populations, its continued action tends
to keep all populations in the same species. Gene flow does not need to be
eliminated altogether, but it must be reduced sufficiently to allow the other
evolutionary forces to make the populations genetically different. Populations must become genetically isolated from one another for speciation to
occur.

The most common form of isolation in animal species is geographic isolation. When two populations are separated by a physical barrier, such as a river or mountain range, or by great distances, gene flow is cut off between the populations. As long as the populations remain isolated, genetic changes occurring in one group will not spread to other groups.

Geographic separation is the most common means of producing reproductive isolation among animal populations, but other mechanisms may also cause isolation. Some of these can operate within a single geographic region. Populations may be isolated by behavioral differences such as feeding habits. Some groups may eat during the day and others at dusk. Because the groups are not in frequent contact with one another, there is opportunity for isolation to develop.

Isolation is the first step in the speciation process. By itself, this isolation does not guarantee speciation. Elimination of gene flow provides the opportunity for speciation. Other evolutionary forces must then act upon this isolation to produce a situation in which the isolated groups have changed sufficiently to make fertile interbreeding no longer possible. Isolation, however, does not always lead to speciation.

How can the evolutionary forces lead to speciation? Mutation might act to increase variation among populations because it occurs independently in the genetic composition of separate groups. Without gene flow to spread them, individual mutations will accumulate in each group, making isolated populations genetically divergent. Genetic drift also contributes to differences in allele frequencies among small populations. In addition, if the two populations are in separate environments, then natural selection will lead to genetic differences. Once gene flow has been eliminated, the other evolutionary forces will act to make the populations genetically divergent. When this process continues to the point where the two populations can no longer interbreed and produce fertile offspring, they are separate species.

There is continued debate over the role of the various evolutionary forces in producing genetic divergence. For many years, speciation was felt to be solely the byproduct of natural selection. In recent years, however, more attention has been given to the contributions to speciation of mutation and genetic drift in small populations.

Adaptive radiation. The process of speciation minimally results in two species: the original parent species and the new offspring species. Under certain circumstances, many new species can come into being in a short period of time. This rapid diversification of species is associated with changing environmental conditions. When new environments open up, or when new adaptations to a specific environment develop, many new species can form—a process known as **adaptive radiation.**

New environments often open up following the demise of other species. One example, discussed in greater detail in Chapter 9, is the rise of mammals following the extinction of the dinosaurs. Once the dinosaurs

adaptive radiation The formation of many new species following the availability of new environments or the development of a new adaptation.

gradualism A model of macroevolutionary change whereby evolutionary changes occur at a slow steady rate over time.

punctuated equilibrium A model of macroevolutionary change in which long periods of little evolutionary change (stasis) are followed by relatively short periods of rapid evolutionary change.

stasis Little or no evolutionary change occurring over a long period of time.

were gone, there were vacant environments for mammals to adapt to. The rise of flowering plants at about the same time also provided many new habitats. The result was an adaptive radiation of mammalian species.

The tempo and mode of macroevolution. During the past two decades, considerable attention has been given to the tempo (how fast?) and mode (the mechanism) of macroevolutionary change. Charles Darwin saw speciation as a slow and gradual process, taking thousands or millions of years. To Darwin, natural selection acted on populations ultimately to produce new species. The view that macroevolution is a slow and gradual process is called **gradualism.** According to this view, small changes in each generation over time result in major biological changes.

Gradualism, then, regards speciation as a slow process that takes a long time to occur. New species form from large portions of an original species. In such large populations, genetic drift and mutation have little impact in each generation. Natural selection, slowly operating on some initial mutation(s), is primarily responsible for speciation. The gradualistic model predicts that, given a suitable fossil record, we will see a smooth and gradual transition from one species into another. Although there are examples of such change in the fossil record, it is not always apparent. An alternative theory has been suggested by Niles Eldredge and Stephen Jay Gould in the form of a model known as **punctuated equilibrium** (Eldredge and Gould 1972; Gould and Eldredge 1977). This theory suggests that the pattern of macroevolution consists of long periods of time when little evolutionary change occurs (**stasis**) and short periods of time when rapid evolutionary change occurs. To Eldredge and Gould, the tempo of macroevolution is not gradual; rather, it is static at times and rapid at other times. Long periods of stasis are punctuated by short periods of rapid evolutionary change. Examples of gradualism and punctuated equilibrium are given in Figure 3.9.

There is little doubt among evolutionary biologists that stasis and rapid speciation have occurred in some organisms in the fossil record. It is also clear that the fossil record shows many examples of gradualism. Neither model is entirely correct in all cases, nor was it meant to be. Both represent different extremes of thinking about the tempo and mode of evolution. Though there is some debate over the genetic mechanisms of punctuated equilibrium, there is less debate on the facts of stasis and rapid speciation (Futuyma 1988).

Extinctions and mass extinctions. In considering macroevolutionary trends, we must not forget the most common pattern of them all—extinction. It is estimated that over 99 percent of all species that ever existed have become extinct (Futuyma 1986). In historic times, humans have witnessed (and helped cause) the extinction of a number of organisms, such as the passenger pigeon.

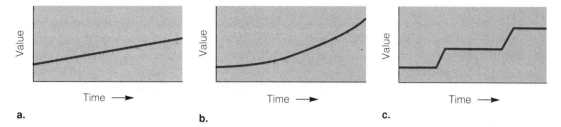

a.   **b.**   **c.**

What causes extinction? When a species is no longer adapted to a changed environment, it may die. The exact causes of a species' death vary from situation to situation. Rapid ecological change may render an environment hostile to a species. For example, temperatures may change and a species may not be able to adapt. Food resources may be affected by environmental changes, which will then cause problems for a species requiring these resources. Other species may become better adapted to an environment, resulting in competition and ultimately the death of a species.

Extinction seems, in fact, to be the ultimate fate of all species. Natural selection is a remarkable mechanism for providing a species with the ability to adapt to change, but it does not always work. When the environment changes too rapidly or when the appropriate genetic variations do not exist, a species can become extinct.

The fossil record shows that extinction has occurred throughout the history of the planet. Recent analyses have also revealed that on some occasions a large number of species became extinct at the same time—a **mass extinction.** One of the best-known examples of mass extinction occurred 65 million years ago with the demise of dinosaurs and many other forms of life. Perhaps the largest mass extinction was the one that occurred roughly 225 million years ago, when approximately 95 percent of all species were wiped out (Gould 1991). Mass extinctions can be caused by a relatively rapid change in the environment, compounded by the close interrelationship of many species. If, for example, something were to happen to destroy much of the plankton in the oceans, then the oxygen content of our planet would drop, affecting even organisms not living in the oceans. Such a change would probably lead to a mass extinction of mammals.

Figure 3.9

The tempo of macro-evolution: gradualism and punctuated equilibrium. Each portion of this figure has a line showing the change in value of a physical trait over time. (a) Gradualism: the change over time is linear and constant. (b) A geometric, gradual pattern. The rate of change increases with time, but the curve is still smooth; there are no discontinuities. (c) Punctuated equilibrium: there are periods of no change (statis) punctuated by periods of rapid change; the net result is a "staircase" pattern.

Misconceptions about Evolution

Evolution is a frequently misunderstood subject. Many of our basic ideas regarding evolution are misconceptions that have become part of the general culture. The often used phrase "survival of the fittest" conjures up

mass extinction When many species become extinct at roughly the same time.

images that are sometimes at odds with the actual findings of evolutionary science. It is common for such misconceptions to continue even after initial exposure to evolutionary theory.

The Nature of Selection

Many people have a basic understanding of the general principles of natural selection. The problem lies in our misinterpretation of the nature of natural selection.

Misconception: Bigger is better. A common misconception is that natural selection will *always* lead to larger structures. According to this idea, the bigger the brain, the better, and the bigger the body, the better. At first, this idea seems reasonable. After all, larger individuals may be more likely to survive since they can compete more successfully for food and sexual partners. Therefore, larger individuals are more likely to survive and pass their genes on to the next generation. Natural selection is expected to lead to an increase in the size of the body, brain, and other structures. However, this isn't always true. There are numerous examples of species in which *smaller* body size or structures were more adaptive and selected for. Keep in mind that in evolution nothing is free! A larger body may be more adaptive because of sheer size, but a larger body also has greater energy needs. Any advantage gained by a larger body may be offset by the disadvantage of needing more food. What we have to focus on is a *balance* between the adaptive and nonadaptive aspects of any biological characteristic. By walking upright, humans have their hands free, which is rather advantageous. However, we pay the price with varicose veins, back pain, fallen arches, and other nonadaptive consequences of walking on two legs. Again, we need to focus on the relative costs and benefits of any evolutionary change. Of course, this balance will obviously vary in different environments.

Misconception: Newer is better. There is a tendency to believe that traits more recent in origin are superior because they are newer. Humans walk on two legs, a trait that appeared at least four million years ago. We also have five digits (fingers and toes) that date back many hundreds of millions of years. Is upright walking better because it is newer? Of course not. Both features are essential to our tool-making way of life. The age of a structure has no bearing on its usefulness.

Misconception: Natural selection always works. The idea that natural selection will always provide an opportunity for some members of a species to survive is not accurate. Occasionally this author has heard statements such as "we will evolve to tolerate air pollution." Such statements are absurdities. Natural selection only operates on variations that are present. If no genetic variation occurs to aid in breathing polluted air, natural selection will not help us. Even in cases where genetic variation is present, the environment may change too quickly to respond through natural selection. All we have to do is to examine the fossil record to see how inaccurate this misconception is—that 99 percent of all past species are extinct shows us that natural selection obviously doesn't always work!

Misconception: There is an inevitable direction in evolution. An idea popular in the nineteenth century was **orthogenesis,** the notion that evolution would continue in a given direction because of a vaguely defined nonphysical "force" (Mayr 1982). As an alternative to the theory of natural selection, orthogenesis suggested that evolutionary change would continue in the same direction either until a perfect structure was attained or a species became extinct. Apart from the problems of dealing with metaphysical "forces," orthogenesis has long been rejected by analysis of the fossil record and the triumph of natural selection as an explanatory mechanism for evolutionary change. Some of its basic notions, however, are still perpetuated. A common belief is that humans will evolve larger and larger brains, as a continuation of earlier trends (Figure 3.10). The view of orthogenesis is tied in with notions of "progress" and with the misconception that bigger is better. There are many examples from the fossil record of nonlinear change, and many examples of reversals in sizes of structures. In the case of human evolution, brains actually stopped getting larger 50,000 years ago. In fact, the average brain size of humans since that time has decreased slightly as a consequence of a general decrease in skeletal size and ruggedness (Henneberg 1988).

Is it possible for a trend to continue to change in a given direction under the right circumstances? Of course, but change comes through the action of natural selection, not some mysterious internal force. Continuation of any trend depends on the environment, present genetic variation, and basic biological limits. (A 50-foot spider can't exist because it wouldn't be able to absorb enough oxygen for its volume.) Such change also depends on the relative cost and benefits of change. Suppose that an increase in human brain size was combined somehow with an increase in pelvic size (assuming genetic variation was present for both features). A larger brain *might* confer some advantage, but a larger pelvis would certainly make pregnancy and childbirth more hazardous because of the relatively narrow birth canal in humans. A larger pelvis would also affect walking. Evolution works on the entire organism and not one trait at a time. Any change can have both positive and negative effects, but it is the net balance that is critical to the operation of natural selection.

Structure, Function, and Evolution

A number of misconceptions about evolution focus on the relationship between biological structures and their adaptive (or nonadaptive) functions.

orthogenesis A discredited idea that evolution would continue in a given direction because of some vaguely defined "force."

Figure 3.10

The theory of orthogenesis predicts continued change in a given direction. The popular but incorrect notion that humans in the future will have progressively larger brains is illustrated.

Misconception: Natural selection always produces perfect structures. There is a tendency to view nature as the product of perfect natural engineering. Granted, there are many marvelous and wondrous phenomena in the natural world, but a closer examination shows that biological structures are often far from perfect. Consider human beings. Is the human body perfect? Hardly. Just to note one aspect, consider your skeleton when you stand upright. What is holding in your internal organs? Skin and muscles. Your rib cage provides little support for lower internal organs because it reflects ancestry from a four-legged form. When humans stood up (adaptive), the rib cage offered less support. The result—a variety of complaints and complications, such as hernias. The human skeleton is not perfect, but rather the result of natural selection operating on the variation that was present.

Misconception: All structures are adaptive. Natural selection is such a powerful model that it is tempting to apply it to all biological structures. Indeed, many anthropologists and biologists have done so. They examine a structure and explain its function in terms of natural selection. Are all structures adaptive? Many structures simply reflect a byproduct of other biological changes and have no adaptive value of their own (Gould and Lewontin 1979). Other structures, such as the human appendix, may have served a function in the past but appear to have no present function.

Misconception: Current structures always reflect initial adaptations. The idea here is that any given structure, with an associated function, originally evolved specifically for that function. Human beings, for example, walk on two legs; this allows them to hold tools and other objects that are constructed with the aid of an enlarged brain. Although it is tempting to say that both upright walking and a larger brain evolved at the same time because of the adaptive value of having both structures, this is not what happened. Upright walking evolved at least 1.5 million years before the use of stone tools and the expansion of the brain (Chapter 10).

As another example, consider your fingers. You have five of these digits on each hand, which allow you to perform a variety of manipulative tasks. Humans use their hands to manipulate both natural and human-made objects. Manipulative digits are essential to our nature as tool-using creatures. We might therefore suggest that our grasping hands *first* evolved to meet this need; this is not the case. Grasping hands *first* developed in early primate ancestors to meet the needs of living in the trees (Chapter 9). Even though we don't live in trees, we have retained this trait and use it *for a different purpose*. Natural selection operates on the variation that is present. Structures are frequently modified for different uses.

SUMMARY

Evolution is understood in terms of microevolution and macroevolution. The study of microevolution looks at changes in allele frequencies from one generation to the next. Such analyses allow detailed examination of the factors that alter allele frequencies in the short term and provide us with inferences about long-term patterns of evolution. Changes in allele frequencies stem from four evolutionary forces: mutation, natural selection, genetic drift, and gene flow.

Mutation is the ultimate source of all genetic variation but occurs at low enough rates that additional factors are needed to explain polymorphic frequencies (whereby two or more alleles have frequencies greater than 0.01). The other three evolutionary forces are responsible for increasing or decreasing the frequency of a mutant allele. Natural selection changes allele frequencies through the process of differential survival and reproduction of individuals having certain genotypes. Genetic drift is the random change in allele frequencies from one generation to the next and has the greatest effect on small populations. Gene flow, the movement of alleles between populations, acts to reduce genetic differences between different groups. Nonrandom mating, such as inbreeding and assortative mating, does not change allele frequencies, but does affect the *rate* of allele frequency change.

Macroevolution, the process of long-term evolution, can occur in two ways: anagenesis, the evolution of a single species over time, or cladogenesis, the splitting off of one or more species from the original parent species. In cladogenesis, new species form through the process of reproductive isolation followed by genetic divergence. Both steps are understood in terms of evolutionary forces. Reduction or elimination of gene flow provides for the beginning of reproductive isolation. Mutation, genetic drift, and selection can then act on this isolation to produce a new species. Two models of macroevolutionary change can be applied to the fossil record. Gradualism states that most evolutionary change is the result of slow but constant change over many generations. Punctuated equilibrium states that there are long periods of time with little evolutionary change (stasis), punctuated by rapid evolutionary events.

There are many misconceptions regarding natural selection and evolution. Some of the more common of these are: that bigger is better, that newer is better, that natural selection always works, and that there is an inevitable direction to evolution. There are also misconceptions regarding the relationship of biological structures, their functions, and their evolutionary origin.

Supplemental Readings

Bodmer, W. F., and L. L. Cavalli-Sforza. 1976. *Genetics, Evolution, and Man*. San Francisco: W. H. Freeman. This text provides a basic, essentially nonmathematical discussion of evolutionary forces.

Futuyma, D. J. 1986. *Evolutionary Biology*. 2d ed. Sunderland, Mass.: Sinauer. An excellent text on the evolutionary process focusing on macroevolution.

Underwood, J. H. 1979. *Human Variation and Human Microevolution*. Englewood Cliffs: N.J.: Prentice-Hall. A basic treatment of human microevolution with some, but not extensive, mathematics; clearly written, and with many excellent examples of case studies from human populations.

In addition, the books by Gould listed at the end of Chapter 1 provide many interesting and relevant essays on macroevolution.

CHAPTER 4

Case Studies of Human Microevolution

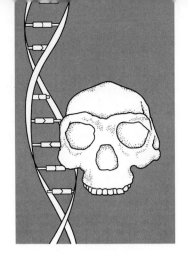

The previous three chapters have provided you with an overview of evolutionary theory, including the genetic aspects and concepts of microevolution and macroevolution. This chapter and the next two further explore microevolutionary change in human populations.

The focus of this current chapter is how genetic drift, gene flow, and natural selection operate to affect patterns of genetic variation within and between populations. Case studies provide examples of the basic concepts of microevolution, demonstrating how microevolution in humans is similar to and different from that observed in other organisms, while emphasizing the interrelationship between biology and culture.

Studying Human Microevolution

Much of the study of human variation is observational. We look to see what patterns of genetic variation exist in populations as they occur. By employing a number of methods, we can compare and contrast patterns of variation to find out more about the specific mechanisms of genetic change in human populations from one generation to the next.

Univariate and Multivariate Approaches

Biological anthropologists rely on a wide variety of traits to analyze human variation. Such traits include single locus traits, such as blood

univariate analysis The analysis of human biological variation focusing on a single trait at a time.

multivariate analysis The analysis of human biological variation that considers the interrelationships of several traits at a time.

genetic distance An average measure of relatedness between populations based on a number of traits.

groups, as well as complex traits, such as height, head length, skin color, dental measures, and fingerprints. Sometimes we analyze these traits one at a time (**univariate analysis**) and sometimes many at a time (**multivariate analysis**). The difference in these approaches relates to the goals of a study and whether we are focusing on the forces of genetic drift and gene flow on one hand, or natural selection on the other.

The basic starting point is that genetic drift and gene flow are expected to affect *all* loci to the same degree, whereas natural selection is expected to affect each locus differently. For example, if you move from one population to another and have offspring in your new population, all of your genetic material moves with you: gene flow should affect all loci the same. Likewise, the *average* effect of genetic drift is expected to be the same for all loci. Natural selection, however, should affect each locus differently—unless, of course, the loci are both related to the same selective force.

As a result, we tend to study natural selection one locus or trait at a time, unless we are looking at related traits. If we wish to study the effects of genetic drift and gene flow, we try to sample as many loci or traits as possible with the goal of getting the best estimate of overall effect. Of course, any study must consider *all* of the evolutionary forces. The univariate and multivariate approaches together often provide us with information regarding a number of these evolutionary forces.

The Analysis of Gene Flow and Genetic Drift

A number of methods are used to examine the joint effect of gene flow and genetic drift on patterns of human variation. Two of the more common approaches are discussed here.

Genetic distance analysis. When comparing a number of biological traits across populations, we frequently compute a summary measure known as a **genetic distance**. This is an average measure of relatedness between groups based on a number of traits (i.e., a multivariate approach). Quite simply, the larger the genetic distance, the *less* similar two populations are to each other. For example, imagine that you have investigated a number of traits for three groups, called A, B, and C. You compute one of a number of genetic distance measures and obtain the following distances (don't worry about the units of measure; most distance measures are relative):

Distance between A and B = 9

Distance between A and C = 16

Distance between B and C = 25

Interpretation of these results is fairly straightforward. Populations A and B have the smallest distance, so they are the *most* similar to each other.

Population C is the most distant and so is the least similar genetically. Further analysis would require additional data on the history and location of these groups to determine *why* population C is the most different.

Interpretation is difficult when there are more than three populations being considered. For that reason, we often take the genetic distance measures and use them to construct what is known as a **genetic distance map,** a picture showing the genetic relationships between groups. These maps are easy to interpret—the closer two populations are on the map, the closer they are genetically. An example of a genetic distance map is shown in Figure 4.1, that shows five hypothetical populations (A, B, C, D, E). It is clear that populations A, B, and C are all similar to one another genetically, as is population D to population E. The most striking feature is that populations D and E are quite distant genetically from the other three populations. Additional data would be needed to determine why. Are D and E separated geographically from the other three populations? This would be easy to check: simply compare the genetic distance map with a geographic distance map. Other hypotheses, such as differences in religion or other cultural variables, could also be tested using a comparative approach.

Demographic measures. Much information regarding the effect of genetic drift and gene flow can be extracted from analysis of demographic measures, especially population size and migration. These measures can be used to estimate the likely effect of genetic drift and gene flow by means of a variety of complex mathematical methods. If information is available for genetic traits, then these estimates can be compared with observed reality. This type of comparison allows us to test various assumptions of models and to determine the relative effect of gene flow and genetic drift.

The relationship between demographic measures and microevolution is relatively straightforward. Since the magnitude of genetic drift is related to population size (the smaller the population, the greater the effect of drift), a knowledge of population size can give us an estimate of the effects of genetic drift. Much gene flow is related to migration, so an analysis of marriage records and other vital statistical data can provide us with an idea of the relative magnitude of gene flow. Using appropriate models, scientists can consider the effects of gene flow and genetic drift simultaneously to predict genetic distances and then compare them with actual genetic distances.

genetic distance map A picture showing the genetic relationships between populations, based on genetic distance measures.

Figure 4.1

Example of a genetic distance map for five hypothetical populations (A, B, C, D, E). The closer populations are genetically, the closer they plot near each other on the map.

The Analysis of Natural Selection

The analysis of natural selection in human populations is complex. Rather than set up laboratory experiments, most of the time we must rely on comparisons of situations existing in nature. Consider the following hypothetical situation. You are interested in testing the hypothesis that mammalian body size is related to temperature. If you were dealing with laboratory animals such as mice, you would set up an experiment in which you would expose different groups of mice to different ambient temperatures and then determine what change, if any, takes place from one generation to the next. But what if you were interested in testing this hypothesis on elephants? It is unlikely that you would be able to overcome the large number of practical difficulties involved in such a project.

If you were interested in humans, the whole laboratory approach would be immoral and illegal in many societies as well as impractical. Does this mean that the hypotheses cannot be tested? No, because you could examine a natural experiment. You would collect data on body size and temperature from human populations across the world to determine if a relationship in fact existed.

There are several approaches to measuring natural selection in human populations. The most direct method involves comparing measures of survival and reproduction (fitness) among individuals with different genotypes. Another method is to look at regional or worldwide variation in a trait to determine if it has any relationship with climate or other environmental factors. A third method is to look at the potential for natural selection by using measures of births and deaths from demographic data.

Individual genetic associations. Because natural selection refers to the process in which individuals with certain genetic characteristics are more likely to survive or reproduce, we want to determine whether individuals with certain genotypes have a greater probability of surviving or reproducing. If you were interested in looking at the potential effects of natural selection on the MN blood group system, you would want to separate your sample into groups of individuals with the same genotype (*MM, MN,* or *NN*). You would then attempt to determine if there were any differences in mortality or fertility among these groups.

These questions, and others, can be answered in principle by looking at the associations among some measure of health, survival, or fertility and different genotypes. Suppose you were interested in whether or not different *MN* genotypes have different susceptibilities to diseases. You could select a group, determine its *MN* genotypes, and monitor its members for the rest of their lives to track their disease histories. Alternatively, you could select a group of individuals having had a given disease and compare their *MN* genotypes with those of a random sample of people who have not had the disease.

Environmental correspondence. One way of looking for the effects of natural selection is to analyze patterns of variation over a large geographic region. Given that natural selection is related to environmental variation, differences among locations might reflect changes in environment and in genotype. The goal is to determine the level of correspondence between some aspect or aspects of the physical environment and a genotype. To test the idea that climate is related to body size, you would look at the distribution of body size and see how well it matches the distribution of climatic variables.

Demographic measures. Natural selection operates on differences in mortality and fertility, both of which may be measured from demographic records. The death rate of a population is a measure of the proportion of deaths occurring within a given period of time. The birth rate measures fertility within a population. These measures can provide an idea of the overall *potential* for natural selection.

A good example of this approach is Meindl and Swedlund's (1977) study of mortality in the populations of Deerfield and Greenfield in historical Massachusetts. Historical data indicated that both populations experienced epidemics of childhood dysentery, a serious disease, between 1802 and 1803. Meindl and Swedlund used death records to determine the effect of these epidemics on the mortality of those who survived the disease. They found that the individuals who survived the disease actually lived longer than those who were not exposed to it. They concluded that the greater longevity of those individuals reflected, in part, genetic differences. One possible interpretation is that those who survived had genetic characteristics that gave them greater resistance to dysentery; this is natural selection in action. Another possibility is that those exposed to the disease developed stronger immune systems as a response. Such augmented resistance is a physiological response, although there is most likely a genetic component involved. Though such demographic analyses cannot provide any definite answers regarding natural selection, they do provide useful supplements to traditional genetic analysis.

Case Studies of Gene Flow and Genetic Drift

This section provides two brief examples of the effects of gene flow and/or genetic drift in human populations.

Genetic Relationships of Jewish and Non-Jewish Populations

The Jewish Diaspora resulted in Jews spreading throughout much of the world. Given religious and ethnic differences, combined with frequent discrimination in their new lands, many Jewish populations remained culturally isolated. From an understanding of microevolutionary theory, we would expect there to be genetic isolation as well. On the other hand, we know historically that intermarriage between Jews and non-Jews has often occurred, although at different rates in different times and places. What are the present-day genetic relationships between Jewish and non-Jewish populations? How much gene flow has there been between groups in the past? Are Jewish populations throughout the world more similar to each other, or more similar to their non-Jewish neighbors? Has genetic drift further complicated the picture, since many Jewish populations were small in size to begin with?

Many studies have addressed these questions, often with mixed results because of disparate methods and the use of data from different populations. One such study was conducted by Kobyliansky and colleagues at Tel-Aviv University in Israel (Kobyliansky et al. 1982). Pooling their own data with those from previous studies, they obtained information on seven genetic marker loci for both Jewish and non-Jewish populations in six geographical regions: Eastern Europe, Central Europe, Southern Europe, the Middle East, North Africa, and Yemen (the latter being representative of isolated groups). Figure 4.2 presents a genetic distance map similar to that shown in Figure 4.1, using the method of Harpending and Jenkins (1973) to compute standard genetic distances among the 12 populations (6 Jewish and 6 non-Jewish).

The first, most obvious feature of this genetic distance map is that the two populations from Yemen are relatively close to each other and quite different from other Jewish and non-Jewish populations in Africa, Asia, and Europe. This fits in with our knowledge of the isolated nature of the small Yemenite populations. Second, all of the remaining Jewish populations cluster together and are distinct from most of the non-Jewish popu-

Figure 4.2

Genetic distance map showing the relationship between six Jewish and six non-Jewish populations. Circles (●) indicate Jewish populations and squares (■) indicate non-Jewish populations. The code letters next to the circles and squares represent the geographic area: CE = Central Europe, EE = Eastern Europe, SE = Southern Europe, ME = Middle East, NA = North Africa, Y = Yemen.
(Based on data taken from Kobyliansky et al. [1982])

lations. This finding suggests that the five remaining Jewish populations are more similar to each other genetically than any to their non-Jewish neighbors. Third, the non-Jewish Middle Eastern population clusters with the Jewish populations, that suggests Middle Eastern Jews and non-Jews share common ancestry. All of these findings are consistent with historical evidence. Except for the isolated Yemenite groups (whose position is most likely due to low levels of gene flow and increased action of genetic drift), there seems to have been relatively little gene flow between Jewish and non-Jewish populations. Of course, this analysis focuses on large geographic regions. Within these, it is likely there exist populations that differ from the overall pattern shown here.

Social Organization and Genetics of South American Indians of the Rain Forest

A number of genetic studies have been carried out on the tribal populations living in the rain forests of South America. Studies of these populations have allowed investigation into the ways in which the social structure of small tribes contributes to genetic diversity. Of course, the small size of the populations and their general isolated nature act to increase the likelihood of genetic drift. What makes these studies so fascinating is the specific social and political structures that act in certain ways to increase drift and in other ways to counter it.

Many of these populations have what is known as a **fission-fusion** structure. As populations grow, the limits of the environment are soon reached. Political factions develop, creating unrest within the local villages resulting from too many people in one place. When populations become too large, they will often fission into separate groups. Some of these separate groups will be too small to remain viable villages, and smaller groups may then undergo fusion to form a large group (Figure 4.3).

The formation of new, smaller villages from old (fission) is expected to lead to increased opportunity for genetic drift. The merging of smaller villages to form large ones (fusion) acts to some extent to counter the effects of genetic drift. Adding to this complex situation is the fact that all villages practice **exogamy** (finding a mate in another group) to some extent. Exogamous marriage results in gene flow between villages, which acts to counter the effects of genetic drift.

Village fissioning is a form of the founder effect and is expected to lead to group differences because of genetic drift. The amount of genetic drift can be predicted and then compared to observed allele frequencies to test the hypothesis that genetic variation is being affected by drift. Following up on pioneering work by James Neel, Smouse (1982) and colleagues have performed extensive analyses on a number of genetic systems for several tribal populations, such as the Yanomamo (Figure 4.4), and have found that the observed level of genetic differences between groups exceeds the level expected under random genetic drift. Closer analysis has

fission-fusion A group breaks into smaller populations (fission) and may later combine with other populations to form a larger group (fusion).

exogamy The tendency to choose mates from outside the local population

Figure 4.3

Fission-fusion social structure. Fissioning is the splitting of a population into two or more smaller populations. Fusioning is the merging of two or more populations into a larger population. Circles in this figure indicate the relative sizes of each population: populations A and B both split into two smaller populations; populations A2 and B1 then merge to form a larger population C.

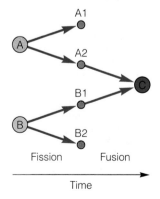

Figure 4.4

The Yanomamo Indians of the South American rain forest. (Courtesy of Napoleon A. Chagnon)

Figure 4.4

The Yanomamo Indians of the South American rain forest. (Courtesy of Napoleon A. Chagnon)

shown that the village fissions were not random. Rather, many fissions take place along kinship lines. Instead of a random group of individuals forming a new village, often a group of related individuals does so. This non-random splitting actually acts to enhance the effects of genetic drift because new villages are less likely to have an equal representation of alleles from the original population. Thus, the individual pattern of village fissioning adds to the effect of genetic drift.

Case Studies of Natural Selection

This section provides several examples of natural selection in human populations. Since natural selection operates differently on different loci, the focus will be on individual loci or traits rather than on specific populations.

Hemoglobin, Sickle Cell, and Malaria

Perhaps the best-known example of natural selection operating on a discrete genetic trait is the relationship of hemoglobin variants to malaria. One of the proteins in red blood cells is hemoglobin, which functions to transport oxygen to body tissues (see Chapter 2). The normal structure of the beta chain of hemoglobin is coded for by an allele usually called hemoglobin A. In many human populations, the A allele is the only one present, and as a result everyone has the AA, or normal adult hemoglobin, genotype.

Hemoglobin variants. Many hemoglobin variants are produced by the mutation of an A allele to another form. The most widely studied mutations include hemoglobin S, C, and E. The S allele is also known as the sickle cell allele. A person who has two S alleles (genotype SS) has **sickle cell anemia,** a condition whereby the structure of the red blood cells is altered and oxygen transport is severely impaired (Figure 4.5). Roughly, only 15 percent of those with genotype SS survive to adulthood. An estimated 100,000 deaths per year throughout the world are from sickle cell anemia.

If the S allele is harmful in homozygotes, we expect natural selection to eliminate S alleles from the population in such a way that the frequency of S should be relatively low. Mutation introduces the S allele, but natural selection eliminates it. Indeed, in many parts of the world the frequency of S is extremely low, fitting the model of mutation balanced by selection. In a number of populations, however, the frequency of S is much higher— often up to 10 to 20 percent. Such high frequencies seem paradoxical, given the harmful effect of the S allele in the homozygous genotype. Why does S reach such high frequencies? Genetic drift might seem likely, except for the fact that there is a definite association of geography and higher frequencies of S. That is, higher frequencies of S occur only in certain environments. Genetic drift is random and influenced by population size, not environment. If genetic drift were responsible for the high frequencies

sickle cell anemia A genetic disease occurring in a person homozygous for the sickle cell allele that alters the structure of red blood cells.

Figure 4.5

Sickle cell anemia. The blood cells on the left are twisted and deformed compared to the shape of normal red blood cells on the right. (© AP/ Wide World Photos)

infectious disease A disease caused by the introduction of an organic foreign substance into the body.

noninfectious disease A disease caused by factors other than the introduction of an organic foreign substance into the body.

of S, we would expect to see high frequencies in isolated groups in many different environments.

Distribution of the sickle cell allele and malaria. The distribution of the sickle cell allele is related to the prevalence of a certain form of malaria. Malaria is an **infectious disease**—that is, caused by the introduction of an organic foreign substance, such as a virus or parasite (a disease that is not caused by an organic foreign substance is a **noninfectious disease**). Malaria is caused by a parasite that enters an organism's body, and four different species of the malarial parasite can affect humans. Malaria remains one of the major infectious diseases in the world today. In the late 1970s, as many as 120 million people in the world had some form of malaria (Encyclopaedia Britannica 1988).

The Old World shows a striking correspondence of the higher frequencies of the S allele (Figure 4.6) and the prevalence of malaria caused by the parasite *Plasmodium falciparum* (Figure 4.7). This parasite is spread

Figure 4.6

Distribution of the sickle cell allele in the Old World. Compare high-frequency areas with the high-frequency areas of malaria in Figure 4.7.

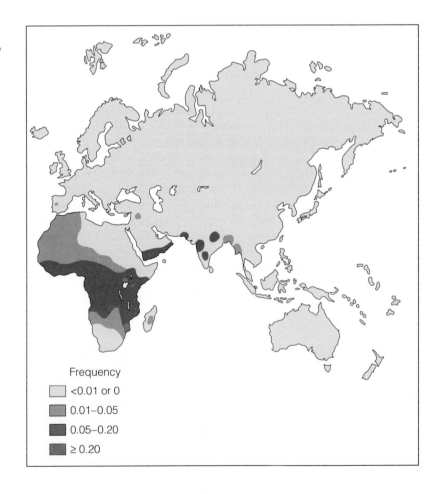

Frequency

<0.01 or 0
0.01–0.05
0.05–0.20
≥ 0.20

through the bites of certain species of mosquitoes. Those areas with frequent cases of malaria, such as Central Africa, also have the highest frequencies of the sickle cell allele. The falciparum form of malaria, the most serious of all forms of malaria, is often fatal.

The strong geographic correspondence suggests that sickle cell anemia and malaria are both related to the high frequencies of the S allele in parts of the world. Further experimental work has confirmed this hypothesis. Because the S allele affects the structure of the red blood cells, it makes the blood an inhospitable place for the malaria parasite.

In a malarial environment people who are heterozygous (genotype AS) actually have an advantage. The presence of one S allele does not give the person sickle cell anemia, but it does change the blood cells sufficiently so that the malaria parasite does not have as serious an effect. Overall, the heterozygote has the greatest fitness in a malarial environment. As discussed in Chapter 3, this is a case of balancing selection in which selection occurs for the heterozygote (AS) and against both homozygotes (AA from malaria and SS from sickle cell anemia). The balance between these two diseases is such that the maximum fitness of an entire population occurs when the frequency of S is somewhere between 10 and 20 percent.

Figure 4.7

Regions where falciparum malaria is common.

An analysis of one African population suggests that for every 100 people with *AS* who survive to adulthood, 88 people with *AA* survive and only 14 of those with *SS* (Bodmer and Cavalli-Sforza 1976). Clearly, the relationship between hemoglobin, sickle cell anemia, and malaria represents a very strong case of natural selection. Instead of a difference in survival between genotypes of only several percent, the differences are quite striking. Such differences can lead to major changes in allele frequencies in a very short period of time. To illustrate the rapidity of such change, Figure 4.8 shows a hypothetical example of changes in the frequency of the sickle cell allele. In this example, the initial frequency of *S* from mutation was set equal to a reasonable estimate of 0.00001. The fitness values mentioned earlier were used to examine the kind of change in the frequency of *S* that could take place. As the frequency of *S* increases, change takes place more rapidly because there are more people with the *AS* genotype to be selected for. After 100 generations, there is little change in the frequency of the *S* allele because it has reached an equilibrium based on the balance between the effects of sickle cell anemia and malaria. In this example, the sickle cell allele would reach an equilibrium frequency of 0.122. Of course, this simple illustration does not take other evolutionary forces into account, but it does show how quickly allele frequencies can change under strong natural selection.

The sickle cell example clearly shows the importance of the specific environment on the process of natural selection. In a nonmalarial environment, the *AS* genotype has no advantage, and the *AA* genotype has the greatest evolutionary fitness. In such cases, the frequency of the *S* allele is

Figure 4.8

Reconstruction of past changes in sickle cell allele frequency in malarial Africa. This simulation assumes an initial allele frequency of 0.00001 caused by mutation. Relative fitness values are assumed constant over time: *AA* = 88%, *AS* = 100%, *SS* = 14%. The first 40 generations would show little change since the initial allele frequency was so low. After 40 generations, the allele frequency would increase rapidly, reaching an equilibrium after roughly 100 generations.

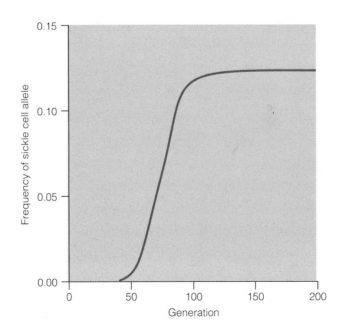

very low, approaching zero. In a malarial environment, however, the situation is different, and the heterozygote has the advantage. Clearly, we cannot label the *S* allele as intrinsically "good" or "bad"; it depends on circumstances.

Effects of culture change on sickle cell frequency. Sickle cell anemia provides an excellent example of the interaction of biology and culture. Livingstone (1958) and others have taken information on the distribution and ecology of the malaria parasite and the mosquito that transmits it, along with information on the prehistory and history of certain regions in Africa, and have presented a hypothesis about changes in the frequency of the sickle cell allele. Several thousand years ago, the African environment was not conducive to the spread of malaria. Large areas of the continent consisted of dense forests.

This situation changed several thousands of years ago when prehistoric African populations brought horticulture into the area. **Horticulture** is a form of farming employing only simple hand tools. As the land was cleared for crops, the entire ecology shifted. Without the many trees, it was easier for sunlight to reach the land surface. Continued use of the land changed the soil chemistry, allowing pools of water to accumulate. Both these changes led to an environment ideal for the growth and spread of mosquito populations, and therefore the spread of the malaria parasite. The growth of the human population also provided more hosts for the mosquitoes to feed on, thus increasing the spread of malaria.

Before the development of horticulture in Africa, the frequency of the sickle cell allele was probably low, as it is in nonmalarial environments today. When malaria increased, there was then an evolutionary advantage to those who had the heterozygote *AS* genotype because they would have greater resistance to malaria without suffering the effects of sickle cell anemia. As shown earlier, this change could have taken place in a short period of time, roughly 100 generations, because of the large differences in fitness among hemoglobin genotypes. The initial introduction of the sickle cell allele, through mutation or gene flow, was followed by a rapid-change reaching an equilibrium point in which the fitness of the entire human population was at a maximum.

This scenario shows that human cultural adaptations (horticulture) can affect the ecology of other organisms (the mosquito and malaria parasite), which can then cause genetic change in the human population (an increase in the frequency of the sickle cell allele). This sequence of events is summarized in Figure 4.9.

Of course, we cannot observe these events directly because they occurred in the past. Nonetheless, all available evidence supports this hypothesis. We know the physiological differences between different hemoglobin types. We also know that low frequencies of *S* occur in nonmalarial environments and higher frequencies occur where there is malaria. Archaeological evidence shows when and where the spread of horticulture took

horticulture A form of farming in which only simple hand tools are used.

Figure 4.9

Sequence of cultural and environmental changes leading to changes in the frequency of the sickle cell allele in malarial Africa.

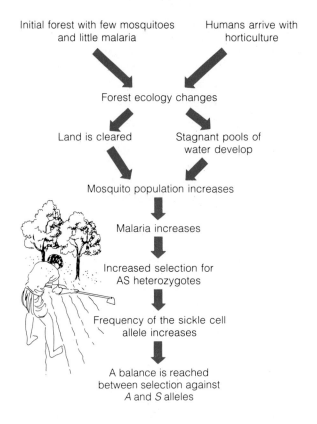

Initial forest with few mosquitoes and little malaria

Humans arrive with horticulture

Forest ecology changes

Land is cleared

Stagnant pools of water develop

Mosquito population increases

Malaria increases

Increased selection for AS heterozygotes

Frequency of the sickle cell allele increases

A balance is reached between selection against *A* and *S* alleles

antibody A substance that reacts to other substances invading the body.

place in Africa. From studies of modern-day agriculture, we also know that malaria spreads quickly following the clearing of land. Taking all this information together, we find the scenario for changes in the frequency of the sickle cell allele in Africa is most reasonable.

The ABO Blood Group and Natural Selection

The relationship between the sickle cell allele and malaria is the most well-studied example of natural selection for a discrete genetic trait in human populations. It is often frustrating that the situation is not as clear for other traits. The differences in fitness between different genotypes is often much less than that seen for the hemoglobin locus. Also, we often find evidence of multiple relationships between genetic traits and natural selection. It is often difficult to determine which factor is the most important or which was initially responsible for the evolution of a trait.

The human blood groups have been the subject of many investigations of natural selection. There are many different blood groups, defined on the basis of the type of molecules present on the surface of the red blood cells. Some blood groups are associated with different **antibodies** that react to various substances invading the blood stream (foreign **antigens**). Two blood groups—MN and ABO—have already been mentioned in previous chapters. Other red blood cell groups include Rhesus, Diego, Duffy, Lutheran, Lewis, and Xg, to name but a few. Some of these blood groups appear to be neutral in terms of natural selection, or perhaps we just have not been able to detect any effects. Also, some may have been selected for or against in the past, but not at present. Others are definitely related to natural selection, but in ways that are difficult to discern. The ABO blood group is discussed here in terms of natural selection.

The ABO blood group is the most widely studied simple genetic trait in human populations. As shown in Chapter 2, there are three different alleles (*A, B, O*) whereby *A* and *B* are codominant and *O* is recessive. There are four possible phenotypes: type A (genotypes *AA* and *AO*), type B (genotypes *BB* and *BO*), type O (genotype *OO*), and type AB (genotype *AB*).

Worldwide, the *O* allele is the most common, the *A* allele is next most frequent, and the *B* allele is the least common. The allele frequencies of all human populations fall within certain limits. The frequency of the *O* allele ranges from 0.4 to 1.0, the frequency of the *A* allele ranges from 0 to 0.55, and the frequency of the *B* allele ranges from 0 to 0.3 (Brues 1977). These allele frequencies are too high to be explained by mutation alone (because mutation occurs at low rates). Gene flow, genetic drift, and natural selection must be considered as possible explanations.

One possible clue to the effects of natural selection on the ABO blood groups is that there are certain antibodies associated with different blood groups. There are two antibodies in the ABO system known as anti-A and anti-B. Unlike some blood group systems, the ABO antibodies are present throughout an individual's life. The anti-A antibody reacts to destroy A-type molecules, and the anti-B antibody reacts to destroy B-type molecules. There is no antibody for O. People with blood type A have the anti-B antibody, people with blood type B have the anti-A antibody, people with blood type O have both, and people with blood type AB have neither (Table 4.1).

antigen A substance invading the body that stimulates the production of antibodies.

T A B L E   4.1
ABO Blood Group Phenotypes and Antibodies

Genotypes	Phenotype	Antigens	Antibodies
AA *AO*	A	A	anti-B
BB *BO*	B	B	anti-A
AB	AB	A, B	none
OO	O	none	anti-A, anti-B

The fact that different blood types have different antibodies has implications for natural selection and susceptibility to different diseases. If you have blood type A, and hence anti-B antibodies, your immune system will tend to fight off any microorganisms that are biochemically similar to type B molecules. For example, the microorganism that causes venereal syphilis is biochemically similar to A molecules. Therefore, people with blood types B and O will have greater resistance to syphilis because they have the anti-A antibodies. People with blood types A and AB will not have this resistance because they lack the anti-A antibodies. It has been suggested that a link exists between various ABO blood types and a number of infectious diseases, such as smallpox, typhoid, influenza, bubonic plague, and others. Many of these diseases were indeed serious in the past, and differential resistance could be a possible factor in explaining the range of allele frequencies for the ABO system.

It has been suggested that each blood type is more susceptible than others to certain diseases. For example, type A seems more susceptible to smallpox, type B seems more susceptible to infantile diarrhea, and type O seems more susceptible to bubonic plague. If these suggestions are verified, it seems that the frequencies of the ABO alleles are subject to a variety of different types of selection. This makes analysis extremely difficult.

The distribution of the ABO alleles is to some extent consistent with selection and infectious disease. India, for example, is a region with a high frequency of the *B* allele (Roychoudhury and Nei 1988). India also has a history of frequent epidemics of both smallpox and bubonic plague. Since blood type O is more susceptible to plague, *O* alleles would be removed from the population. Since type A is more susceptible to smallpox, *A* and *O* alleles would be removed from the population. The net result would be a relatively higher frequency of the *B* alleles—precisely what is found in India.

ABO blood types also appear to be related to noninfectious diseases. Some hospital studies have suggested that people with blood type O have a greater chance of getting duodenal and stomach ulcers. People with blood type A have a greater chance of getting certain forms of cancer. The differences between the phenotypes appear strong, but we do not understand the reasons for these associations. In any case, it is unclear what evolutionary importance these associations have. Most of the noninfectious diseases have severe effects late in life and therefore should not be subject to natural selection because they usually occur after an individual's reproductive life is over. Some people, however, do acquire these diseases early enough in life so that at least the possibility exists that natural selection could be operating through differential survival to noninfectious diseases. We must demonstrate, however, that such selection did (or does) in fact take place, and not merely that it is possible.

Natural selection may also be operating on ABO blood groups as a consequence of incompatibility between mother and fetus. Incompatible matings will often lead to the destruction of red blood cells in the fetus.

Most often, ABO incompatibility will lead to spontaneous abortion early in prenatal life. Incompatibility occurs when the mother's blood has an antibody corresponding to the type of molecule present in the fetus's blood. An example of incompatibility is a woman with blood type A whose fetus is blood type AB. The woman's blood contains anti-B antibody, which reacts with the B molecules present in the fetus's blood. All possible types of incompatibility between mother and fetus are listed in Table 4.2. Note that in each case the genotype of the fetus is heterozygous. This suggests selection against some heterozygotes.

There seems to be little doubt that natural selection has affected allele frequencies for the ABO blood group system. Studies have shown the relationship among blood type and incompatibility, infectious disease, and noninfectious disease. It does not appear likely that any one of these factors is solely responsible for the observed allele frequency range in human beings. It is also possible that there are other factors of which we are unaware. A further complication is that we generally have data on ABO phenotypes and not on genotypes. Our blood tests can tell us if someone is blood type A, but they cannot tell us if that person has the *AA* or *AO* genotype. Simply because we cannot tell the difference does not mean that natural selection does not affect these genotypes in different ways. As we develop more sophisticated methods of genetic analysis, we may be able to look more closely at the relationship between selection and genotype for the ABO system.

lactase deficiency When an older child or adult lacks the ability to produce the lactase enzyme needed to digest milk sugar.

**T A B L E 4.2
ABO Blood Group
Maternal-fetal
Incompatibilities**

Mother's genotype	Incompatible fetal genotypes
AA	*AB*
AO	*AB, BO*
BB	*AB*
BO	*AB, AO*
AB	*None*
OO	*AO, BO*

Lactase Deficiency

As shown in the sickle cell example, cultural variation can affect genetic variation. **Lactase deficiency** is another example of a genetic trait that is influenced by cultural factors. As mammals, human infants receive nourishment from mother's milk. Infants have an enzyme, lactase, that allows milk sugar, lactose, to be digested. In most human populations, the manufacture of the lactase enzyme is "turned off" by four years of age as it is in most mammals after infancy. A person who has a deficiency of this enzyme as a child or adult will not be able to digest milk efficiently and can develop severe cramps, diarrhea, and other intestinal problems if he or she consumes it. The genetics of adult lactase deficiency are not fully understood, but it may be caused by a recessive allele. The environment may also exert some influence because individuals who are lactase-deficient may be able to build up some ability to digest milk over time. Though lactase deficiency is probably not a "simple" discrete trait, the available evidence does suggest a relatively simple mode of inheritance.

Most human populations have high frequencies of lactase deficiency, but some populations do not. The enzyme continues to be produced throughout life, and these people can continue to digest milk sugar. Interestingly, a clear relationship exists between the frequency of lactase defi-

T A B L E   **4.3**
Frequencies of Lactase Deficiency in Some Human Populations

Population		Percentage of lactase deficiency
African ancestry	African Americans	70–77
	Ibos	99
	Bantus	90
	Fulani	22
	Yoruba	99
	Baganda	94
Asian ancestry	Asian Americans	95–100
	Thailand	97–100
	Eskimos	72–88
	Native Americans	58–67
European ancestry	European Americans	2–19
	Finland	18
	Switzerland	12
	Sweden	4

Sources: Lerner and Libby (1976:327); Molnar (1992:124).

ciency in a population and whether or not the population is involved in dairy farming. Table 4.3 lists the frequency of lactase deficiency in a number of populations of African, Asian, and European ancestry. In general, the lowest frequency is found in populations of European ancestry with a known history of dairy farming. The highest frequency of lactase deficiency occurs in populations of African and Asian ancestry that did not practice dairy farming. Populations that rely extensively on cheese products generally do not conform to this pattern, probably reflecting the fact that the lactose is broken down in the process of cheese making. The digestion of cheese is not accomplished by the lactase enzyme but by certain intestinal enzymes and bacteria.

The correspondence of low frequencies of lactase deficiency and dairy farming suggests that the ability to digest milk later in life is selected for in environments where milk is a major source of nutrition. This circumstance suggests that humans originally had very high frequencies of lactase deficiency and that as populations grew to rely more and more on milk in their diet after infancy, natural selection acted to decrease the proportion of those with lactase deficiency. After all, we would expect higher survival and reproduction in those individuals best able to utilize available nutrition. An examination of some discrepancies in the usual pattern of frequencies in Table 4.3 supports this hypothesis. Many African populations, such as the Ibos and Bantus, are known horticultural populations that do not practice dairy farming. The Fulani, however, are a group of nomadic cattle herders who rely extensively on milk in their diet. The percentage of lactase deficiency among the Fulani is low (22 percent) and similar to the percentage found in European populations. African Americans have high rates of lactase deficiency, but much lower than those populations found in West Africa from whom they are descended. The reduction in the frequency of lactase deficiency among African Americans may represent European admixture, physiological adaptation to milk diets, and/or some degree of natural selection. Lactase deficiency provides a good example of rapid natural selection in human populations. Dairy agriculture is less than 12,000 years old and the observed differences among dairy- and nondairy-producing economies must have arisen since then.

SUMMARY

The study of human microevolution focuses on the effects of genetic drift, gene flow, and natural selection on patterns of genetic variation within and between populations. Assessments of genetic drift and gene flow rely on multivariate measures of genetic variation that deal with a number of traits at the same time, because drift and gene flow are expected to have the same effect on all loci. Natural selection is expected to have different effects on different traits, leading researchers to examine one trait at a time.

Genetic drift and gene flow exert critical impact on genetic variation in a wide range of populations. Factors such as geographic distance, cultural change, social organization, culture contact, and religious differences, among others, have all been shown to affect genetic differences between groups.

Studies of natural selection have produced mixed results because of the difficulty in measuring natural selection over short time periods and because selective forces that shaped our past are not always working today. The strong relationship of hemoglobin variants and certain blood groups with the presence of malaria represents the strongest evidence for natural selection on relatively simple genetic traits. Other traits, such as the ABO blood groups, have been linked to a number of selective factors, but it is difficult at present to determine which ones have been most significant.

Supplemental Readings

Crawford, M. H., and P. L. Workman, eds. 1973. *Methods and Theories of Anthropological Genetics.* Albuquerque: University of New Mexico Press.

Crawford, M. H., and J. H. Mielke, eds. 1982. *Current Developments in Anthropological Genetics,* Vol. 2, *Ecology and Population Structure.* New York: Plenum Press.

Mielke, J. H., and M. H. Crawford, eds. 1980. *Current Developments in Anthropological Genetics,* Vol. 1, *Theory and Methods.* New York: Plenum Press. These three volumes provide detailed, although somewhat advanced, reviews of theory, methods, and applications in the study of human microevolution.

Harrison, G. A., J. M. Tanner, D. R. Pilbeam, and P. T. Baker. 1988. *Human Biology: An Introduction to Human Evolution, Variation, Growth, and Adaptability.* 3rd ed. Oxford: Oxford University Press.

Molnar, S. 1992. *Human Variation: Races, Types, and Ethnic Groups.* 3rd ed. Englewood Cliffs, N.J.: Prentice-Hall. These two texts provide summaries of the field of human variation and microevolution. Although not as detailed as the first three, they are better designed for new students.

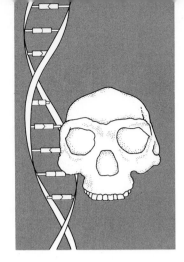

CHAPTER 5

Approaches to the Study of Human Variation

We each encounter human biological diversity every day of our lives, but we seldom speak of what we see in terms of evolutionary forces. Instead, we use words like "race" without actually defining them. What do phrases like the "white race," the "Japanese race," and the "Jewish race" mean to you? They are extremely confusing because the term "race" is used to stand for a variety of factors such as skin color, national origin, and religion. Sometimes we use the term in a biological sense, sometimes in a social sense.

Race and Racial Classifications

Obviously, race is an important concept in our lives. But what exactly is it? How many races are there? What are the differences between races? This chapter looks at the biological definition of race and compares the utility of this definition to a microevolutionary approach.

The Biological Concept of Race

From a biological standpoint, a **race** is generally defined as "a division of a species that differs from other divisions by the frequency with which certain hereditary traits appear among its members" (Brues 1977:1). Race

race A group of populations sharing certain traits that make them distinct from other groups of populations. The concept of race is difficult to apply to patterns of human variation.

in this definition has two characteristics. First, it is a group of populations that share some biological characteristics. Second, these populations differ from other groups of populations according to these characteristics. Race is meant to provide a classification of biologically similar populations.

The race concept works better biologically with some organisms than with others. For other organisms, such as humans, the concept has less utility. Humans inhabit a wide number of environments and move between them frequently. The high degree of gene flow among human populations, compared to many other organisms, means that clear-cut boundaries among groups of populations are difficult to establish.

The race concept presents a number of problems that are outlined in the next section. Given these problems, race and racial classifications provide only a crude tool for description, one with little utility for today's biologist or anthropologist, when sophisticated statistical methods and computers allow us to analyze patterns of biological variation more precisely than ever before.

Problems with the Concept of Race

What is wrong with classifying people into races? After all, we can do it accurately. Or can we?

The number of human races. A major problem with the race concept is that scientists have never agreed on the number of human races. Some have suggested that there are three human races: Europeans, Africans, and Asians (often referred to by the archaic terms "Caucasoid," "Negroid," and "Mongoloid," which are almost never used in scientific research today). But many populations do not fit neatly into these three basic categories. What about native Australians (aborigines)? As shown in Figure 5.1, these are dark-skinned people who frequently have curly or wavy hair that is sometimes blond and who have abundant facial hair. On the basis of skin color, we might be tempted to label these people as African, but on the basis of hair and facial shape they might be classified as European. One approach has been to create a fourth category, the "Australoid" race.

As we travel around the world, we find more and more populations that do not fit a three- or four-race system. As a result, some authors added additional races to their list. There has never been clear consensus on the actual number, however. Different authors have suggested four, five, and nine major races, among other numbers. Additional populations that are the result of admixture, such as African Americans, are often referred to as "composite races." In each case there has been little agreement on the number of races or subraces.

Two points emerge from a study of the history of attempts to classify and apply the race concept to human populations. First, the lack of agreement among different researchers indicates that the entire concept of race is arbitrary as it applies to humans. How useful is a classification system

Figure 5.1

An Australian aborigine with
dark skin and curly hair.
(Neg. no. 330831. Photo
by A. P. Elkin. Courtesy
Department of Library Services,
American Museum of Natural
History)

when there is so much disagreement about the number of units? Second,
something is being described here, although in a crude manner. All racial
classifications, for example, note the wide range in skin color among human populations and note further an association with geography. The
native peoples of Africa tend to have darker skin than those of northern
Europe. Then why doesn't the race concept work well when describing
biological variation?

The nature of continuous variation. Biological variation is real; the
order we impose on this variation by using the concept of race is not. Race
is a product of human minds, not of nature. One reason race fails to
describe variation accurately is that much variation is continuous, whereas
race is a discrete unit. In other words, we must reduce variation into a few
small categories.

Consider human height as an example. Most of us cannot describe a
person's height to the nearest centimeter without actually measuring that
person. When we look at someone, we are unlikely to know *exactly* how
tall that person is. We would not, however, describe everyone as the same
height simply because we do not know the exact values. Instead, we use

relative terms such as "short," "medium," and "tall." But are these categories real?

The same problem applies to races. Many racial classifications in Western societies use skin color as a major distinguishing feature. The races correspond to different measures of skin color—"white," "yellow," "red," "brown," and "black," for example. We know, however, that skin color does not fall into 5, or even 50, different categories. Skin color is a continuous variable. This means that any attempt to divide the continuous range into discrete units (races) is going to be arbitrary.

Since the 1950s, biological anthropologists have used an objective method of measuring skin color—reflectance spectrophotometry. According to this method, a light source is held up next to a person's skin, and the amount of light reflected back from the skin surface is measured. Skin color is measured as the percentage of light reflected. The higher the percentage of reflectance, the lighter the skin color.

Figure 5.2 shows the average skin reflectance for males in 22 samples. For each sample, the dot represents the average value, and the lines represent 1 standard deviation below and above the average. (A standard deviation is a statistical measure of variation. Roughly 68 percent of the cases in each sample lie between the ends of the lines drawn in Figure 5.2. Each sample contains some individuals who are even lighter or darker than the range shown.) There are no discrete boundaries between different groups. The ranges of skin reflectance overlap one another. In other words, on the basis of skin color it is not possible to tell where one population ends and another starts.

There is also overlap in skin color among traditional racial groupings. Using published data on male skin reflectance, the average skin reflectance for 27 Sub-Saharan African populations is 30 percent. The average skin reflectance for 22 South Asian populations is 49 percent. Generally, Sub-Saharan Africans are darker than South Asians (the lower the percentage reflectance, the darker the skin). However, considerable overlap occurs between these two geographic groups. Individual Sub-Saharan African populations range from 18 to 46 percent reflectance, and individual South Asian populations range from 32 to 56 percent. Some South Asian populations are darker than some Sub-Saharan African populations!

If we look only at the darkest and lightest of these samples, we might be tempted to describe two races, "black" and "white." The range of variation in the entire world, however, shows that we cannot describe different races. Where does one race end and another begin? There are no discrete boundaries, even with a handful of samples. How many races would you use for description? Two? Three? The number is arbitrary.

Despite these arguments, many people are still convinced that human races are easily identifiable. After all, they say, you can walk down any city street in the United States and point out who is "white" and who is "black". Under such circumstances, race is easily identifiable (or is it?). Races seem distinct in certain situations because disproportionate num-

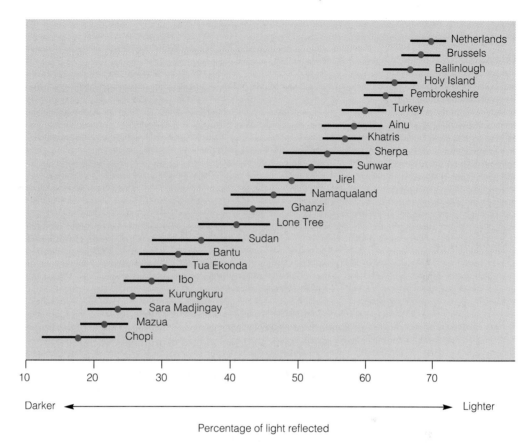

Darker ←————————————————————————————→ Lighter

Percentage of light reflected

Figure 5.2

Variation in skin color in 22 human populations (males). Dots indicate the mean skin reflectance measured at a wavelength of 685 nanometers; lines indicate 1 standard deviation on each side of the mean. (All data from published literature)

bers of peoples from different geographic regions are present. We do not find equal representation of all human populations on most U.S. city streets. For example, we tend to see far fewer Australian aborigines than we see people of predominantly European or African ancestry.

In short, the overall composition of the U.S. population tends to give us a distorted view of the total variation in the world. The majority of early settlers in the United States came from Western Europe, one of the regions in the world whose human populations show the lightest skin color. During the next few centuries, many slaves were brought from West Africa, one of the regions where human skin color is darkest. The result has been a disproportionate representation of the range of skin color. More people in the United States have either very light or very dark skin than any shade in between (Figure 5.3).

Not all biological traits show continuous variation. Blood group phenotypes, for example, are discrete traits. We do not, however, often find situations in which all members of one race have one phenotype and all

Figure 5.3

Original settlement of the United States from the perspective of skin color. From the continuous range of skin color in the human species, the majority of earliest settlers were from the two extreme ends—dark-colored West Coast Africans and light-colored Western Europeans. This differential settlement gives rise to the seeming existence of two distinct races in the United States based on skin color.

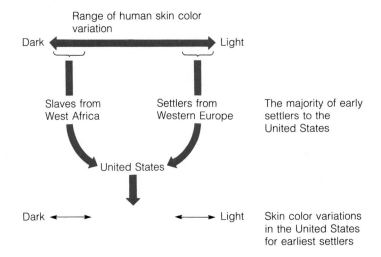

members of another race have a different phenotype. For example, the frequency of the *a* allele for the Diego blood group is moderately high in native South American populations, ranging up to 0.32. In both Africa and Europe, however, the frequency is 0 (Roychoudhury and Nei 1988). This allele is useful in separating South America from other regions but does not separate Africa and Europe—two regions typically assigned to different races. In addition, there are populations in South America that have a near-zero allele frequency. If we used the Diego blood group, we would have to assign these South American populations to a mixed European/African race!

Correspondence of different traits. If race were to be a useful biological concept, the classifications would have to work for a number of independent traits. A classification developed from skin color would also need to show the same racial pattern in other traits, such as head shape, nasal shape, and hair color. If each trait produces a different set of races, then the race concept is not very useful as a description of overall biological similarity. In fact, racial classifications vary according to the biological trait used. This lack of correspondence is expected, given Mendel's work on independent assortment.

High frequencies of the sickle cell allele are found not only in populations belonging to "African races," but also in parts of Europe and India. Any racial classification based on high or low frequencies of the sickle cell allele in a population would not produce the same distribution as skin color. Another example comes from the work of Bodmer and Cavalli-Sforza (1976), who looked at the relationships among four "racial groups": Native Americans, Europeans, Australian aborigines, and Africans. Using body and cranial measurements, they found that Native Americans were more similar to Europeans and Australian aborigines were more similar to Africans. When they used a number of genetic marker systems, however, they found a different pattern. Native Americans were more similar to Australian aborigines and Europeans were more similar to Africans.

With the proper choice of variables, however, we can find combinations that are useful in looking at the relationships between populations on a worldwide basis. By examining a number of traits presumed neutral in terms of natural selection, we try to come up with an average pattern that reflects the tendency of gene flow and genetic drift to affect all loci to the same extent. Often we find clusters of populations that agree in a limited sense with geography. That is, we can identify some separation between Sub-Saharan African populations, European populations, Middle Eastern populations, and so on. This is expected, given the close relationship of geographic distance and gene flow in human populations. Sub-Saharan African populations should be more similar to each other, on average, than to European populations. This does not, however, support the race concept. Genetic distances within regional groups are often greater than those found between regions. Also, it is sometimes still difficult, if not impossible, to draw lines clearly delineating different races. We can identify rough geographic clusters that, in some cases, have a *rough* correspondence with predetermined notions of races. However, because races are often defined in part on the basis of geography, the entire process is somewhat circular.

Variation between and within groups. Racial classifications represent a form of **typology,** a set of discrete groupings. Instead of looking at the continuous range of variation, populations are placed into different races. The problem with typologies and typological thinking is that it tends to ignore the variation and focus exclusively on the "types." An average is considered representative of the entire group. Take, for example, the fact that the average height in Finland is 171 cm (Molnar 1992). Does this mean that *everyone* in Finland is exactly this height? Of course not. There is always variation within the group.

Racial classifications focus on the difference between groups and deemphasize the variation that exists within groups. Lewontin (1972) examined the actual levels of variation between and within seven designated "races": Africans, Europeans, Asians, Native Americans, South Asians, Oceanians, and Australian aborigines. Lewontin took this list of races and then looked at a number of loci for each race. He found that 94 percent of the total variation occurred *within* races and 6 percent of the variation *between* races. His study shows clearly how limited the race concept is for classification.

typology A set of discrete groupings in classification that emphasize average tendencies and ignore variation within groups.

What use is the race concept? Even if we acknowledge the many problems associated with race as a concept, does it have any use? In the scientific study of human variation, the concept of race has little, if any, use. It is a descriptive tool, not an analytic one. If we examine the biological characteristics of a population and then assign the population to a given race, all we have accomplished is giving a label to some observed phenomenon. We have not explained the causes of variation, nor why some groups are more similar, or different, from others. The name explains nothing.

Until the 1950s, much of biological anthropology was devoted to racial description and classification. Most sciences go through a descriptive phase, followed later by an explanatory phase in which hypotheses are proposed and tested. Indeed, at least until the work of Charles Darwin, much of biology was basically a descriptive science. Today biological anthropologists rarely treat race as a concept. It has no utility for explanation, and its value for description is limited.

In contemporary society, however, race is still a common category. In this context the term has more a social connotation than a biological one. In state and federal government reports, "race" identifies some aspect of geographic origin and ethnic identity. For example, "black" refers to African or African-American descent. "Hispanic" refers to Spanish speakers but actually encompasses a wide variety of peoples from Mexicans to Bolivians. Such classifications have their use, particularly in defining groups of people who have suffered social inequities, but they are not without their own problems. Classification into discrete groups always means that we obscure the subtle gradations of human variation.

Human variation is best analyzed using an approach that focuses on microevolutionary forces and uses individuals or local populations as the unit of analysis. This approach, aided by modern statistical and computer methods, allows better description than the race concept, avoids the problems of classification, and provides a focus for *explanation*.

Skin Color: An Example of Racial versus Microevolutionary Approaches

Skin color has been a widely used characteristic in racial classifications. Typical classifications equate a different skin color with each race, such as "black" (African), "white" (European), "yellow" (Asian), and "red" (Native American). Perhaps the major reason for the popularity of skin color as a racial characteristic is that you can see it: skin color is one of the most noticeable forms of human variation. This was particularly true when the early European explorers first met darker-skinned peoples. You could just as easily attempt to construct a racial classification using frequencies of the ABO blood group system, except that in this case you would not be able to assign people to races just by looking at them.

A common reaction of many people when they look at skin color variation is to see distinct colors. This is particularly true in the United States, for reasons discussed earlier. Once we identify distinct classes of colors, we label each color as a different race. The problem here is that our observations are not always objective. We often emphasize differences among groups to the exclusion of variation within groups. Do all "white" people have the same skin color? Figure 5.2 shows that we cannot break up the range of human skin color variation into discrete categories.

Racial approaches to skin color do not take into account the processes behind the variation. The real issues are why people have different skin color. To answer this question, we must abandon typical racial classifications and look more closely at the biological nature of skin color.

The Biology of Skin Color

Human skin color is a complex trait. A number of researchers have suggested that skin color has a strong genetic component (e.g., Williams-Blangero and Blangero 1992) and is affected by the environment, such as the amount of direct sunlight present.

Skin color is caused by three pigments. One pigment, *melanin*, is responsible for the majority of variation in lightness and darkness in skin color. Melanin is a brown pigment secreted by cells in the bottom layer of the skin. All human populations appear to have the same number of melanin-producing cells. Variation in the darkness of the skin depends on how many cells actually produce melanin and how they cluster together (Szabo 1967). The more melanin-producing cells are present or the more they cluster, the darker the skin color. Another pigment affecting skin color is *hemoglobin*, which gives oxygenated blood cells their red color. A third pigment is *carotene*, a yellowish pigment obtained from certain foods. A person who eats these foods in sufficient amounts may notice a yellowish tinge to the skin.

Skin Color and Natural Selection

The distribution of skin color. The worldwide distribution of human skin color among native populations shows a striking correspondence with latitude. Figure 5.4 shows the relationship between skin color and distance from the equator for 93 male samples from the Old World. Native populations closer to the equator tend to be the darkest, while those farther from the equator tend to be the lightest. Note that there are no discrete breaks. The distribution of skin color and latitude corresponds to the amount of ultraviolet radiation received at the earth's surface. Because of the way sunlight strikes the earth, ultraviolet radiation is strongest at the

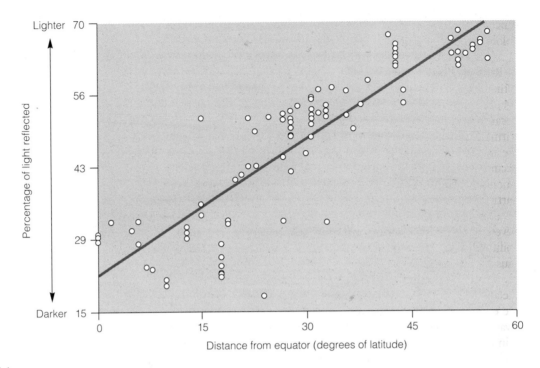

Figure 5.4

Geographic distribution of human skin color for 93 human Old World populations (males). Circles indicate the mean skin reflectance measured at a wavelength of 685 nanometers plotted against the distance, in degrees of latitude, from the equator. The solid line indicates the best-fitting linear curve relating skin reflectance and latitude.   (All data from published literature)

equator and diminishes in strength as we move away from the equator. It is even more diminished where cloud cover is extensive.

Skin cancer, sunburn, and ultraviolet radiation. What are the biological effects of ultraviolet radiation? This radiation causes the skin to tan—that is, to produce more melanin. Too much exposure burns the skin, leading to infection. In sufficient amounts, ultraviolet radiation can lead to skin cancer. The greater the intensity of ultraviolet radiation, the greater the risk for skin cancer at a given level of pigmentation. Among the European-American population of the United States, skin cancer rates are much higher in Texas than in Massachusetts (Damon 1977). Dark-skinned individuals have lower rates of skin cancer, since the heavy concentration of melanin near the surface of the skin blocks some of the ultraviolet radiation. Accordingly, the correspondence of latitude and skin color may reflect, in part, the differential effects of skin cancer.

Researchers have argued against skin cancer as a selective factor, suggesting that skin cancer, like many cancers, affects mostly older individuals past their reproductive years. If someone dies from skin cancer after reproducing, their death does not affect the process of natural selection. According to this line of reasoning, some researchers have suggested that skin cancer has had a minimal effect, at best, on the evolution of human skin color (e.g., Blum 1961).

The problem with this argument is that the evidence does not support it. Robins (1991) points out that all albinos studied in Nigeria and Tanzania either had skin cancer or precancerous skin lesions by 20 years of age. People are normally dark skinned in these countries, and the albinos, because of a rare genetic condition, would be particularly susceptible to harmful effects of ultraviolet radiation. From an evolutionary standpoint, the important finding is that skin cancers and precancerous conditions occur *early* in life, contrary to the opinion that they are generally found among the elderly. Skin cancer could have been a powerful selective agent, particularly among early humans that had limited protection from the sun.

Sunburn could also have been an important factor in natural selection. Severe sunburn can lead to infection and can interfere with the body's ability to sweat efficiently. Dark skin could protect from these effects, and thus be selected for.

Natural selection related to skin cancer and sunburn may be part of the answer to the question of worldwide skin color variation, but it is not the entire answer. Even though there is less ultraviolet radiation farther away from the equator and light-skinned people would have less risk for skin cancer and sunburn, this does not explain *why* light skin evolved in such regions. The model only shows that light skin *could* evolve.

The vitamin D hypothesis. A more subtle effect of ultraviolet radiation is the synthesis of vitamin D, a nutrient needed by humans for proper bone growth. Today we may receive vitamin D either through vitamin supplements or through the injection of vitamin D into our milk. Formerly, humans had to obtain their vitamin D through diet or from stimulation of the synthesis of certain chemical compounds by ultraviolet radiation. For most human populations in the past the major source of vitamin D was the sun.

Because vitamin D synthesis depends on ultraviolet radiation, it seems reasonable to assume that more of it will be produced near the equator, where ultraviolet radiation is strongest. It has been suggested that too much or too little of the vitamin is harmful to the human body. An excess of vitamin D can lead to vitamin poisoning, cause calcification of soft tissues, and interfere with proper kidney functioning while a lack of it can lead to poor bone development and maintenance, including diseases, such as rickets, that lead to deformed bones.

The idea that vitamin D intake must lie in a certain range, without excess or deficit, is at the core of the vitamin D hypothesis of skin color evolution (Loomis 1967). According to this hypothesis, in regions close to the equator, where ultraviolet radiation is the greatest, darker skin serves to block the harmful effects of excessive vitamin D production. In areas farther away, dark skin blocks too much of the sun's rays, which leads to insufficiency of vitamin D. Natural selection thus produced a change toward lighter skin color, that would be adaptive in such environments.

The vitamin D hypothesis thus explains the entire distribution of human skin color, showing the adaptive significance of both dark skin and light skin in different environments. Although logical, some investigations have suggested that this model is *not* correct. Holick and colleagues (1981) have shown that vitamin D synthesis reaches a maximum level during continued exposure to ultraviolet radiation. A light-skinned person's prolonged exposure to ultraviolet radiation will *not* lead to toxic vitamin D levels.

Though the vitamin D hypothesis does not hold up for explaining dark skin near the equator, can it still be used to explain the occurrence of light skin farther away from the equator? Robins (1991) listed a number of reasons why the vitamin D hypothesis fails here as well. First, rickets is a disease associated with recent urbanization. It is essentially absent in rural areas, and there is little evidence of rickets in the fossil record of our ancestors (who lived in rural, not urban, conditions). Second, although dark skin is not as effective as light skin in synthesizing vitamin D, it is still effective enough for production and maintenance of proper vitamin D levels. Laboratory studies have shown that African Americans can produce their maximum quota of vitamin D in three hours. Though this is not as fast as for European Americans (30 minutes), it is still effective enough for proper health except under conditions of modern urbanization, such as smog and tall buildings that cut down on exposure. Studies have also determined that dark-skinned peoples could produce and maintain sufficient vitamin D in northern climates even with only their heads, necks, and hands exposed to ultraviolet radiation. In sum, the relationship between rickets and limited vitamin D appears confined to recent urban areas and is also associated with lower social class (the poor have less money for milk). For conditions typical of our ancestors, dark skin would *not* be at a disadvantage in terms of limited vitamin D production.

Skin color and cold injury. The vitamin D hypothesis does not hold true when explaining the distribution of human skin color. One possibility for the occurrence of light skin at distances away from the equator is cold injury. Reviewing a wide range of data, Post and colleagues (1975) noted that, in cold climates, dark-skinned individuals are at greater risk for frostbite than light-skinned individuals. Data reporting this difference are available on soldiers in world wars I and II, the Korean War, and those stationed in Alaska during the late 1950s. For example, during the Korean War, African-American soldiers were over four times more likely to get frostbite than European-American soldiers. Closer analysis of the data from the Korean War shows that this difference persists even after controlling for other sociological and health factors.

At present, the evidence supports skin cancer and sunburn as selective factors for dark skin in equatorial regions. Farther away from the equator, there is less of an advantage for dark skin, and more of an advantage for light skin, the former being more vulnerable to severe cold injury. Further study will be needed to strengthen support for both of these ideas and to explore the possibility that other factors affect skin color variation. Recent observations that ultraviolet radiation affects functioning of the immune system (Robins 1991) are also worth investigating.

The IQ Controversy

The area that generates the most controversy in any discussion of race is behavior, especially aspects of personality and intelligence. Inferences about race and behavior run deep in most cultures. Scientists, though often seeking to be objective, are members of cultures and have often contributed their share of misunderstanding.

In the United States a continuing source of controversy has been the evaluation of racial differences in intelligence test scores. Part of the confusion in this controversy arises from the designation of groups, identified as European-American, African-American, and Asian-American, as biological races. Given typological thinking, there is a tendency to consider each group as homogeneous, with little variation within the group. In reality, these groups are defined in part on the basis of ancestry and contain a highly varied mixture of genetic and social backgrounds. By now it should be clear that the use of general terms such as *black* and *white* has limited utility if we take these groups as "types" or "races."

Results of IQ Testing

Regardless of how we define "black" and "white," one fact emerges from numerous studies of intelligence testing—the average IQ score for African Americans is 15 points below the average IQ score for European Americans. In general, Asian Americans score higher than European Americans. The controversy comes from interpreting exactly what these differences mean.

IQ tests have certain problems. There is a certain amount of individual variation, and people may show different scores when tested at different stages of maturation. Physical factors such as stress have been shown to affect individual scores by as much as 15 points. Also, the usual IQ tests are often biased to a specific culture, and there has not been much success in developing a culture-free IQ test. An interesting finding is that African Americans score higher than European Americans on average on IQ tests designed around aspects of African-American language and culture.

Regardless of the exact relationship, or lack of relationship, between intelligence and IQ scores, the fact that African Americans score lower on average than European Americans would seem to indicate a substantial group difference in *some* aspect of learning or problem-solving abilities. In looking at these results, however, remember not to fall into the trap of associating a group's average value with all members of the group. Both groups show appreciable variation in IQ scores.

The nature of variation means that we cannot make any predictions about the IQ scores of an individual based on group averages. Because African Americans and European Americans differ in one obvious biological trait—skin color—it is often tempting to explain differences in average IQ score as also the result of genetic differences between the two groups. It is important to realize that the two groups differ in many environmental factors. On average, African Americans have fewer educational and economic opportunities, less available health care, lower socioeconomic status, and poorer nutrition than European Americans. Do these differences account for the observed difference in IQ test scores? Or are there genetic differences between the two groups?

Genetic and Environmental Effects on IQ Scores

To date, there is evidence that *both* genetic and environmental factors affect IQ scores. Studies of twins and other relatives reveal strong association between the IQ scores of parents, children, and other relatives. In a recent and comprehensive study of identical twins raised apart, Bouchard and colleagues (1990) found that roughly 70 percent of the variation in observed IQ scores could be related to genetic factors. However, being born to two parents with a high IQ does not guarantee a high IQ; the social and physical environment must also be appropriate. Numerous studies have shown that IQ scores are associated with social class, educational background, nutrition, health status, and other factors.

These studies show us that IQ scores are not a fixed innate trait reflecting a person's genetic code but can be affected by environmental factors. The studies also show us that, all other factors being equal, inherited abilities contribute to performance on these tests.

Faulty reasoning has often been used in evaluating genetic differences between African Americans and European Americans and their effect on IQ test scores. A typical argument runs as follows: if IQ scores have a genetic basis and if two groups are genetically different, then the two groups will have different average IQ scores. The problem with this argument is that it relies on the myth of correspondence. The fact that skin color is different between two groups does not mean that any other trait, such as intelligence, will also be different. Many traits are "fixed" within the human species, such as the number of legs, arms, and eyes.

Actually, we need not rely on logical reasoning to look at the issue of genetic differences in IQ scores. The hypothesis that population differences in IQ scores are caused by genetic differences has been repeatedly tested. They are not.

One type of test examines the IQ scores of African Americans according to their amount of European admixture (see Chapter 3). If there are genetic differences between African Americans and European Americans for IQ scores, then African Americans with more European ancestry should have higher IQ scores than those with less European ancestry. Overall, there should be a positive relationship between the extent of European ancestry and IQ scores. In one test of this hypothesis, hundreds of African Americans from Philadelphia had blood testing to determine their degree of European admixture. The results showed no relationship between admixture and IQ scores (Scarr and Weinberg 1978).

Another type of test looks at differences between European Americans and African Americans in IQ scores after adjusting for variation in the social and physical environment. One well-known study analyzed the massive amounts of data collected on U.S. Army recruits during World War I. When the total sample of European-American and African-American recruits was tallied, the former had, on average, higher test scores. When comparisons were made between literate European Americans and literate African Americans, however, the difference virtually disappeared.

Another large-scale study of IQ differences was carried out using 650,000 school children. Although the average score for European Americans was higher than for African Americans, there were also strong relationships between test scores and social factors. "Race" was found to be less important in predicting IQ scores than a variety of social factors. When differences in socioeconomic status and other factors were controlled for, the difference between African Americans and European Americans was insignificant (Molnar 1992).

Studies of adopted children also shed light on the relative effects of genetics and environment. One study focused on 130 African-American children that had been adopted by fairly well-off European-American parents. These children had an average IQ of 106, compared to an average of 94 for children that remained in their old neighborhoods. This finding suggests that simply a change in environment resulted in a 12-point increase in IQ. Another study of 63 African-American children adopted into upper-income families showed a difference of 21 points between the children (mean IQ = 106) and their biological mothers (mean IQ = 85) (Woodward 1992).

The available data suggest that differences between African Americans and European Americans reflect environmental differences rather than genetic differences. Based on such studies, the general conclusion is that if the environmental differences are changed, then the differences in IQ scores will disappear. This is not an easy hypothesis to test for the entire country, since prejudice and differential treatment of European Americans and African Americans are realities that will take a long time to change. Several studies, however, have shown this predicted effect. One of the most famous was conducted in Milwaukee, where efforts were made to improve the environment of African-American children living in the poorest section of the city. A random sample of children received special education, including extensive individual attention for the first six years of life. This group scored much higher on IQ tests than a control group that did not receive such attention (Loehlin et al. 1975).

Performance on IQ tests clearly reflects an interaction of both genetic *and* environmental factors. Despite many of these findings, people continue to argue about whether IQ is related to genetics *or* to environment. Suggestions that IQ has a strong genetic component have sometimes been considered socially improper and racist. This logic runs as follows: if there is a genetic component to IQ, and because African Americans and European Americans are by definition genetically different, then any difference in average IQ between the races must therefore be genetic. Finally, the argument goes, if the difference is genetic, then the suggestion of a genetic component to IQ implies a "natural" superiority of one race over another, which is a racist attitude. Can you spot the logical problems with this argument? The fact that IQ scores do have a genetic component is *not* justification for assigning labels of inferiority. Just because a trait has a genetic basis does not mean that it will necessarily differ from one group to another. A number of traits do differ between African Americans and European Americans, and a number of traits do *not*. There is no way to determine beforehand whether any particular trait will be different in the two groups. The only way of solving the problem is to test the specific hypothesis. Our findings to date indicate that IQ scores have a strong genetic component, are strongly affected by the environment, and that differences *between* so-called racial groups are environmental in nature.

SUMMARY

The biological concept of race emphasizes differences between groups and deemphasizes variation within groups. In the past, race was moderately useful as a crude means by which to describe patterns of human variation. A major problem in using race as a concept is that distinct "races" take on a reality of their own in people's minds. The race concept has limited use in analyses of biological variation, particularly for widespread species such as human beings. The race concept uses arbitrary classifications of predominantly continuous variation, ignores Mendel's work on independent assortment, does not account for differences in patterns of variation among different traits, and does not account for variation within groups. Apart from these problems, the race concept is further limited because it offers no explanation of variation.

Variation in skin color has often been used as a characteristic for racial classification. Skin color does not come in a handful of shades but rather is a continuous trait. Examination of the distribution of human skin color suggests several environmental factors in its evolution, particularly the relationship of intense ultraviolet radiation with skin cancer and sunburn in equatorial regions, and the greater susceptibility of dark skin to cold injury in northern climates.

The issue of whether populational differences in behavior exist, especially in intelligence, has long been controversial. The most widely studied fact is the 15-point difference in IQ test scores between African Americans and European Americans in the United States. Numerous studies have shown that this difference reflects environmental, not genetic, differences between these groups. Intelligence has a genetic component, but it has not been shown to vary among "races." Prejudice is an unfortunate feature of human nature, but such biases cannot be "supported" by scientific evidence.

Supplemental Readings

Brues, A. M. 1977. *People and Races*. New York: Macmillan. This text, which represents a "traditional" view of human races, contains a great deal of information on variation in human biological traits.

Gould, S. J. 1981. *The Mismeasure of Man*. New York: W. W. Norton. A well-written book tracing the historical development of several methods used to demonstrate racial differences in mental abilities, and their shortcomings.

Molnar, S. 1992. *Human Variation: Race, Types, and Ethnic Groups*. 3rd ed. Englewood Cliffs, N. J.: Prentice-Hall. Provides information on human biological variation as well as a general introduction to the history of racial classification and the controversy on race and behavior.

Montagu, M. F. A., ed. 1964. *The Concept of Race*. New York: Free Press. A collection of articles written by anthropologists and biologists, criticizing the utility of the race concept in biology.

Robins, A. H. 1991. *Biological Perspectives on Human Pigmentation*. Cambridge: Cambridge University Press. An excellent review of the biology, variation, and evolution of human skin color. The final chapter on the evolution of skin color is the best treatment of the subject to date.

CHAPTER **6**

Human Biology and Culture

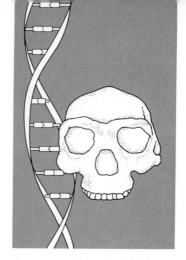

As discussed in Chapter 1, a main focus of biological anthropology is the interrelationship of biological and cultural variation. This chapter expands on the biocultural approach by looking at several areas of human biological variation that are affected strongly by cultural behaviors. Given that many biological traits are the joint product of genetic and environmental factors, the close relationship of human biology and culture is to be expected.

This chapter examines four biocultural approaches to the study of human variation: human growth, human adaptation, human health and disease, and demography. These are all fields of study in which close links exist between biological and cultural change in human populations. These are also the areas of biological variation most affected by rapid cultural changes in today's world. As human technology continues to expand precipitately, it has many effects on our biology, especially in those areas we are about to discuss.

Human Growth

The study of human growth and development clearly demonstrates the interrelationship of biology and culture. The growth patterns of any species have both genetic and environmental components. As our environment changes (including our cultural environment), so do our patterns of physical growth. Some of the effects, such as changes in health care and nutrition, are direct. Others, such as the relationship of socioeconomic class and nutrition, are indirect. For example, the poorer a family is, the less likely it is that the children will obtain proper nutrition, which in turn affects the growth of the children. Cultural changes are often mirrored in patterns of physical growth.

Stages of Human Growth

Before considering cultural influences on human growth, it is necessary to review some basic concepts. First, **growth** refers to the change in size of a living structure. Tissues can become larger because of an increase in the number of cells, an increase in the size of cells, or an increase in the amount of material between cells. Another common term, **development,** refers to the process of differentiation and specialization of cells that produces tissues and organs. From the perspective of growth and development, the life cycle can be divided into prenatal life (before birth) and postnatal life (after birth). Prenatal life is the period from conception through childbirth. After conception, the fertilized egg (**zygote**) develops into a cluster of identical cells. During the first week, the fertilized egg multiplies as it travels into the uterus. Then cell differentiation begins. During the second week, the outer layer of the cluster of cells forms the beginning of the placenta. The embryonic stage lasts from roughly two to eight weeks after conception. The **embryo** is very small, reaching an average length of 25 mm (1 inch) by the eighth week. During this time the basic body structure reaches completion and many organ systems have developed (Figure 6.1). From this point until birth the offspring is known as a **fetus.** Development of body parts and organ systems continues, along with a tremendous amount of body growth.

The Pattern of Human Postnatal Growth

The stages of postnatal life are defined somewhat arbitrarily and in different ways for varying purposes. From the perspective of human biological growth, the postnatal stages can be labeled according to basic patterns of physical growth and maturation. *Infancy* often refers to the first year of life, a time characterized by rapid body growth. *Childhood* is the period from infancy through puberty, characterized mostly by a slow, but constant, rate of growth. **Puberty** marks the period in which physical and sexual maturity is reached. Occurring normally somewhere between 8 and 16 years for females and 10 and 22 years for males (Malina 1975), puberty is characterized by rapid body growth, maturation of the reproductive system, and development of secondary sexual characteristics. *Adulthood* follows puberty and continues until death.

growth A change in the size of a living structure, most often because of an increase in cell size or number.

development The process of differentiation and specialization of cells that produces specific tissues and organs.

zygote A fertilized egg.

embryo The stage of human prenatal life lasting from roughly two to eight weeks following conception, characterized by structural development.

fetus The stage of prenatal growth from roughly 8 weeks following conception until birth, characterized by further development and rapid growth.

puberty The point in the human life cycle when sexual and physical maturity is attained.

Figure 6.1

A 2-month-old embryo. The fingers have developed and the eye is oval in shape. The total body length at this stage is 3.18 cm (1.25 in). (Copyright Lennart Nilsson; *A Child Is Born,* Dell Publishing Company)

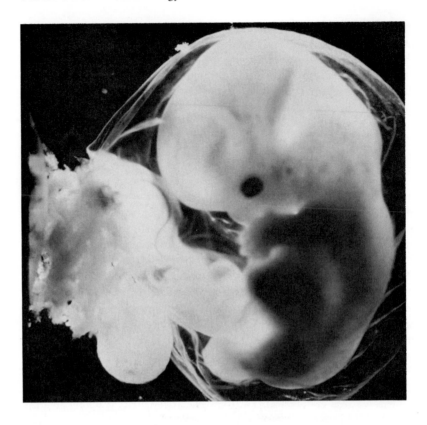

distance curve A measure of size over time. For example, a distance curve would show how tall someone is at different ages.

velocity curve A measure of the rates of change in growth over time.

Distance and velocity curves. Human growth is not simply a process of getting larger as you get older. For one thing, some components of your body (e.g., the lymph tissues) get smaller as you get older. For another thing, different parts of your body grow at different rates. Growth patterns vary according to age and body part. Simple graphs, called growth curves, convey information about patterns of physical growth.

The two most commonly used types of growth curves are distance curves and velocity curves. **Distance curves** simply measure overall size as a function of age—that is, how large you are at a given age. A typical distance curve for human height is shown in Figure 6.2. Note that the curve is not a straight line—humans do not get larger by the same amount each year. The curve shows a rapid increase in total height during infancy. Height continues to increase by a fairly constant amount during childhood and then increases quickly for a short time during puberty. By adulthood, there is little additional growth in height.

Whereas distance curves measure the actual amount of growth, **velocity curves** measure the rate of change in growth. Velocity refers to how fast you are moving. If you gain 4 inches in height in a single year, your

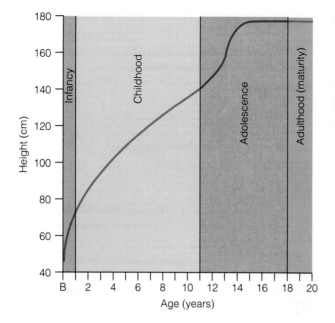

Figure 6.2

Typical distance curve for human height. (From *Growth and Development* by Robert M. Malina © 1975, publisher Burgess Publishing Company, Minneapolis, MN)

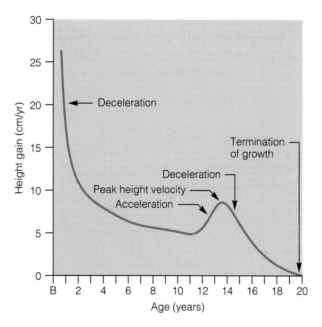

Figure 6.3

Typical velocity curve for human height. (From *Growth and Development* by Robert M. Malina © 1975, publisher Burgess Publishing Company, Minneapolis, MN)

growth velocity is 4 inches per year. Figure 6.3 shows a typical velocity curve for human height. Note that the greatest rate of change in height occurs immediately after birth. At no other time in your life will you be growing as fast. During infancy, the rate of change decreases quickly. You

adolescent growth spurt
The increase in rate of body growth during the adolescent years because of hormonal changes.

continue to get taller, but at a slower rate in each succeeding month. During childhood, the rate of change is fairly constant, but low. During puberty, the rate of growth in height increases again—a phenomenon known as the **adolescent growth spurt.** This increase is related to hormonal changes taking place during puberty. Following puberty, the rate of growth decreases again, reaching a level of zero growth by roughly 20 years of age in contemporary Western populations. Velocity curves are similar in males and females, except that females reach the growth spurt two years on average earlier than males. Adult human males are generally taller than adult human females, in part because they have had two years of extra growth prior to their growth spurt.

Differential growth. Not all parts of the body change at the same rate as overall body size. The distance and velocity curves for the brain and head look quite different. Figure 6.4 compares a distance curve for body size and brain growth. Brain growth is much more rapid in early postnatal life. This makes sense because humans rely on large brains, intelligence, and learned behavior. Given that only a certain amount of brain growth can occur before birth (the size of the mother's birth canal puts a limit on this), much brain growth must occur early in a person's postnatal life. Our growth patterns reflect our need for large brains, capable of learning, early in life.

Sexual maturation also follows a different growth path from body size. There is little growth of the reproductive organs during infancy or childhood. During puberty, these organs experience rapid growth, pro-

Figure 6.4

Distance curves for (a) body size and (b) brain growth, each measured as the percentage of adult size attained at a given age. (From *Growth and Development* by Robert M. Malina © 1975, publisher Burgess Publishing Company, Minneapolis, MN)

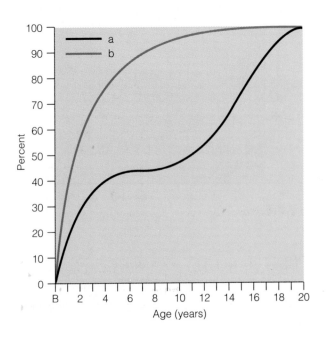

ducing the transition to biological maturity. In evolutionary terms, delayed sexual maturation is understandable. If young children were biologically able to have children, they would not yet have had the chance to acquire adequate knowledge to care for them.

The growth process. Growth curves often are used to get an idea of average patterns of growth in a population. Individuals deviate from the average patterns for a variety of reasons, both genetic and environmental, including hormonal deficiencies, physical illness, poor nutrition, and psychological stress. Even though the growth process is susceptible to a number of stresses, it also has the ability to recover if a stress is removed and even catch back up to where it should have been had the stress not occurred. This recovery process is aptly named **catch-up growth.** Consider children whose nutritional levels drop. Their growth will be reduced unless the nutritional stress is removed, whereupon they may show an increase in growth velocity and "catch up" to where they might have been under optimal conditions. However, because any system can be put under too much stress, catch-up growth does not always work. There are times during the growth process, known as **sensitive periods of growth,** in which catch-up growth is not possible. Prenatal life and the first year of postnatal growth are particularly sensitive periods of growth.

Influences on Human Growth

Human growth is affected by biological factors (genetics and hormones) and by a variety of environmental factors, including nutrition, disease, and the physical environment. Cultural differences also affect growth by causing changes in one or more of these environmental factors.

Biological influences. Comparisons of growth patterns among related individuals have shown that human growth is partially affected by genetic factors. The adult sizes of parents and children, for example, show a close resemblance for height and other linear body measurements. This relationship reflects similarity in patterns of bone growth, though the resemblance is less for measures of body width and circumference. Rates of growth and maturation are also influenced by genetic factors.

Growth is regulated by the body's secretion of chemical messengers known as **hormones,** which stimulate and regulate biological processes in different tissues. The release of hormones is controlled by a structure in the brain called the **hypothalamus.** A variety of hormones are known to affect human growth.

Nutrition. Proper nutrition is a critical factor in determining whether or not a person reaches his or her genetic potential for growth. Too little nutrient energy can result in a reduction in overall size and in delayed maturation. Too much nutrient energy can result in accumulation

catch-up growth An increase in growth that can occur following the removal of a limiting factor to growth.

sensitive period of growth A time during the life cycle when catch-up growth is not possible.

hormone Chemical released by endocrine glands that travels to body tissues and stimulates and regulates biological processes.

hypothalamus A structure of the brain that regulates the secretion of hormones.

▶

malnutrition Poor nutrition, either from too much or too little food, or the improper balance of nutrients.

of fat. Inadequate amounts of certain critical nutrients can also affect biological processes. Basic nutritional needs include calories (energy), amino acids from dietary proteins, fatty acids, vitamins, and minerals.

Malnutrition, which occurs in many human populations, includes problems caused by undernutrition and overnutrition. We tend to equate malnutrition with starvation, but too much food can also lead to problems. Obesity, for example, can lead to conditions such as hypertension, heart disease, and diabetes that require medical treatment. Excessive intake of calories, and resulting obesity, is a continuing health problem in the United States today.

Throughout much of the world today, however, the major nutritional problem is lack of food, or at least lack of a varied diet. Poor nutrition acts to slow down the growth process, leading to smaller adult body size. Distance curves for weight and height are shown in Figure 6.5 for two samples of Mexican boys, one well nourished and one suboptimally nourished. These curves show clearly that lowered nutritional levels result in smaller body size throughout childhood and puberty.

If nutritional levels do not become so low that they cause medical problems, smaller body size may be a desirable human trait. In fact, reduced growth and smaller body size are an adaptation to decreased nutritional intake. In environments where the food supply is limited, a smaller person who uses up less energy might be at an advantage.

Figure 6.5

Distance curves for weight (*top*) and height (*bottom*) for well-nourished and poorly nourished Mexican boys. At all ages, the well-nourished boys are taller and heavier. (From *Growth and Development* by Robert M. Malina © 1975, publisher Burgess Publishing Company, Minneapolis, MN)

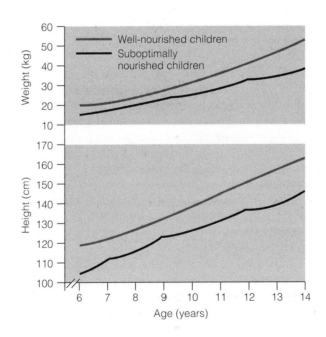

Severe undernutrition, especially in infancy, can have equally severe effects. Not only is physical growth stunted, but mental retardation may also result. Without an adequate diet, infants and children are more susceptible to infectious diseases. Severe undernutrition is highly prevalent in today's world, particularly in Third World nations, where poor nutrition is associated with overpopulation, poverty, inadequate waste disposal, contaminated water, high rates of infectious disease, and economic and political conflicts. Of course, undernutrition is not limited only to the Third World—the problem can also be found in parts of the United States.

A number of nutritional disorders are collectively known as **protein-calorie malnutrition,** which is an inadequate amount of protein and/or calories in the diet. Protein-calorie malnutrition is the most serious nutritional problem on the planet. Its various forms have different physical symptoms, but all stem from the basic problems of a poor diet in poverty conditions and have the same ultimate effects, ranging from growth retardation to death.

The two most severe types of protein-calorie malnutrition are **kwashiorkor** (severe deficiency in proteins but not calories) and **marasmus** (severe deficiencies in both proteins and calories). In protein-scarce environments, kwashiorkor results in growth retardation, muscle wasting, swelling of the body, and lowered resistance to disease. Marasmus also leads to growth retardation, muscle wasting, and even death. Although the physical appearance of children with kwashiorkor and marasmus differs, both disorders are caused by poverty and an inadequate diet. They also share the same ultimate outcomes—growth retardation and possibly death. The devastating effects of protein-calorie malnutrition should not be underestimated; between 5 and 45 percent of children in some developing countries suffer from one of these nutritional diseases.

Infectious disease. Infectious diseases generally do not affect a child's growth if they are treated and if the child is well nourished. In undernourished populations, the situation is different. Here, infectious disease and poor nutritional status affect each other. Undernutrition causes a lowering of the body's resistance to infectious disease, because the body cannot produce antibodies if it lacks proteins and calories. Infection can also influence nutritional status by reducing the efficient absorption of nutrients, particularly infections in the gastrointestinal tract. Infectious diseases may also result in a loss of appetite, which further reduces nutritional intake. As nutritional status deteriorates, the body's resistance to disease is lowered further (Martorell 1980). Thus, the negative effects of poor nutrition and infectious disease compound one another.

Social and cultural influences. A variety of social and cultural factors can affect patterns of physical growth, including ethnicity, family size, and socioeconomic status. Variation in nutritional status and health care is

protein-calorie malnutrition A group of nutritional diseases resulting from inadequate amounts of protein and/or calories.

kwashiorkor An extreme form of protein-calorie malnutrition, resulting from a severe deficiency in proteins but not calories.

marasmus An extreme form of protein-calorie malnutrition resulting from severe deficiencies in both proteins and calories.

Fetal Alcohol Syndrome
A group of birth defects resulting from major alcohol intake by the mother early in pregnancy.

secular trend A change in the average pattern of growth in a population over different generations.

often associated with such variables. For example, in situations where money is needed for adequate nutrition and health care, we see a relationship between social class and growth. Children belonging to upper-class families are often larger and grow more quickly because of better nutrition and health care (Tanner 1989). In Western societies, on the other hand, obesity is more prevalent in lower social classes because foods high in calories are less costly.

The number of children in a family also has an influence on growth. Children from larger families tend to grow more slowly. Of course, family size and socioeconomic status are often interrelated (larger families tend on average to be found in lower social classes), so this is perhaps a consequence of reduced food availability for each child.

The personal behaviors of parents can also affect the growth of their offspring. Two major habits shown to have strong effects on human growth are smoking and alcohol consumption. When a pregnant woman smokes cigarettes, she affects her child's prenatal development adversely. Numerous studies have shown that mothers who smoke during pregnancy weigh less when they conceive, gain less weight during pregnancy, give birth earlier, and have babies that weigh less at birth. Even among women who carry their offspring full term, the birth weight of the children is lower than that of children born to women who did not smoke during pregnancy (Garn 1985). Table 6.1 summarizes this effect by comparing the birth weight of children born to nonsmokers and to smokers for different levels of prepregnancy weight of the mother.

Alcohol consumption is also harmful during pregnancy. Many studies have shown drinking during pregnancy to be associated with an increase in miscarriages, birth defects, and infant mortality. Alcohol consumption can also result in physical and mental retardation among offspring. Alcohol affects prenatal development by introducing toxic substances and by reducing oxygen levels (Abel 1982). One pattern of observable birth defects caused by major alcohol intake early in pregnancy is referred to as **Fetal Alcohol Syndrome.** The defects include smaller body size, smaller heads, facial deformities, organ disorders, and reduced intelligence, apparently the result of impaired brain development. Though the more extreme problems are associated only with chronic drinkers, serious medical and behavioral problems can also result from even small amounts of alcohol during pregnancy.

Studies of secular trends. Environmental factors clearly influence growth. Given the vast number of environmental changes in the past few centuries, it should be possible to record their biological impact by comparing growth patterns from one generation to the next. Many growth studies do precisely this, in an attempt to discover secular trends in human growth. A **secular trend** is simply a change in the pattern of growth across generations.

T A B L E 6.1
Effects of Mother's Smoking
During Pregnancy on Birth Weight
of European-American U.S. Infants

Mother's prepregnancy weight (in pounds)	Average birth weight of infants (in kilograms)	
	Nonsmokers	Smokers
<100	3.10	2.93
100–119	3.27	3.08
120–139	3.42	3.22
140–159	3.53	3.32
160–179	3.59	3.37
180–199	3.66	3.46
200–219	3.65	3.46
220–239	3.65	3.45

These data represent 10,435 women who did not
smoke during pregnancy and 11,200 women who
did. This table does not include a few women in the
study who weighed more than 240 lbs.

Source: Garn (1985:518).

Two basic secular trends have been observed in many Western nations during the past century: an increase in body size and earlier sexual maturation. Children in many Westernized nations are taller and heavier than children of the same age a century or so ago. This finding is demonstrated in Figure 6.6, which compares the average height of European-American males in North America in 1880 and 1960. Although both generations have roughly the same height at birth, children born in 1960 are taller at every subsequent age than children born in 1880. Studies have shown that the difference in height reflects earlier maturation among children born in 1960.

A commonly used measure of maturation is **age at menarche,** which is the age at which a female experiences her first menstrual period. Figure 6.7 plots the average age at menarche for the United States and several European industrial nations over time. The age at menarche has clearly decreased in recent decades, the general trend being one of earlier biological maturation.

The secular trends observed in industrial nations over the past century show how environmental change has allowed some human populations to attain more of their genetic potential for growth (the time period has been

age at menarche The age at which a female experiences her first menstrual period.

too short for genetic change). Numerous environmental factors have been suggested as responsible for these past secular trends, including improved nutrition, reduction of childhood infectious disease, improved availability of health care, improved standard of living, and reduction in family size.

Figure 6.6

Secular trend in European-American males in North America. At all ages the males living in 1960 have greater height than those who lived in 1880.   (From *Growth and Development* by Robert M. Malina © 1975, publisher Burgess Publishing Company, Minneapolis, MN)

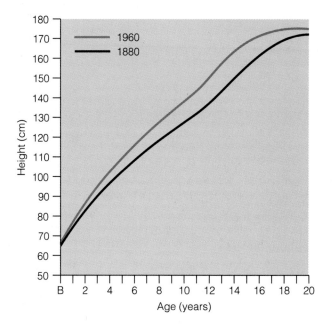

Figure 6.7

Secular trend in age at menarche (the age of the female's first menstrual period) in the United States and several European countries.   (From *Growth and Development* by Robert M. Malina © 1975, publisher Burgess Publishing Company, Minneapolis, MN)

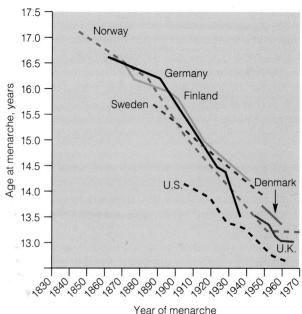

Many of these factors are interrelated, making interpretation difficult (Roche 1979). Malina (1979) suggests that one of the most important factors was an improvement in health conditions, resulting in the reduction of childhood infectious diseases. Because infectious diseases reduce growth rates, the elimination of such diseases most probably resulted in quicker rates of growth.

Human Adaptation

As explained in Chapter 1, adaptation is the successful interaction of a population with its environment. Thus far, adaptation has been discussed in terms of genetic adaptation—that is, natural selection. In this section, we will examine a broader biocultural perspective. Central to the study of adaptation is the concept of **stress,** broadly defined as any factor that interferes with the normal limits of operation of an organism. Organisms maintain these limits through an ability known as **homeostasis.** As ways of dealing with the stresses that alter your body's functioning, adaptations restore homeostasis. For example, when you stand outside in a cold wind you may shiver. This is your body's way of adapting to cold stress. You might also choose to put on a heavy jacket.

As human beings, we can adapt both biologically and culturally. It is important to note, however, that our biocultural nature can work against us. In adapting to stresses culturally, we can introduce other stresses as a result of our behavior. Pollution, for example, is a consequence of cultural change and has negatively impacted our physical environment in numerous ways.

Key to the interaction between human biology and culture, human adaptation operates on a number of levels—physiologic, developmental, genetic, and cultural—all of which are interrelated, for better or for worse. Thus the countering of a biological stress such as disease by the cultural adaptation of medicine can lower the death rate for human populations but also can increase population size, which in turn can lead to further stresses, such as food shortages and environmental degradation.

Types of Adaptation

How do humans adapt? What are the different ways we have to cope with the stresses of the physical and cultural environment? Besides genetic and cultural adaptation, humans are capable of two other forms of adaptation that are physiologic in nature: acclimatization and developmental acclimatization. **Acclimatization** refers to changes in organ or body structure that occur within an individual's lifetime in response to one or more stresses. Examples include shivering when cold and sweating when overheated. Some changes may be temporary; others may be more permanent.

stress Any factor that interferes with the normal limits of an operation of an organism.

homeostasis In a physiologic sense, the maintenance of normal limits of body functioning.

acclimatization Changes in organ or body structure that occur within an individual's lifetime in response to one or more stresses.

developmental acclimatization Changes in organ or body structure that occur during the physical growth of any organism.

plasticity The ability of an organism to respond physiologically or developmentally to environmental stress.

vasoconstriction The narrowing of blood vessels, which reduces blood flow and heat loss.

vasodilation The opening of the blood vessels, which increases blood flow and heat loss.

Bergmann's rule (1) Among mammals of similar shape, the larger mammal loses heat less rapidly than the smaller mammal, and (2) among mammals of similar size, the mammal with a linear shape will lose heat more rapidly than the mammal with a nonlinear shape.

Allen's rule Mammals in cold climates tend to have short, bulky limbs, allowing less loss of body heat; mammals in hot climates tend to have long, slender limbs, allowing greater loss of body heat.

When a change occurs during the physical growth of any organism, it is known as **developmental acclimatization.** The ability to respond physiologically or developmentally to environmental stress is often referred to as **plasticity.**

Climate and Human Adaptation

Though originally tropical primates, we humans have managed to expand into virtually every environment on our planet. Such expansion has been possible largely because of multiple adaptations to the range of temperatures around the world.

Physiologic responses to temperature stress. As warm-blooded creatures, humans have the ability to maintain a constant body temperature. This homeostatic quality works well under certain limits. When the temperature becomes too cold or too hot, the body attempts to maintain this temperature through physiologic responses. When you are cold, your body is losing heat too rapidly. One response is to increase heat production temporarily through shivering, which also increases your metabolic rate. This response is not very efficient and is costly in terms of energy. A more efficient physiologic response to cold stress is minimization of heat loss through alternate constriction and dilation of blood vessels. **Vasoconstriction,** the narrowing of blood vessels, reduces blood flow and heat loss. **Vasodilation,** the opening of blood vessels, serves to increase blood flow and heat loss. Neither vasoconstriction nor vasodilation by itself provides an effective physiologic response to cold stress. *Both* must operate, back and forth, to maintain a balance between heat loss and damage to the extremities.

When experiencing heat stress, your body is not removing heat quickly enough. One way of countering heat stress is evaporation, which is the loss of heat through the conversion of water to vapor. As you sweat, heat energy is burned up in the process of evaporating the sweat (Frisancho 1979).

Evaporation has its drawbacks. The removal of water from the body during the process can be harmful or even fatal. The efficiency of evaporation is also affected by humidity. In humid environments, evaporation is less efficient, making heat loss more difficult under hot and humid conditions than under hot and dry conditions.

Climate and morphological variation. Differences in physiologic responses and certain morphological variations, most notably the size and shape of the body, affect people's ability to handle temperature stress.

Among mammals, including humans, there is a strong relationship between average body size and temperature. In general, human populations in colder climates tend to be heavier than those in hotter climates.

This does not mean that all people in cold climates are heavy and all people in hot climates are light. Every human group contains a variety of small and large people. Some of this variation is caused by factors such as diet. However, a strong relationship of *average* body size and *average* temperature does exist among indigenous human populations (Roberts 1978).

A nineteenth-century English zoologist, Carl Bergmann, noted the relationship between body size and temperature in a number of mammal species. Bergmann explained his findings in terms of mammalian physiology and principles of heat loss. **Bergmann's rule** states that if two mammals have similar shapes but different sizes, the smaller animal will lose heat more rapidly and will therefore be better adapted to warmer climates, where the ability to lose heat is advantageous. Larger mammals lose heat more slowly and are therefore better adapted to colder climates (see Figure 6.8 for a geometric explanation of these principles).

Another aspect of Bergmann's rule involves the shape of an organism and its relationship to heat production and loss. Linear organisms will be at an advantage in hot climates because they lose heat more quickly, and organisms that are less linear will be at an advantage in cold climates because they lose heat less quickly (see Figure 6.9 for a geometric explanation). Bergmann's rule predicts that mammals in hot climates will have linear body shapes and mammals in cold climates will have less linear body shapes. Another zoologist, J. Allen, applied these principles to body limbs and other appendages. **Allen's rule** predicts that mammals in cold climates should have shorter, bulkier limbs, whereas mammals in hot climates should have longer, narrower ones.

Do the Bergmann and Allen rules hold for human body size and shape? Figure 6.10 shows !Kung men from Africa and an Eskimo. Note the thinness and length of the tribesmen's body and limbs. Those of the Eskimo are shorter and bulkier. These physiques do in fact conform to Bergmann and Allen's predictions. Analysis of data from many human populations has found the rules to be accurate in describing the *average* trends among populations. Again, don't forget that extensive variation exists within populations. Also, some populations are exceptions to the general rule. African pygmies, for example, are short and have short limbs, yet they live in a hot climate. In this case, the pygmy's short size appears to be due to a hormonal deficiency (Shea and Gomez 1988).

The Bergmann and Allen rules apply to adult human body size and shape. Are these average patterns the result of natural selection (i.e., genetic adaptation) or changes in size and shape during the growth process (i.e., developmental acclimatization)? Do infants born elsewhere who move into an environment attain the same adult size and shape as native-born infants? If so, this suggests a direct influence of the environment on growth. If not, then the growth pattern leading to a certain adult size and shape may be genetic in nature and determined by natural selection. Of course, if *both* environmental and genetic factors are responsible for adult size and shape, then the expected pattern is more complex. Unraveling the

Figure 6.8

Geometric representation of Bergmann's rule relating body size and heat loss. The larger cube has a larger volume (heat production) and a larger surface area (heat loss). The larger cube also has a smaller surface area/volume ratio, however, indicating that it would lose heat less rapidly and therefore be adaptive in colder climates.

Surface area = 24
Volume = 8
Surface area/volume = 3

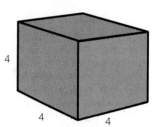

Surface area = 96
Volume = 64
Surface area/volume = 1.5

Figure 6.9

Geometric representation of Bergmann's rule relating body shape and heat loss. The cube has a lower surface area/volume ratio than the rectangular block and would therefore lose heat less rapidly.

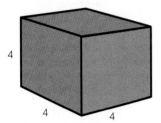

4

4   4

Surface area = 96
Volume = 64
Surface area/volume = 1.5

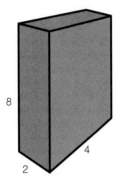

8

4

2

Surface area = 112
Volume = 64
Surface area/volume = 1.75

potential genetic and climatic effects is a difficult process because other contributing influences, such as nutrition, also vary with climate.

The evidence to date suggests that both genetic and environmental factors influence the relationship between climate, growth, body size, and shape. When children grow up in a climate different from that of their ancestors, they tend to grow in ways the indigenous children do (Malina 1975; Roberts 1978). This finding supports the idea that environment directly influences the growth process. The relationship between growth and climate in such children, however, is not as strong as it is among indigenous children. Therefore, long-term genetic adaptation is also responsible for the association of size, shape, and climate observed in adults. Natural selection leads to changes in growth potential that are further modified by environmental factors. It appears that climate can alter the growth patterns of all children, although those with a certain genetic predisposition may show greater response.

Cultural adaptations. In Western societies we tend to take cultural adaptations to temperature stress for granted. Housing, insulated clothing, heaters, air conditioners, and other technologies are all around us. How do people in other cultures adapt to excessive cold or heat? The Inuit, or Eskimo people, of the Arctic have realized effective cultural adaptations to cold stress, most notably in their clothing and shelter. It is not enough just to wear a lot of clothes to stay warm; if you work hard you tend to overheat. The Inuit wear layered clothing, trapping air between layers to act as an insulator. Outer layers can be removed if a person overheats. Also, the Inuit design their clothing with multiple flaps that can be opened, to prevent build-up of sweat while working.

While outside hunting or fishing, the Inuit frequently construct temporary snow shelters, or igloos, that are quite efficient protection from the cold. The ice is an excellent insulator, and its reflective surface helps retain heat. More permanent shelters also provide ample protection from the cold. Inuit houses have an underground entry, which is curved to reduce incoming wind. Inside, the main living area lies at a higher level than the fireplace; this architectural feature serves to increase heat and minimize drafts (Moran 1982).

Not all cold-weather housing is as effective as the types constructed by the Inuit. Among the Quechua Indians of the Peruvian highlands, the temperature inside temporary houses is often not much warmer than it is outside. However, these shelters do provide protection against rain and to some extent the cold. The bedding used by the Quechua is their most effective protection against heat loss (Frisancho 1979).

Cultural adaptations are also useful in adapting to heat stress. Human populations live in environments that are dry and hot (i.e., deserts) and that are humid and hot (i.e., tropical rain forests). Moran (1982) has summarized some basic principles of clothing and shelter that are used in desert environments, where the objectives are fourfold: to reduce heat

Figure 6.10

!Kung men (*left*) and an
Eskimo (*right*) illustrate the
relationship among body size,
body shape, and climate
predicted by the Bergmann
and Allen rules.   (Richard Lee/
Anthro-Photo; Joel Halpern/
Anthro-Photo)

production, to reduce heat gain from radiation, to reduce heat gain from conduction, and to increase evaporation. Clothing is important because it protects from both solar radiation and hot winds. Typical desert clothing is light and loose, thus allowing circulation of air to increase evaporation. The air between the clothing and the body also provides excellent insulation.

Shelters are frequently built compactly to minimize the surface area exposed to the sun. Light colors on the outside help reflect heat. Doors and windows are kept closed during the day to keep the interior cool. Building materials are also adaptive. Adobe, for example, is efficient in absorbing heat during the day and radiating it at night (nighttime temperatures drop precipitously in desert environments).

Heat stress in tropical environments is often a problem because the extreme humidity greatly reduces the efficiency of evaporation through sweating. Cultural adaptations to tropical environments are similar throughout the world. Clothing is minimal, helping to increase the potential for evaporation. In some cultures, shelters are built in an open design, without walls, to augment cooling during the day; in others, shelters are built closed to increase warmth at night. The combination of high heat and

hypoxia Oxygen starvation; occurs frequently at high altitudes.

humidity obviously affects daily routines. Generally people start work early in the day, taking long midday breaks to keep from overheating.

High-Altitude Adaptation

Some human populations have lived for long periods of time at elevations of over 2,500 m, or roughly 8,200 ft. An estimated 25 million people currently live at elevations between 2,500 and 5,000 m (Harrison et al. 1988).

High-altitude stresses. High-altitude environments produce several stresses, including oxygen starvation, cold, and sometimes poor nutrition. Studies of high-altitude populations have gained us insight into how humans cope with multiple stresses. Oxygen starvation, or **hypoxia,** is more common at high altitudes because of the relationship of barometric pressure and altitude. Barometric pressure decreases quickly with altitude. Because air is less compressed at high altitudes, its oxygen content is less concentrated and less oxygen is thus available to the hemoglobin in the blood. The percentage of arterial oxygen saturation decreases rapidly with altitude. At rest, hypoxia generally occurs above 3,000 m; for active persons it can occur as low as 2,000 m (Frisancho 1979).

Hypoxia is not the only stress resulting from high altitude. Because the air is thinner at high altitudes, the concentration of ultraviolet radiation is greater and the air itself offers less protection against it. The thinner air also causes considerable heat loss from the atmosphere, resulting in cold stress. In many high-altitude environments conditions are also extremely dry, because of mountain winds and low humidity. In addition, hypoxia affects plants and animals; due to lack of oxygen, trees cannot grow above 4,000 m. The limited availability of plants and animals means that nutritional stress is likely in many high-altitude environments.

Numerous studies have compared the physiology and morphology of high-altitude and low-altitude populations. Early research tended to attribute any differences to the effects of hypoxia on the human body. More recent studies have shown that other stresses of high altitude are significant factors as well (Frisancho 1990). When dealing with human adaptation, it is best to consider the effect and interaction of *multiple* stresses.

Physiologic responses to hypoxia. People who live at low altitudes experience several physiologic changes when they enter a high-altitude environment. Some of these happen immediately; others occur after several months up to a year. Such physiologic responses help to maintain sufficient oxygen levels. Respiration increases initially but returns to normal after a few days. Red blood cell production increases for roughly three months. Other changes include possible hyperventilation and higher hemoglobin concentration in the blood. In addition to these adaptive responses, loss of appetite and weight loss are common. Memory and sensory abilities may be affected, and hypoxia may influence hormone levels.

The physiologic differences between high-altitude and low-altitude natives are primarily acquired during the growth process. Studies of children who were born at low altitudes but moved into high altitudes during childhood clearly substantiate this phenomenon. In terms of aerobic capacity, for example, the younger the age of migration, the higher the aerobic capacity (Frisancho 1979). In other words, the longer a child lives in a high-altitude environment, the greater the developmental response to that environment. Age at migration has no effect on the aerobic capacity of adults, however, further indicating that most physiologic changes are the result of developmental acclimatization.

Physical growth in high-altitude populations. Studies of high-altitude and low-altitude Indian populations in Peru, conducted by Paul Baker and his colleagues, found two unique characteristics of growth. Chest dimensions and lung volume were greater at all ages in the high-altitude group, and high-altitude populations were shorter at most ages than low-altitude populations (Frisancho and Baker 1970). The shorter stature is related to delayed maturation, and the increase in chest size is due to growth acceleration of this part of the body during childhood.

Initially, the researchers interpreted both patterns of physical growth as direct developmental responses to hypoxia and cold stress at high altitude. Larger chests and larger lung volumes relative to body size would be better able to provide sufficient oxygen levels. The more energy devoted to growth of oxygen transport systems, however, would leave less energy available for growth in other organ systems, especially the skeletal and muscle systems. As discussed below, this view is now being questioned.

Studies in high-altitude environments around the world show a similar pattern of growth in chest dimensions, although the extent of growth varies. Migrants to high-altitude populations also show an increase in chest dimensions, particularly among those that migrate at an early age. Increased growth of oxygen transport systems appears to be a developmental response to hypoxia.

Are the developmental changes in chest and lung growth in high-altitude populations genetic in nature? Were they shaped by natural selection? Most research to date assigns a relatively minor role to genetic factors. A recent study examined high-altitude and low-altitude populations of European ancestry in Bolivia (Greska 1990). Because these groups do not have a long history of residence at high altitude, they would not possess any genetic predisposition for high-altitude adaptations. The study showed there was an increased capacity of the oxygen transport system in these populations at high altitude even though they were not of high-altitude ancestry. The observed changes were instead direct effects of a chronic hypoxic stress.

epidemiology The study of patterns of human disease and their causes.

The delayed maturation and small stature of the Peruvians have not been found in all studies of growth in high-altitude populations. As a result, some researchers have questioned the initial premise that hypoxia and cold stress have necessarily led to these characteristics, suggesting instead that other causal factors might be at work. A recent study undertaken in Peru in fact has shown that nutrition has been a major influence on stature (Leonard et al. 1990). Although high altitude may play a role in the Peruvian highlands, income levels and access to land are of greater consequence. Also, other high-altitude populations, such as those found in Ethiopia, have a higher standard of living but do not show the growth deficits observed in Peru. Thus, it appears that although increased chest growth is a functional adaptation to hypoxia, the smaller body size is not necessarily related to high altitude. These results amply illustrate the complexity in assessing the relative value of stresses in any given environment.

Human Health and Disease

One of the most recent and rapid changes in human biology has been in human disease patterns. In the last 100 years, the major causes of death in developed regions of the world have shifted from infectious diseases to noninfectious diseases. Some infectious diseases, such as smallpox, have been eradicated. Others have been reduced, although certain infectious diseases, such as malaria, continue to take their toll in tropical environments. In developed nations, noninfectious diseases, such as diabetes, have risen in occurrence.

These changes are the consequence of cultural innovations. Improvements in public health and sanitation have accounted for major reductions in the spread of many infectious microorganisms. Advances in medical technology, such as the use of immunizations and antibiotics, have also reduced the risk for many infectious diseases.

The field of medical anthropology focuses on human health and disease in a comparative framework, with an emphasis on the interrelationship between biological and cultural aspects of disease patterns. This section looks at some basic principles of health and disease and then considers changing patterns of health throughout human history and prehistory.

Epidemiology

The study of human disease patterns and their causes is known as **epidemiology.** Epidemiology is an interdisciplinary field that focuses on the analysis of rates of diseases in human populations. The study of medical anthropology shares many of the goals and methods of epidemiology.

Types of diseases. Diseases can be classified in a number of ways. Diseases can be infectious or noninfectious. Infectious diseases are those caused by the introduction of organic matter, such as a virus, bacteria, or parasite, into the body. Infectious diseases can also be classified as *communicable* or *noncommunicable,* depending on whether the disease can be transmitted directly from one person to another. Malaria, for example, is an infectious disease transmitted by a parasite, but it is not a communicable disease because it cannot be transmitted directly from one human to another. Measles, another infectious disease, is communicable because it can be transmitted from one human to another. Diabetes, by contrast, is a noninfectious disease that is caused by a variety of genetic and environmental factors.

Rates of diseases. Epidemiological research looks at the rates of incidence and prevalence of both infectious and noninfectious diseases in populations over time and space. Rates are proportions of population size. The **incidence rate** is the rate of new cases of a disease that develop within a given population in a given period. For example, an annual incidence rate for spinal cord injury of 4 per 100,000 means that 4 out of every 100,000 people will have a spinal cord injury each year. The **prevalence rate** is the rate of the total number of cases, old and new, within a given population within a given period. For example, a prevalence rate for spinal cord injury of 90 per 100,000 means that 90 out of 100,000 people now living have a spinal cord injury, regardless of when they had it.

Several terms are used to describe the overall magnitude of disease rates. An **epidemic** pattern is one in which new cases of a disease spread quickly. An **endemic** pattern has a low but constant rate—a few cases are always present, but no major spread occurs. A **pandemic** pattern is an epidemic that takes place over large geographic ranges, such as the major bubonic plague pandemics that spread throughout Europe during the Middle Ages. Another example is the 1918 influenza pandemic. Pandemics are not just something that happened in the past; pandemics occur today as well. Currently, the world has been experiencing a cholera pandemic since 1961, and epidemic spread of the disease has now reached four continents (Table 6.2).

Causes of diseases. Incidence and prevalence rates are analyzed to determine their relationship with possible factors affecting susceptibility. We might examine the geographic distribution of rates to determine the first outbreak of a disease and factors that might hinder or accelerate its spread. Rates are also looked at over time. An increase in disease rates in a population may indicate the start of an epidemic. Changes over time can also be used to evaluate changes in disease prevention or environmental changes.

incidence rate The rate of new cases of a disease developing in a population in a specified period of time.

prevalence rate The rate of total cases of a disease, old and new, in a population in a specified period of time.

epidemic When new cases of a disease spread rapidly through a population.

endemic When new cases of a disease occur at a relatively constant but low rate over time.

pandemic An epidemic that occurs over a large geographic range.

TABLE   6.2
Cholera: An Example of a Current Pandemic

Year	Occurrence of Epidemic
1961	Indonesia (first outbreak)
1963	Bangladesh
1964	India
1965	Former Soviet Union
1970	Africa
1990	Parts of Europe
1991	South America

Source: Dixon and McBride (1992).

paleopathology The study of disease in prehistoric populations based on analysis of skeletal remains and archaeological evidence.

zoonose A disease transmitted directly from animals to humans.

Individual characteristics are also an important focus of epidemiology. These include age, sex, ethnicity, health status, occupation, and others (Lilienfeld and Lilienfeld 1980). For example, a person's behavior can affect the probability of contact with an infectious microorganism. People with many sexual partners have a higher risk, all other factors being equal, of acquiring a sexually transmitted disease. Individual behaviors can also affect the probability of acquiring a noninfectious disease. Smokers, for example, are more likely to get lung cancer than nonsmokers.

The Evolution of Human Disease

A unique contribution of anthropology to epidemiological research has been its investigation of the evolution of human diseases. A technological shift began roughly 12,000 years ago from hunting and gathering to agriculture. During the past few centuries further changes have led to the development and spread of large industrial societies. What effects have these rapid shifts, and related environmental and cultural changes, produced on patterns of human health and disease? This section examines disease in hunting-gathering, agricultural, and industrial societies.

Disease in hunting-gathering societies. Humans have relied on hunting and gathering as a way of life until very recently—12,000 years ago. While there are few hunting-gathering populations in existence today, the few that remain give us clues as to likely patterns of disease and death associated with this way of life. Analysis of prehistoric disease (**paleopathology**) contributes additional information.

In terms of infectious diseases, the two most common types in hunting-gathering populations are caused by parasites and **zoonoses** (diseases transmitted from other animals to humans). Parasites include lice and pinworms. The zoonoses are introduced through insect bites, animal wounds, and contaminated meat and include diseases such as sleeping

Figure 6.11

!Kung women gathering
vegetables. The small size and
nomadic nature of hunting-
gathering populations means
that infectious disease is
endemic, not epidemic.
(M. Shostak/Anthro-Photo)

sickness, tetanus, and schistosomaisis (Armelagos and Dewey 1970). Of
course, the prevalence of many of these diseases depends in large part on
the specific environment. Disease organisms found in arctic or temperate
environments are generally not found in tropical environments.

In general, hunting-gathering populations do not experience epidemics of infectious disease. This is because of two ecological factors associated
with a hunting-gathering way of life: small population size and nomadism
(Figure 6.11). Hunter-gatherers live in small groups of roughly 25 to 50
people that interact occasionally with other small groups in their region.
Under such conditions, infectious diseases do not spread rapidly—there
are not enough people to become infected to keep the disease going at
high rates. Without more people to infect, the disease microorganisms die.
This does not apply to chronic infectious diseases, such as those caused by
certain parasitic worms, because the microorganisms can survive long

life expectancy A measure of the average length of life in a population.

enough to infect other people coming into the group. In such cases, the prevalence rates are low. Most infectious diseases in hunting-gathering populations are endemic rather than epidemic (McElroy and Townsend 1989).

The noninfectious diseases common in industrial societies, such as heart disease and hypertension, are rare in hunting-gathering societies. Part of the reason for these low rates might be the diet and lifestyle of hunter-gatherers, but it might also be due to the fact that fewer individuals in hunting-gathering societies live long enough to develop the noninfectious disorders.

Nutrition in hunting-gathering populations is varied and provides a well-balanced diet. The major nutritional problem is the scarcity of food during bad times, such as drought. To some extent, hunting-gathering populations have adapted to occasional fluctuations in food supply by having reduced rates of growth and smaller body sizes. Overall, the rate of malnutrition and starvation in hunting-gathering societies is usually very low (Dunn 1968).

Hunter-gatherers generally have a low **life expectancy** (a measure of the average length of life). Life expectancy at birth is low in hunting-gathering populations—roughly 20 to 30 years (Weiss 1973). Given low rates of infectious disease and few other health problems, what accounts for this low life expectancy? Deaths by injury are one factor. Injuries can result from hunting accidents, fires, falling, drowning, and other hazards. In some hunting-gathering groups, injuries are the leading cause of death (Dunn 1968). For females, an additional factor is death during childbirth.

Agriculture and disease. The pattern of human disease is quite different in agricultural societies (both slash-and-burn agriculture discussed in Chapter 4 and intensive agriculture). Agriculture allows larger population size and requires a sedentary life. The increased population size and lack of mobility has certain implications for the spread of infectious disease. Large populations of susceptible individuals allow the spread of short-lived microorganisms. Such conditions exist in agricultural populations because of increased population size and increased probability of contacting someone with the disease. As a result, agricultural populations often show epidemics of diseases such as smallpox, measles, and mumps (McElroy and Townsend 1989). Sedentary life increases the spread of infectious disease in other ways. Large populations living continuously in the same area can accumulate garbage. Poor sanitation and contamination of the water supply increase the chance for disease epidemics.

Agricultural practices also cause ecological changes, making certain infectious diseases more likely. The introduction of domesticated animals adds to waste accumulation and provides the opportunity for exposure to diseases carried by animals. Cultivation of the land increases the probability of contact with insects carrying disease microorganisms. Irrigation can also further the spread of infectious disease. One of the major problems

Figure 6.12

Chinese farmers planting rice. The larger size and sedentary nature of agricultural populations contributes to epidemics of infectious disease. (Courtesy Kenneth Feder and Michael Park, Central Connecticut State University)

today in tropical agricultural populations is the increased snail population that lives in irrigation canals and carries the disease schistosomiasis. Irrigation can also pass infectious microorganisms from one population to the next (Figure 6.12).

Although agriculture provides populations with the ability to feed more people, this way of life does not guarantee an improvement in nutrition. Extensive investment in a single food crop, such as rice or corn, may provide too limited a diet for many people, and certain nutritional deficiency diseases can result. For example, populations relying extensively on corn as the major food source may show an increase in pellagra (a disease caused by a deficiency in niacin) as well as protein deficiency. Agriculture can also lead to dental problems. The increased amount of starches in an agriculturalist's diet, combined with an increase in dirt and grit in the food, can lead to an increase in dental wear and cavities.

Urbanization and disease. Following the origin and spread of agriculture, some human populations became urbanized. Preindustrial cities date back several thousand years. Such cities developed as market or administrative centers for a region, and their increased population size and density provided ample opportunities for epidemics of infectious disease. In addition, a number of early cities often had inadequate waste disposal and contaminated water, both factors increasing the spread of epidemics.

epidemiologic transition
The change in disease patterns in which infectious diseases are replaced by noninfectious diseases as the leading causes of death.

Perhaps the best-known example of an epidemic in preindustrial cities is the Black Death in Europe during the fourteenth century. The Black Death is another name for bubonic plague, which is caused by a bacterium and is spread by fleas from field rodents. With the development of large urban areas and a correspondingly large indoor rat population, the disease spread from field rats to rats in the cities. From there, fleas infected humans. The spread of bubonic plague during this time was pandemic, affecting populations throughout Europe. It is estimated that up to 20 million Europeans died from bubonic plague between 1346 and 1352 (McEvedy 1988). The ecological changes accompanying urbanization in Europe provided an opportunity for the rapid spread of rats, fleas, and the disease.

As industrialization began several centuries ago, the population of urban areas increased even more. Technological changes allowed more efficient methods of agriculture and provided the ability to support more people than in previous times. The increased growth of urban areas was accompanied initially by the further spread of infectious diseases. As industrialization continued, however, the rate of infectious disease declined and the rate of noninfectious disease increased. This shift in disease patterns was accompanied by a reduction in mortality, especially infant mortality, and an increase in life expectancy.

The epidemiologic transition. The shift from infectious disease to noninfectious disease as the primary cause of death is a feature of the **epidemiologic transition** model, developed by Omran (1977). According to this model, a pretransition population has high death rates, particularly because of epidemics of childhood infectious diseases. As a culture's public health, sanitation, and medical technologies improve, epidemics become less frequent and less intense. Following the transition, the primary cause of death is not infectious disease but degenerative noninfectious disease. This shift in disease patterns is also accompanied by an increase in life expectancy at birth.

Figure 6.13 presents death rates per 100,000 people in the United States in 1900 and 1975 for several selected diseases. Note the tremendous decline in the death rates for infectious diseases such as tuberculosis and pneumonia. On the other hand, there has been an increase in death rates from cardiovascular diseases, cancers, and diabetes. In addition, the overall death rate declined from 1,622 per year per 100,000 people in 1900 to 890 per year per 100,000 people in 1975. A large proportion of this decrease has been a consequence of the reduction of infant mortality (death during the first year of life). In 1900, the infant mortality rate was 162 deaths per 1,000 live births. By 1975, the infant mortality rate had dropped to 14 deaths per 1,000 live births.

The epidemiologic transition has also affected life expectancy in developed societies. In the United States in 1900, life expectancy at birth was 49 years. In 1990, this figure had risen to 75.4 years (Haub 1992). Not all people in the United States today have the same life expectancy. On average, females have a higher life expectancy than males, and European Americans have a higher life expectancy than African Americans (Table 6.3).

A specific example of the epidemiologic transition is presented in Figure 6.14, which shows changes in the overall death rate in New York City from 1800 through 1970. Before the 1860s, the overall death rate was high and had frequent spikes, primarily because of cholera epidemics. Following the mid-1860s, both the overall death rate and the intensity of epidemics declined. This decrease corresponds with the establishment of the Health Department. After the 1920s, the spread of better sanitation and water supplies along with an improvement in drugs and health care and the introduction of pasteurized milk caused the death rates to decline even more.

Figure 6.13

Death rates for selected diseases in the United States in 1900 and 1975. Note the decrease in infectious disease deaths and the increase in noninfectious disease deaths. (Source of data: Molnar [1983:219])

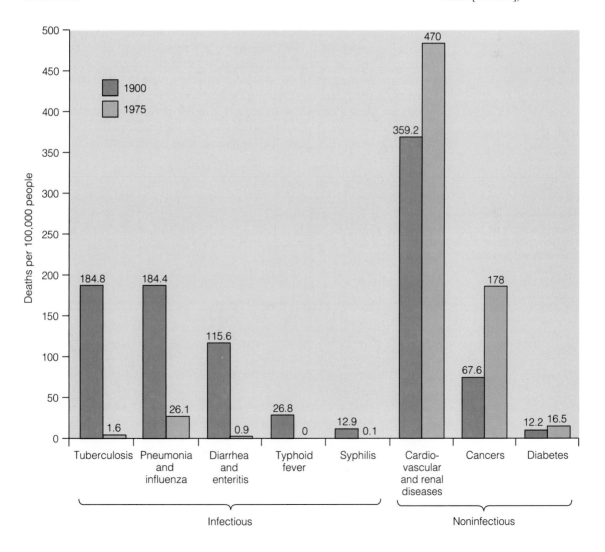

T A B L E   6.3
Life Expectancy at Birth in the United States, 1990

Group	Life expectancy at birth (years)
European-American females	79.3
African-American females	74.5
European-American males	72.6
African-American males	66.0
All groups	75.4

Source: Haub (1992).

What are the specific reasons for the epidemiologic transition? Cultural changes in industrial societies have often resulted in average improvements in health care, public sanitation, and water quality. These factors aid in reducing the spread and effect of infectious diseases, particularly in infancy. As a result, more people are likely to live to older ages—long enough, therefore, to develop long-term noninfectious diseases, such as cancer. These diseases often require lengthy periods of time to reach a debilitating stage. A person who dies in early life from an infectious disease will obviously not have had sufficient time to develop noninfectious disorders.

Figure 6.14

Changes in the death rate in New York City during the nineteenth and twentieth centuries.   (Source: Omran [1977:12]. Courtesy of the Population Reference Bureau, Inc., Washington, D.C.)

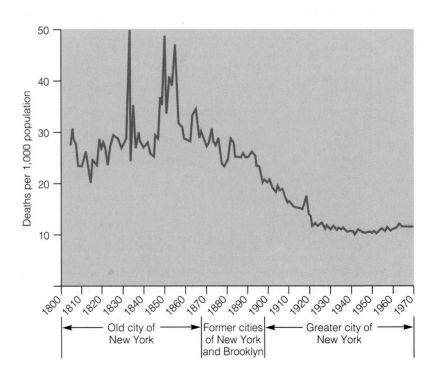

Other contributing factors are the changes in the physical environment brought about by urbanization and industrialization. Industrial pollution of the air and water can lead to elevations in cancer rates and other noninfectious diseases. Technological and social changes have also led to the abundance of drugs such as alcohol and tobacco, which increase disease. Such factors as stress, lifestyle, crowding, and noise levels also appear to play a role in the disease process.

The Demography of Human Populations

The interrelationship of biology and culture in human populations is perhaps most visible in demographic patterns. **Demography** is the study of the size, composition, and distribution of human populations. Like epidemiology, demography is an interdisciplinary subject to which anthropology brings comparative, evolutionary, and holistic perspectives. Anthropologists do not focus only on demographic processes within a single society such as the United States. We examine all types of societies, from hunter-gatherers to industrialized nations. Using a holistic perspective, we link demographic processes with patterns of biological and cultural variation.

The Study of Demography

Demographic studies focus on the measurement of three characteristics: fertility, mortality, and migration.

Demographic measures. The measure of fertility provides us with information on the rate of actual births in a population. When we count birth records or interview people to find out how many children they have had, we are measuring the **fertility** of a population. On the other hand, we are also sometimes interested in measurements of **fecundity,** or the number of individuals capable of having children. Fertility and fecundity are not always the same; people that are capable of having children do not necessarily have them.

The analysis of fertility is particularly interesting to anthropologists because fertility reflects both biological and cultural variation. Some individuals may have more children than others because of biological differences. One example, discussed in Chapter 4, is incompatibility of blood types. In addition, some individuals may have more, or fewer, children for cultural reasons. Economic factors, for example, often play a role in determining fertility, as do educational and religious factors, among others.

Availability of contraceptive technologies also affects fertility. But how is fertility regulated in societies that generally have not had access to such devices? Studies of fertility among the !Kung San, a group of hunter-

demography The study of the size, composition, and distribution of human populations.

fertility Actual reproduction: the number of births per individual.

fecundity Potential reproduction: the number of people capable of having children.

mortality Death.

life table A table that provides an estimate of the probability that an individual will die by a certain age, used to estimate life expectancy.

natural increase Number of births minus number of deaths.

gatherers living in the Kalahari Desert in southern Africa, provide one such example (the "!" preceding their name indicates a clicking sound made in their language). Except for occasional droughts, the !Kung are adequately nourished and do not have very high levels of mortality. How then, do they regulate their fertility? If they did not, the population might soon grow too large for the local environment to support them. The !Kung obviously have some control over fertility because the average interval between successive births is 44 months (Potts 1988). This long spacing between births acts to moderate fertility.

One major factor in fertility control among the !Kung is breast feed-ing. When a woman nurses her child, hormonal changes take place that act to prevent ovulation, especially when body fat levels are low. This finding has sometimes been dismissed by scientists who have noted many cases of women returning to their monthly cycle of ovulation before their child was weaned. As a result, many Western physicians caution women against using breast feeding as a form of contraception. The case of the !Kung is different because the pattern of nursing is different from that practiced in Western nations and because their body fat levels are lower. In the United States today, nursing tends to occur for long periods of time (10 to 20 minutes) several times a day. Among the !Kung, breast feeding may occur as frequently as every 15 minutes but only for a minute or so each time. The frequency of nursing is the important component acting to prevent ovulation among the !Kung (Ackerman 1987).

Demographic studies also look at measures of **mortality,** that is, mea-surements of death. Like fertility, mortality can be influenced by biological and cultural factors. The age at death and cause of death may relate to biological factors such as susceptibility to certain diseases or to cultural factors such as differences in social class, which may affect the quality of health care. Warfare may increase the probability of early death, as will hazardous employment. A long history of drug use or poor nutrition also affects the probability of death.

As discussed earlier in this chapter, measures of life expectancy can tell us something about the average age of death and, by extension, about the average health of individuals in a population. Life expectancy is most often determined from a **life table,** a compilation of the numbers of deaths for different age groups in a population. A given life expectancy does not mean that everyone will live to that age. It is only an average. Many people die before this age, and many live beyond it. As an average measure, how-ever, life expectancy does tell us something about the net patterns of health and mortality in a population.

Population growth. Rates of fertility and mortality affect the overall size of a population. Births increase the size of a population and deaths decrease it. **Natural increase** refers to the number of births minus the number of deaths. If more people are born than die in a certain period of time, then the population grows. If the number of deaths exceeds the number of births, the natural increase is negative. In reality, we also have to factor in the net effect of migration: people can move into, or out of, a population. Migration can either increase or decrease the size of a population. The overall change in population size can be expressed as

Change in population size = births − deaths ± migration

The Age-Sex Structure of Populations

Demographers also study the composition of populations. Who makes up the population in terms of sex, age, ethnicity, occupation, and religion, among other characteristics? Most demographic studies focus special attention on the number of males and females per age group in a population, that is, on the **age-sex structure** of a population. A device known as a **population pyramid** is the best way to describe a population's age-sex structure at a particular point in time. The population pyramid is simply a graph showing the numbers of both sexes at different age groups.

Developing nations. Figure 6.15 shows the age-sex structure of developing regions of the world as of 1984 (those regions where industrial development was fairly recent, such as Mexico, Cuba, and Taiwan). The bottom axis of the graph shows the number of males on the left and the

age-sex structure A measure of the composition of a population in terms of the numbers of males and females at different ages.

population pyramid A diagram of the age-sex structure.

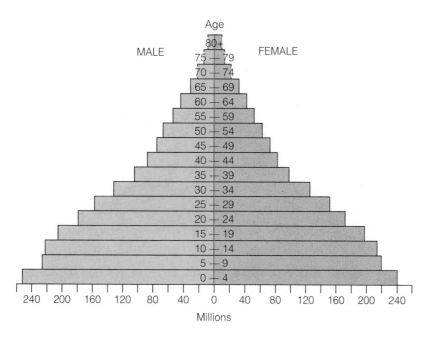

Figure 6.15

The age-sex structure of developing regions of the world in 1984. (Source: Bouvier [1984:12]. Courtesy of the Population Reference Bureau, Inc., Washington, D.C., and United Nations, *Demographic Indicators of Countries: Estimates and Projections as Assessed in 1980* [New York: 1982], pp. 61 and 63, data for 1985)

Figure 6.16

The age-sex structure of developed regions of the world in 1984.   (Source: Bouvier [1984:12]. Courtesy of the Population Reference Bureau, Inc., Washington, D.C., and United Nations, *Demographic Indicators of Countries: Estimates and Projections as Assessed in 1980* [New York: 1982], pp. 61 and 63, data for 1985)

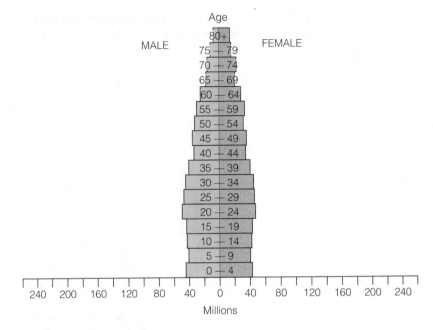

number of females on the right. The vertical axis represents different age groups, from 0 to 4 years in the first group, to 80-plus years of age in the top group. The population pyramid allows a succinct display of basic demographic patterns. It is obvious that infants and children greatly outnumber young adults or the elderly.

The age-sex structure of developing nations illustrates the nature of fertility and mortality in these populations. High fertility results in the large numbers of people in young age groups. The pyramid shape results from the fact that fewer people live to the next age group (high mortality).

Developed nations. The age-sex structure of a developed nation, such as the United States or Sweden, is quite different. Figure 6.16 shows the age-sex structure of the developed regions of the world as of 1984. This population pyramid is more rectangular in shape. The largest section of the population is not infants and young children but young adults. This shape results from a reduction in infant mortality combined with a decrease in fertility. Fewer people are born, making the younger age groups smaller. Because more people live longer, the older age groups stay fairly numerous.

Demography and the Modern World

Today's world is constantly changing. Advances in communications technologies bring the peoples of the world in closer contact with one another. The average life expectancy in developed nations continues to increase, and more and more, the economic systems of many nations are becoming interconnected. Many demographic changes are taking place as well, acting as both cause and effect of social, political, and economic changes.

The demographic transition. The demographic changes that have taken place in many industrialized nations over the past century have been described by demographic transition theory. Though the universal applicability of this theory is still being debated, it does serve as a convenient summary of basic demographic trends that have occurred in a number of societies.

Demographic transition theory states that as a population becomes more economically developed, a reduction in death rates will take place first, followed by a reduction in fertility rates. Three stages are usually identified in this model (Swedlund and Armelagos 1976). Stage 1 populations are those of undeveloped areas with high mortality and high fertility. Because the number of births is balanced by the number of deaths, the overall population size remains more or less stable. The age-sex structure of a Stage 1 population resembles a true pyramid, with a very wide base and a very narrow apex. The broad base, corresponding to infants and young children, is a product of the high fertility. Because mortality rates are high, fewer and fewer people survive to each successive age group—thus the pyramid shape.

Stage 2 populations are found in developing regions where demographic and economic factors are changing rapidly. A Stage 2 population is characterized by high fertility and lowered mortality. The transition to lowered mortality, especially in childhood, is a consequence of improvements in health care and medical technologies. Because the fertility rate remains high, there are more births than deaths. As a result, the population grows in size. The age-sex structure still resembles a pyramid, but with the top portion becoming wider as more people survive to older ages (see Figure 6.15). The base of the pyramid is broad because fertility rates are high.

Stage 3 populations are found in developed regions and are characterized by low rates of fertility and mortality. Because of technological, social, economic, and educational changes, people in developed regions have more of an opportunity to control family size. As is often the case, the fertility rate declines. Because the rates of births and deaths are both low, such populations may show little growth. The age-sex structure becomes more and more rectangular as the base decreases (lowered fertility) and more people live to older ages (lowered mortality) (see Figure 6.16). Some nations, such as Sweden, show this pattern clearly. Others, such as the United States, are still in the process of becoming a Stage 3 population.

The demographic transition model has several problems. Mortality and fertility rates are not easily separated into "low" and "high" phases. Situations unique to certain countries may result in fluctuating rates of

demographic transition theory A model of demographic change that states that as a population becomes economically developed, a reduction in death rates (leading to population growth) will take place first, followed by a reduction in birth rates.

fertility, such as the "Baby Boom" in the United States following World War II. In spite of these problems, the model does provide a rough summary of the types of average changes found accompanying economic and industrial development.

World population growth. The total human population of the world has increased throughout human evolution, especially during the last several centuries. Estimates of prehistoric population size are crude, but they do provide us with an idea of the extent of population growth. For example, the total world population 50,000 years ago was most likely in the neighborhood of 1.3 million people. By 10,000 years ago, the estimated population was 6 million people (Weiss 1984). These low numbers are consistent with what we know about hunting-gathering societies and their potential population sizes.

Following the development and spread of agriculture starting some 12,000 years ago, the population of the world increased more and more rapidly. The major acceleration came following the Industrial Revolution (roughly 1750). Since this time, the world's population increased at an exponential rate to the present figure (see Figure 6.17). Between 1750 and 1950, the world's population tripled in size. Between 1950 and 1975 the world's population increased almost 63 percent (Weeks 1981). The world population was estimated to be 5,384,000,000 people in mid-1991 and

Figure 6.17

World population growth since the origin of agriculture. (From *Population: An Introduction to Concepts and Issues,* Second Edition, by John R. Weeks © 1978 by Wadsworth Publishing Company)

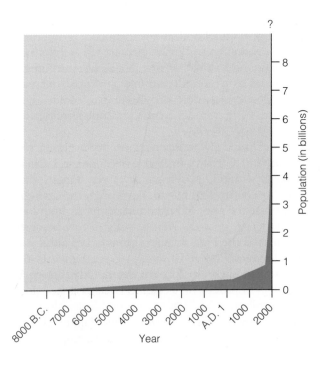

was growing at an annual rate of 1.76 percent. The projected world population in the year 2000 is 6.26 billion, and in the year 2050, 8.50 billion (Haub 1992).

Regardless of the specific estimate, the current trend is toward continued population growth. Many people are concerned with a probable lack of resources, such as food and energy. Others feel less concerned and believe new technologies will help bridge the gap between population size and resources. Many developing nations today are making efforts to control fertility, in particular, by providing increased awareness of birth control.

SUMMARY

Analysis of the interrelationship between biology and culture is a major focus of contemporary biological anthropology. The biocultural nature of anthropology helps us to understand how cultural changes can affect patterns of biological variation.

The study of human growth provides many examples of the interrelationship of biology and culture. While growth patterns are affected by genetic and hormonal influences, they are also affected by a variety of environmental influences, such as nutrition and disease. These influences are further modified by cultural variables, such as family size, socioeconomic status, and personal behaviors. Studies of generational changes in human growth (secular trends) show clearly the effects of rapid cultural change on human growth.

Studies of human adaptation examine the interplay between physiologic, genetic, and cultural modes of adaptation. Differences in human adaptation to temperature stress reflect differences in growth patterns, genetic potential, and cultural mechanisms, such as clothing and shelter. Human adaptation to high-altitude environments has also exhibited considerable variation.

The study of human health and disease clearly demonstrates how culture and biology influence each other. Research on prehistoric, historic, and contemporary human populations allows analysis of changing patterns of health and disease, from hunting-gathering to agricultural and industrial societies. Many industrial nations have undergone an epidemiologic transition during the past century, whereby noninfectious diseases have replaced infectious diseases as the primary cause of death and life expectancy at birth has increased. These biological phenomena are a direct result of a cultural environment in which unprecedented changes in subsistence, public-health, sanitation, and medical technologies have occurred.

Demography studies the relationship of fertility, mortality, and migration to the size, distribution, and composition of human populations.

Reflecting both biological and cultural factors, fertility and mortality measures demonstrate how rapid cultural change has significantly modified demographic patterns in today's world.

Supplemental Readings

Bogin, B. A. 1988. *Patterns of Human Growth*. Cambridge: Cambridge University Press. A general text focusing on influences on human postnatal growth and the evolutionary implications of human growth patterns.

Frisancho, A. R. 1979. *Human Adaptation: A Functional Interpretation*. St. Louis, Mo.: C. V. Mosby. This text provides a thorough review of adaptation studies through the late 1970s, focusing on biological responses to stress.

Lilienfeld, A., and D. E. Lilienfeld. 1980. *Foundations of Epidemiology*. 2d ed. New York: Oxford University Press. A well-written introduction to the field of epidemiological research.

McElroy, A., and P. K. Townsend. 1989. *Medical Anthropology in Ecological Perspective*. 2d ed. Boulder, Colo.: Westview Press. This text is perhaps the best single introduction available to the field of medical anthropology, dealing with both cultural and biomedical approaches to the field.

Moran, E. F. 1982. *Human Adaptability: An Introduction to Ecological Anthropology*. Boulder, Colo.: Westview Press. This general text provides a good review of human adaptation, with a special focus on cultural issues.

Swedlund, A. C., and G. J. Armelagos. 1976. *Demographic Anthropology*. Dubuque, Iowa: Wm. C. Brown. Even though dated and, unfortunately, out of print, this book furnishes a lucid general review of demography that includes examples from anthropology.

Tanner, J. M. 1989. *Foetus into Man: Physical Growth from Conception to Maturity*. 2d ed., rev. and enl. Cambridge, Massachusetts: Harvard University Press. Along with Bogin's text, this book provides a valuable introduction to the study of human growth.

Weeks, J. R. 1981. *Population: An Introduction to Concepts and Ideas*. 2d ed. Belmont, California: Wadsworth. Although not anthropologically oriented, this is a sound introduction to the study of demography.

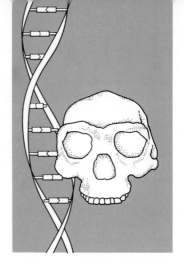

CHAPTER *7*

Our Place in Nature

What are humans? This question has been a focus of science, art, and literature. Many different fields, from theology to psychology, have addressed its ultimate significance. Our perspective on ourselves is not abstract; the way we define what we are has great impact on the way we treat each other and the rest of the world.

What is the scientific definition of humans? Many sciences attempt to answer this question, zoology, biochemistry, and even computer science among them. In addition, a wide range of disciplines, such as history, geography, economics, political science, sociology, psychology, and anthropology, deal exclusively with human beings and their behaviors. From a scientific viewpoint, we are interested in a definition of humans that incorporates differences and similarities with other living creatures.

Taxonomy

Taxonomy was discussed briefly in Chapters 1 and 3. Here, we turn to a more detailed examination of the philosophies and methods used in constructing biological classifications.

Methods of Classification

Two species may have the same characteristic for several reasons. First, they both may have inherited the trait from a common ancestor.

153

homologous trait Physical trait in two species that has a similar structure but may or may not show a similar function.

analogous trait Physical trait that has a similar function in two species but a different structure.

primitive trait A trait that has not changed from an ancestral state. The five digits of the human hand and foot are primitive traits inherited from earlier vertebrate ancestors.

derived trait A trait that has changed from an ancestral state.

Humans and monkeys, for example, both have five digits on each limb because they both inherited this trait from a distant common ancestor. Second, the two species may have developed the same trait independently in their evolution. The canary and bat are both small animals capable of flight. The shared characteristic of flight is not because they share common ancestry but rather because both species evolved flight independently.

Homologous and analogous traits. One of our first steps is to look at a biological trait and determine its structure (how it is put together) and its function (how it is used). **Homologous traits** are traits that show similar structure but may or may not show the same function. For example, each of your arms or legs is composed of a single upper bone and two lower bones. These bones are found in many other organisms, including creatures that use their limbs in quite different ways. Figure 7.1 illustrates the arm bones of a human, a bird, and a whale. These three animals use their limbs for different purposes, but the basic structure is the same, with the same bones, but differing in size, shape, and function. The correspondence of the arm and hand bones of the animals in Figure 7.1 indicates these bones are homologous structures. The reason for this correspondence is that these traits have been inherited from a common ancestor.

Traits that have the same function but not the same structure are called **analogous traits.** Figure 7.2 illustrates the wings of a bird and a flying insect. The two structures are quite different, but they serve the same function—flight. In this case, evolution has led to the same function from two different starting points.

Primitive and derived traits. Biological traits can also be characterized as primitive or derived. When a trait has been inherited from an earlier form, we refer to that trait as **primitive.** Traits that have changed from an ancestral state are referred to as **derived.** As an example, consider the number of digits in humans and horses. Both humans and horses are

Figure 7.1

Homologous structures: the forelimbs of a human, whale, and bird. Note that the same bones are found in all three vertebrates. Even though the limbs are used differently by all three organisms, the bones show a structural correspondence, reflecting common ancestry. (Adapted with permission from T. Dobzhansky, F. J. Ayala, G. L. Stebbins, and U. W. Valentine, *Evolution,* 1977, page 264, publisher W. H. Freeman)

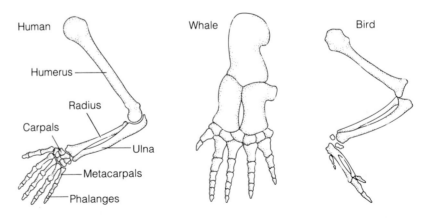

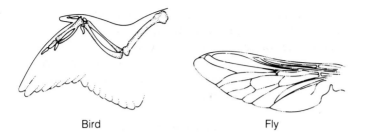

Bird   Fly

Figure 7.2

Analogous structures: the
wings of a bird and a fly.
Even though both structures
provide the same function
(flight), they are structurally
different, reflecting independent evolutionary origin.
(Adapted with permission from
T. Dobzhansky, F. J. Ayala, G. L.
Stebbins, and U. W. Valentine,
Evolution, 1977, page 264,
publisher W. H. Freeman)

mammals. From fossil evidence (see Chapter 9) we know that the first
mammals had five digits on each hand and foot (as did other early land
vertebrates). Humans have retained this condition, and we refer to the five
digits of the human hand and foot as primitive traits. The horse's single
digit (a toe), however, is a derived trait relative to the first mammals.

The Vertebrates

As with all living creatures, human beings can be classified according
to the different levels of Linnean taxonomy—kingdom, phylum, class, and
so on. The complete taxonomic description of modern humans is given in
Table 7.1.

The animal kingdom. Kingdom is the most inclusive taxonomic category. All living organisms can be placed into one of five kingdoms: plants,
animals, fungi, nucleated single-celled organisms, and bacteria. Major differences between these kingdoms are their source of food and their mobility. Whereas plants produce their own food through photosynthesis,
animals must ingest food. Humans belong to the animal kingdom.

T A B L E   7.1
Taxonomic Classification of
Human Beings

Taxonomic category	Placement of humans
Kingdom	Animals
Phylum	Chordates
Subphylum	Vertebrates
Class	Mammals
Subclass	Placental mammals
Order	Primates
Suborder	Anthropoids
Superfamily	Hominoids
Family	Hominids
Genus/Species	*Homo sapiens*

Chordata A vertebrate phylum consisting of organisms that possess a notochord at some period during their life.

Vertebrata A subphylum of the phylum Chordata, defined by the presence of an internal, segmented spinal column and bilateral symmetry.

bilateral symmetry When the right and left sides of the body are approximate mirror images.

Vertebrate characteristics. Humans belong to the phylum **Chordata** (the chordates, animals with a spinal cord). Humans belong to the subphylum **Vertebrata** (the vertebrates, animals with backbones). One characteristic of vertebrates is that they have **bilateral symmetry,** which means that the left and right sides of their bodies are approximately mirror images. This pattern contrasts with other phyla of animals such as starfish. Another characteristic of vertebrates is an internal spinal cord covered by a series of bones known as vertebrae. The nerve tissue is surrounded by these bones and has an enlarged area of nerve tissue at the front end of the cord—the brain.

The general biological structure of human beings can be found in many other vertebrates. Figure 7.1 showed the limb bones of three vertebrates—human, bird, and whale. It is important to note the similarity among these three different organisms. All, like most vertebrates, have the same basic skeletal pattern: a single upper bone and two lower bones in each limb, and five digits. Some vertebrates have changed considerably from this basic pattern. For example, a modern horse has one digit (a toe) on the end of each limb. Humans may seem to be rather specialized and sophisticated creatures, but actually they have retained much of the earliest basic vertebrate skeletal structure.

The subphylum of vertebrates also includes several classes of fish along with the amphibians, reptiles, birds, and mammals. Humans belong to the class of mammals, and much of our biology and behavior can be understood in terms of what it is to be a mammal.

Characteristics of Mammals

The first primitive mammals evolved from early reptiles approximately 200 million years ago. The distinctive features of modern mammals and modern reptiles are the result of that long period of separate evolution in the two classes. It is important to realize that the further back in time we look, the more difficult it is to tell one form from another.

Because mammals and reptiles are related through evolution, it is logical and useful to compare these two classes to determine the unique features of each. Modern mammals differ from modern reptiles in reproduction, temperature regulation, diet, skeletal structure, and behavior.

Reproduction

Some mammals, such as the platypus, lay eggs. Others, such as kangaroos, give birth to an extremely immature fetus that completes development inside a pouch in the mother. The most common mammal found today belongs to the subclass of placental mammals, characterized by the development of the fetus inside of the mother's body. Humans are placental mammals.

Placental mammals. The **placenta** is an organ that develops inside the female during pregnancy. It functions as a link between the circulatory system of the mother and child, acting to transport food, oxygen, and antibodies as well as to filter out waste products. The efficiency of the placenta means that the developing offspring of placental mammals have a much greater chance of survival than a reptile developing in an egg or in a nonplacental mammal.

A main feature of mammals is that the female has mammary glands that provide food for the newborn infant. Important immunities are also provided in mother's milk. The ready availability of food increases the child's chance of survival. While advantageous, nursing also has a price; energy is expended by the mother during this process, and only a limited number of offspring can be taken care of at one time.

r-selection and K-selection. The **prenatal** (before-birth) and **postnatal** (after-birth) patterns of offspring care in mammals contrast with those of reptiles, which expend less energy during reproduction and care of offspring. Pregnancy and raising offspring take energy; the more offspring an organism has, the less care a parent can give each of them. Some animals produce large numbers of offspring but provide little care to them, a pattern known as **r-selection.** Other animals have few offspring but provide much more care to each of them, a pattern known as **K-selection.** These two patterns represent the extremes in reproductive biology.

From an evolutionary standpoint, which strategy is better? That is, which provides the maximum probability of survival of a population? In reality, each reproductive strategy has advantages and disadvantages. r-selection has the advantage of producing large numbers of offspring, but because little care is given to them, many, if not most, will die before reaching maturity. On the other hand, K-selection has the advantage of extensive child care, but the disadvantage that only a few offspring are produced at any one time. There is no clear-cut answer to which strategy is "better"; it all depends on specific circumstances.

Human reproduction and child care. As mammals, human beings are relatively K-selected. We are, however, actually less K-selected than many other mammals, including our closest relatives, the apes. In general, the more closely related a mammal is to humans, the more K-selected it is. Humans differ from this pattern. We continue to invest a great amount of parental care in our children, but we are also able to have more children than a typical highly K-selected organism. The difference is that we do not wait until our children are fully mature before having another child. We

placenta An organ that develops inside a pregnant placental mammal that provides the fetus with oxygen and food and helps filter out harmful substances.

prenatal The period of life from conception until birth.

postnatal The period of life from birth until death.

r-selection A reproductive pattern characterized by large numbers of offspring and little parental care.

K-selection A reproductive pattern characterized by few offspring but extensive parental care.

homoiotherm Organism capable of maintaining a constant body temperature under most circumstances.

most often have one child at a time, but their periods of dependency on us overlap (Figure 7.3).

Cultural adaptations provide numerous ways in which additional babies can be born without seriously affecting the amount of care each child receives. In our own society, such adaptations include labor-saving devices in the home, babysitting, participation in child rearing by the father, the convenience of social networks to help in child care (such as families and friends), improved transportation, easier access to shelter and food, and many others.

Temperature Regulation

Modern mammals are **homoiotherms;** they are able to maintain a constant body temperature under most circumstances. Modern reptiles are cold-blooded and cannot keep their body temperature constant; they need to use the heat of the sun's rays to keep them warm and their metabolism active. Mammals maintain a constant body temperature in several ways. Mammals are covered with fur or hair that insulates the body, preventing heat loss in cold weather and reducing overheating in hot weather.

Figure 7.3

Birth spacing in apes and humans over a 15-year period. The letter *O* refers to different offspring born during this time period. In apes, the female gives birth to an offspring roughly every five years: the time required for the offspring to reach maturity. Modern humans do not wait for a child to reach maturity (roughly 15 years) before having another child. Instead, births overlap one another (in this example the overlap is two years). This overlap is possibly a consequence of cultural adaptations that allow the care of more than one child at a time. The result is that humans can have more offspring in a given period of time without sacrificing parental care.

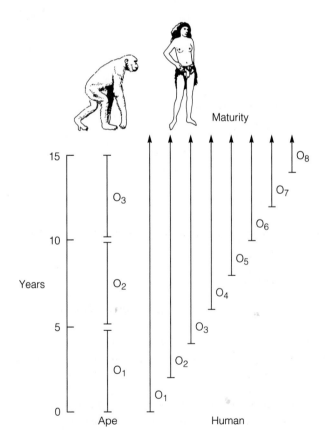

Mammals also maintain a constant body temperature by ingesting large quantities of food and converting the food to energy in the form of heat. When you feel hot, your body is not losing the produced heat quickly enough. When you feel cold, you are losing heat too quickly. The ability to convert food energy to heat allows mammals to live comfortably in many environments where reptiles would slow down or even die.

Mammals are thus able to exploit a large number of environments. Heat production and temperature regulation, however, though obviously useful adaptations in certain environments, are not without a price. To obtain energy, mammals need to consume far greater quantities of food than reptiles. In environments where food resources are limited, mammals may be worse-off than reptiles. Again, the evolutionary benefit of any trait must be looked at in terms of its cost.

Teeth

The saying, "You are what you eat," is not usually made literally, but in fact it embodies an important truth of ecology and evolution. The nutritional requirements of organisms dictate, in part, their environmental needs. Also, diet is reflected in the physical structure of organisms, particularly the teeth and jaws. Because mammals maintain a constant body temperature by converting food energy to heat, they require a considerable amount of food. The physical features of mammalian teeth reflect this need.

The teeth of reptiles (as well as amphibians and fish) are all the same; they all have sharp sides and continue to grow throughout life. The function of reptilian teeth is to hold and kill prey. The food is then most often eaten whole. Mammals, on the other hand, have different types of teeth in their jaws. Mammals only have two sets of teeth during their lives: a set of deciduous ("baby") teeth and a set of permanent teeth. As a mammal grows and matures, the baby teeth fall out and are replaced with the adult teeth. In modern humans this replacement normally starts around age 6 and takes the first 18 or 20 years of life to complete.

Mammals have four types of teeth: **incisors, canines, premolars, and molars.** These teeth are shown for a chimpanzee and a human in Figure 7.4. The incisor teeth are flat and located in the front of the jaw. Both the human and the chimpanzee (and other higher primates) have a total of four incisors in each jaw. These teeth are used for cutting and slicing of food. Behind the incisors are the canine teeth, which are often long and sharp, resembling fangs or tusks. Apes and humans have two canine teeth in each jaw. In many mammals the canine teeth are used as weapons or to kill prey. While the canine teeth of most mammals are rather large and project beyond the level of the rest of the teeth, human canines are usually small and nonprojecting.

The premolar and molar teeth are also known collectively as the back teeth. Both of these types of teeth are often large in surface area and are

incisor The flat front teeth used for cutting, slicing, and gnawing food.

canine The teeth located in the front of the jaw behind the incisors that are normally used by mammals for puncturing and defense.

premolar One of the types of back teeth used for crushing and grinding food.

molar The teeth furthest back in the jaw used for crushing and grinding food.

Figure 7.4

The lower jaws and teeth of a chimpanzee and a modern human.

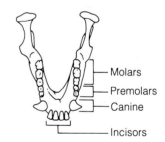

Chimpanzee

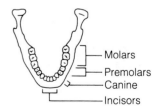

Human

cerebrum The area of the forebrain that consists of the outermost layer of brain cells, associated with memory, learning, and intelligence.

used for grinding and chewing food. When you chew food between your back teeth, you do not simply move your lower jaw up and down. Instead, your upper and lower back teeth grind together in a circular motion as your jaw moves up and down and sideways as well.

The nature of mammalian diet and teeth relates to their warm-bloodedness. Mammals need more food than reptiles, and their teeth allow them to utilize a wider range of food and to process it more productively. The benefits of differentiated teeth lie in these abilities. The cost is the fact that the teeth tend to wear out over time.

Skeletal Structure

Both mammals and reptiles share the basic skeletal structure of all vertebrates, but there are some differences, especially in movement. In reptiles the four limbs come out from the side of the body for support and movement (Figure 7.5). In four-legged mammals, the limbs slope downward from the shoulders and hips. Having the limbs tucked in under the body allows more efficient and quicker movement. The weight of the body is supported better.

Figure 7.5

The orientation of the limbs to the body in reptiles and in mammals.

Reptile

Mammal

Behavior

The brains of all vertebrates have similar structures but differ in size, relative proportions, and functions. All vertebrates have a hindbrain, a midbrain, and a forebrain. In most vertebrates, the hindbrain is associated with hearing, balance, reflexive behaviors, and control of the autonomic functions of the body, such as breathing. The midbrain is associated with vision, and the forebrain is associated with chemical sensing such as smelling ability.

The brain of a mammal reveals several important shifts in structure and function. The mammalian brain has a greatly enlarged forebrain that is responsible for the processing of sensory information and coordination. In particular, the forebrain contains the **cerebrum,** the outermost layer of brain cells, which is associated with learning, memory, and intelligence. The cerebrum becomes increasingly convoluted, which allows huge numbers of interconnections between brain cells. It accounts for the largest proportion of the mammalian brain.

The overall functions of a brain include basic body maintenance as well as the ability to process information and respond accordingly. Mammals rely more on learning and flexible responses than do reptiles. Behaviors are less instinctual and rigid. Previous experiences (learning) become more important in responding to stimuli. As a consequence, mammals are more capable of developing new responses to different situations and are capable of learning from past mistakes. New behaviors are more likely to develop and can be passed on to offspring through the process of learning. Humans have taken this process even further; our very existence depends on flexible behaviors that must be learned. While our behavior is to a large extent cultural, our ability to transfer information through learning relies on a biological trait: the mammalian brain.

The behavioral flexibility of mammals ties in with their pattern of reproduction. Extensive parental care requires increased intelligence and the ability to learn new behaviors in order to provide maximum care for infants. The increased emphasis on learning requires in turn an extended period of childhood during which to absorb the information needed for the adult life. Furthermore, the extension of childhood requires more extensive child care, so that offspring are protected during the time they need to complete their growth and learning. Thus it is no surprise that the K-selected pattern of reproduction is associated with greater intelligence and flexibility of behaviors.

Variations on a Theme

Modern reptiles and modern mammals differ markedly in biology and behavior. A major reason for this sharp difference is the fact that mammals and reptiles have evolved separately for almost 200 million years. Mammals and reptiles have certain features in common that they inherited from a common ancestor. Other features, such as the teeth and the reproductive system, are different because each line has evolved independently from the common ancestor. In the analysis of fossil remains, this means that the older a given form is, the more closely it resembles a common ancestor and the harder it is to classify the fossil as a reptile or a mammal. This difficulty shows a basic problem with taxonomy: evolution leads to change, and a classification system works best when things stay the same.

There is another point to keep in mind when we draw up lists of characteristics that distinguish modern reptiles from modern mammals. The modern forms of these creatures are those that have survived until the present. Modern reptiles include organisms as varied as crocodiles, turtles, and snakes. Many other variations on the basic theme have existed in the past and have become extinct. For example, modern reptiles are often characterized as slow-moving, cold-blooded creatures. This does not mean that all past reptiles had these characteristics. One group, the dinosaurs, became extinct 65 million years ago but were once the dominant form of life on land. Though they are also classified as reptiles, the dinosaurs were nonetheless quite different from modern reptiles. According to some recent interpretations, they moved fast, took care of their young, and were warm-blooded (Bakker 1986). Accordingly, a number of the usual characteristics used to classify reptiles may not be appropriate for dinosaurs. Change over time means that taxonomic classification is often difficult and should best be regarded as a tool to describe general trends.

Primate Characteristics

primates The order of mammals that has a complex of characteristics related to an initial adaptation to life in the trees.

arboreal Living in trees.

terrestrial Living on the ground.

prehensile Capable of grasping.

There are many different forms of mammals, as diverse as mice, whales, giraffes, cats, dogs, and apes. The mammalian class is broken down into a number of orders. Humans are **primates,** as are the apes, such as the chimpanzee and gorilla, which are our closest living relatives. Monkeys are also primates, along with more biologically primitive forms known as prosimians.

No single characteristic identifies primates; rather, they share a set of features. Many of these features relate to living in the trees. Though it is clear that humans, as well as other modern primates, do not live in the trees, they still retain certain features inherited from ancestors who did.

An **arboreal** (tree-living) environment presents different challenges than a **terrestrial** (ground-living) environment. Living in the trees requires an orientation to a three-dimensional environment. Animals that live on the ground generally contend with only two dimensions: length and width. Arboreal animals must also deal with the third dimension, height. Perception of distance and depth is vital to a tree-living form, which moves quickly from one branch to the next, and from one level of the forest to another. Agility is also important, as is the ability to anchor oneself in space.

Many forms of animals, such as squirrels and birds, have adapted to living in the trees. Primates, however, are capable of extensive rapid movement through the trees and are able to move to all areas of a tree, including small terminal branches. The two major characteristics of primates that account for their success in the trees are the ability to use hands and feet to grasp branches (rather than digging in with claws), and the ability to perceive distance and depth.

The Skeleton

Let us consider some general characteristics in the primate skeletal structure.

Grasping hands. A characteristic of the earliest known mammals (and reptiles) is five digits on each hand or foot. Certain mammals, such as the horse, have changed from this ancestral condition and only have a single toe on each limb. Other mammals, such as the primates, have kept the ancestral condition.

Primates, including humans, are primitive in the number of digits on the hands and feet. In the case of primates, the retention of the primitive characteristic of five digits on the hands and feet turned out to be an important adaptation. The hands and feet of primates are **prehensile,** meaning that they are capable of being used to grasp objects. The ability to grasp involves the movement of the fingers to the palm, thus allowing the fingers to wrap around an object. In many primates, the toes can also wrap around an object. This grasping ability provides a remarkable adaptation to living in the trees. Primates can grab onto branches to move about, to provide support while eating, and in general to allow for a high degree of flexibility in moving about their environment.

Another feature of primate hands and feet is their expanded tactile pads (such as the ball of your thumb) and nails instead of claws. These nails serve to protect the sensitive skin at the ends of the fingers and the toes. The numerous nerve endings in the tips of fingers and toes of primates provide an enhanced sense of touch that is useful in the manipulation of objects.

Generalized structure. Biological structures are often classified as specialized or generalized. **Specialized structures** are used in a highly specific way, whereas **generalized structures** can be used in a variety of ways. The hooves of a horse, for example, are a specialization that allows rapid running over land surfaces. The basic skeletal structure of primates is generalized because it allows movement flexibility in a wide variety of circumstances.

The arm and leg bones of primates follow the basic pattern of many vertebrates: each limb consists of an upper bone and two lower bones (refer back to Figure 7.1). This structure allows limbs to bend at the elbows or knees. That the lower part of the limb is made up of two bones provides even greater flexibility. This flexibility is obtained by the retention of a generalized skeletal structure.

Vision

The three-dimensional nature of arboreal life requires keen eyesight, particularly depth perception. This feature has evolved from the need to judge distances successfully. (Jumping through the air from branch to branch demands the ability to judge distances. After all, it is not very adaptive to fall short of your target and plunge to the ground!)

Depth perception involves **binocular stereoscopic vision.** *Binocular* refers to overlapping fields of vision. The eyes of many animals are located at the sides of the skull so that each eye receives a different image with no overlap (Figure 7.6). The eyes of primates are located in the front of the skull so that the fields of vision overlap. Primates see objects in front of them with both eyes. The *stereoscopic* nature of primate vision refers to the way in which the brain processes visual signals. In nonstereoscopic animals, the information from one eye is received in only one hemisphere of the brain. In primates, the visual signals from both eyes are received in both hemispheres of the brain. The result is an image that has depth. Moving in three dimensions makes use of depth perception.

specialized structure A biological structure adapted to a narrow range of conditions and used in very specific ways.

generalized structure A biological structure adapted to a wide range of conditions and used in very general ways.

binocular stereoscopic vision Overlapping fields of vision with both sides of the brain receiving images from both eyes, thereby providing depth perception.

Figure 7.6

Binocular stereoscopic vision in primates. The fields of vision for each eye overlap, and the optic nerve from each eye is connected to both hemispheres of the brain.   (From *Human Antiquity: An Introduction to Physical Anthropology and Archaeology,* 2d ed., by Kenneth Feder and Michael Park. Fig. 5.1. Copyright © 1993 by Mayfield Publishing Company)

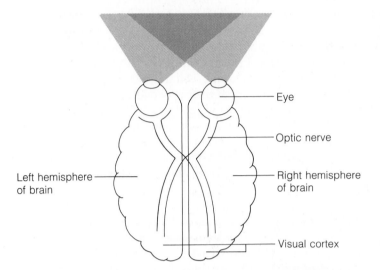

Primates are vision-oriented. On average, their sense of smell is less keen. As a result, the areas of the face devoted to smelling are reduced in primates. Compared to other mammals, primates have short snouts.

The Brain and Behavior

Primates have expanded on the basic pattern of mammalian brains. Their brains are even larger relative to body size. Primate brains have larger visual areas and smaller areas for smelling, corresponding to their increased emphasis of vision over smell as the main sense. Also, primate brains are even more complex than those of most other mammals. Primates have larger proportions of the brain associated with learning and intelligence. Areas of the brain associated with body control and coordination are also proportionately larger, as expected from the demands of arboreal life. Hand–eye coordination, for example, is crucial for moving about in the trees.

Learning. The greater size and complexity of primate brains are reflected in their behaviors. Primates rely even more extensively than other mammals on learned behaviors. As a result, it is often difficult to assign specific behaviors to a given species of primate because the increased emphasis on learning allows a great deal of flexibility in behavior patterns.

The increased emphasis on learning means that primates spend a greater proportion of their lives growing up, both biologically and socially, than other animals. The more an animal needs to learn, the longer the period of time needed for learning. An increase in the amount of time spent as an infant or child further means that greater amounts of attention and care are required from parents. Again, we see the intimate relationship among reproduction, care of offspring, learning, and intelligence.

Figure 7.7

A macaque washing food in water.   (Steve Gaulin/Anthro-Photo)

An example of learning in primates. Primate studies have provided many good examples of the introduction of new behaviors to a group by one or more individuals, which are then learned by other individuals. Studies of the Japanese macaque monkeys on the island of Koshima during the 1950s revealed a number of cases of cultural transmission of new behaviors. (Figure 7.7).

In 1953, a young female macaque named Imo began washing sweet potatoes in a stream before eating them. Within three years, this behavior had been learned by almost half of the troop. Two years later, only two adults continued this practice. Of the 19 younger monkeys 15 had adopted this behavior, however, and thereafter almost all newborn infants acquired it by observing their mothers (Bramblett 1976).

Another food-related behavior developed among the troop in 1956 when scientists began feeding the monkeys grains of wheat. The wheat was scattered on a sandy beach to slow down the monkeys' eating so that researchers would have more time to study them. Imo developed a new method of eating the grains of wheat. She took handfuls of sand and wheat down to the water and threw them in. The sand sank while the wheat floated, thus letting her skim the grains off the surface of the water. This new behavior provided a much quicker way of getting the wheat than picking out grains from the sand. The young female's method of wheat washing spread quickly through most of the rest of the troop (Bramblett 1976).

The studies of cultural transmission among the Japanese macaques show the importance of learning in primate societies. The washing of

monogamy An exclusive sexual bond between an adult male and an adult female for a long period of time.

polygamy A sexual bond between an adult male and an adult female in which either individual may have more than one mate at the same time.

sweet potatoes and the separation of wheat and sand are not innate behaviors in Japanese macaques. These behaviors are transmitted through learning, not genetic inheritance.

Reproduction and Care of Offspring

As with all mammals, primates are characterized by a small number of offspring and a great deal of parental care. Indeed, primates are the most K-selected mammals of all.

The mother-infant bond. The K-selected nature of primates is seen in the strong and long-lasting bond between mother and infant. Unlike some mammals, infant primates are entirely helpless. They depend on their mothers for food, warmth, protection, affection, and knowledge, and they remain dependent for a long time. Of all the different types of social bonds in primate societies, the mother-infant bond is the strongest. In many primate species this bond continues well past childhood. Chimpanzees, for example, regularly associate with their mothers through their adult lives (Goodall 1986).

Paternal care. Paternal care is highly variable among primate species. In general, primates that are **monogamous** (characterized by a more or less permanent bond forming between a single male and female) are most likely to show high levels of paternal care. By contrast, species that are polygamous tend, on average, to show less paternal involvement with offspring. This difference may relate to the fact that in monogamous species it is easy for the male to tell he is the father! In a **polygamous** species, paternal behaviors may be less appropriate from a genetic perspective since a male can never be sure if he is the father.

Growing up. The importance of the extended period of infant and child growth in primates cannot be overstated. The long period of growth is necessary for learning motor skills and social behaviors. The close bond between mother and infant provides the first important means by which an infant primate learns. It is not the only important social contact for a growing primate, however. The process of socialization in most primates depends to a large extent on close contact with peers. Interaction with other individuals of the same age provides the opportunity to learn how to interact socially in general, along with specific types of social behaviors.

Social Structure

Primates are essentially social creatures. The close bond between mother and infant, the importance of learning, and the great flexibility in behaviors all point to this fact. Apart from this general need, primates show an amazing amount of variation in the ways in which their societies are structured. The main social group of primates can range in size from two individuals up to several hundred and can have different proportions of males, females, young, and old.

Social groups. A social group is generally defined as a group within which there is frequent communication or interaction among members. This definition is a bit arbitrary but provides us with a starting point for looking at primate societies. **Social structure** consists of the composition of the group and the way in which it is organized. Primates display four basic types of social structure, with many variations on these basic types. The **mother-infant group,** consisting of the mother and her infant, is the smallest social group. Adult males are solitary and tend to interact with adult females only when mating. The **family group** consists of an adult male, an adult female, and their offspring. Although this is a common pattern among humans in Western nations, it is actually not that common among primates or even among human cultures. In family groups, both adult males and adult females care for their offspring. The **one-male group** consists of a single adult male, several adult females, and their offspring. The **multimale group** is composed of several adult males, several adult females, and offspring. The multimale group is the most common form of social structure found in nonhuman primates, although there are many variations on this basic theme because of factors such as group size and the ratio of adult males to adult females.

Social organization and dominance. Nonhuman primate societies show a ranking of individuals in terms of their relative dominance in the group. A **dominance hierarchy** is the ranking system within the society and reflects which individuals are most and least dominant. Dominance hierarchies are found in most nonhuman primate societies, but they vary widely in their overall importance in everyday life. The dominance hierarchy provides stability in social life. All individuals know their place within the society, eliminating to some extent uncertainty about what to do or who to follow.

The dominance hierarchy in nonhuman primates is usually ruled by those individuals with the greatest access to food or sex or those that control social behaviors to the greatest extent. Societies with strong male dominance hierarchies are likely to show a moderate to large difference in the sizes of adult males and adult females. The **sexual dimorphism** in body size has often been considered the result of competition among males for breeding females. The males who are larger and stronger are considered more likely to gain access to females and hence pass on their genetic potential for larger size and greater strength.

This pattern does not always hold, however. The adult male most likely to attract mates may not be the male most likely to have access to

social structure The composition of a social group and the way it is organized, including size, age structure, and number of each sex in the group.

mother-infant group Social structure in which the primary social group consists of mother and her dependent offspring.

family group Social structure in which the primary social group consists of a single adult male, a single adult female, and their offspring.

one-male group Social structure in which the primary social group consists of a single adult male, several adult females, and their offspring.

multimale group A type of social structure in which the primary social group is made up of several adult males, several adult females, and their offspring.

dominance hierarchy The ranking system within a society that indicates which individuals are dominant in social behaviors.

sexual dimorphism The average difference in body size between adult males and adult females.

food. Fedigan (1983) has reviewed the literature on the relationship between dominance rank of males and access to breeding females for a
number of primate species and has found that this expected relationship is
not always present.

An example of a primate species with a strong dominance hierarchy
is the savanna baboon, a monkey living on the open grasslands of Africa.
Baboons live in large multimale groups. Adult males are dominant over
adult females, and there is a constant shift in the relative position of the
most dominant males (Figure 7.8). Adult males are larger than adult females, and the largest and strongest adult males have a greater chance of
becoming the most dominant.

Size and strength are not the only determinants of a male baboon's
dominance status. Coalitions of two or more lower-ranking baboons have
often been observed to displace a more dominant male who was actually
larger and stronger than either of the lower-ranking males. The ability to
enlist aid from others is an important determinant of dominance rank.

In other primate societies we also see that dominance may reflect
additional factors. In the Japanese macaque monkeys, for example, the
rank of a male's mother has an influence on the male's dominance rank
(Eaton 1976). Males born to high-ranking mothers have a greater chance
of achieving high dominance themselves, all other factors being equal.

In a number of primate societies, the dominance hierarchy of females
is more stable over time than that of the males. Whereas the position of
most dominant male can change quickly, the hierarchy among females
remains more constant over time. Even in cases where all males are dominant over females, the female dominance hierarchy exerts an effect on
social behaviors within the group, such as the case discussed earlier of
mother's rank affecting the rank of male offspring.

Figure 7.8

Two adult male baboons
engaged in a dominance
dispute. Though physical
violence does occur in such
encounters, much of the
display is bluff.   (Irven
Devore/Anthro-Photo)

Primate Suborders

In terms of both biology and behavior, primates are an extremely variable group of mammals. Though the general characteristics discussed earlier are useful in understanding the basic primate adaptations, it becomes difficult to make additional generalizations without considering different subgroups of primates. General primate characteristics may reflect arboreal adaptations, but not all modern primates are arboreal. To understand what humans are, we must consider biological and behavioral variation within primates.

The primate order is divided into suborders, which are further divided into other taxonomic categories, such as infraorders, superfamilies, families, and so on. A list of the complete taxonomic designations of many living primates is given in the Appendix. This chapter covers only the major categories and a few selected examples from each to give an idea of the relationships between primate groups.

The two major divisions of primates that are traditionally used are the suborder **prosimians** and the suborder **anthropoids.** Each of these suborders is broken down into infraorders, and so on. Figure 7.9 shows the traditional primate taxonomy discussed in the next few pages.

Prosimians

The word *prosimian* means literally "before simians" (monkeys and apes). In biological terms, prosimians are more primitive, or more like early primate ancestors, than monkeys and apes.

prosimians A suborder of primates that are biologically primitive compared to anthropoids.

anthropoids The suborder of primates consisting of monkeys, apes, and humans.

Figure 7.9

Summary of traditional primate taxonomy. Only the major groups discussed in this chapter are listed. A more complete taxonomy is provided in the Appendix.

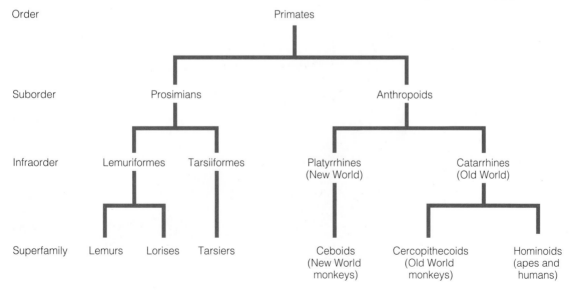

nocturnal Active during the night.

diurnal Active during the day.

loris Nocturnal prosimian found today in Asia and Africa.

tarsier Nocturnal prosimian found today in Indonesia.

lemur A prosimian found today on the island of Madagascar.

Prosimian characteristics. The prosimians often lack one or more of the general characteristics of primates. For example, some prosimians lack color vision, and some have a single claw on each hand or foot.

Another primitive characteristic of prosimians is that they rely to a much greater extent on the sense of smell than do the anthropoids. Prosimian brains are also generally smaller relative to body size than the brains of anthropoids. Prosimians are usually small in size, tend to be solitary, and are often **nocturnal** (active at night). These characteristics and others point to the basic primitive nature of many prosimians.

Prosimians themselves show considerable variation. Some prosimians have larger body sizes, some have larger social groups, and some are **diurnal** (active in daylight). This variation makes classification difficult, but it does show us both the general trends of the prosimians as well as specific differences among them.

Types of prosimians. There are three different groups of prosimians in the world today, each with a number of different species. One group, the **lorises,** are small, solitary, nocturnal prosimians found in Asia and Africa (Figure 7.10). Another group, the **tarsiers,** also small, solitary, and nocturnal, are found in Indonesia. The nocturnal nature of tarsiers is evidenced by their large eyes, the size of which serves to gather available light (Figure 7.11).

The most biologically diverse group of prosimians are the **lemurs,** which are found only on the island of Madagascar off the southeast coast

Figure 7.10

A loris, a prosimian from Southeast Asia.   (Animals Animals © Stouffer Enterprises)

Figure 7.11

A tarsier, a prosimian from Southeast Asia. Unlike other prosimians, the tarsier does not have a moist nose. (© Zoological Society of San Diego)

of Africa (Figure 7.12). Some species of lemurs are nocturnal and some are diurnal. Social structure is highly variable among the lemurs: some have the family group structure, some have the one-male structure, and some have the multimale structure. Other characteristics, such as body size, diet, and group size, are also variable among lemur species.

Anthropoids

The anthropoids are the higher primates and consist of monkeys and hominoids (apes and humans). Anthropoids are generally larger in overall body size, have larger and more complex brains, rely more on visual abilities, and show more complex social structures than other primates. Except for one monkey species, all anthropoids are diurnal. The anthropoids include both arboreal and terrestrial species.

All living prosimians are found in the Old World, but anthropoids are found in both the New World and the Old World. (The Old World consists of the continents of Africa, Asia, and Europe; the New World is the Americas.) New World anthropoids are found today in Central and

Figure 7.12

Ring-tailed lemur from the island of Madagascar. (© Zoological Society of San Diego)

quadrupedal A form of movement in which all four limbs are of equal size and make contact with the ground and the spine is roughly parallel to the ground.

South America. Old World anthropoids are found today in Africa and Asia (and one monkey species in Europe). The only New World anthropoids are monkeys, whereas Old World anthropoids include monkeys, apes, and humans. Because humans are anthropoids, the rest of this chapter focuses mainly on the biology and behavior of this group.

The Monkeys

Anthropoids include monkeys and hominoids (apes and humans). Monkeys and apes are often confused in the popular imagination. In reality, they are easy to tell apart. Monkeys have tails, apes and humans do not. Monkeys also have smaller brains relative to body size than apes or humans. The typical pattern of monkey movement is on all fours (**quadrupedal**), and their arms and legs are generally of similar length so that their spines are parallel to the ground. By contrast, apes have longer arms than legs and humans have longer legs than arms.

New World monkeys. The monkeys of Central and South America are biologically different from the Old World monkeys. Some of these differences are important in reconstructing evolutionary relationships, such as the fact that New World monkeys have four more premolar teeth than Old World monkeys. The dental formulae for many New World monkeys is 2-1-3-3, compared to the 2-1-2-3 dental formula of all Old World monkeys. Other differences relate to the way in which the monkeys live, such as the fact that many New World monkeys have prehensile tails.

Because the tail of many New World monkeys is capable of grasping, it is highly useful in moving about and feeding in the trees (Figures 7.13 and 7.14). Typically, the monkey will use this "fifth limb" to anchor itself while feeding on the ends of small branches. Old World monkeys have tails, but none of them have prehensile tails. Those New World monkeys with prehensile tails are thus more proficient in terms of acrobatic agility. This difference probably relates to the fact that all New World monkeys are arboreal, whereas some Old World monkeys are terrestrial. The prehensile tail of many New World monkeys appears to be a biological specialization that either did not develop in the Old World monkeys or was lost in that line's evolution from some earlier common ancestor of all monkeys.

Old World monkeys. Old World monkeys are biochemically and physically more similar to humans than are New World monkeys. For example, Old World monkeys have the same number of teeth as apes and humans (a dental formula of 2-1-2-3). Old World monkeys inhabit a wide range of environments. Many species live in tropical rain forests, but other species have adapted to the **savanna** (open grasslands). One species has even learned to survive in the snowy environment of the Japanese mountains (Figure 7.15).

The Old World monkeys, like the New World monkeys, are quadrupedal, running on the ground and branches on all fours. Though Old World monkeys are agile in the trees, many species have adapted to spending more time on the ground in search of food. Most Old World species

savanna An environment consisting of open grasslands in which food resources tend to be spread out over large areas.

Figure 7.13

A Bolivian red howler monkey, one of the New World monkeys with a prehensile tail. (© Zoological Society of San Diego)

Figure 7.14

A spider monkey, also capable of using its tail as a "fifth limb." (© Zoological Society of San Diego)

Figure 7.15

Japanese macaques adapted to living in the snow.   (© Steven Kaufman/Peter Arnold, Inc.)

Figure 7.16

A mandrill, an Old World monkey.   (© Zoological Society of San Diego)

eat a mixed diet of fruits and leaves (Figure 7.16), although some show dental and digestive specializations for leaf eating.

Social structure is highly variable among Old World monkeys. Most species have the multimale group structure, but several species, such as the hamadryas baboon, have the one-male structure. This social structure appears to be adaptive in environments where food is less abundant. One male seems to be sufficient for protection and reproduction; additional adult males consume food without adding much to group survival.

Although studies of prosimians and monkeys tell us much about primate biology and behavior, the study of the apes provides even more valuable information for understanding the human species. Our close relationship to apes furnishes us with additional information with which to answer the question, "What is human?" The apes and their biological and behavioral similarities to humans are discussed in the next chapter.

SUMMARY

The biological and behavioral nature of human beings is revealed in the different levels of taxonomic classification to which humans belong. Humans are animals, chordates, and vertebrates. We share certain characteristics with other creatures in these categories, such as a more developed nervous system. Humans are mammals, which means that we rely a great deal on a reproductive strategy of few births and extensive parental care. This reproductive pattern is associated with higher intelligence and a greater capacity for learned behaviors. Other adaptations of mammals include differentiated teeth, a skeletal structure capable of swift movement, and the ability to maintain a constant body temperature.

Humans belong to a specific order of mammals known as primates. The primates have certain characteristics, such as skeletal flexibility, grasping hands, and keen eyesight, that evolved in order to meet the demands of life in the trees. There is a great deal of biological and behavioral variation among the living primates. The order Primates is composed of the more biologically primitive prosimians and the higher primates, the anthropoids. The anthropoids are the monkeys (New World and Old World) and the hominoids (apes and humans). Studies of primate behavior show behavior patterns common to certain species but also a great deal of variation. The importance of the basic pattern of social learning in primates provides us with the most useful generalization we can extend to the study of human behavior.

Supplemental Readings

Passingham, R. 1982. *The Human Primate*. San Francisco: W. H. Freeman. A detailed examination of human beings in comparison to that of other mammals.

Jolly, A. 1985. *The Evolution of Primate Behavior,* 2d ed. New York: Macmillan.

Richard, A. F. 1985. *Primates in Nature*. New York: W. H. Freeman. These two textbooks provide a comprehensive review of primate biology and behavior.

CHAPTER **8**

Apes and Humans

Perhaps one of our most memorable images of apes comes from the 1933 movie *King Kong*. The giant gorilla discovered on "Skull Island" is captured and brought back to New York City for display as the eighth wonder of the world. Ignoring the fantastic nature of some of the plot elements (gorillas could not be that large and still walk), the film draws close comparisons between Kong's behavior and that of the humans in the film. Kong shows love, curiosity, and anger, among other emotions and behaviors. Kong is a mirror for the humans, and the humans a mirror for Kong.

The Hominoids

Whether we choose to look at apes as humanlike or humans as apelike, the fact remains that of all living creatures, the apes are the most similar to humans in both biology and behavior. From a scientific perspective, we acknowledge this similarity by placing apes and humans in a taxonomic category to distinguish them from the other anthropoids. Apes and humans make up the superfamily of **hominoids,** which literally means "humanlike." Hominoids have certain biological and behavioral characteristics that distinguish them from the monkeys.

Hominoid Characteristics

Unlike monkeys, hominoids do not have tails. Another hominoid characteristic is size: in general, apes and humans are larger than monkeys.

hominoids A superfamily of anthropoids consisting of apes and humans.

176

Hominoid brains as a rule are larger than monkey brains, both in terms of absolute size and in relationship to body size. Their brains are also more complex, which correlates with the hominoid characteristics of greater intelligence and learning abilities. Hominoids are also the most K-selected of the primates; they invest the most time and effort in raising their young.

Hominoids have the same number of teeth as Old World monkeys. The structure of the molar teeth, however, is different in monkeys and hominoids. The most noticeable difference is that the lower molar teeth of hominoids tend to have five **cusps** (raised areas) as compared to the four cusps in the lower molars of monkeys. The deeper grooves between these five cusps form the shape of the letter Y. As such, this characteristic shape is called the "Y-5" pattern (Figure 8.1).

Perhaps one of the most important characteristics of hominoids is their upper body and shoulder anatomy. Hominoids can raise their arms above their heads with little trouble, whereas a monkey would find this difficult. Three basic anatomical features allow hominoids to raise their arms above their heads. First, hominoids have a larger and stronger collarbone than monkeys. Second, the hominoid shoulder joint is very flexible and capable of a wide angle of movement. Third, the hominoid shoulder blades are located more toward their backs. By contrast, monkeys' shoulder blades are located more toward the sides of the chest (Figure 8.2). Hominoid shoulder joints face outward, compared to the downward-facing shoulder joints of monkeys.

Most hominoids have longer front limbs than back limbs. Modern humans are an exception to this rule, with longer legs than arms. This trait facilitates upright walking (discussed later). In apes, the longer front limbs represent an adaptation to hanging from limbs. In addition, hominoids generally have long fingers that help them hang suspended from branches. The wrist joint of hominoids contains a disc of cartilage (called a meniscus) between the lower arm bones and the wrist bones. This disc cuts down on

cusp A raised area on the chewing surface of a tooth.

Figure 8.1

The Y-5 lower molar pattern of hominoids. Circles represent cusps. The heavier line resembles the letter Y on its side.

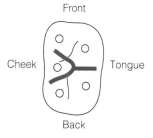

Front

Cheek ··· Tongue

Back

Figure 8.2

Top view of the shoulder complex of a monkey (*right*) and a human (*left*) drawn to the same scale top to bottom. In hominoids (apes and humans), the clavicle is larger and the scapula is located more toward the rear of the body.

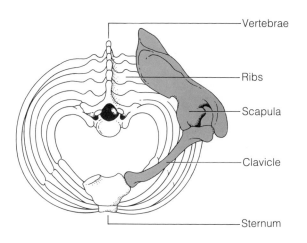

Vertebrae

Ribs

Scapula

Clavicle

Sternum

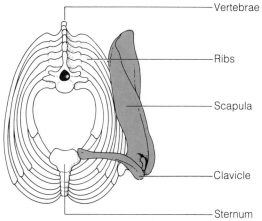

Vertebrae

Ribs

Scapula

Clavicle

Sternum

suspensory climbing and hanging The ability to raise the arms above the head and hang on branches and to climb in this position.

contact between bones. As a result, the wrist joints of hominoids are more flexible than those of monkeys, allowing greater hanging ability.

Hominoid anatomy allows them a different type of movement from that of monkeys. Hominoids are adept at climbing and hanging from branches. They are **suspensory climbers and hangers.** Living hominoids all share this basic ability but vary quite a bit in terms of their normal patterns of movement. Some apes, for example, are proficient arm swingers, whereas others are expert climbers. Humans have evolved a totally different pattern in which the arms are not used for movement, allowing us to carry things while walking on two legs. In spite of these differences in function, the close relationship between apes and humans is seen in their shared characteristics of the upper body and shoulder.

Classification of the Hominoids

Between 8 and 20 million years ago there were many different types of hominoids. Today we have only the representatives of a few surviving species from this once diverse, widespread group. Living hominoids are divided into three categories: the lesser apes, the great apes, and humans. The lesser apes are the gibbon (eight species) and the siamang (one species), and are the least related to humans. The great apes are the Asian orangutan and the African apes, the gorilla and chimpanzee (two species). A list of the scientific and common names of all living hominoids is given in Table 8.1.

T A B L E   8.1
Taxonomy of Living Hominoids

General group	Genus	Species	Common name
Lesser apes	*Hylobates*	*agilis*	Agile gibbon
	Hylobates	*concolor*	Black gibbon
	Hylobates	*hoolock*	Hoolock gibbon
	Hylobates	*klossi*	Kloss's gibbon
	Hylobates	*lar*	White-handed gibbon
	Hylobates	*moloch*	Silvery gibbon
	Hylobates	*muelleri*	Mueller's gibbon
	Hylobates	*pileatus*	Pileated gibbon
	Symphalangus	*syndactylus*	Siamang
Great apes	*Gorilla*	*gorilla*	Gorilla
	Pan	*paniscus*	Pygmy chimpanzee
	Pan	*troglodytes*	Common chimpanzee
	Pongo	*pygmaeus*	Orangutan
Humans	*Homo*	*sapiens*	Human

Source: Jolly (1985:11).

Methods of analysis. For many years, the standard approach has been to compare the physical structure (**morphology**) of these living forms in order to come up with some measure of relatedness. Scientists are now relying on a different type of comparison by looking directly at the biochemistry and genetics of the various hominoid species. Similarities and differences between species are revealed by a number of methods that compare proteins and even the genetic code. Constructing taxonomies from biochemical and genetic data has a definite advantage. If we focus on proteins or sections of DNA not affected by natural selection (or at least those we assume not to be affected), then any degree of similarity should reflect relative evolutionary relationships.

One biochemical method consists of looking at immunological reactions. When foreign molecules are introduced into an animal's blood, the animal's immune system provides a defense by producing antibodies to attack the foreign molecules (antigens). If you mix the antibodies from one species with proteins from the blood serum of another species, this reaction will not be as strong. The strength of this reaction relates to the degree of similarity between the two species being compared. Stronger reactions indicate closer molecular similarity. Because molecular structure reflects genetic factors, the stronger the reaction, the more similar genetically the two species being compared.

Comparison of immunological reactions can be used to assess evolutionary relationships and to construct taxonomies. In the case of the hominoids, such research has shown that the orangutan is distinct from the chimpanzee, gorilla, and human. In other words, the African apes and humans resemble each other more than either resembles the orangutan.

The structure of proteins for two or more species can also be compared. The amino acid sequence for a given protein is compared between two or more species to determine the minimum number of genetic differences between one form and another. The smaller the number of differences, the more closely related the two species.

When applied to many proteins, this method produces the same result as obtained from looking at immunological reactions. Chimpanzees, gorillas, and humans form a closely related group; orangutans are set apart from this group. Gibbons and siamangs are even less similar to African apes and humans. This finding supports the idea that the African apes and humans shared a more recent common ancestor than any of them shared with the orangutan. In terms of a family tree, orangutans split off the main branch earlier than the African apes and humans. Put another way, the African apes are the closest living relatives of humans.

Another method of molecular comparison is DNA hybridization. **DNA hybridization** involves, first, heating the DNA of a given species until the strands separate. Single strands from another species are combined with those from the first species, causing the two strands partially to reassociate. The degree to which the two strands reassociate depends on their overall similarity in DNA. The more closely related two species are,

morphology The physical structure of organisms.

DNA hybridization A method of separating and reassociating strands of DNA in different species to assess their genetic similarity.

Figure 8.3

Traditional taxonomic classification of hominoids. To emphasize certain aspects of behavior and physical characteristics, the orangutan, gorilla, and chimpanzee are placed together in a separate category from humans. Although useful, this classification does not reflect that humans and African apes are more similar to each other than either is to the orangutan. Compare this classification with the one shown in Figure 8.4.

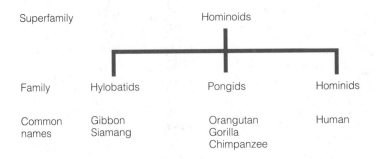

the greater the extent of this reassociation. Similarity between the DNA of two species is assessed by determining the amount of heat needed to break the associated strands apart—the more heat necessary, the more similar the DNA. Such methods have again shown that humans and the African apes are the most similar to each other, followed by the orangutan and then the gibbon.

Models of relationship. What conclusions about hominoid classification can we draw based on these different methods? Anatomical, biochemical, and genetic analyses all support classifications in which the lesser apes (gibbons and siamangs) are distinct from the great apes and humans. In other words, all great apes and humans are more similar to one another than any are to the lesser apes.

The *exact* nature of the relationship among the great apes and humans has long been debated. The oldest of these ideas places all the great apes in a group separate from humans (humans were classified as hominids and all great apes were classified as pongids), implying that all great apes are equally similar to one another and that humans are quite distinct. This model, which had its roots in the then-prevailing concept of human uniqueness, is now rejected. Anatomical and genetic data show that humans and the African apes are more similar to one another than any are to the Asian great ape, the orangutan.

Biochemical and genetic comparisons clearly demonstrate that the African apes and humans are most similar to one another. In a classic study of protein differences and DNA sequences between chimpanzees and humans, King and Wilson (1975) found that the two species are 99 percent identical. Subsequent research confirmed this finding and also found the gorilla to be equally similar. This finding implies that the three species all split from a common ancestor at the same time. (The Asian great ape, the orangutan, is considered separate from these three hominoids.)

The traditional view of humans as separate from all apes is shown in Figure 8.3, which illustrates the traditional taxonomy of hominoids. This perspective is still widespread, in part because it necessitates a separate family (hominids) for human beings and their immediate ancestors. Although many question humans' uniqueness, it is still useful to separate us

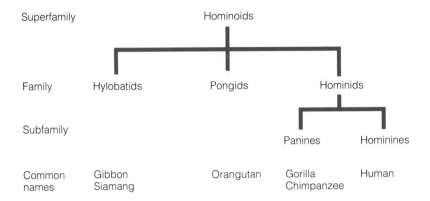

Figure 8.4

Revised taxonomic classification of hominoids. To emphasize evolutionary relationships, the African apes are placed in a separate category from the orangutan. Although useful, this classification does not reflect common and unique aspects of behavior or physical appearance. Compare this classification with the one shown in Figure 8.3.

from the great apes for certain discussions of anatomy, behavior, and evolution.

A different view, based on the cladistic approach, is shown in Figure 8.4, where hominids are considered a family made up of two subfamilies, the African apes and humans. Despite the accuracy gained in reflecting evolutionary relationships, it becomes confusing for some purposes to classify the African apes with humans and apart from the orangutan. Part of the confusion (especially for introductory students) lies in the practice of using taxonomic names. For instance, Figures 8.3 and 8.4 both use the term *hominid,* but in different ways. In this text, we use the traditional taxonomic scheme presented in Figure 8.3.

Another problem in hominoid classification is determining the exact evolutionary relationship between gorillas, chimpanzees, and humans. Figure 8.5 illustrates the two major schools of thought. The traditional view, shown in Figure 8.5a, states that gorillas and chimpanzees are more similar to each other than either is to humans. An alternative view, shown in Figure 8.5b, states that chimpanzees and humans are more similar to each other than either is to gorillas. There continues to be controversy over which view is correct. The close genetic relationship among *all* three hominoids makes precise identification of which two are closer very difficult (Figure 8.6).

Figure 8.5

Alternative evolutionary relationships between humans and the African apes. (a) The African apes are more similar to one another than either is to humans. (b) Chimpanzees and humans are more similar to each other than either is to gorillas. To date, evidence exists to support both views to some extent; the final answer awaits further analysis.

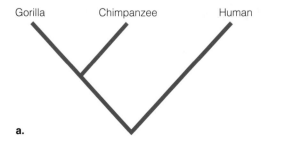

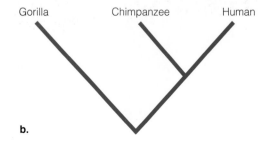

brachiation A method of movement that uses the arms to swing from branch to branch.

The Living Apes

To provide a better comparison of the biology and behavior of the apes and humans, it is necessary to consider briefly the physical characteristics, distribution, environment, and social structure of all of the hominoids. Although the living hominoids all share a number of features, they also show a great deal of biological and behavioral variation.

Gibbons and Siamangs

Physical characteristics. The gibbon and closely related siamang are the smallest of the living apes. There are eight recognized species of gibbon and one species of siamang. For the purpose of this discussion, the term *gibbon* applies to all these forms.

The physical characteristics of gibbons reflect adaptation to life in the trees. The climbing and hanging adaptations of hominoids have evolved in the gibbon to allow highly agile movement through the trees. The gibbon's usual form of movement, known as **brachiation**, consists of hand-over-hand swinging from branch to branch. Many primates are often portrayed as arm swingers, but only the gibbon can perform this movement quickly and efficiently (Figure 8.7).

A number of anatomical adaptations allow gibbons efficient arm swinging. They have small body sizes, weighing 5.5 kg on average (12 lbs) (Richard 1985). Their arms are extremely long relative to their trunks and legs. Gibbon fingers are elongated and their thumbs are relatively short. The long fingers allow gibbons to form a hook with their hands while swinging from branch to branch. The thumb is short enough to prevent its getting in the way while swinging, but still long enough to allow manipulation.

Distribution and environment. Gibbons and siamangs are found in the tropical rain forests of Southeast Asia, specifically Thailand, Vietnam, Burma, and the Malay Peninsula. The rain forest environment is characterized by heavy rainfall that is relatively constant throughout the year. Rain forests have incredibly rich and diverse vegetation. The gibbons' diet consists primarily of fruits supplemented by leaves.

Social structure. The social group of gibbons is a monogamous family structure: an adult male, an adult female, and their offspring. The male and female form a mating pair for their entire lives. For the most part, neither males nor females are dominant over the other. Both exhibit equal levels of aggression. Also, gibbons show almost no sexual dimorphism in body size.

Figure 8.6

The genetic structure of apes is very similar to that of humans. In this picture, a small piece of human DNA from a gene called "U2" is fluorescently labeled (greenish-yellow dots) and hybridized to chromosomes from a gorilla (blue). Because of the similarity of base pairs of humans and apes, the human DNA binds to its complementary sequence in the gorilla, revealing the location of the gene in that species.   (© Jon Marks from the *Journal of Human Evolution*, March 1993; with permission of the Academic Press, London)

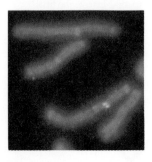

Figure 8.7

A siamang holding onto a rock with one of its long arms. Siamangs and gibbons are the most acrobatic of the apes and can swing by their arms. (© Zoological Society of San Diego)

Orangutans

The orangutan is a large ape found only in certain areas of Southeast Asia. The word *orangutan* translates from Malay as "man of the forest."

Physical characteristics. One of the orangutan's most obvious physical features is its reddish brown hair (Figure 8.8). Males are roughly twice the size of females; an average adult male weighs between 80 and 90 kg (roughly 175 to 200 lbs), and an average adult female weighs between 33 and 45 kg (roughly 73 to 99 lbs) (Markham and Groves 1990). Males also have large pads of fat on their faces.

Orangutans are agile climbers and hangers. In the trees, they use both arms and legs to climb in a slow, cautious manner. They will use one or more limbs to anchor themselves to branches while using the other limbs to feed (Figure 8.9). Younger orangutans occasionally brachiate, but the larger adults generally move through the trees in a different manner. A large orangutan will not swing from one tree to the next; rather, it will rock the tree it is on slowly in the direction of the next tree and then move

over when the two trees are close together. The orangutan's great agility in climbing is due, in part, to its basic hominoid shoulder structure.

Orangutans are largely arboreal. Males, however, frequently come to the ground and travel along the forest floor for long distances. On the ground, orangutans walk on all fours but with their fists partially closed. Unlike monkeys, who rest their weight on their palms, orangutans rest on their fists: a form of movement often called fist walking.

Distribution and environment. The orangutan is found today only in Sumatra and Borneo in Southeast Asia. Orangutans are vegetarians, with over 60 percent of their diet consisting of fruit (Jolly 1985). As does the gibbon, the orangutan lives in tropical rain forests.

Figure 8.9

An orangutan foraging in
the trees.   (Animals Animals
© Mickey Gibson)

Social structure. The basic social group of orangutans is the mother-infant group. Males are not needed for protection because there is little danger from predators (Horr 1972). Adult males generally live by themselves, interacting only during times of mating. Orangutans are polygamous; they do not form long-term bonds with any one partner. The small group size of orangutans appears to be related to the nature of the environment; when food resources are widely scattered, there is not enough food in any one place for large groups (Denham 1971).

knuckle walking A form of movement used by chimpanzees and gorillas that is characterized by all four limbs touching the ground, with the weight of the arms resting on the knuckles of the hands.

Gorillas

Gorillas, the largest living primates, are found only in equatorial Africa.

Physical characteristics. An adult male gorilla weighs 160 kg (roughly 350 lbs) on average. Adult females weigh less but are still very large for primates (70 kg/155 lbs) (Leutenegger 1982). Besides a much larger body size, the adult males also have larger canine teeth and often large crests of bone on top of their skulls for anchoring their large jaw muscles. Gorillas usually have blackish hair; fully mature adult males have silvery gray hair on their backs. These adult males are called "silverbacks."

Their large size makes gorillas predominantly terrestrial. Their typical means of movement is called **knuckle walking:** they move about on all fours, resting their weight on the knuckles of their front limbs. This form of movement is different from the fist walking of orangutans. Gorilla hands have well-developed muscles and strengthened joints to handle the stress of resting on their knuckles. Because their arms are longer than their legs, gorilla spines are at an angle to the ground. In contrast, the spine of a typical quadrupedal animal, such as a monkey, is roughly parallel to the ground when walking (Figure 8.10).

Distribution and environment. Gorillas are found only in certain forested areas in Africa. Their range is disappearing rapidly, primarily as

Figure 8.10

An adult male gorilla knuckle walking. Note the angle of the spine relative to the ground, because of the longer front limbs.   (© Zoological Society of San Diego)

Figure 8.11

A gorilla social group.
(© Michael K. Nichols/Magnum
Photos Inc.)

the result of the replacement of forests by human farming land and human poaching (Fossey 1983). Gorillas live in humid rain forests in both the lowlands and in the mountain regions. Compared to the rain forests of the orangutans, the gorilla's environment is characterized by greater clumping of food resources (Denham 1971).

Many myths have circulated about the gorilla's lust for human and nonhuman flesh, but the truth of the matter is that gorillas are exclusively vegetarian. Over 85 percent of their diet consists of leaves (Jolly 1985). In fact, the intestinal tracts of gorillas are somewhat specialized for the digestion of leaves.

Social structure. Gorillas live in small social groups of about a dozen individuals. The social group consists of an adult male (the silverback), several adult females, and their immature offspring (Figure 8.11). Occasionally one or more younger adult males are part of the group, but they tend not to mate with the females. Though dominance rank varies among the females and subadult males, the adult silverback male is the most dominant individual in the group and is the leader. The silverback sets the pace for the rest of the group, determining when and how far to move in search of food.

Chimpanzees

The chimpanzee is perhaps the best known of all the nonhuman primates. Most of our experience with chimpanzees, however, is with captive or trained animals. We like to watch chimpanzees perform "just like humans" and delight in a chimpanzee's smile (which actually signals tension, not pleasure).

From a scientific perspective, chimpanzees are equally fascinating. Genetic studies during the last 20 years have shown that humans and chimpanzees are even more similar than they were previously thought to be. Laboratory and field studies have shown that chimpanzees are capable of behaviors we once thought of as unique to humans, such as toolmaking and language acquisition. Any examination of the human condition must take these remarkable creatures's accomplishments into account.

Physical characteristics. There are two living species of chimpanzee, both found in Africa: the common chimpanzee and the lesser-known pygmy chimpanzee (Figure 8.12). Unless otherwise indicated, all information here refers to the common chimpanzee. Chimpanzees are smaller than gorillas and show only slight sexual dimorphism. Adult males weigh about 45 kg (99 lbs) on average and adult females weigh about 37 kg (82 lbs) on average (Leutenegger 1982). Chimpanzees have extremely powerful shoulders and arms. Like humans, chimpanzees show great variation in facial features and overall physical appearance (Figure 8.13).

Chimpanzees, like gorillas, are knuckle walkers with longer arms than legs. Chimpanzees, however, are more active and agile than gorillas. Chimpanzees are both terrestrial and arboreal. They spend considerable time in the trees, either sleeping or looking for food. They often hang by their

Figure 8.12

A pygmy chimpanzee.
(© Frans Lanting/Minden Pictures)

Figure 8.13

Variation in chimpanzee faces.
(© Wrangham/Anthro-Photo)

arms in the trees. On the ground, they sometimes stand on two legs to carry food or sticks.

Distribution and environment. Most chimpanzees are found in the African rain forests, although some groups are also found in the mixed forest–savanna environments on the fringe of the rain forests. The chimpanzee diet consists mainly of fruit (almost 70 percent), although they also eat leaves, seeds, nuts, insects, and meat. Chimpanzees have been observed hunting small animals, such as monkeys, and sharing the meat.

Social structure. Chimpanzees live in rather large multimale groups of 50 or more individuals. All chimpanzees in the social group recognize and interact with others in the group. Chimpanzee groups are less rigid than other multimale primate societies such as baboons. Although all members of the group do interact to some extent, it is common for smaller subgroups to form much of the time. The actual composition of these subgroups also changes frequently.

Most social behaviors revolve around the bond between mother and child (Figure 8.14). Chimpanzees tend to associate with their mothers and other siblings throughout their lives, even after they are fully grown. As with other primates, young females watch and observe their own mothers taking care of children and learn mothering behaviors. There is no close bond between adult males and infants except for associations through the mother. Overall, chimpanzee society can be seen as a collection of smaller

groups, defined in terms of mothers and siblings, forming a larger community. Other associations are also common, such as temporary all-male
groups. Some chimpanzees are even solitary for periods of time.

Adult males are generally dominant over adult females, although
there is much more overlap than found in baboon societies. Some females,
for example, are dominant over the lower-ranking males. As with other
primates, dominance is influenced by a variety of factors such as size,
strength, and the ability to form alliances. Individual intelligence also
appears to affect dominance, as was revealed in Jane Goodall's study of the
chimpanzees in the Gombe Stream National Park near Lake Tanganyika.
In 1964 the community studied by Goodall had 14 adult males. The

lowest-ranking male (Mike) replaced the most dominant male (Goliath) after inventing a particularly innovative display of dominance. There were a number of empty kerosene cans lying around Goodall's camp that the chimpanzees generally ignored. Mike would charge other males while hitting the cans in front of him, creating an unusual and very noisy display. This behavior was so intimidating to other males that Mike rose from the lowest to the highest rank at once (Goodall 1986).

Studies of the Gombe Stream chimpanzee community have also revealed a number of other interesting features of chimpanzee social behaviors and intelligence. The chimpanzees have been observed to make and use tools (discussed at length later in this chapter), hunt in cooperative groups, and sometimes engage in widespread aggression against other groups. We will examine some of these findings when we consider what behaviors may be considered uniquely human.

hominid Humans and humanlike ancestors.

Modern Humans

Humans are the last of the primates we will study and the most widely distributed in spite of our origin in a specific environment. Humans and humanlike ancestors are also known by the term **hominid.**

Distribution and Environment

As later chapters will outline, humans evolved in a tropical environment. In fact, much of our present-day biology reflects the fact that we are tropical mammals. During the course of human evolution, however, we have expanded into many different environments. Biological adaptations have aided humans in new environments, such as cold weather and high altitude. The cultural adaptations of humans have allowed even greater expansion. Today there is no place on the planet where we cannot live, given the appropriate technology. Humans can live in the frozen wastes of Antarctica, deep beneath the sea, and in the vacuum of outer space.

Brain Size and Structure

One very obvious biological characteristic of the human species is the large brain. Our bulging and rounded skulls and flat faces contrast with these features in other animals, including the rest of the hominoids. Whereas an ape's skull is characterized by a relatively small brain and large face, modern humans have relatively large brains and small faces.

Table 8.2 lists the brain size (in milliliters) for a number of primate species. There is a clear relationship between taxonomic status and brain size: monkeys have the smallest brains, followed by the lesser apes, great apes, and humans. Absolute brain size is not as useful a measure of intel-

TABLE 8.2
Brain Volume of Selected Living Primates (in Milliliters)

Primate species	Range	Average
Macaque monkey		100
Baboon		200
White-handed gibbon	82–125	102
Siamang	100–152	124
Orangutan	276–540	404
Gorilla	340–752	495
Common chimpanzee	282–500	385
Modern human	900–2000	1345

Averages for macaque and baboon from Campbell (1985:233).
Hominoid data from Tobias (1971:34–40), where the averages
were taken as the means of males and females.

allometry The change in proportion of various body parts as a consequence of different growth rates.

lectual ability because larger animals tend to have larger brains. Elephants and whales, for example, have brains that are four to five times the size of the average human brain.

Among mammals, the relationship of brain and body weight is not linear. That is, as the body size increases, the brain size increases—although not at the same rate. Differences in size because of disparate growth rates among various parts of the body (known as **allometry**) are common. Parts of the body grow at different rates. Brain size increases at a nonlinear rate with body size. For example, consider two species of primates in which one species is twice the body weight of the other. If the ratio of brain size to body size were linear, we would expect the brain size of the species with the larger body size to be twice that of the lighter species. Actually, the brain size of the larger-bodied species is on average only 1.6 times as large. Because of this relationship, larger species appear to have smaller brain/body size ratios.

This allometric relationship between brain size and body size is quite regular among almost all primate species. The most notable exception is humans. We have brains that are three times the size we would expect for a primate of our size (Passingham 1982). In addition, our brains have proportionately more cerebral cortex than other primate brains. The cerebral cortex is the part of the brain involved in forming complex associations.

What exactly is the relationship between brain size, relative to body size, and intelligence? This question has been long debated, but with little resolution. A recent study by Willerman and colleagues (1991) helps resolve some of the conflict. They measured the brain size of 40 adults using magnetic resonance imaging and compared these values, adjusted for body size, with IQ test scores. Adjusting their results to the general population, they found a correlation of 0.35 between relative brain size and IQ scores (a positive correlation can take on a value from 0 to 1; the higher the value, the closer the correspondence). In statistical terms, this finding means that roughly 12 percent of the observed variation in IQ test scores is related to variation in relative brain size. However, this also indicates that 88 percent of the observed variation in IQ scores is *not* related to such variation. Overall, the results show that relative brain size is a contributing factor, but not the only one. In terms of evolution, the correlation is sufficient to show that natural selection has had an impact over many generations. However, the correlation is also low enough that one could not predict accurately a person's IQ from his or her relative brain size.

Recent studies have also looked at the relationship among brain size, body size, and metabolism. Larger mammals have larger brain sizes and produce greater amounts of metabolic energy. Mammals show a great deal of variation, however, in the amount of energy used by the brain. The brains of many mammals, such as dogs and cats, use 4 to 6 percent of their body metabolism. Primate brains use a considerably greater proportion of energy; the Old World macaque uses 9 percent and modern humans use 20 percent (Armstrong 1983).

What does all this mean? The human brain is not merely large; it also has a different structure than other primates, with the cortex being disproportionately larger. This difference in structure is also probably related to the higher proportion of metabolic energy used by the human brain. The bottom line is that brain size does not tell the whole story. Thus, the human brain is not only larger than the brain of a chimpanzee; it is also structurally different. The increased convolution of the human cerebral cortex (the folding of brain tissue) means that the brain of a human child with the same volume of that of a chimpanzee has more cerebral cortex.

Bipedalism

Another striking difference between humans and apes is the fact that humans walk on two legs. We are **bipedal** (meaning "two legs"). This does not mean that apes cannot walk on two legs. They can, but not as well and not as often. The physical structure of human beings shows adaptations for upright walking as the normal mode of movement.

The human form of bipedal movement is best characterized as a "striding gait." Consider walking in slow motion. What happens? First, you stand balanced on two legs. Then you move one leg forward. You shift your body weight so that your weight is transferred to the moving leg. As that leg touches the ground on its heel, all your body weight has been shifted. Your other leg is then free to swing forward. As it does so, you push off with your other foot.

Human bipedalism is made possible by anatomical changes involving the toes, legs, spine, pelvis, and muscles. In terms of actual anatomy, these changes are not major: after all, no bones are added or deleted; the same

bipedal Moving about on two legs. Unlike the movement of other bipedal animals such as kangaroos, human bipedalism is further characterized by a striding motion.

bones can be found in humans and in apes. The changes involve shape, positioning, and function. The net effect of these changes, however, is dramatic. Humans can move about effectively on two legs, allowing the other limbs to be free for other activities.

The feet of human beings reflect adaptation to bipedalism. The feet of a human and a chimp are shown in Figure 8.15. The big toe of the chimp sticks out in the same way that the thumb of all hominoids sticks out from the other fingers. The divergent big toe allows chimps to grasp with their feet. The big toe of the human is tucked in next to the other toes. When we walk, we use the nondivergent big toe to push off during our strides.

Our balance while we stand and walk is partly the result of changes in our legs. Figure 8.16 shows a human skeleton from the frontal view. Note that the width of the body at the knees is less than the width of the body at the hips. Humans are literally "knock-kneed." Our upper leg bones (the femurs) slope inward from the hips. When we stand on one leg, the angle of the femur transmits our weight directly underneath us. The result is that we continue to be balanced while one leg is moving. In contrast, the angle of an ape femur is very slight. The legs of an ape are almost parallel from hips to feet. When an ape stands on two legs and moves one of them, the ape is off balance and tends to fall toward one side. When an ape walks on two legs, it must shift its whole body weight over the supporting leg to stay on balance. This shifting explains the characteristic waddling when apes walk on two legs.

Figure 8.15

The skeletal structure of the feet of a chimpanzee (*left*) and a modern human (*right*). Note how the big toe of the human lies parallel to the other toes.

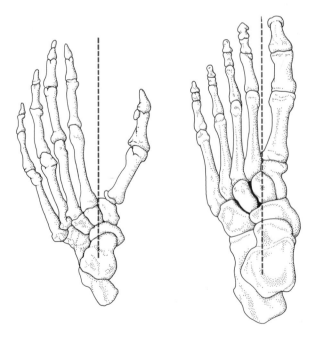

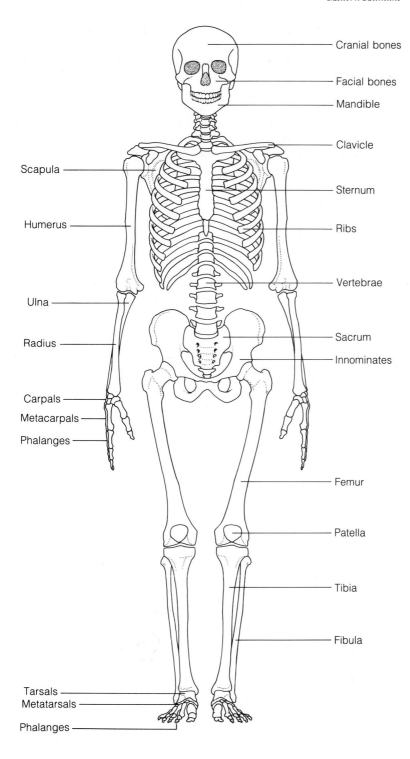

Cranial bones

Facial bones

Mandible

Clavicle

Scapula

Sternum

Humerus

Ribs

Vertebrae

Ulna

Radius

Sacrum

Innominates

Carpals

Metacarpals

Phalanges

Femur

Patella

Tibia

Fibula

Tarsals

Metatarsals

Phalanges

Figure 8.16

The modern human skeleton from a frontal view.

The human spine also allows balance when we walk upright (Figure 8.17). The spinal column of humans is vertical, allowing weight to be transmitted down through the center of the body. In knuckle-walking apes, the spine is bent in an arc so that when they stand on two legs the center of gravity is shifted in front of the body. The ape is off balance and must compensate greatly to stay upright. What is difficult for apes is easy for humans. The human spine is vertical but not straight. It curves in several places, allowing it to absorb the shocks occurring while we walk.

The human pelvis is shaped differently than an ape pelvis (Figure 8.18). It is shorter top to bottom, and wider side to side. The sides of the pelvis are broader and flair out more to the sides, providing changes in

Figure 8.17

Side view of the skeletons of a chimpanzee (*left*) and a modern human (*right*), illustrating the shape and orientation of the spine.   (Adapted with permission from: Bernard Campbell, *Human Evolution,* Third Edition [New York: Aldine de Gruyter]. Copyright © 1985 Bernard Campbell)

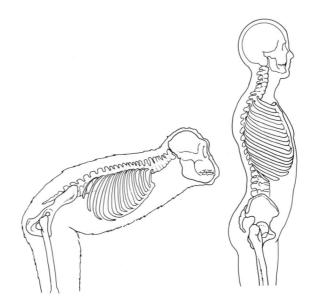

Figure 8.18

The trunk skeletons of a modern human (*left*) and a chimpanzee (*right*) drawn to the same size. Note the proportionately shorter and wider pelvis of the human being, reflecting adaptations to upright walking (see text).   (Adapted with permission from: Bernard Campbell, *Human Evolution,* Third Edition [New York: Aldine de Gruyter]. Copyright © 1985 Bernard Campbell)

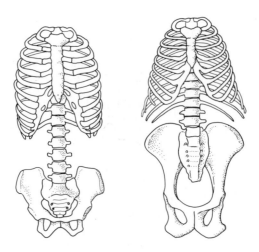

muscle attachment that permit striding bipedalism. The shortness of the human pelvis allows greater stability when we stand upright. The changes in the human pelvis also involve changes in the positioning of various muscles.

Canine Teeth

As we saw in the last chapter, human canine teeth are different from canine teeth in many other mammals. Human canines are small and do not project beyond the level of the other teeth. Human canine teeth serve much the same function as the incisor teeth.

That we have small nonprojecting canines has led to much speculation concerning causes and effects of human evolution. Given that canine teeth serve as weapons in many primate species, the lack of large canine teeth in humans seems to imply that we do not need them for weapons anymore. One scenario is that when human ancestors began using tools, they no longer required large canines. As you will see in later chapters, the uniqueness of human canine teeth is a bit more complex a topic than we once thought.

Sex and Reproduction

We humans consider ourselves the sexiest primates. That is, we are more concerned with sex than is any other primate. The fact that humans do not have the estrus cycle has often been cited as a unique aspect of human sexuality. For the most part, temperate-zone domestic animals breed only during certain seasons and mate around the time of ovulation. Human females, in contrast, cycle throughout the year and often mate at any time during the cycle. This may be a primitive characteristic, however. Some mice and rats cycle continuously. Also, as noted earlier in this chapter, it now appears that orangutans also lack the estrus cycle. In addition, recent field studies on other primates suggest that many individuals mate outside the usual cycle to some extent, such as pygmy chimpanzees (Jolly 1985).

The human pattern of reproduction is basically the same as that of most primates: single births. Unlike apes, humans have additional children before the previous children have grown up socially or physically. Because of cultural adaptations, humans have reduced their amount of K-selection without sacrificing parental care. In fact, a greater proportion of the human life span is taken up in infancy and childhood. Compared to the other hominoids, we mature more slowly and require a greater amount of our life for learning.

Social Structure

Human social structure is a topic of almost infinite complexity that is thoroughly explored in cultural anthropology textbooks. One observation

polygyny A form of marriage in which a husband has several wives.

polyandry A form of marriage in which a wife has several husbands.

is obvious—there is extensive variation. Because variation in social structure is great even among the apes, it should come as no surprise that humans, with an even greater emphasis on learned behavior, show greater variation.

A common Western assumption is that the "normal" social structure of human beings is the nuclear monogamous family group: mother, father, and children. Actually, the majority (almost 90 percent) of human societies prefer **polygyny**—a pattern in which one husband has several wives (Harris 1987). In such societies, however, it is still common for many men to have only a single wife. Though multiple wives are permitted, and preferred, many men lack the necessary economic or political status required for many wives. A very few cultures practice **polyandry,** in which one woman has several husbands. The common element in all human social structures is the existence of some mechanism for the care and education of the children.

Are Humans Unique?

Humans and apes show a great many similarities as well as a great many differences. When we ask whether humans are unique we do not suggest that we cannot tell an ape and a human apart. Rather, we ask what the extent of these differences is. Are the behaviors of apes and humans completely different, or are differences present only in the expression of specific behaviors? Can we say, for example, that humans make tools and apes do not? Or should we say instead that there are differences in the way in which these two groups make and use tools?

Tool Use and Manufacture

Tool use has often been cited as a unique human behavior. As defined here, a tool is an object that is not part of the animal. Human tools include pencils, clothes, eating utensils, books, and houses. All of these are objects that are not part of the biological organism (humans) but are used for a specific purpose. Tool use, however, does not seem to even be a unique primate characteristic. Birds use sticks for nests and beavers use dirt in their dams. Both sticks and dirt could be considered tools by this definition.

A more common definition of modern humans focuses on humans as toolmakers (this definition is complicated by the fact that the earliest hominids may not have made tools—see Chapter 10). The key element of this definition is that some object is taken from the environment and modified to meet a new function. Humans take trees to make lumber to build houses. It can be argued that birds modify sticks and beavers modify dirt, but tool manufacture implies something different. Birds, for example, use sticks for building nests but do not use these sticks for defensive or offensive weapons. Humans, on the other hand, can take sticks and use them to make shelters, defend themselves, hunt, dig up roots, and draw pictures in the sand. When we discuss tool manufacture, we mean the new and different ways to modify an object for a task. Humans can apply the same raw materials to a variety of tasks.

In this sense, tool manufacture has long been considered a unique human activity. But research on apes, particularly Goodall's work on chimpanzees, has since shown that this is not true. Apes make and use tools. Though their tools are extremely simple by modern human standards, it is clear that the difference between apes and humans cannot be reduced to humans making tools and apes not making tools. Differences exist in the method and uses of manufactured tools, but not the presence or absence of toolmaking.

Chimpanzee termite fishing. In the early 1960s, Jane Goodall reported a remarkable finding—chimpanzees were making and using tools! Though chimpanzees are predominantly fruit eaters, they also enjoy a variety of other foods, including termites. One group of chimpanzees demonstrated a method for capturing termites. They took a grass stem or a stick, went up to a termite mound, and uncovered one of the entrance holes left by the termites. They inserted the stick into the hole, twirled the stick a bit to attract termites down in the mound, and then withdrew the stick. Termites attached themselves to the stick, and the chimpanzees ate the termites directly off the stick.

Close analysis of this "termite fishing" behavior shows it to be true tool manufacture along with rather complex tool use. Chimpanzees often spent a great deal of time selecting the appropriate stick. When a suitable stick was not available, they pulled a branch out of the ground or off a bush and stripped away the leaves. This is deliberate manipulation of an object in the environment—toolmaking. The act also reflects a conscious decision-making process.

Termite fishing is not an innate chimpanzee behavior. It is passed on to others in the group by means of learning. Young chimpanzees watch their elders and imitate them, thus learning the methods and also developing practice. Termite fishing has become part of the local group's culture.

Other examples of toolmaking. Termite fishing is only one of many types of tool manufacture reported among chimpanzees. Sticks are also used to hunt for ants (Figure 8.19). A chimpanzee will dig up an underground nest with its hands and then insert a long stick into the nest. The ants begin swarming up the stick and the chimpanzee withdraws it to eat the ants. Sticks have also been used to probe holes in dead wood and to break into ant and bee nests (Goodall 1986).

Chimpanzees have also been observed to make sponges out of leaves. After a rainfall, a chimpanzee often drinks out of pools of water that collect in the holes of tree branches. Often the holes are too small for the chimp

Figure 8.19

The chimpanzees have fashioned simple tools to fish for ants. The infant chimpanzee watches and learns this process.   (James Moore/Anthro-Photo)

to fit its head into, so the chimp creates a tool to soak up the water: he takes a leaf, puts it in his mouth, and chews it slightly. (Chewing increases the ability of the leaf to absorb water.) The chimp inserts this "sponge" into the hole in the branch to soak up the water. Other examples of chimpanzee toolmaking and tool use include using leaves as napkins and toilet paper, using sticks as weapons, and using rocks to break open nuts and hard fruits (Goodall 1986).

In recent years, researchers have observed that toolmaking and tool use are not specieswide characteristics among chimpanzees. Not all groups have shown the same behaviors. Some use sticks for ant or termite fishing or sponges for drinking; others do not (McGrew 1992).

Human and chimpanzee toolmaking.   It is obvious that chimpanzees make and use tools in a systematic manner. It is also clear that they use genuine problem-solving abilities in their toolmaking. They see a problem (e.g., termites in the mounds) and create a tool to solve the problem. The implication of these studies is that we can no longer define humans as the only toolmakers. Our definition must be modified, and we must focus on differences in toolmaking between apes and humans.

There are several important differences between chimpanzee and human toolmaking and tool use. First, humans depend on tools; chimpanzees do not. Termite fishing provides a tasty treat for the chimpanzees, but it is not essential for their survival. Chimpanzees survive without tools in many places. Humans, on the other hand, depend on tools for survival. Toolmaking and tool use are not an option for humans; they are an imperative.

A second difference is that humans save their tools. Chimpanzees start over each time they make a tool. Chimpanzees who fish termites do not save the sticks they have made. Humans save their tools, presumably because of the greater importance tools have for human survival.

Third, humans use tools to make other tools. This allows for the construction of a complex technological system. Thus far, no one has seen chimpanzees do this. A further key distinction of modern humans is that we accumulate our knowledge of toolmaking, building on it generation after generation.

Language Capabilities

Language has long been considered a unique human property. Language is not merely communication but rather a symbolic form of communication. The nonhuman primates communicate basic emotions in a variety of ways. Chimpanzees, for example, have a large number of vocalizations that they use to convey emotional states such as anger, fear, or stress (Figure 8.20). Many primates also use their sense of touch to communicate some emotions by **grooming,** the handling and cleaning of another individual's fur (Figure 8.21). Grooming helps keep the animals clean and also acts to soothe and reassure tense or frightened individuals. Grooming is a common form of social communication among primates.

What is language? Primate communication through vocalizations, grooming, or other methods does not constitute language. Language, as a symbolic form of communication, has certain characteristics that distin-

grooming The handling and cleaning of another individual's fur or hair. In primates, grooming serves as a form of communication that soothes and provides reassurance.

Figure 8.20

A chimpanzee hooting. (Marine World Africa USA/ Darryl W. Bush, Photographer)

Figure 8.21

Two chimpanzees grooming. (Marine World Africa USA/ Darryl W. Bush, Photographer)

guish it from simple communication. Language is an *open system;* that is, new ideas can be expressed that have never been expressed before. Chimpanzee vocalizations, on the other hand, form a closed system capable of only conveying a few basic concepts or emotions. Human language can use a finite number of sounds and create an infinite number of words, sentences, and ideas from these sounds.

Another important characteristic of language is *displacement*. Language allows discussion of objects and events that are displaced—that is, not present—in time and/or space. For example, you can say, "Tomorrow I am going to another country." This sentence conveys an idea that is displaced in both time ("tomorrow") and space ("the other country"). We can discuss the past, the future, and faraway places. Displacement is very important for our ability to plan future events—imagine the difficulty in planning a hunt several days from now without the ability to speak of future events!

Language is also arbitrary. The actual sounds we use in our languages need not bear any relationship to reality. Our word for "book" could just as easily be "gurmf" or some other sound. The important point is that we understand the relationship of sounds to objects and ideas. This in turn shows yet another important feature of language—it is learned.

Apes and American Sign Language. Early efforts to teach English to apes were failures. One classic experiment was conducted on a young female chimpanzee named Vicki. After years of extensive work Vicki could only speak four words: "Mama," "Papa," "up," and "cup." Later researchers noted that the failure of this experiment might mean only that apes cannot speak English; it said nothing about their ability to understand. Looking back at this study, it is no surprise that Vicki could not speak very well, because the vocal anatomy of chimpanzees makes speaking a human language next to impossible.

In the 1960s, two scientists, Allen and Beatrice Gardner, began teaching the American Sign Language to a young female chimpanzee named Washoe. Devised for the deaf, American Sign Language (ASL) is a true symbolic language that does not require vocalization but instead uses hand and finger gestures. Because chimpanzees are capable of making such signs, ASL is the most suitable medium to determine whether or not they are capable of using language (Figure 8.22). Washoe quickly learned many signs and soon developed an extensive vocabulary.

Washoe also demonstrated the ability to generalize: to take a concept learned in one context and apply it to another. For example, she would use the sign meaning *open* to refer to boxes as well as doors. This suggests that Washoe truly understood the general concept of *open* and not just the use of the sign in one specific context. Washoe also invented new signs and "talked" to herself while playing alone, an act human children perform when learning language. Washoe was even observed to swear!

Figure 8.22

A chimpanzee is using the American Sign Language to convey the message "more eat." (H. S. Terrace/Anthro-Photo)

One of the most intriguing findings of the Gardners' research was that Washoe would form simple two- and three-word sentences (for example, "You tickle me"). Early observations suggested that Washoe was not only capable of symbolism but also of grammar and sentence construction.

Washoe was the first ape taught American Sign Language. Since then there have been many experiments into the nature of language capabilities of the apes. Gorillas, as well as chimpanzees, have been taught ASL. Other languages were also invented, including one based on plastic tiles and another using a computer keyboard. Experiments were devised that required two chimpanzees to interact with each other using language. These experiments confirmed the ability to generalize signs and to create new ones.

Human and ape language abilities. The purpose of the original research with Washoe was to determine what was unique about the way in which a human child learns language. It was suggested that a comparison of human and chimpanzee language acquisition would reveal at what point human abilities surpassed those of the ape. Washoe's abilities exceeded early expectations, and soon the research focus shifted to the language capabilities of the apes themselves. The ability of Washoe and other apes to learn a symbolic language suggested that language acquisition could no longer be regarded as a unique human feature.

There is considerable debate about the meaning of these studies. Some claim that many of the positive results are the result of unconscious cues given to the apes by humans. Also, there is the problem of interpreting the data and seeing what one wants to see. For example, Washoe signed "water bird" the first time she saw a swan. Some researchers have interpreted this as a true invention. Others have suggested that Washoe simply saw the water and then the bird, and responded with the two signs in sequence.

In spite of the debates, there is little doubt that apes can learn and understand the meaning of many signs. Chimpanzees, gorillas, and orangutans have all mastered a certain number. Some chimps have learned over 150 signs by the time they were 7 years old (Snowden 1990). Carefully controlled experiments have shown that the basic vocabulary of apes is not a reflection of unconscious cues given by the scientists. The behavior of signing correctly while playing alone strongly suggests that the apes actually do understand, *in some manner,* the meaning of signs.

Much of the controversy over language acquisition in apes revolves around two different training approaches. Many studies, including the Washoe project, attempted to teach language in an environment similar to that in which human children develop linguistic skills, one offering continued exposure in an unstructured environment with many opportunities for creativity and expression. Other ape studies used controlled, less flexible environments. The controlled experiments were of course designed to minimize cues from humans and to provide more definitive measurements. The problem is that this type of sterile approach is not the most conducive to learning language.

One of the most interesting observations came about by accident during a study conducted by Savage-Rumbaugh, in which researchers were attempting to teach a female pygmy chimpanzee a keyboard-based language. At the time, the chimp was caring for an infant, Kanzi, who frequently interrupted his mother. Later, when the mother was returned to the breeding colony, Kanzi began to use the keyboard to make requests. Over time, he performed well on a variety of measures (Snowden 1990). Significantly, he learned language by observation, and not through direct training. (After all, the experiment was not designed to teach him; he was simply there to be nursed.) In other words, Kanzi learned elements of language in the same way that human children do.

The suggested ability of apes to understand grammar and to construct sentences is also controversial. Though apes do create correct two- and three-word sentences, the few longer sentences they create are often grammatically incorrect. There has also been evidence that the apes respond to unconscious cues in constructing sentences (as opposed to simple vocabulary identification). Though some see definite evidence of grammar (e.g., Linden 1981), others see little evidence (e.g., Terrace 1979). The debate continues.

Regardless of the outcome, it is clear that the difference between human and ape is not as great as we once thought. We can no longer define modern humans in terms of the capability to learn certain aspects of symbolic language. Apes are certainly capable of symbolic behavior, even if we can debate over exactly how much. Both humans and apes can learn symbols, though humans are clearly better at it. Perhaps one of the major differences is the fact that humans rely on language and apes do not. In their natural habitat, apes do not use sign language. The fact that they are capable of learning language to a certain extent should not detract from the point that they do not use language in their natural environment. As with tool manufacture, we see evidence of capabilities in the apes for behaviors that are optional for them but mandatory for modern humans.

SUMMARY

The hominoids (apes and humans) are a group of anthropoids that share certain characteristics, such as the lack of a tail, similar dental features, larger brains, and a shoulder complex suitable for climbing and hanging. The hominoids consist of the lesser apes (gibbon and siamang), the great apes (orangutan, gorilla, and chimpanzee), and humans. Biochemical analyses show that the African apes—the gorilla and chimpanzee—are the most similar to modern humans.

The living apes show a great deal of environmental and anatomical variation. Some are arm swingers (gibbon, siamang), others are knuckle walkers (gorilla, chimpanzee), and one is a climber (orangutan). In spite of the fact that the apes are all similar genetically and have a fairly recent common ancestor (less than 20 million years ago), they show a great deal of social variation. Gibbons and siamangs live in family groups, the orangutan lives in mother-infant groups, the gorilla lives in one-male groups, and chimpanzees live in large multimale communities.

Humans share many features with the other hominoids but also show a number of differences. The main biological characteristics of humans are the large and complex brain, bipedalism, and small canine teeth. All humans live in groups, but a great deal of variation exists from one culture to the next in the exact form of social structure.

Past behavioral definitions of humans have often focused on humans as toolmakers and users of symbolic language. Recent studies of toolmaking and language acquisition in apes show that this definition must be modified. Modern humans remain unique in the specific ways they use tools and language and in their reliance on these behaviors for survival. What is mandatory for modern humans is optional for apes.

Supplemental Readings

Goodall, J. 1986. *The Chimpanzees of Gombe: Patterns of Behavior*. Cambridge: Harvard University Press. A comprehensive review of Jane Goodall's research on chimpanzee behavior since the early 1960s, this is a well-written and superbly illustrated description of all aspects of chimpanzee behavior.

Fossey, D. 1983. *Gorillas in the Mist*. Boston: Houghton Mifflin. A popular and well-written account of the late Dian Fossey's researches on the behavior of the mountain gorilla. Deals specifically with the problem of human intervention and the likely extinction of the mountain gorilla.

Linden, E. 1981. *Apes, Men, and Language*. Middlesex, England: Penguin.

McGrew, W. C. 1992. *Chimpanzee Material Culture: Implications for Human Evolution*. Cambridge: Cambridge University Press. A recent review of the nature of chimpanzee tool use, with an emphasis on variation in behaviors.

Passingham, R. 1982. *The Human Primate*. San Francisco: W. H. Freeman. A detailed examination of the human species from both a biological and behavioral perspective.

Patterson, F., and E. Linden. 1981. *The Education of Koko*. New York: Holt, Rinehart and Winston.

Terrace, H. S. 1979. *Nim: A Chimpanzee Who Learned Sign Language*. New York: Alfred A. Knopf. This book, along with Linden (1981) and Patterson and Linden (1981), presents different views of the research into the abilities of apes to learn American Sign Language.

CHAPTER 9

The Origin and Evolution of the Primates

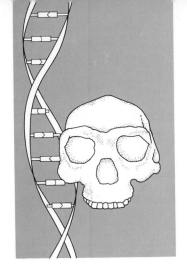

This chapter reviews the fossil evidence for the origin and evolution of the primates, emphasizing the major events in primate evolution between 5 and 65 million years ago. Since the past 65 million years is but a fraction of the 4.6-billion-year history of our planet, and since the origin of primates has its roots in previous patterns of vertebrate and mammalian evolution, it is necessary to review briefly some major events in evolution *before* the primates.

The Fossil Record

Before proceeding to a review of evolution before the primates, it is necessary to look briefly at some of the methods used in paleontological analysis. The two major questions discussed here are: How can we assign dates to the fossil record? and How can we reconstruct past environments?

Dating Methods

Two basic classes of methods are used to date fossil remains. **Relative dating** determines which fossils are older but not their exact date. **Chronometric dating** determines an "exact" age (subject to some measurement of possible error and statistical fluctuation).

When we refer to exact dates in the fossil record, we conventionally use the term **B.P.**, which means "Before Present." "Present" has been set

relative dating Estimating the older of two or more fossils or sites but not a specific date.

chronometric dating Estimating the specific date of fossils or sites.

B.P. Before Present (1950), the internationally accepted form of designating past dates.

stratigraphy A relative dating method based on the fact that older remains are found deeper in the earth because of cumulative buildup of the earth's surface over time.

faunal correlation Assigning an approximate age to sites based on the similarity of animal remains with other dated sites.

arbitrarily as the year 1950. Some people use the term B.C., meaning "Before Christ," but since not all peoples share the belief in Christ, the term B.P. is preferable and has been agreed on internationally. A date of 800,000 years B.P. would mean 800,000 years before the year 1950.

Relative dating methods. If we have two sites containing fossil material, relative dating methods can tell us which is older, but not by how much. It is preferable to have exact dates, but this is not possible for all sites. Relative dating methods can tell us the basic time sequence of fossil sites. **Stratigraphy** makes use of the geological process of superposition, which refers to the cumulative buildup over time of the earth's surface. When an organism dies or a tool is discarded on the ground, it will ultimately be buried by dirt, sand, mud, and other materials. Winds move sand over the site, and water can deposit mud over the site. In most cases, the older a site is, the deeper it is. If you stand on the ground and dig down through the earth, the deeper you go, the older the deposits.

A number of other methods provide relative dates for fossils. One such method is **faunal correlation,** which involves comparison of animal remains found at different sites to determine any similarity in time levels. Imagine that you have discovered a site that contains a certain species of fossil pig. Suppose that you know from previous studies that this species of pig has always been found between 1.5 and 2.0 million years B.P. Logically, this suggests that your newly discovered site is also between 1.5 and 2.0 million years old.

There are chemical methods that also provide relative dates. Fluorine dating, for example, is a method that looks at the accumulation of fluorine in bones. When an organism dies, its bones lose nitrogen and gain fluorine. The rate at which this process occurs varies, so we cannot tell exactly how old a bone is by using the method. The method does, however, allow us to determine if two bones found at the same site are the same age.

Chronometric dating methods. Chronometric dating methods provide an "exact" date, subject to statistical variation. Chronometric dating relies on constant physical and chemical processes in the universe. Many of these methods utilize the fact that the average rate of radioactive decay is constant for a given radioactive atom no matter what chemical reaction it might be involved in. If we know that a certain element decays into another at a constant rate, and if we can measure the relative proportions of the original and new elements in some object, then we can mathematically determine the age of the object. Radioactive decay is a probabilistic phenomenon, meaning that we know the average time for decay over many atoms. Such processes allow us to specify an average date within limits of statistical certainty.

Carbon-14 dating is one such method. Living organisms take in the element carbon throughout their lives. Ordinary carbon (C^{12}) is absorbed by plants that take in the gas carbon dioxide from the air, and by animals that eat the plants (or animals that eat the animals that ate the plants). Because of cosmic radiation, some of the carbon in the atmosphere is a radioactive isotope known as carbon-14 (C^{14}). An organism takes in both C^{14} and C^{12}, and the proportion of C^{12} to C^{14} is constant during its life, since the proportion is constant in the atmosphere. When an organism dies, no additional C^{14} is ingested, and the accumulated C^{14} begins to decay. The rate at which C^{14} decays is constant—it takes 5,730 years for one half of the C^{14} to decay into N^{14}. Carbon-14 is therefore said to have a **half-life** of 5,730 years. The half-life is the time it takes for half of a radioactive substance to decay.

Carbon-14 dating uses this constant rate of decay to determine the age of materials containing carbon. The process of radioactive decay of C^{14} results in the emission of radioactive particles that can be measured. In theory, any sample containing carbon can be used. In practice, however, bone tends not to be reliable in all cases because of the chemical changes during fossilization in which carbon is replaced. In most circumstances, charcoal is the best material to use.

Carbon-14 dating is only useful for sites during the past 50,000 years at most (newer techniques may be able to extend this range, but they are still under development). Any older samples would contain too little C^{14} to be detected. Though carbon-14 dating is extremely valuable in studies of recent hominid evolution, it is not useful for dating the majority of earth's geological history.

Another chronometric dating method that utilizes the process of radioactive decay is **potassium-argon dating.** Here, an isotope of potassium (K^{40}) decays into argon gas (Ar^{40}) with a half-life of approximately 1.31 billion years. This rate of radioactive decay means that this method is best used on samples older than 100,000 years (Figure 9.1).

Potassium-argon dating requires rocks that did not possess any argon gas to begin with. The best material for this method is volcanic rock, for the heat generated by volcanic eruptions removes any initial argon gas. Thus, we are sure that any argon gas we find in a sample of volcanic rock is the result of radioactive decay. By looking at the proportions of K^{40} and Ar^{40}, we can determine the number of elapsed half-lives and therefore the age of the volcanic rock (within probabilistic limits).

Another method of dating involves paleomagnetism. When we use a compass to find direction, we rely on the fact that the needle points north. During many times in the past, this was not the case. The magnetic pole has at times shifted to the southern end of the planet. These **paleomagnetic reversals** provide a means by which to date certain rocks. When rocks initially form, they retain the magnetic orientation at the time they came into being—either "normal" (north) or "reversed" (south). By using other dating methods, such as potassium-argon, a chart of the reversals over the last eight million years has been developed. Because these reversals

half-life The average length of time it takes for half of a radioactive substance to decay into another form.

carbon-14 dating A chronometric dating method based on the half-life of carbon-14 that can be applied to organic remains such as charcoal over the past 50,000 years.

potassium-argon dating A chronometric dating method based on the half-life of radioactive potassium that can be used to date volcanic rock older than 100,000 years.

paleomagnetic reversal Dating sites based on the fact that the earth's magnetic pole has shifted back and forth from the north to the south in the past at irregular intervals.

Figure 9.1

Hypothetical example of the use of potassium-argon dating. Hominid remains are found between two layers of volcanic ash, one dating to 3.8 million years B.P. and the other dating to 3.2 million years B.P. The hominid can therefore be dated at between 3.2 and 3.8 million years B.P. (From *Human Antiquity: An Introduction to Physical Anthropology and Archaeology*, 2d ed., by Kenneth Feder and Michael Park, Fig. 7.7. Copyright © 1993 by Mayfield Publishing Company)

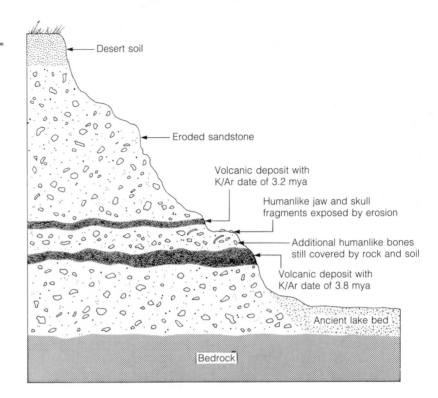

Desert soil

Eroded sandstone

Volcanic deposit with K/Ar date of 3.2 mya

Humanlike jaw and skull fragments exposed by erosion

Additional humanlike bones still covered by rock and soil

Volcanic deposit with K/Ar date of 3.8 mya

Ancient lake bed

Bedrock

dendrochronology A chronometric dating method based on the fact that trees in dry climates tend to accumulate one growth ring per year.

fission-track dating A chronometric dating method based on the number of tracks made across volcanic rock as uranium decays into lead.

last for different amounts of time, they form a varying pattern. A section of rock can then be compared to the chart to determine the age.

Many other types of chronometric dating methods can be used in certain circumstances. Some utilize radioactive decay and some use other constant effects for determining age. Archaeologists working in the relatively recent past (within the last 10,000 years) often use a method known as **dendrochronology,** or tree ring counting. We know that a tree will accumulate a new ring for every period of growth. The width of each ring depends on available moisture and other factors during that specific period. In dry areas there is usually only one growth period in a year. By looking at the width of tree rings, archaeologists have constructed a master chart of tree ring changes. Any new sample, such as a log from a prehistoric dwelling, can be compared to this chart to determine its age.

In addition to radioactive decay, other physical constants allow an estimate of age to be assigned to a sample. **Fission-track dating** relies on the fact that when uranium decays into lead in volcanic glass (obsidian), it leaves small "tracks" across the surface of the glass. We can count the number of tracks and determine the age of the obsidian from the fact that these tracks occur at a constant rate.

Thermoluminescence is a dating method that relies on the fact that certain heated objects accumulate trapped electrons over time, thus allowing us to determine, in some cases, when the object was initially heated. This method has been applied to pottery, bronze, and burned flints. Thermoluminescence can be used to date objects as far back as one million years.

Electron spin resonance is a fairly new method that provides an estimate of dating from observation of radioactive atoms trapped in calcite crystals present in a number of materials, such as bones and shells. This method is also useful for dating sites back to roughly one million years.

Reconstructing the Past

In addition to dating fossil and archaeological sites, we also need to consider other sources of evidence when putting together a sequence of evolutionary events, and for interpreting them.

Taphonomy. When describing the behavior of early hominids, or other organisms, we rely on a wide variety of data to reconstruct their environment and to provide information on population size, diet, presence or absence of predators, and other ecological aspects. Some of these questions can be answered by methods developed within the field of **taphonomy,** the study of what happens to plants and animals after they die. This field provides us with valuable information about which bones are more likely to fossilize, which bones are more likely to wash away, the distribution of bones left over by a predator, the likely route of pollen dispersal in the air, and many other similar topics.

Paleoecology. When reconstructing the past, we need to know more than just what early organisms looked like. We also need to know about the environment in which they lived. What did they eat? Were they predators, or prey? What types of vegetation were available? Where were water sources? These questions, and many others, deal with **paleoecology,** the study of ancient environments.

One example of the many methods used in reconstructing ancient environments is **palynology,** the study of fossil pollen. By looking at the types of pollen found at a given site, experts can identify the specific types of plants that existed at that time. They can then make inferences about yearly and seasonal changes in temperature and rainfall based on the relative proportion of plant species. Further information on vegetation can be extracted from analysis of fossil teeth. Microscopic analysis of scratch patterns on teeth can tell us whether an organism relied more heavily on leaves, fruits, or meat. Chemical analysis of teeth can also tell us something about diet.

thermoluminescence A chronometric dating method based on the capacity of certain heated objects to accumulate trapped electrons over time, that allows the date when the object was initially heated to be determined.

electron spin resonance A chronometric dating method that estimates dates from observation of radioactive atoms trapped in calcite crystals present in a number of materials, such as bones and shells.

taphonomy The study of what happens to plants and animals after they die.

paleoecology The study of ancient environments.

palynology The study of fossil pollen.

Evolution before the Primates

era The major subdivision of geologic time.

period Subdivision of a geologic era.

epoch Subdivision of a geologic period.

Precambrian The time in earth's history preceding the first major appearance of life.

Looking at the early beginnings of life helps us realize the short length of time humans have been in existence. Astronomers estimate the age of our universe to be roughly 15 billion years old. Geological evidence shows the earth to be roughly 4.6 billion years old. Compared to these numbers, 4 million years is a short time.

The Origin of Life

Geologists and paleontologists divide the history of the earth into five geological **eras,** known as the Archean, Proterozoic, Paleozoic, Mesozoic, and Cenozoic. Each era is broken down into different geologic **periods,** each of which is further broken down into **epochs.** Table 9.1 presents a list of the eras and periods and the major evolutionary events that occurred during each.

The fossil record shows that the initial radiation of many life forms took place during the Cambrian period of the Paleozoic era. We often refer to the time before this as the **Precambrian,** which includes the Archean and Proterozoic eras. The Precambrian takes up most of the 4.6 billion years of the earth's existence. It dates from the beginning of the planet until 550 million years B.P. During this time, life existed in the form of algae and some early invertebrates. Our oldest fossils preserve some of these organisms, but we lack direct fossil evidence for the first signs of life. We must rely on a knowledge of the early conditions of the planet and combine these observations with laboratory evidence suggesting possible origins of life.

Such evidence indicates that life first began through a process of chemical evolution. Laboratory experiments in the 1950s demonstrated that amino acids could be produced by discharging electrical energy into a mixture of chemicals representing the atmosphere of the ancient earth. Other experiments have produced the same results using somewhat different combinations of gases and forms of energy. Further experiments have shown that certain combinations of chemical molecules, called microspheres, will form. These look and act much like simple cells (Reader 1986). Though they are not life, the laboratory creations show us how a process of chemical evolution could have started.

Though we have no fossil evidence of these very first beginning steps, the evidence we do have is quite old. Fossilized microscopic cells have been found dating back to 3.3 to 3.5 billion years, along with evidence for the origin of photosynthesis (Schopf and Packer 1987). Fossils that indicate cell division have been found in deposits dating back to 850 million years ago, and evidence for multicelled organisms goes back to at least 750 million years ago (Reader 1986).

T A B L E   9.1
Geological Eras and Periods

Era	Period	Millions of years B.P.	Major evolutionary events
Archean		2,500–4,550	The origin of life
Proterozoic		550–2,500	Early invertebrates
Paleozoic	Cambrian	500–550	"Explosion" of life; marine invertebrates
	Ordovician	440–500	Early vertebrates, including jawless fishes; trilobites and many other invertebrates
	Silurian	410–440	First fish with jaws; land plants
	Devonian	360–410	Many fishes; first amphibians; first forests
	Carboniferous	290–360	Radiation of amphibians; first reptiles and insects
	Permian	250–290	Radiation of reptiles; mammallike reptiles
Mesozoic	Triassic	210–250	First dinosaurs; egg-laying mammals
	Jurassic	140–210	Dinosaurs dominate; first birdlike reptiles
	Cretaceous	65–140	Extinction of dinosaurs; first birds and placental mammals
Cenozoic	Tertiary	1.8–65	Origin and evolution of primates; origin of hominids
	Quaternary	0–1.8	Evolution of the genus *Homo*

Note: The Archean and Proterozoic eras are often collectively referred to as the Precambrian eon. *Source for dates:* Schopf (1992).

The Paleozoic Era

The **Paleozoic era** lasted from 250 million to 550 million years B.P. The first geological period of the Paleozoic era is the Cambrian, which was a time of rapid evolution of many life forms. In fact, the term *Cambrian explosion* is often used to describe the beginning of this period. The "explosion" actually took place over millions of years (Gould 1977a).

Early life forms included organisms similar to modern sponges and jellyfish, and a wide variety of marine invertebrates that have no living counterpart (Figure 9.2). From a human perspective, the most interesting of the Paleozoic organisms are the first vertebrates—the jawless fishes. These creatures possessed the internal segmented vertebral column com-

Paleozoic era The third geologic era, dating roughly between 250 and 550 million years B.P., when the first vertebrates appeared.

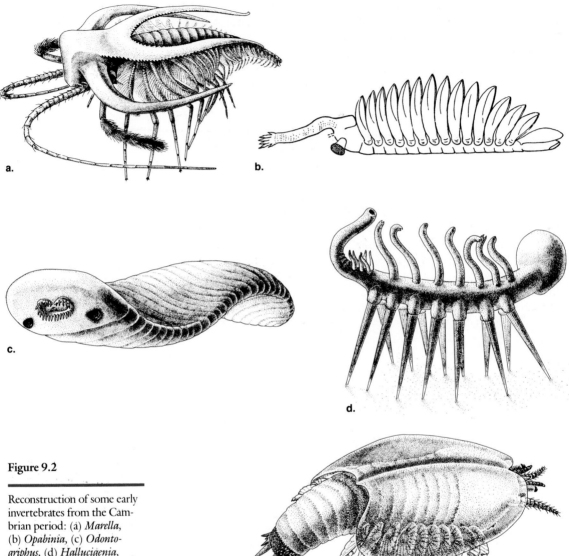

Figure 9.2

Reconstruction of some early invertebrates from the Cambrian period: (a) *Marella*, (b) *Opabinia*, (c) *Odontogriphus*, (d) *Hallucigenia*, (e) *Canadaspis*. Recent studies of *Hallucigenia* have suggested an alternative reconstruction. (a, c, d, e: The illustrations by Marianne Collins from *Wonderful Life*, The Burgess Shale and the Nature of History, by Stephen Jay Gould, are reproduced by permission of W. W. Norton & Company, Inc. Copyright © 1989 by Stephen Jay Gould; b: reprinted with permission from Cambridge University Press)

mon to all vertebrates but lacked jaws and teeth. The jawless fishes came in many forms and were quite successful from 350 to 410 million years ago. Today only two specialized descendants of this once widespread group survive—the hagfish and the lamprey.

Some of these jawless fishes developed armor plating around their heads from a hard material known as dentin. The first teeth were nothing more than spikes of this material that folded inward. This new feature provided a powerful adaptation for those that had it because it allowed them to eat a greater variety of food. Many scientists believe that the development of teeth meant that the jawed fishes ate the jawless fishes (Reader 1986). Later the teeth developed further and jaws evolved.

If we trace the embryological development of a bird or mammal, we can see how the bones and blood vessels that once served the gill arches of fish have been elaborated to form structures that do other things in higher vertebrates. The first gill arch of jawless fish forms the jaws of the rest of the vertebrates. The bones of mammalian ears come from the second gill arch. Evolution often does not build structures from scratch but rather modifies and revises what already exists.

The next major evolutionary step in the history of life was the invasion of land by early amphibians. We are used to thinking that fish have gills that allow oxygen to be absorbed from water, and land animals have lungs that allow oxygen to be absorbed from the air. Actually, many fishes, such as the lungfish, have lunglike structures.

Many fish are bottom dwellers. They rest on strongly developed fins. In the Paleozoic era a group of fish called lobe-fins evolved this ability. Some of these adaptations survive in a fish commonly called the "walking catfish," which often moves on land to get from one stream to another, obtaining oxygen from the air as well.

The movement of lobe-fins is not the most efficient form of locomotion on dry land, but this ability was crucial in the changing environment of the Paleozoic. The lobe-fins could survive when lakes and streams dried up by crawling from pond to pond. An additional bonus of land exploration for these fish was the great availability of new plants that had evolved. Over time these adaptations were selected for, and ultimately amphibians evolved. The fossil evidence shows that these changes took place during the Devonian period of the Paleozoic.

Amphibians represent a transitional form of vertebrate that lives both in water and on land. The early amphibians were successful and many of these forms evolved into modern amphibians. Some early amphibians became highly successful on the land and evolved into early reptiles during the Carboniferous period. This was facilitated by the development of eggs with leathery shells that did not dry out, thus freeing reproduction from the need for a watery environment. The Permian period witnessed an adaptive radiation of reptiles. Reptiles were the dominant form of animal life on the land surface of the planet for more than the next 200 million years.

Mammals and birds eventually evolved from the reptiles. The evolution of mammals from reptiles suggests that an intermediate form of animal intervened. To many, an intermediate form implies some sort of strange-looking creature with a mixture of *modern* reptilian and mammalian features. This is an incorrect view of evolution. Modern reptiles and mammals represent millions of years of evolution from a common ancestor.

therapsid An early group of reptiles also known as the mammallike reptiles. Therapsids were the ancestors of later mammals.

Mesozoic era The fourth geologic era, dating roughly between 65 and 250 million years B.P., when the first mammals and birds appeared.

The first reptiles did not look exactly like modern-day reptiles. In fact, some of the earliest primitive reptiles included a group referred to as the **therapsids,** or mammallike reptiles.

The therapsids are classified as reptiles because they have more features that we would call reptilian. They also possessed certain mammalian features, however, such as differentiated teeth. We therefore call them, for lack of a better term, mammallike reptiles. Therapsids underwent an adaptive radiation during the Permian period of the Paleozoic era, with a wide variety of shapes and sizes.

The dental adaptations of the therapsids were well suited to life on land, allowing them to forage plants effectively. Although this group was highly successful, it ultimately declined following an adaptive radiation of what we might term "true reptiles" during the Mesozoic. Recent fossil evidence shows that some of the mammallike reptiles survived at least until 60 million years ago (Fox et al. 1992).

The Mesozoic Era

The **Mesozoic era,** lasting from 65 million to 250 million years B.P., is often called the "Age of Reptiles" because it was the time when reptiles became the dominant form of life on the earth's surface. One of the most successful groups of reptiles were the dinosaurs (Figure 9.3). The major characteristic of the dinosaurs was the modification of the leg and pelvic structures. Many dinosaurs were bipedal, and some appear to have been extremely quick movers and efficient walkers and runners (Wilford 1985). The therapsids, on the other hand, did not change much beyond the earliest land vertebrates except for modifications in their teeth.

Unfortunately for the therapsids, the ancestors of the dinosaurs developed quicker and more efficient locomotion as well as powerful hands and teeth to capture prey. Ultimately, the dinosaurs emerged as the dominant animal life on land and the therapsids declined in numbers. Some of the therapsids, however, evolved into what we call "true mammals."

During the Triassic period the monotremes, or egg-laying mammals, evolved. Some, such as the platypus, have survived until the present day. The first placental mammals evolved during the Jurassic period, which was the heyday of the dinosaurs. Birdlike reptiles also evolved during this time period. At the end of the Cretaceous period the dinosaurs became extinct, and mammals became the dominant animal life.

It is widely thought that the emergence of mammals led to the disappearance of the dinosaurs. After all, mammals have more efficient systems of reproduction, temperature regulation, and an emphasis on social learning, among other adaptations. The story is not that simple. There is growing evidence that at least some of the dinosaurs possessed a measure of temperature regulation and had a complex form of social organization (Wilford 1985, Bakker 1986). Also, mammals and dinosaurs coexisted for tens of millions of years. Regardless of the adaptations of the earliest

Figure 9.3
───────────────

Two well-known dinosaurs:
Triceratops (*top*) and
Tyrannosaurus (*bottom*).

mammals, they were limited in their expansion by the success of the dinosaurs. The mammals were confined to a few small environmental niches.
Most were small and probably nocturnal, existing on insects and living in
the trees. Only when the dinosaurs became extinct and flowering plants
evolved did the mammals undergo an adaptive radiation. Until that time
they remained in the shadow of the dinosaurs. Evolution requires
opportunities.

   Why did the dinosaurs (and many other organisms) become extinct?
Recent explanations of dinosaur extinction have relied on the idea that an
asteroid or comet hit the earth with tremendous force, kicking up clouds
of dust and blocking the sun. Temperatures dropped and many plant forms
became extinct. As plants died, so did the plant eaters and those who ate
the plant eaters. In other words, the entire ecology of the planet was
altered. There is growing geologic evidence for such a catastrophic event

Cenozoic era The fifth, and most recent, geologic era, dating roughly to the last 65 million years, when the first primates appeared during the Cenozoic era.

(e.g., Sheehan et al. 1991), although many researchers suggest other factors may have also played a part.

In any case, the fossil record shows clearly that dinosaurs died out and mammals took their place during the last of the Cretaceous period. New opportunities opened up for the mammals, and they began an adaptive radiation, filling vacant environmental niches. The last 65 million years of the earth's history is the **Cenozoic era,** often called the "Age of Mammals." Some mammals ultimately evolved to exploit the grasslands. Others developed adaptations that allowed them to become sea creatures, such as the whale and dolphin.

Early Primate Evolution

Primates evolved during the Cenozoic era, whose epochs are listed in Table 9.2. Each epoch is associated with a major event in primate evolution. Primate evolution should not be thought of as a simple evolutionary "tree" with a few branches. A better analogy would be a series of "bushes" with many different branches at each stage of primate evolution. One or more adaptive radiations of primate forms occurred during each epoch. Many of the new forms became extinct, some evolved to become present-day representatives, and some evolved into the next phase of primate evolution.

TABLE 9.2
Epochs of the Cenozoic

Epoch	Millions of years B.P.	Major events in primate evolution
Paleocene	55–65	Primatelike mammals
Eocene	38–55	First primates (primitive prosimians); first anthropoids?
Oligocene	22–38	Anthropoid evolution
Miocene	5–22	Radiation of early apes
Pliocene	1.8–5.0	First hominids and first members of the genus *Homo*
Pleistocene	0.01–1.8	Evolution of the genus *Homo* (*Homo erectus* and *Homo sapiens*)
Holocene	0–0.01	Humans develop agriculture and industry, explore outer space

Source for dates: Conroy (1990).

Overview of Early Primate Evolution

During the Paleocene epoch an adaptive radiation of primatelike mammals led to the origin of what we would call "true primates." The Paleocene primatelike mammals show evidence of the initial adaptation to life in the trees. Many of these forms died out, but some evolved into primitive prosimians, which were fully adapted to living in the trees. These early prosimians underwent an adaptive radiation during the Eocene epoch. Some of the descendants of this adaptive radiation survive as the modern-day prosimians. Many other prosimian species became extinct. Some of these early prosimians evolved into early anthropoids. A subsequent adaptive radiation of anthropoids during the Oligocene epoch led to separate groups of New World monkeys, Old World monkeys, and apes.

The Paleocene Epoch

The **Paleocene epoch** lasted from 55 to 65 million years B.P. A major event during the Paleocene was the origin of primates. At the end of the Mesozoic era there were a number of mammals called **insectivores** that were arboreal, were nocturnal, and ate insects. A modern-day representative of this group is the tree shrew (Figure 9.4), that illustrates the probable morphology of the ancestor of primates. Of all living mammals, the insectivores are most similar to the primates, suggesting that they are ancestral to primates. Paleoanthropologists look at the variation in this early group to try to identify forms that show the transition to the primates.

Continental drift and primate evolution. Most of the fossil evidence on primate origins comes from Paleocene deposits in North America and

Paleocene epoch The first epoch of the Cenozoic era, dating roughly between 55 and 65 million years B.P., when the primatelike mammals appeared.

insectivore An order of mammals adapted to insect eating.

Figure 9.4

A tree shrew, an insectivore similar in certain respects to primates.   (© Zoological Society of San Diego)

continental drift The movement of continental land masses on top of a partially molten layer of the earth's mantle that has altered the relative location of the continents over time.

postorbital bar The bony ring that separates the eye orbit from the back of the skull in primates.

mosaic evolution The concept that major evolutionary changes tend to take place in stages, not all at once.

Europe of a group of insectivores known as the primatelike mammals. This widespread distribution may seem strange, given the fact that North America and Europe are now separated by the Atlantic Ocean. This was not, however, their configuration during the Paleocene. The continents continually move about on large crusted plates on top of a partially molten layer of the earth's mantle—a process known as **continental drift.** This process continues today. The placement of the different continents at various times in the past is shown in Figure 9.5.

An understanding of past continental drift is crucial in interpreting the fossil evidence for primate evolution. As continents move, their environments change. When continents separate, populations become isolated; when the continents join, there is an opportunity for large-scale migrations of populations. Roughly 230 million years ago, all the continents were joined together as one large land mass. By 180 million years B.P., this large mass had split in two: one containing North America, Europe, and Asia, and the other containing South America, Africa, Australia, and Antarctica. By the time of the primatelike mammals, South America had split off from Africa, but North America and Europe were still joined.

The primatelike mammals. The primatelike mammals were small creatures, usually no larger than a cat and often smaller. They were quadrupedal (four-footed) mammals whose arms and legs were well adapted for climbing. Within this general group there was considerable diversity. Remains have been assigned to 27 different genera (Conroy 1990). Most of this extensive variation was in body size and dental specializations. Some of the primatelike mammals had large incisors for heavy gnawing, others had teeth better adapted for slicing, and still others had teeth adapted for eating nectar and insects. Such variation is expected from an adaptive radiation. These small insectivores had some ability to climb and thus were able to exploit many different types of food.

In spite of their arboreal adaptations, these creatures are not considered true primates. A picture of the skull of one of these creatures (Figure 9.6) shows why. The front teeth are far apart from the rest of the teeth, a feature not found in primates. The eyes are located more toward the sides of the skull, unlike the forward-facing eyes of primates. In addition, the primatelike mammals lack a **postorbital bar,** a bony ring separating the orbit of the eye from the back of the skull. Primates have a postorbital bar. Also, the hands and feet of these animals did not have the grasping ability of primates, and they had claws instead of nails.

If these Paleocene forms are not primates, then how can we say they are related to primates? You should not expect to examine the fossil record and see some point at which modern-day primate structure immediately appears. Evolution is **mosaic,** meaning that not all new structures appear at the same time. Examination of the primatelike mammals shows a number of primate features, such as changes in the teeth and development of climbing abilities. Not enough changes have occurred that we would call

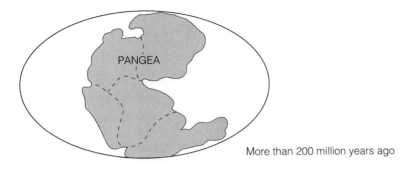

PANGEA

More than 200 million years ago

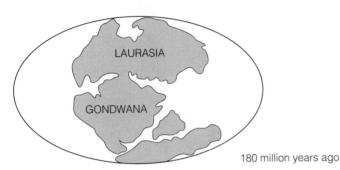

LAURASIA

GONDWANA

180 million years ago

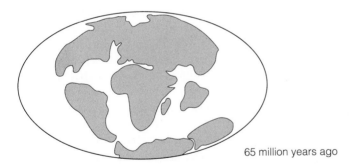

65 million years ago

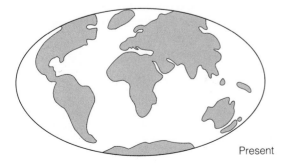

Present

Figure 9.5

Continental drift. Over 200 million years ago all of the continents formed a single land mass (called Pangea). By 180 million years ago, two major land masses had formed (Laurasia and Gondowana). By 65 million years ago (the beginning of primate evolution), South America had split from Africa, but North America and Europe were still joined. (From *Human Antiquity: An Introduction to Physical Anthropology and Archaeology*, 2d ed., by Kenneth Feder and Michael Park. Copyright 1993 by Mayfield Publishing Company)

Figure 9.6

Side view of a skull of a Paleocene primatelike mammal. (Redrawn from Fleagle, *Primate Adaptation and Evolution*, 1988, with permission, Academic Press, Inc.)

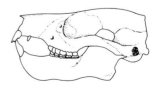

Eocene epoch The second epoch of the Cenozoic era, dating roughly between 38 and 55 million years B.P., when the first true primates, early prosimians, appeared.

them primates, but enough have taken place that we call them primatelike mammals. They are another example of transitional forms in the fossil record.

Models of primate origins. The first true primates evolved from a population of primatelike mammals. The general scenario for this change involves continuing adaptation to life in the trees. The primatelike mammals had the beginnings of arboreal adaptations, and many also possessed the more generalized teeth capable of exploiting different types of foods and environments. In an arboreal environment, natural selection would favor those individuals better able to cope with the demands of life in the trees. As discussed in Chapter 7, living in the trees is quite a different experience than living on the ground. First, a three-dimensional orientation is needed. Leaping from branch to branch requires depth perception, which involves forward rotation of the eyes so that the visual fields overlap.

Second, living in the trees also requires an agile body capable of bending and twisting in midair. The early insectivores retained the early generalized vertebrate skeletal structure, and the first primates made use of this flexibility in the trees. The retention of the primitive trait of five digits was also important because having five digits on hands and feet allows the grasping of limbs and branches. Finally, good hand-eye coordination and a brain capable of rapidly processing a large volume of visual information are essential.

The early primatelike mammals already had traits on which natural selection could act. They had a generalized skeletal structure and five digits. Individuals possessing certain variations such as more forward-facing eyes and grasping abilities would be selected for. Over time, the primatelike mammals adapted to life in the trees and became the first true primates.

Another scenario for the initial origin of the primates has been offered by Matthew Cartmill (1974), who sees the initial changes in grasping ability and vision as adaptations to insect eating. The early insectivores hunted out their prey on the ground and on low-lying slender branches in the forest. The development of grasping hands allowed more successful hunting of prey along small branches. The development of stereoscopic vision made it easier for them to locate prey. According to Cartmill's model, primate adaptations first arose as adaptations to more successful insect predation. Once these traits were established, these adaptations later allowed further exploitation of the trees. The fossil record is not complete enough to test fully Cartmill's model, but the dental evidence does show that many of the early primatelike mammals were insect eaters.

The Eocene Epoch

The **Eocene epoch** lasted from 38 to 55 million years B.P.

Eocene environments. The climate during the Eocene was warm and humid, and the predominant land environment was tropical and subtropical forests. At the beginning of the Eocene, North America and Europe were still joined, resulting in migration and similarity among the fossils we find in these regions. Many orders of modern-day mammals first appeared during the Eocene, including aquatic mammals (whales, porpoises, and dolphins), rodents, and horses. It was also during this epoch that some surviving primatelike mammals evolved into "true primates." The remainder of the primatelike mammals became extinct, most likely as the result of competition with the new species of rodents.

The Eocene primates. Fossil primates from the Eocene epoch have been found in North America and Europe. During the Eocene there was an adaptive radiation of the first true primates—the early prosimians. This adaptive radiation was part of the general increase in the diversity of mammals associated with the warming of the climate and related environmental changes. Five families of primates containing as many as 67 new genera evolved during the Eocene (Fleagle 1988).

The Eocene forms possessed stereoscopic vision, grasping hands, and other anatomical features characteristic of primates. A picture of the skull of an Eocene primate (Figure 9.7) shows many of these changes. Compared to the Paleocene primatelike mammals, the snout is reduced and the teeth are closer together. These forms possessed a postorbital bar, had larger brain cases, and had features of cerebral blood supply similar to that of modern primates (Fleagle 1988). The large size of the eyes of some of the Eocene primates suggests they were still nocturnal.

Oligocene epoch The third epoch of the Cenozoic era, dating roughly between 22 and 38 million years B.P., when the first anthropoids appeared.

Figure 9.7

Side view of a skull of an Eocene primate.   (Redrawn from Fleagle, *Primate Adaptation and Evolution*, 1988, with permission, Academic Press, Inc.)

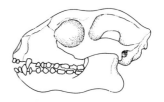

The Oligocene Epoch

The **Oligocene epoch** lasted from 22 to 38 million years B.P.

Oligocene environments. The temperature cooled during the Oligocene and there was an expansion of grasslands and a reduction in forests. North American and European vertebrates were still similar to one another as the result of interchange, although this similarity decreases by the end of the Oligocene. Carnivores became widespread during the Oligocene, probably as a result of the change to open grasslands and the resultant increase in herbivores on which they could feed.

Old World anthropoids. At the end of the Eocene epoch, climatic change seems to have resulted in the southward movement of some prosimian populations. After this, we see little further evidence of primate evolution in North America or northern Europe. During the Oligocene

Aegyptopithecus A genus of fossil medium-sized, arboreal anthropoids found in Egypt dating to 33 million years B.P., a possible common ancestor of later Old World monkeys and apes.

epoch we find evidence of further primate evolution in southern climates in Africa and South America.

Most of the Old World evidence comes from an area known as the Fayum beds in Egypt. During the Oligocene the Fayum was a rich tropical forest, in contrast to much of the area today. While limited geographically, the Fayum fossil evidence shows that there was an adaptive radiation of anthropoids, the higher primates. The Fayum had a warm and wet climate, with plants similar to those found today in tropical regions of Southeast Asia. New evidence shows that all the Fayum primates lived before 31 million years ago (Fleagle et al. 1986).

The Oligocene primates show the continued radiation of anthropoid forms in both the Old World and the New World. To date, there have been eight genera of Old World anthropoids and three genera of New World anthropoids discovered at Oligocene sites (Conroy 1990). The Oligocene anthropoids show continued reduction of the snout and nasal area, indicating greater reliance on vision than on smell. In addition to the postorbital bar shared with all primates, the Oligocene anthropoids have a fully enclosed eye socket, characteristic of modern anthropoids. All of the Oligocene anthropoids were small and arboreal and were generalized quadrupeds; none show signs of specialized locomotion. Their diet appears to have consisted primarily of fruit supplemented with insects and leaves. The smaller eye orbits of many Oligocene anthropoids suggest that these forms were diurnal.

One of the most interesting Oligocene anthropoids is the genus ***Aegyptopithecus*** (Figure 9.8), which has been found in Fayum deposits dating to 33 million years B.P. In most ways *Aegyptopithecus* represents a

Figure 9.8

Side view of the skull of *Aegyptopithecus*. (Peabody Museum of Natural History, Yale University)

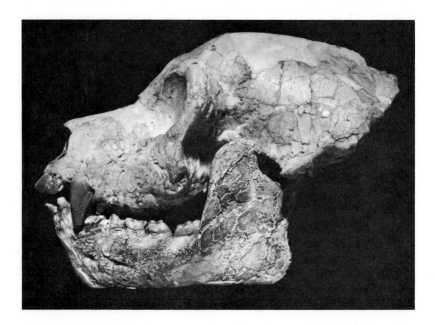

typical Oligocene anthropoid. It was monkeylike in general appearance, roughly the size of a cat, a generalized quadruped, and totally at home in the trees. Some scientists have suggested that *Aegyptopithecus* represents the first ape because of its teeth. This view was based on the presence of Y-5 molars in *Aegyptopithecus* and the assumption that Y-5 molars were derived traits in the hominoid line. Recently, however, further evidence shows that Y-5 molars were primitive and that *Aegyptopithecus* most likely represents a common ancestor of all later Old World anthropoids (monkeys and hominoids).

Evolution of the New World monkeys. Where did the New World monkeys come from? One suggestion is that some prosimians had moved into South America from North America. If so, then any biological similarities between New World and Old World monkeys represent parallel evolution. Recent evidence, however, shows so many similarities between Old World and New World monkeys (living and extinct) that it is very unlikely that monkeys evolved from prosimians twice. It is much more likely that the monkeys evolved once and then spread to different continents.

Two possibilities exist for the initial origin of the New World monkeys. Monkeys either migrated from North America to South America, or from Africa to South America. But by the end of the Eocene these continents had already separated. How, then, did monkeys migrate across the water?

One explanation is that anthropoids reached South America by "rafting." No, this does not mean that these early primates built rafts and sailed to South America! Ocean storms often rip up clumps of land and trees near the shore, which are then pulled out into the ocean. Sometimes these trees contain helpless animals. Often they drown, but occasionally they will be washed up on an island or continent.

Present geological evidence supports the rafting hypothesis. This still leaves the problem of where the anthropoids first came from, however. At present, the available evidence suggests that the Old World is a more likely point of origin than North America (Fleagle 1988).

Miocene Apes

Miocene Evolution

The **Miocene epoch** lasted from 5 to 22 million years B.P. Most Miocene mammals are fairly modern in form, and roughly half of all modern mammals were present during this time. South America and Australia were isolated by this time because of continental drift. The land mass of **Eurasia** (a term given to the combined land masses of Europe and

Miocene epoch The fourth epoch of the Cenozoic era, dating roughly between 5 and 22 million years B.P., when the first apes appeared.

Eurasia The combined land masses of Europe and Asia, joined during the Miocene epoch.

Asia) and Africa were joined during part of the Miocene (approximately 16–17 million years B.P.).

The early and middle Miocene (before 16 million years B.P.) was a time of heavy tropical forests, particularly in Africa. Subsequently, the climate became cooler and drier, and there was an increase in open grasslands and mixed environments consisting of open woodlands, bushlands, and savannas.

Evidence exists of the adaptive radiation of early hominoids at the beginning of the Miocene, and at the end evidence suggests the first appearance of hominids (i.e., the bipedal primates). We identify many Miocene primates as apes because of their dental characteristics and not their total appearance. For this reason, many researchers call the Miocene hominoids "dental apes."

Table 9.3 lists the genera of Miocene apes known at present according to geographic region and geologic date (this list is likely to have changed by the time you read it; new Miocene hominoids are found almost every

TABLE 9.3

Genera of Miocene Apes

Region	Date		
	Early Miocene	Middle Miocene	Late Miocene
Africa	*Afropithecus*		
	Dendropithecus	*Kenyapithecus*	
	Limnopithecus		
	Micropithecus		
	Nyanzapithecus		
	Proconsul	*Otavapithecus*	
	Rangwapithecus		
	Turkanapithecus		
Asia	*Dionysopithecus*		*Gigantopithecus*
			Laccopithecus
			Lufengpithecus
		Sivapithecus	
Europe		*Dryopithecus*	
			Oreopithecus
		Pliopithecus	
		Sivapithecus	

Note that *Sivapithecus* is represented in both Asia and Europe. *Gigantopithecus* is also found in Asia during the Pliocene and Pleistocene epochs.

Source: Conroy (1990) and Conroy et al. (1992), with the exception that *Kenyapithecus* is considered here as a separate genus.

year!). Miocene hominoids have been discovered in Africa, Asia, and Europe. The 18 genera listed show how diverse the Miocene apes were relative to modern hominoids (only 6 genera exist today). Of course, different scholars still debate the assignment of specific fossils to different genera and species. Some see evidence for fewer groups and some see evidence for more. In any case, that many genera have been found demonstrates the great diversity in Miocene apes.

In light of this diversity, only a few selected Miocene apes that appear to be related to modern-day apes and humans will be discussed here. Keep in mind that there existed many other forms of Miocene apes that have no living counterpart.

The Fossil Evidence

Proconsul. Table 9.3 lists a number of primitive apes that lived during the early and middle Miocene. One of these, the genus **Proconsul,** lived in Africa between 17 and 23 million years B.P. Specimens assigned to this genus show considerable variation, particularly in overall size, making assignment to specific species somewhat difficult. The skeletal structure of *Proconsul* shows a mixture of monkey and ape features (Figure 9.9). Like modern apes, *Proconsul* did not have a tail. The limb proportions, however, are more like that of a monkey than an ape, with limbs of roughly the same size. In a modern ape, the front limbs are generally longer than the rear limbs, reflecting knuckle walking. The arms and hands are monkeylike, but the shoulders and elbows are more like those of apes. The most recent analyses of the limb structure suggest that *Proconsul* was an unspecialized quadruped that lived in the trees and ate fruit (Pilbeam 1984; Walker and Teaford 1989).

The skull of a typical *Proconsul* specimen (Figure 9.10) is more like that of an ape in being large relative to overall body size. The teeth also

Proconsul A genus of fossil apes that lived in Africa between 17 and 23 million years B.P. that also shows a number of monkey characteristics.

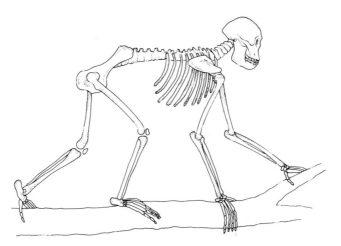

Figure 9.9

Reconstructed skeleton of *Proconsul.* (Redrawn from Fleagle, *Primate Adaptation and Evolution,* 1988, with permission, Academic Press, Inc.)

Figure 9.10

Side view of the skull of *Proconsul africanus,* the smaller of several species of *Proconsul.* (Courtesy of Milford Wolpoff, University of Michigan)

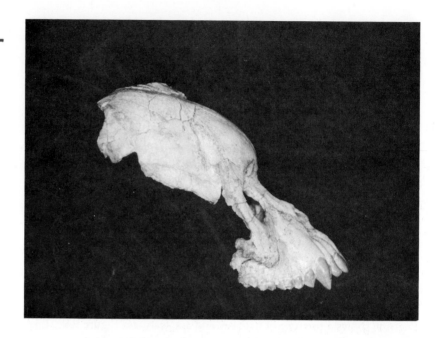

diastema A gap next to the canine teeth that allows space for the canine on the opposing jaw.

Sivapithecus A genus of fossil ape found in Asia and Europe dating between 7 and 14 million years B.P., probably an ancestor of the modern-day orangutans, great apes, and humans.

demonstrate that these forms were hominoid. They possessed Y-5 molars and had large protruding canines (Figure 9.11). The shape of the lower premolar is like that of modern apes, with a single dominant cusp rather than two more or less equal-sized cusps as found in humans. In apes, the single large cusp rubs against, and sharpens, the upper canine tooth. Ape jaws also have noticeable gaps (called **diastema**) next to the canine teeth, which allow the jaws to close.

The mixture of monkey and ape traits points to them as typical of a transition from early generalized anthropoid to what we think of as an ape. Though definitely not identical to a modern ape, their overall structure is more like that of an ape than a monkey; hence we refer to them as an early form of hominoid.

Proconsul was adapted to forest living and was a successful group for millions of years. As the climate cooled and became drier in certain regions during the Miocene, their habitat shrank. As competition for dwindling resources increased, other apes developed that were more successful in dealing with the new environments.

Sivapithecus. The genus ***Sivapithecus*** lived in Asia and Europe between 7 and 14 million years ago. The genus name means "Siva's ape," after the Indian deity Siva (pronounced "SHE-va"). Like *Proconsul, Sivapithecus* was a diverse genus ranging in size and geographic distribution. Because of this variation it is not clear exactly how many species actually existed. Current estimates suggest as many as six different species (Kelly 1988; Conroy 1990).

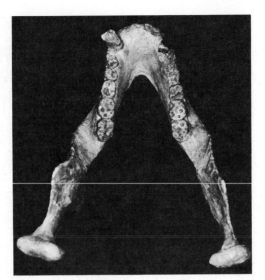

Figure 9.11

The lower jaw of a specimen of *Proconsul nyanzae,* a medium-sized species of *Proconsul.* Note in particular the large canine tooth. (Courtesy of Milford Wolpoff, University of Michigan)

A major distinguishing feature of *Sivapithecus* lies in the jaws and teeth. First, the molars are relatively large, are low-cusped, and have thick enamel. Second, the jaws are relatively massive but do not protrude forward as much as in other apes. Third, in many forms the canines are relatively smaller than in other apes and do not protrude as much. These features are all probably related to a change in diet from soft fruits to foods that are harder to chew, such as nuts, seeds, and hard fruits. This change in diet seems to be associated with the fact that the climate was on average cooler and drier, leading to a change in available foods.

Environmental data suggest that *Sivapithecus* lived in a mosaic of mixed woodland, grassland, and forest regions. Our reconstructions of *Sivapithecus* are hampered by the fact that we know very little about their form of locomotion. Recent reviews of the **postcranial** (the skeleton below the skull) structure of Miocene apes suggest generalized quadrupeds from which modern forms of ape locomotion could have been derived (Fleagle 1983). The few postcranial bones of *Sivapithecus* (Pilbeam et al. 1977; Rose 1986) seem to support this theory. The arm and leg bones are highly mobile, the big toe was capable of grasping in much the same way as does an orangutan, and there is no evidence of bipedalism. To the best of our knowledge, the modern specialized patterns of hominoids, such as knuckle walking, brachiation, and bipedalism, do not appear in these fossil apes.

In the late 1970s and early 1980s, a number of *Sivapithecus* specimens were found with rather complete skulls, offering us for the first time a glimpse at something other than jaws and teeth. One of these specimens (Figure 9.12) was discovered by David Pilbeam in 1980 during excavations in Miocene deposits in Pakistan (Pilbeam 1982). Its general appearance is extremely similar to a modern orangutan, as shown in Figure 9.13.

postcranial Referring to that part of the skeleton below the neck.

Figure 9.12

Side view of *Sivapithecus* specimen from Pakistan. (From Clark Spencer Larsen, Robert M. Matter, and Daniel L. Gebo, *Human Origins: The Fossil Record, Second Edition,* p. 36. Copyright © 1991, 1985 by Waveland Press, Inc., Prospect Heights, Illinois. Reprinted with permission from the publisher)

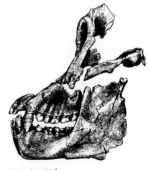

0   cms   5

Figure 9.13

Side views (*top*) and frontal views (*bottom*) comparing the *Sivapithecus* specimen GSP 15000 (*center*) with a modern chimpanzee (*left*) and a modern orangutan (*right*). (Peabody Museum, Harvard University)

Figure 9.14

Comparison of the lower jaws of *Gigantopithecus* (*left*), a modern gorilla (*middle*), and a modern human (*right*). *Gigantopithecus* has the largest overall size, but relatively small canines compared to the gorilla. (From *Gigantopithecus*, by E. L. Simons and P. C. Ettel. Copyright © 1970 by *Scientific American*, Inc. All rights reserved)

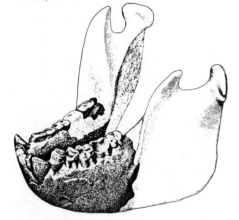

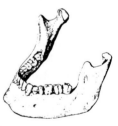

The overall shape and orientation of the two skulls is very similar and quite unlike that of either the chimpanzee or gorilla. The eye orbit of the *Sivapithecus* skull is oval in shape and the two eyes are close together, both features found in the orangutan. The unique triangular appearance of an orangutan's nasal region is also found in *Sivapithecus*. Other similarities also include the shape and size of the incisor teeth.

Not every species of *Sivapithecus* exhibits all of these features. Specimens in China, for example, share certain features of the incisor teeth and jaw shape with the Pakistani specimen shown in Figures 9.12 and 9.13. However, the shape of the eye orbits and the distance between the eyes is different. This variation suggests that there were a number of Asian species of *Sivapithecus,* one of which appears ancestral to the modern-day orangutan.

Gigantopithecus. A genus of fossil ape that shows many dental similarities to *Sivapithecus* is **Gigantopithecus,** which means "giant ape." This genus has been found in China, India, and most recently Vietnam (Ciochon 1988). The Indian finds date between 5 and 9 million years B.P., and the Chinese finds may only be 500,000 years old. To date, only lower jaws and isolated teeth have been found. The most striking aspect of the *Gigantopithecus* finds is their size; the teeth, especially the molars, are huge, and the jaws are incredibly thick and massive (see Figure 9.14 for comparisons with teeth and jaws of humans and gorillas). Based on the large size of the jaws and teeth, some have estimated that *Gigantopithecus* was over 6 feet tall.

The teeth of *Gigantopithecus* show the typical features of all sivapithecines: large molars with thick enamel. They also have relatively small canines whose tips are usually worn down, showing the effects of grinding. Little more is known about this creature other than its diet and dental characteristics.

Kenyapithecus. Fossils similar to *Sivapithecus* have been discovered in Africa. One species, named **Kenyapithecus,** has been dated to 14 to 17 million years B.P. This species is known only from teeth, jaws, and fragmentary facial remains (Figure 9.15). *Kenyapithecus* shares certain features with *Sivapithecus* (some lump the two in the genus *Sivapithecus*), including thick molar enamel. This species also has relatively small canines. While fragmentary, the fossil evidence for *Kenyapithecus* suggests it might be a common ancestor of later African hominoids (the African apes and humans).

Afropithecus. During the 1980s, Richard Leakey and colleagues discovered dental and cranial fragments of a form closely related to *Sivapithecus* at several sites in Kenya, Africa (Leakey and Walker 1985; Leakey and Leakey 1986a, 1986b). In fact, they first classified it as an African form of *Sivapithecus* and later assigned these fossils to a new genus—*Afropithecus.* The specimens have been dated to 16 to 18 million years B.P. A frontal and side view of an *Afropithecus* skull is shown in Figure 9.16. Similarities with *Sivapithecus* include large central incisors that project outward and a long upper jaw. The facial profile of *Afropithecus* is different, however, in that it is more linear than the concave shape of *Sivapithecus.* The date and morphology suggest that *Afropithecus* might be a common ancestor for *Sivapithecus* and later Asian and African hominoids.

Gigantopithecus A genus of fossil ape found in Asia dating between 0.5 and 9 million years B.P.

Kenyapithecus An African Miocene ape, similar to *Sivapithecus* in some ways, but with relatively small canines. The genus dates to 14 to 17 million years B.P. It is a possible common ancestor of modern African apes and humans.

Afropithecus An African Miocene ape that lived between 16 and 18 million years ago, that is perhaps a common ancestor of modern great apes and humans. This genus is similar in some ways to *Sivapithecus.*

Figure 9.15

Jaw fragments of *Kenyapithecus*. Note the small canine teeth. (Courtesy of Dr. Alan Walker, The Johns Hopkins University School of Medicine)

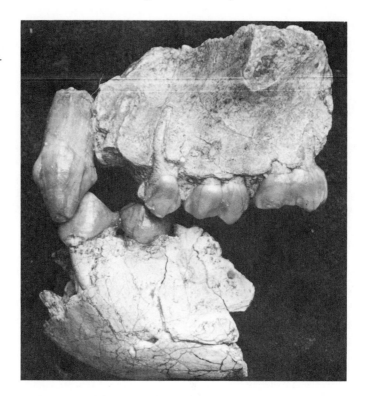

Figure 9.16

Frontal and side views of *Afropithecus,* an African hominoid dated to 16 to 18 million years B.P. that shows certain similarities with *Sivapithecus* and with earlier hominoids.   (From Clark Spencer Larsen, Robert M. Matter, and Daniel L. Gebo, *Human Origins: The Fossil Record, Second Edition,* p. 27. Copyright © 1991, 1985 by Waveland Press, Inc., Prospect Heights, Illinois. Reprinted with permission from the publisher)

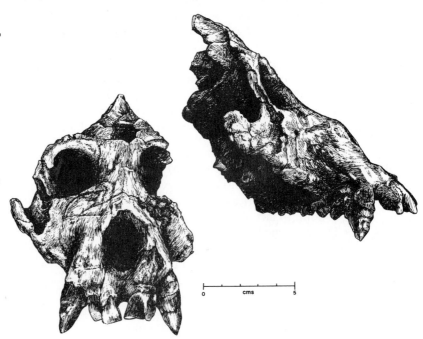

Interpretations of Miocene Evolution

Are the Miocene apes discussed here related to modern apes and humans? If so, then how? Do we have enough data to answer these questions, or are we missing important pieces from fossils not yet discovered? Since discoveries are now happening at a rapid rate, any interpretation of Miocene evolution must be tentative. Don't be surprised if some of this material is out of date by the time you read it!

Molecular dating. The analysis of Miocene hominoid evolution relies heavily on the fossil evidence, but that is not the only source of information we have. Since the late 1960s, the comparison of the genetics of living organisms using a set of methods known as **molecular dating** has shed new light on hominoid evolution.

In Chapter 8 you read about how scientists use molecular information to judge the relative relationship between living hominoids. These methods provide some idea of which primates are most closely related. If certain assumptions are made, these methods can be used to provide an estimate of the date at which two species split from a common ancestor. When two species separate, mutations occur and neutral mutations accumulate in each line independently. If the rate of accumulation is constant in both lines, then a comparison of molecular differences in living forms would provide us with a relative idea of how long the two species have been separated.

Molecular dating rests on two major assumptions. First, we assume that our calibration date is correct. As more fossil evidence accumulates, we might have to change our estimate of the date at which species C first split off. The second, more critical, assumption is that neutral mutations do accumulate at the same rate in different lines. There are methods for testing this assumption, and it does appear to hold true for some molecular estimates (Cronin 1983).

Different methods of analysis give different estimates from molecular dating. For example, Cronin (1983) computed a split of human and chimpanzee at roughly 5 million years ago, with the orangutan splitting off at roughly 10 million years ago and the gibbon splitting off at roughly 12 million years ago. Arguing that the data should be interpreted using nonlinear rates of change, Gingerich (1985) computed an average date of 9 million years for the chimpanzee, 16 million years for the orangutan, and 19 million years for the gibbon. The controversy still continues, but the predominant view from molecular dating is that humans and the African apes split sometime between 5 and 10 million years ago.

A tentative evolutionary tree. Given the fossil and molecular evidence, what is the most likely scenario for the evolution of the hominoids? The ideas proposed here are hypotheses for further testing, not definitive statements. As new data are discovered, some ideas will be rejected and others will gain support.

molecular dating Estimating the sequence and timing of divergent evolutionary lines by applying methods of genetic analysis.

Figure 9.17

Tentative evolutionary tree of
Miocene hominoid evolution
based on fossil and molecular
evidence. Question marks
indicate greater uncertainty.

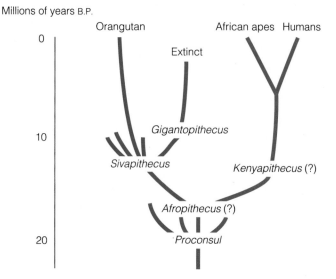

One current idea is that *Sivapithecus* is a direct ancestor of the modern-day orangutan and is not ancestral to the African apes or humans (Pilbeam 1984). This hypothesis is based on the strong similarities between *Sivapithecus* and the orangutan. *Gigantopithecus* is felt to have split off later from the *Sivapithecus* line, perhaps 10 million years ago.

Figure 9.17 presents a tentative evolutionary tree, with question marks indicating areas of uncertainty. According to the hypothesis outlined by the tree, some species of *Proconsul* evolved into an early form of thick-enameled ape—*Afropithecus*. The date and primitive features of *Proconsul* make it a reasonable common ancestor of later Miocene apes. *Afropithecus* has been found to have a number of features similar to both earlier and later Miocene apes, suggesting it might be a reasonable candidate for the common ancestor of the great apes and humans. The location and date of *Afropithecus* are also important. Approximately 16 million years ago, the land masses of Eurasia and Africa came into contact through the action of continental drift, when many animal species moved from one continent to the other. It is after this time that we see the first evidence of *Sivapithecus* in Europe and Asia. This, along with the similarity between *Afropithecus* and *Sivapithecus* in a number of features, suggests that *Sivapithecus* evolved from populations of *Afropithecus* expanding out from Africa. Judging from the strong similarity of the Pakistani form of *Sivapithecus* and the orangutan, it appears that the former is an ancestor of the latter. Given geography and dental similarities, *Gigantopithecus* may have evolved from a species of Asian *Sivapithecus*.

Figure 9.17 suggests another evolutionary lineage of thick-enameled apes in Africa. According to this model, a descendant of *Afropithecus* became the common ancestor of the African apes and humans. Although new fossils are being discovered every year, the fossil evidence for this part of African prehistory is still rather sparse. *Kenyapithecus,* which shows similarities with *Afropithecus* and with later hominids, is a *possible* candidate, particularly since it is in the right place at the right time.

New data will most likely modify the specifics of this tentative tree. You may assume the basic pattern, however, to be fairly accurate. We see evidence of primitive early apes with thin enamel giving rise to a number of lines of later apes with thick enamel and relatively larger molars. This change appears related to the changing climate and its effect on food resources. Many of these later apes became extinct, but some became the ancestors of present-day orangutans, gorillas, chimpanzees, and humans. As is often the case in paleoanthropology, we have a good idea of the *general* picture but are still uncertain about all of the *specifics.*

S U M M A R Y

A discussion of primate origins and evolution requires information on patterns of evolution before the primates, as well as an understanding of methods used to reconstruct evolutionary patterns from the fossil record.

Life on earth began following a period of chemical evolution. The earliest life forms evolved in ancient oceans. The first vertebrates were the jawless fishes, which evolved into fish with jaws. One group of jawed fishes, the lobe-fins, were the ancestors of all later land vertebrates. After the amphibians conquered the land, an adaptive radiation of reptiles fully adapted to land conditions began. One of the first sort of reptiles were the mammallike reptiles, who possessed certain dental adaptations that allowed them to exploit new forms of food. The later adaptive radiation of dinosaurs ultimately led to the extinction of the therapsids. Before they disappeared, however, some therapsids evolved into the first true mammals. The extinction of the dinosaurs opened up many ecological opportunities for the mammals, starting 65 million years ago.

Some early insectivores began to adapt to life in the trees, developing grasping hands and depth perception. The origin of the primates began with the primatelike mammals in the Paleocene epoch, followed by the evolution of early prosimians in the Eocene epoch and the adaptive radiation of anthropoids in the Oligocene epoch. Several adaptive radiations of early apes occurred during the Miocene epoch. Because of the diversity in Miocene apes, it is difficult to assign ancestors to every living hominoid. One of the Asian species of the genus *Sivapithecus* is most likely an ancestor of the modern orangutan, based on the close similarity of dental and facial traits. An earlier related form, *Afropithecus,* may be a common ancestor of all later hominoids. Some evidence suggests that another related form, *Kenyapithecus,* was a common ancestor of the African apes and humans, although there is not sufficient data to rule this as more than a tentative hypothesis.

Supplemental Readings

Conroy, G. C. 1990. *Primate Evolution*. New York: W. W. Norton.

Fleagle, J. G. 1988. *Primate Adaptation and Evolution*. San Diego: Academic Press. These two texts are the best current sources for information on primate evolution.

Lewin, R. 1982. *Thread of Life: The Smithsonian Looks at Evolution*. New York: W. W. Norton.

———. 1987. *Bones of Contention: Controversies in the Search for Human Origins*. New York: Simon & Schuster. A lively summary of controversies in human evolution. Chapters 5 and 6 deal with human origins, Miocene hominoids, and molecular dating.

Reader, J. 1986. *The Rise of Life: The First 3.5 Billion Years*. New York: Alfred A. Knopf. This and the earlier Lewin text are both well-written, superbly illustrated introductions to evolution from the origin of life to the present.

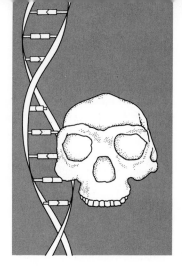

CHAPTER **10**

The First
Hominids

This chapter examines the fossil record for human evolution from the time of the oldest known hominids through the beginnings of the evolution of the genus *Homo*. The oldest known hominids are classified in the genus *Australopithecus,* characterized primarily by their small brains, large faces and teeth, and bipedal locomotion. The first two sections cover what we presently know about the distribution, anatomy, and behavior of the first hominids. The last two sections discuss past and present evolutionary models and general evolutionary trends.

The Genus *Australopithecus*

All fossil hominids can be placed into two genera: the genus ***Australopithecus*** and the genus ***Homo.*** The first hominids belonged to the genus *Australopithecus.* There may have been four or more species of *Australopithecus,* one of which evolved into an early form of the genus *Homo.* By 1 million years B.P., all australopithecines became extinct and the genus *Homo* continued to evolve, with an increase in brain size and cultural adaptations.

General Characteristics

The genus named *Australopithecus* translates as "southern ape," so named because the first specimen was found in southern Africa and it was

Australopithecus A genus of fossil hominid that lived in Africa between 1 and 4 million years B.P., characterized by bipedal locomotion, small brain size, large face, and large teeth.

Homo A genus of hominid with three recognized species (*Homo habilis, Homo erectus,* and *Homo sapiens*), dating from over 2 million years ago and characterized by large brain size and dependence on culture as a means of adaptation.

australopithecines All species in the genus *Australopithecus*.

Pliocene epoch The fifth epoch of the Cenozoic era, dating from 1.8 to 5 million years B.P., when hominids appeared.

Pleistocene epoch The sixth epoch of the Cenozoic era, dating from 0.01 to 1.8 million years B.P., marked by the continued evolution of the genus *Homo*.

Plio-Pleistocene The time frame of the australopithecines (from 1 to 4 million years B.P.).

cranial capacity A measurement of the interior volume of the brain case, used as an approximate estimate of brain size.

regarded as more apelike than humanlike. **Australopithecines** (a general term referring to all members of the genus *Australopithecus*) were the first hominids and were basically bipedal apes. They were hominids because they were bipedal, a derived characteristic of hominids not found in any other primate. Australopithecines, however, still retained a number of primitive ape characteristics, and we should not equate them directly with "humans." To do so implies that their behavior and biology were in many ways similar to our own. We do share certain characteristics with the australopithecines, but we are also different in many ways.

Distribution in time and space. Australopithecines have been found dating between 1 and 4 million years B.P. This time period includes portions of the **Pliocene epoch** (1.8 to 5 million years B.P.) and the **Pleistocene epoch** (0.01 to 1.8 million years B.P.). The time period of the australopithecines is often called the **Plio-Pleistocene.**

An important fact about australopithecines is that they have all been found in Africa. No australopithecines have been discovered outside Africa. This fact supports Darwin's early idea that Africa was the birthplace of hominids. It also means that the australopithecines were limited to a specific environment—tropical grasslands.

Australopithecines have been discovered in two major areas within Africa: South Africa and East Africa. Figure 10.1 provides a map of the major australopithecine sites. Historically, the South African sites were discovered first. The geology of South Africa and the nature of fossilization in that area have made absolute dating difficult. As a result, for many years we were not sure exactly how old the australopithecines were. Sites in East Africa have since been discovered and their absolute dates have been determined: extensive volcanic activity in East Africa during the time of the australopithecines allows us to use potassium-argon dating on these sites.

Australopithecine characteristics. Although four species of *Australopithecus* have been identified, a number of physical characteristics are common to all species. These features are discussed here briefly, followed by a more extensive look at variation within the genus and illustrations of their morphology.

The australopithecines were bipedal, as we can tell by their pelvic structure, nondivergent big toe, and angle of the femur. Though they were definitely bipedal, the specific nature of australopithecine bipedalism has been debated. Some scientists believe they were completely adapted to upright walking, and others believe there are indications of considerable climbing ability.

All the australopithecines had relatively small **cranial capacities** (a measurement of the interior volume of the brain case, measured in milliliters). Their cranial capacities ranged from 400 to 530 ml, roughly the size of an ape's. Estimates of body weight vary by species and sex, ranging

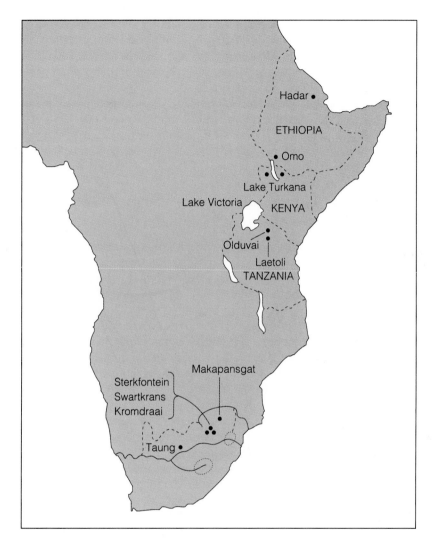

Figure 10.1

Location of the major sites in Africa where *Australopithecus* and *Homo habilis* specimens have been found.

from 40 to 49 kg (88 to 108 lbs) in males, and from 29 to 34 kg (64 to 75 lbs) in females (McHenry 1992). Body weight is estimated from statistical relationships known to occur between overall body weight and the size of different bones. In any case, the size of their brains relative to body weight makes the australopithecine brain similar to, or even larger than, that of modern apes, but considerably smaller than the brain of modern humans. Studies of casts of the interior portions of the skulls provide estimates of brain size, shape, and surface features. These casts show that the australopithecine brains were most likely apelike in structure (Falk 1992).

The overall appearance of all australopithecine skulls shows a small brain case and a large, protruding face. Though a small brain and a large

Australopithecus afarensis
The most primitive of the
australopithecines, dating
between 3 and 4 million years
B.P. and found in East Africa.

face are ape features, the australopithecine skulls do not resemble those of modern apes. The jaws and teeth of *Australopithecus* are large compared to those of modern humans. Most australopithecine species have small canine teeth, as do modern humans. The back teeth of all four species are relatively large and have thick molar enamel.

Were the australopithecines toolmakers? It is entirely possible and even likely that the australopithecines used simple wood tools. Most evidence to date suggests that they did not manufacture stone tools. In every case where stone tools have been found, even at the same time level as australopithecines, remains have been found of hominids with larger brains—those in the genus *Homo*.

Australopithecine Variation

Keeping in mind the general characteristics of *Australopithecus,* we can now turn to a closer investigation of variation within the genus. We will look at three different groups of australopithecines and trace their possible evolutionary relationships.

Australopithecus afarensis. The oldest known australopithecines lived in East Africa between 3 and 4 million years B.P. Their discovery is fairly recent; much of our data on these forms comes from Donald Johanson's fieldwork in the early 1970s at the site of Hadar, Ethiopia (see Figure 10.1). The fossils collected by Johanson and colleagues date between 2.9 and 3.5 million years B.P. Additional fossils collected by Mary Leakey at the site of Laetoli, Tanzania, date back to 3.75 million years B.P. Johanson and colleagues (1978) noted the close similarity between the Hadar and Laetoli finds and placed them together in a different species from all other known australopithecines—*Australopithecus afarensis.* The species name, *afarensis,* comes from the Afar region where the Hadar site is located. Recent discoveries in southern Ethiopia may date back as far as 4.3 million years B.P. (Fleagle et al. 1991).

A. afarensis (the *A.* is scientific shorthand for the genus name *Australopithecus*) is the most primitive of the australopithecines. Consequently, *A. afarensis* is more apelike in certain features than the other australopithecine species. Nonetheless, it is definitely hominid, for it possesses the human form of bipedalism. The most dramatic find showing bipedalism is the fossil nicknamed "Lucy," a 40 percent complete skeleton of an adult female (Figure 10.2). We know she was an adult because her third molar teeth had fully erupted, an event that occurs in young adulthood in hominids. We also know she was a female because her pelvis is fairly intact. Determining the sex of a fossil is best done by examination of the pelvis (Figure 10.3). Females have a wider and more rounded pelvic opening. Such comparisons show that Lucy was a female.

Although an adult, Lucy was small. She was a little over a meter tall (about 3 ft 3 in) and weighed roughly 27 kg (60 lbs) (McHenry 1992).

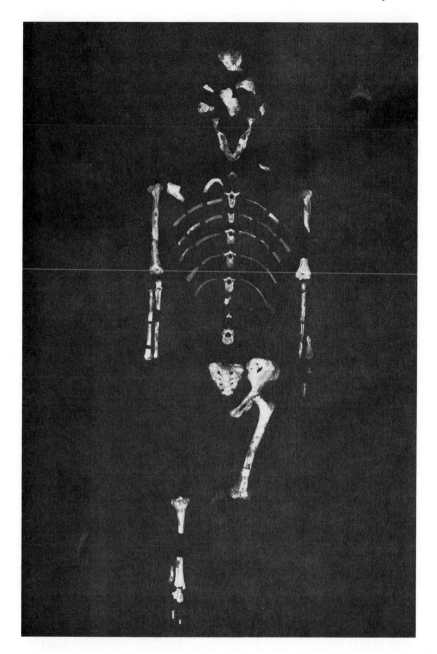

Figure 10.2

The skeletal remains of "Lucy," a 40 percent complete specimen of *Australopithecus afarensis*. (The Cleveland Museum of Natural History)

Her pelvic bones and femur show bipedal locomotion. In addition to Lucy, other fossils from Hadar show bipedalism, including a knee joint. Also, fossil footprints have been found at the site of Laetoli dating back to 3.75 million years B.P. These prints show the bipedal characteristics of a non-divergent big toe, heel strike, and a well-developed arch.

Figure 10.3

Comparison of the pelvic anatomy of modern human males and females.   (From *Human Antiquity: An Introduction to Physical Anthropology and Archaeology,* 2d ed., by Kenneth Feder and Michael Park, Fig. 7.17. Copyright © 1993 by Mayfield Publishing Company)

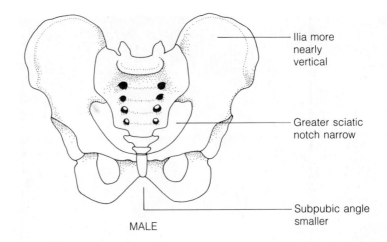

Ilia more nearly vertical

Greater sciatic notch narrow

Subpubic angle smaller

MALE

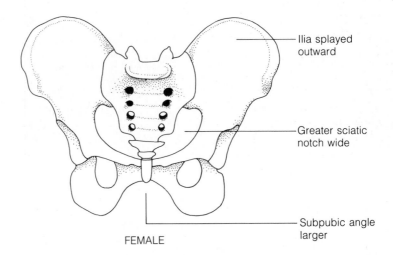

Ilia splayed outward

Greater sciatic notch wide

Subpubic angle larger

FEMALE

Some have noted certain ape tendencies in the postcranial material, such as relatively long arms and curved toe bones. These data suggest that even though *A. afarensis* was bipedal, it was not completely modern and did not walk in exactly the same way we do. Also, this evidence suggests that *A. afarensis* had considerable climbing ability (Stern and Susman 1983).

Cranial material for *A. afarensis* is scarce, but enough exists to allow a composite reconstruction (Figure 10.4). Examination of all cranial remains shows that *A. afarensis* had a small brain, ranging in size between 400 and 500 ml (Blumenberg 1985). These remains also show a number of primitive hominoid features, such as a well-developed crest on the back of the skull for neck muscle attachment and the shape of the external ear canal (Johanson and White 1979). Overall, the skull of *A. afarensis* resembles that of a small ape.

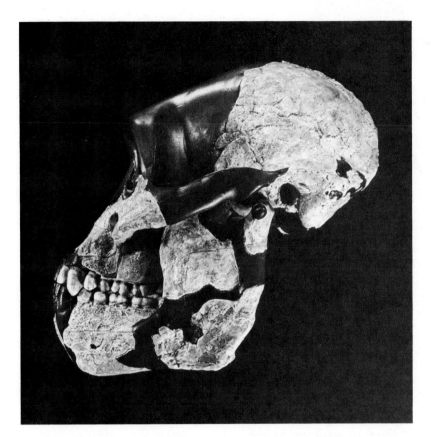

Figure 10.4

Reconstruction of the *Australopithecus afarensis* skull. (Institute of Human Origins)

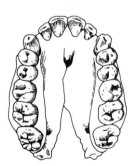
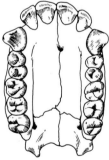
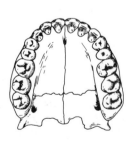

Chimpanzee
upper jaw

Australopithecus afarensis
upper jaw

Modern human
upper jaw

Figure 10.5

Comparison of the teeth and upper jaws of a modern chimpanzee, *Australopithecus afarensis*, and of a modern human. In most features, the teeth and jaws of *Australopithecus afarensis* are intermediate between those of modern apes and modern humans (see text).

The teeth of *A. afarensis* show a number of characteristics intermediate between those of apes and humans. The teeth of modern apes and humans can be easily distinguished (Figure 10.5). The canines of modern apes are large and project past the surface of the other teeth, whereas modern humans have small, nonprojecting canine teeth. The canine teeth

Australopithecus boisei The most robust of the australopithecines, dating between 1 and 2.5 million years B.P. and found in East Africa.

of *A. afarensis* are intermediate; they are larger and more projecting than modern humans, but smaller than most modern apes. An ape's upper jaw has a diastema (gap) between the canine and the adjacent incisor. This space is needed for the large lower canine to fit into when an ape closes its jaw. Modern humans do not have a diastema. The jaws of *A. afarensis* show a small diastema, larger than modern humans but smaller than modern apes. The lower first premolar of a modern ape is pointed with one cusp, whereas the lower premolar of a modern human has two cusps ("bicuspid"). The lower premolar teeth of *A. afarensis* show two cusps, but one cusp is more developed than the other—an intermediate condition. The orientation of the cusps to the jaw is like that of an ape. Indeed, most features of the jaws and teeth of *A. afarensis* show a state intermediate between that of ape and human.

What can we tell about the behavior of *A. afarensis?* No evidence for stone tool manufacture has been found with *A. afarensis.* This does not mean that they may not have been using tools made of perishable materials, such as wooden digging sticks.

In summary, *A. afarensis* shows a number of primitive features in its jaws, teeth, skull, and postcranial skeleton. These features often show an intermediate condition between those found in apes and humans. Because *A. afarensis* was bipedal, it is a hominid, but its primitive features suggest it was not far from the split between ape and hominid evolutionary lines. This hypothesis is supported by molecular evidence (Chapter 8), which suggests a relatively recent ape-human split, roughly five to eight million years ago.

Robust australopithecines. Environmental reconstructions show us that climatic factors, such as temperature and rainfall, have varied in the past. In East Africa temperatures dropped roughly 2.5 million years ago, leading to a reduction in woodlands and an increase in open grasslands. Along with this change came an increase in the number of species of certain mammals, such as antelopes, that adapted to this new environment (Vrba 1985). There is also evidence of two or more hominid species appearing at this time, presumably as a consequence of the same set of ecological changes. One was *Australopithecus boisei* (the species name comes from the Boise fund, which sponsored the research leading to the discovery of the first specimen assigned to this species).

A. boisei had very large back teeth and a massive facial structure. This species has been found at the east and west shores of Lake Turkana, Olduvai Gorge, and several other East African locations. Specimens have been found dating from 1 to 2.5 million years B.P.

A. boisei was somewhat larger and heavier than *A. afarensis.* It was roughly 1.5 m tall (slightly less than 5 ft). Males weighed roughly 49 kg (108 lbs) and females weighed roughly 32 kg (71 lbs) (McHenry 1992). Like *A. afarensis,* this species had a small brain, ranging from 410 to 530 ml (Blumenberg 1985; Walker et al. 1986). The major differences between this species and other australopithecines are in the skull, jaw, and teeth. By this stage in australopithecine evolution, the overall structure of the teeth has become human. That is, the canines are small and nonprojecting, there is no diastema, and the lower premolar has two cusps. In terms of size, however, the teeth of *A. boisei* are quite different from most modern humans. The front teeth (incisors and canines) are small, both in absolute size and in relationship to the rest of the teeth. The back teeth (premolars and molars) are huge, over four times the size of those of modern humans. Figure 10.6 shows the lower jaw of an *A. boisei* specimen. Note how massive the jaw is and how large the back teeth are, especially in relationship to the front teeth. Also note that the premolars are larger side to side than front to back. These features all show a huge surface area for the back teeth, indicating heavy chewing.

The skulls of *A. boisei* also reflect heavy chewing. A picture of an *A. boisei* skull is shown in Figure 10.7. These skulls show massive dished-in faces, large flaring cheek bones, and a large bony crest running down the top. All these features are related to large jaws and back teeth and powerful

Figure 10.6

Lower jaw of *Australopithecus boisei* from the Lake Natron site, Tanzania. Note the small front teeth (incisors and canines) and the massive back teeth (premolars and molars). (From Clark Spencer Larsen, Robert M. Matter, and Daniel L. Gebo, *Human Origins: The Fossil Record, Second Edition*, p. 67 (bottom). Copyright © 1991, 1985 by Waveland Press, Inc., Prospect Heights, Illinois. Reprinted with permission from the publisher)

Figure 10.7

Side, top, and frontal views of an *Australopithecus boisei* skull, specimen KNM-ER 406, from Lake Turkana, Kenya. (© The National Museums of Kenya)

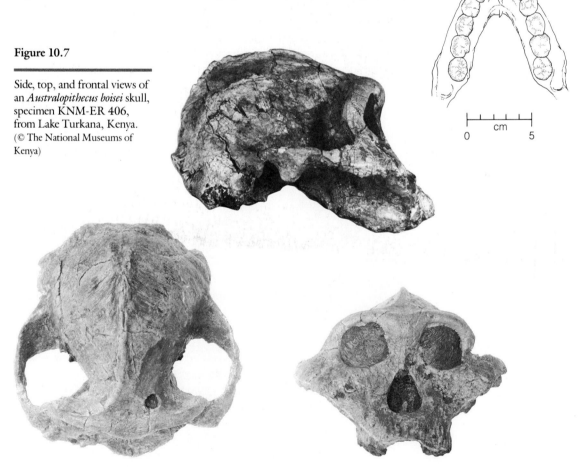

zygomatic arch The bone on the side of the skull connecting the zygomatic and temporal bones that anchors muscles used in chewing.

sagittal crest A ridge of bone running down the center of the top of the skull that serves to anchor chewing muscles.

Australopithecus robustus A robust species of australopithecine, dating between 1 and 2 million years B.P. and found in South Africa.

chewing muscles. Two muscles are responsible for closing the mouth during chewing. One, the masseter, runs from the back portion of the jaw to the forward portion of the **zygomatic arch** (the bone on the side of the skull connecting the zygomatic and temporal bones). The zygomatic arch and facial skeleton anchor this muscle. In hominids with large jaws and masseter muscles, the face and zygomatic arch need to be massive to withstand the force generated during chewing. The other muscle, the temporalis, runs from the jaw up under the zygomatic arch and attaches to the sides and top of the skull. The larger this muscle is, the more the zygomatic arch must flare out from the side of the skull. To anchor the temporalis muscle on the sides and top of the skull, a ridge of bone develops down the center of the skull (called a **sagittal crest**).

A link between *A. afarensis* and *A. boisei* was discovered at West Turkana (Walker et al. 1986). This skull, specimen WT 17000 (also known as the "Black Skull"), dates to 2.5 million years B.P. This date is 500,000 years earlier than all previously discovered specimens of *A. boisei*. This skull shows the characteristic *A. boisei* features such as a large face and zygomatic arch and a sagittal crest (Figure 10.8). In other points it is somewhat different, showing primitive hominid features. This specimen shares those features with *A. afarensis*.

Another robust australopithecine species, ***Australopithecus robustus,*** has been identified based on specimens found in South Africa, dated approximately from 1 to 2 million years B.P. The species was so named

Figure 10.8

The "Black Skull," specimen KNM-WT 17000, Lake Turkana, Kenya. This australopithecine shows a mixture of specialized robust features (the sagittal crest) and primitive features (the forward jutting of the jaw). This mix of features makes it a good candidate for a transitional form between *Australopithecus afarensis* and *Australopithecus boisei*.   (A. Walker/© The National Museums of Kenya)

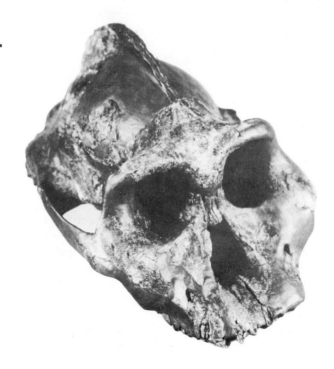

Figure 10.9

Skull of *Australopithecus robustus*, specimen SK 48, Swartkrans, Republic of South Africa. (Transvaal Museum)

because it was the first discovered "robust" species. In cranial and dental features, *A. robustus* is very similar to *A. boisei* but is generally not as large. An *A. robustus* skull is shown in Figure 10.9. Like *A. boisei*, it has a large, flat face and large cheekbones. It also has a sagittal crest. Though not as massive in size *A. boisei*, this skull is clearly robust. *A. robustus* had small front teeth and large back teeth, similar to *A. boisei* but not as huge.

Australopithecus africanus. Australopithecine specimens found in South Africa between 2 and 3 million years B.P. have been placed in the species ***Australopithecus africanus*** (named after Africa). Similar specimens in East Africa dating to roughly 1.5 million years B.P. have also been assigned to this species by some scholars (although there is continuing debate about whether the East African specimens belong to this or another species).

A. *africanus* had reduced canines, large faces, and an average brain size of 440 ml. Compared to the robust australopithecines, *A. africanus* had a smaller face and teeth. For this reason, *A. africanus* has often been called the "gracile" form, indicating its slender appearance relative to the robust forms *A. robustus* and *A. boisei*. The term *gracile* is somewhat misleading, because *A. africanus* was still robust, compared to modern humans, in its face and teeth.

A skull of *A. africanus* is shown in Figure 10.10. Like other australopithecines, it had a small brain and a large face. The face is not as massive

Australopithecus africanus
A species of australopithecine dating between 3 and 4 million years B.P. and found in South Africa.

Figure 10.10

Skull of *Australopithecus africanus*, specimen STS 5, Sterkfontein, Republic of South Africa.   (Transvaal Museum)

Homo habilis The oldest known species in the genus *Homo*, dating between 1.5 and 2.4 million years B.P. and found in Africa, similar in appearance to australopithecines but with a larger cranial capacity.

as the robust forms, however, and there is no sagittal crest. Compared to the robust forms, the front teeth are not as small relative to the back teeth. In overall size, however, the back teeth of *A. africanus* are still larger than those of modern humans.

Homo Habilis

Starting in the 1930s, Louis and Mary Leakey conducted fieldwork at the site of Olduvai Gorge in Tanzania. Among their early finds were the remains of the then oldest known stone tools, dating back throughout the Pleistocene. For many years the Leakeys searched Olduvai Gorge looking for the maker of these tools. In 1960, they found a jaw, two cranial fragments, and several postcranial remains dating to 1.75 million years B.P. These finds represented a hominid with smaller teeth and a larger brain than that of any of the australopithecines found up to that time. Continued work led to the discovery of several more specimens, and in 1964 Leakey and colleagues proposed a new species based on this material—***Homo habilis*** (Leakey et al. 1964). The species name literally translates as "handy man," named for its association with manufactured stone tools. Since that time, additional fossils attributed to *H. habilis* have been found at East Turkana by the Leakeys' son Richard. *H. habilis* has also been found in South Africa (Clarke 1985). *H. habilis* has been dated to 1.5 to 2.4 million years B.P. Until recently, the oldest specimens of *Homo* were dated to roughly 2 million years ago. After reanalysis, a cranial bone originally found in 1967 has been dated to 2.4 million years (Hill et al. 1992).

General Physical Characteristics

The major distinguishing feature of *Homo habilis,* compared to the australopithecines, is its larger brain size. The teeth and postcranial skeleton also show differences.

Brain size. The most noticeable difference between *H. habilis* and the australopithecines is the larger average brain size of *H. habilis.* The average cranial capacity of *A. africanus* is roughly 440 ml. The average cranial capacity of *H. habilis* is 660 ml, which is 50 percent larger than that of *A. africanus* (Blumenberg 1985).

The cranial capacity of *H. habilis* specimens ranges from 509 to 810 ml, overlapping the range of australopithecines and the later species *Homo erectus.* Some anthropologists have suggested that the large range in cranial capacity is evidence that two different species are being lumped together in the fossils we call *H. habilis* (Stringer 1986; Lieberman et al. 1988).

One of the first skull fragments assigned to the species *H. habilis* is shown in Figure 10.11. This specimen (OH 16), dating to 1.7 million years B.P., was discovered at Olduvai Gorge. The specimen consists of a reconstructed skull cap. Its estimated cranial capacity is 650 ml. Another example of *H. habilis,* ER 1470, is shown in Figure 10.12. This specimen was discovered near Lake Turkana, Kenya, and is dated to 1.8 million years B.P. Its cranial capacity is 752 ml (Blumenberg 1985), and it has a rather well-rounded brain case compared to that of the australopithecines.

Evidence exists that the brains of *H. habilis* were structurally different than those of the australopithecines in addition to being larger. Falk (1983) investigated an **endocast** (a cast of the interior brain case) of one

endocast A cast of the interior of the brain case used in analyzing brain size and structure.

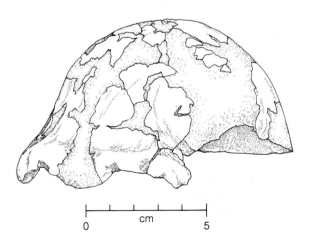

Figure 10.11

Skull of *Homo habilis,* specimen OH 16, Olduvai Gorge, Tanzania. Although this skull is small compared to that of a modern human, its cranial capacity (650 ml) marks it as much larger than the australopithecine skull.   (Figure from *Atlas of Human Evolution,* Second Edition by C. Loring Brace and Harry Nelson, copyright © 1979 by Holt, Rinehart and Winston, Inc., reprinted by permission of the publisher)

cm

0   5

Figure 10.12

Side and frontal views of
Homo habilis, specimen
KNM-ER 1470, Lake
Turkana, Kenya.   (© The
National Museums of Kenya)

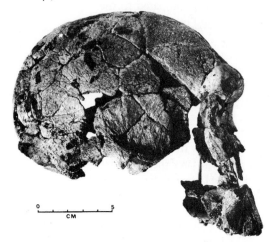

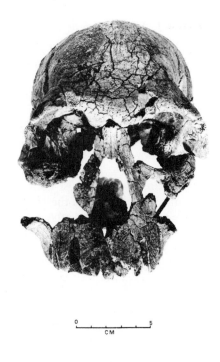

Figure 10.13

Lower jaw of *Homo habilis*,
specimen OH 7, Olduvai
Gorge, Tanzania.   (Figure
from *Atlas of Human Evolution*,
Second Edition by C. Loring
Brace and Harry Nelson,
copyright © 1979 by Holt,
Rinehart and Winston, Inc.,
reprinted by permission of the
publisher)

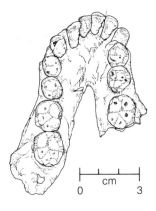

H. habilis specimen and found fissures in the area of the frontal lobes similar to those of modern humans but different from those of apes and australopithecines. This pattern seems to be associated with the development of brain structures linked to language abilities.

Teeth. The teeth of *H. habilis* are in general smaller than those of most australopithecine species, but larger than those of modern humans. In particular, the back teeth are not as large relative to the front teeth as they are in the australopithecines (Figure 10.13). The shape of the premolars of *H. habilis* is more similar to that of modern humans; they are more elongated than the premolars of the robust australopithecines.

The skeleton. For many years little was known about the postcranial skeleton of *H. habilis*. The few fossil remains were isolated parts. In 1986, a partial adult skeleton assigned to *H. habilis* was discovered (Johanson et al. 1987). Preliminary analysis suggests this skeleton is similar to that of *A. afarensis* with small size and relatively long arms. Johanson and colleagues assigned this specimen to *H. habilis* on the basis of fragmentary cranial and dental remains; other anthropologists argue that it might be an australopithecine (Falk 1992). Until further discoveries, with more definitive cranial remains, are found, the nature of the postcranial skeleton of *H. habilis* remains unclear.

Behavior

What can we say about the behavior of *H. habilis?* The increase in brain size and changes in brain structure suggest some associated behavioral evolution compared to the australopithecines. When *H. habilis* was first described, there was a tendency to ascribe a variety of modern human behaviors to it, including use of shelter, manufacture of stone tools, and coordinated hunting. Recent work has suggested that the behavior of *H. habilis* was not like that of modern hunting-gathering societies. Certain behaviors, such as stone tool manufacture, did take place.

Stone tool technology. The earliest known stone tools date to 2.5 million years B.P. Many of these stone tools have been found in association with fossil remains of *H. habilis.*

The stone tool culture of *H. habilis,* referred to as the **Oldowan tradition,** consists of relatively simple chopping tools. Several examples of Oldowan tools are shown in Figure 10.14. These tools were made by striking several flakes off a rounded stone to give it a rough cutting edge. They are normally made from materials such as lava and quartz. The stone was held steady and was then struck with another stone at the right angle to remove a flake of stone. Several strikes often produced a rough edge capable of cutting through animal flesh or other objects that hominids could not tear themselves. The chipped-off flakes could also be used as small cutting tools. This type of tool manufacture sounds extremely easy but actually involves a great deal of skill.

Until recently, the emphasis on archaeological investigations of *H. habilis* had been on the stone cores produced by flaking. The small flakes, often found in great abundance, were felt to be nothing more than waste material. Analysis of the scratch marks on these flakes, however, shows that they were often used for a variety of tasks, including sawing wood, cutting meat, and cutting grass stems (Klein 1989). Archaeologists analyze these scratches by comparing them to those produced under experimental conditions.

Hunting or scavenging? The older interpretation that *H. habilis* was a hunter has given way to a new interpretation that it was a scavenger. This hypothesis is based on analyses of the stone tools and the distribution of animal bones found alongside these tools. Much of this research is based on *H. habilis* sites at Olduvai Gorge, where both the animal bones and the stone tools had been brought to these sites from further away. To complicate matters, there is extensive evidence of carnivore activity at these sites. One interpretation is that *H. habilis* was responsible for the tools, and the carnivores were responsible for the animal carcasses. In this view, *H. habilis* would bring tools to carnivore dens to scavenge from the remains. It seems unlikely that early hominids would bring stone tools to carnivore dens

Oldowan tradition The stone tool culture of *Homo habilis.*

Figure 10.14

Oldowan tools. (From *The Old Stone Age* by F. Bordes, 1968. Reprinted with permission of the publisher, Weidenfeld and Nicolson, Ltd.)

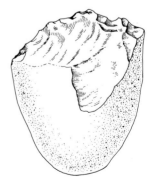

because of the danger (Potts 1984). Another interpretation is that *H. habilis* was responsible for bringing both carcasses and tools to these sites, and carnivores frequented these sites to scavenge meat.

Electron-scanning microscopes have been used to investigate the cut patterns on stone tools to distinguish marks made by tool use from other factors, such as erosion. These analyses show that the Oldowan tools were used for cutting; many animal bones show the characteristic grooves left by stone tools. Many of these bones, however, also show tooth marks from carnivores. In some cases the tool marks overlap the tooth punctures, showing that stone tools were used on an animal *after* it had been gnawed on by carnivores. Other tools show the opposite pattern. The dead animals were a source of food for both *H. habilis* and carnivores.

But what exactly took place at these sites? One possibility is that *H. habilis* hunted animals and brought the carcasses to sites where they would be disarticulated and the meat would be removed and eaten. Bones would be broken open to get at the nutritious marrow. Carnivores would then scavenge the rest of the meat. Another interpretation is that *H. habilis* was a scavenger, taking the remains of dead animals killed by carnivores or left behind from other nonhuman scavengers, such as hyenas.

The available evidence suggests that *H. habilis* was a scavenger. Over half the cut marks left by stone tools are found on bones with little meat, such as the lower legs. This suggests that *H. habilis* was taking what was left over from carnivores. Also, there is no evidence of complete carcasses of larger animals brought to the Olduvai sites, only portions—and these are most often the bones left over by carnivores (Wolpoff 1980; Potts 1984). In addition, the animal bones are not completely processed and considerable meat and marrow was often left over. This type of behavior is strikingly different from that of modern hunters, who utilize the entire remains of an animal.

Though it is likely that *H. habilis* did hunt occasionally, perhaps in a manner similar to living chimpanzees, the available evidence does not support the idea that it was an organized hunter. Instead, *H. habilis* appears to have been a scavenger of meat from dead and dying animals. Though this might not sound like our idea of a "noble ancestor," the act of scavenging did expand the food resources of early hominids.

The archaeological evidence shows that *H. habilis* was the first step in future cultural evolution. Though the stone tools were crude and most likely used for scavenging, they marked the beginning of an adaptive pattern that relied more and more on technological advances and increased problem solving. From this point on, the mainstream of human evolution consists of further associated changes in both biology and cultural behaviors. The rest of this story is told in the next chapter. Before ending this discussion of Plio-Pleistocene hominids, though, we must answer one more general question—when and how did *H. habilis* evolve from the australopithecines?

Models of Plio-Pleistocene Hominid Evolution

The following section discusses the history of discoveries and interpretations of the australopithecines and *H. habilis*.

The Discovery of Plio-Pleistocene Hominids: A Historical Perspective

A great many scenarios have been proposed for hominid origins, some logical and some fanciful. Fossil data have been used to test models and also to construct new models based on available evidence.

Early ideas about the first hominids. Since the eighteenth century, many scientists have noted the close relationship of modern humans to modern apes, particularly the chimpanzee. It seemed reasonable for early scholars to suggest that there was some evolutionary relationship between ourselves and the African apes. These similarities led Charles Darwin to suggest that Africa was the birthplace of the hominids.

Early theories of hominid origins seldom dealt with the fact that both apes and humans had evolved. Instead, humans were considered to be "more evolved" and evolutionary models were constructed to deal with the nature of the changes in humans. Because few data on fossils were available at the beginning of the twentieth century, the issue of hominid origins had to be addressed through comparisons of modern apes and modern humans. Such comparisons show that four major human features must be explained by any model of hominid origins: (1) large brain, (2) bipedalism, (3) small canine teeth, and (4) a dependence on culture.

At the beginning of the twentieth century a popular model hypothesized that brain size evolved first, followed by bipedalism. Scientists predicted that reduction of the teeth would come later. The hypothetical "missing link" would have the large brain of a modern human and the face and teeth of a modern ape. We now know this is not the way things happened, but at the time fossil evidence uncovered at the site of Piltdown in England seemed to support this view.

Piltdown Man was discovered in 1911 and 1915 alongside remains of prehistoric animals such as mastodons and in association with prehistoric stone tools. The specimen consisted of a large skull and an apelike jaw. The teeth, however, were worn flat, more closely resembling the condition of human teeth. This specimen showed the predicted mix of modern human and modern ape traits. Because of the Piltdown find, other known fossil material now assigned to the genus *Homo* (and discussed in the next chapter) was accordingly judged to be not on the main line of human evolution.

For a time, any other fossil hominid remains were rejected because they did not fit the model supported by Piltdown Man. Some scientists were more skeptical about the Piltdown find. Continued investigation

Piltdown Man Forged fossil specimens found in England and once thought to be a "missing link" between apes and humans.

single species hypothesis
A model of Plio-Pleistocene hominid evolution, no longer accepted, that stated that only one species of hominid was present at any point in time.

dietary hypothesis A model first developed in the 1960s that posits two major evolutionary lines in hominid evolution during the Plio-Pleistocene, one line adapted to a vegetarian diet and the other to an omnivorous diet.

showed eventually that the find was a fake. In 1953, fluorine analysis (see Chapter 9) confirmed that the jaw bones and skull bones did not come from the same time period. Close inspection showed the skull was a fossil of a modern human and the jaw was an orangutan's. The teeth had been filed down, and all the bones had been chemically treated to simulate age. The remains of other animals found at the site had been taken from a variety of localities around the world. To this day, no one knows who was responsible for the Piltdown hoax, although several suspects are known to have had both motive and opportunity.

By the 1960s, most anthropologists no longer ranked *Australopithecus* as an unusual ape but as a hominid. As additional adult specimens were discovered, it was found that the dental traits found in *Australopithecus* were hominid, not those of apes. Research in South Africa led to the discovery of enough postcranial data to show conclusively that *Australopithecus* was a biped. The hypothesis that large brains evolved first was rejected. The first hominids were upright walkers with large faces and teeth and small brains. As is common in science, however, the discoveries that led to the rejection of one hypothesis gave rise to additional hypotheses and debates.

The single species and dietary hypotheses. By the late 1950s, two major evolutionary hypotheses were proposed. The first, known as the **single species hypothesis,** proposed that the two species were actually only a single species—*A. africanus*. The robust specimens were thought to be within the range of variation of that species. In other words, all along there had been only one species showing a certain amount of variation in dental size.

Another hypothesis was also proposed. In the **dietary hypothesis,** the two forms were considered to be separate species, each with a different form of adaptation. The robust species, with its large teeth and chewing muscles, was a specialized herbivore. *A. africanus* was a more generalized species, eating both meat and plant food and capable of using simple stone tools (which had been found by this time). According to this model, *A. africanus* evolved into the genus *Homo*.

The evidence today clearly rejects the single species hypothesis as it was first formulated. Evidence given in this chapter and the next show that at *least* two species of hominids coexisted for a long time. But even though the multiple species idea is now accepted, we also realize that the situation is not as simple as first formulated in the dietary hypothesis, either. Other specimens ultimately assigned to additional species were discovered in the 1960s and 1970s, complicating the picture of Plio-Pleistocene evolution.

The East African discoveries. The East African evidence has led to the naming of three additional Plio-Pleistocene hominid species: *Australopithecus boisei* in 1959, *Homo habilis* in 1964, and *Australopithecus afarensis* in 1978. In all three cases, the announcement of the new species has met with resistance and the suggestion that the fossils could be placed in other known species. One of these suggestions has been to place *A. boisei* in the species *A. robustus* because both are robust australopithecines.

The naming of *Homo habilis* was also controversial (see Lewin 1987). Some scientists argued that there were insufficient data to warrant the naming of a new species. The specimens assigned to *H. habilis* might be considered as transitional forms between *A. africanus* and later forms of the genus *Homo*. The discovery of the large-brained specimen ER 1470 seemed to validate the distinctiveness of the species *Homo habilis,* but the situation is still not clear. For one thing, ER 1470 is in some ways different than the first assigned specimens of *H. habilis.* Perhaps another species name is warranted, but is it necessarily the one first proposed for somewhat different fossils? Do all the *H. habilis* specimens belong in a single variable species, or are several species present in the fossil record?

The naming of the most recently discovered species, *Australopithecus afarensis,* has also been the subject of much debate. Some think that these specimens are not sufficiently different from *A. africanus* to warrant a different species name. Others think that there is evidence that what we call *A. afarensis* is in reality two separate species.

Alternative Family Trees

Five species of fossil hominid have been discussed in this chapter: four species of *Australopithecus* and one species of *Homo*. The next chapter will examine two additional species, *Homo erectus* and *Homo sapiens,* which show further increases in brain size and technological advances. The most common interpretation is an evolutionary sequence within the genus *Homo* from *H. habilis* to *H. erectus* to *H. sapiens.* But from which species of australopithecine did *H. habilis* evolve?

As a starting point, examine the family tree shown in Figure 10.15. This model starts with *A. afarensis* as the common ancestor of several later hominid species, based on its age and primitive characteristics. By 2.5 million years ago, one or more species branched off of this line to become the robust australopithecines, who in turn became extinct by 1 million years ago. There is continuing debate over whether there were actually two different species of robust australopithecine, or whether *A. robustus* and *A. boisei* represent geographic variants of a single species. For this discussion, it hardly matters, since the main point is that the robust forms evolved from *A. afarensis.* The Black Skull, with its mixture of robust and primitive features, provides us with evidence linking *A. afarensis* with the robust forms. By 3 million years ago another species, *A. africanus,* also evolved from a population of *A. afarensis.* By 2.5 million years ago, *A. africanus* gave rise to *Homo.* At this point, *A. africanus* is taken as an intermediate form between *A. afarensis* and *Homo,* based on similarities in facial structure, cranial shape, and other anatomical features.

Figure 10.15

Proposed model of Plio-
Pleistocene hominid
evolution. *A. afarensis* is seen
as the common ancestor of
two evolutionary lines. One
line shows evolution into *A.
africanus* into *Homo*. The
other line leads to the robust
australopithecines. The
dashed lines for *A. africanus*
indicate uncertainty regarding
the survival of this species in
East Africa until 1.5 million
years ago.

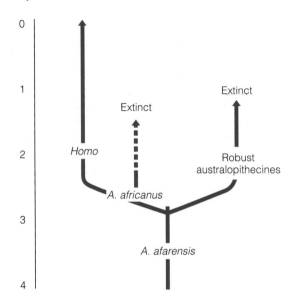

Millions of years B.P.

The family tree shown in Figure 10.15 may not be correct in all details. For this section of the chapter, however, it serves as a useful starting point to introduce a number of current controversies that modify the tree.

***Who was the ancestor of* Homo?** A key feature of the suggested model in Figure 10.15 is that *A. africanus* is the direct ancestor of *Homo*. From this perspective, *A. africanus* is our ancestor some 2.5 to 3 million years ago. Not all anthropologists accept this hypothesis, some believing that *A. africanus* was *not* the ancestor of *Homo* but was instead a separate evolutionary line (Kimbel et al. 1988). Based on their interpretations of the fossil evidence, these anthropologists argue instead that there is a direct evolutionary connection between *A. afarensis* and *Homo*. This alternative model is shown in Figure 10.16.

How many species? Another continuing controversy centers on the assignment of fossil hominids into the species *A. afarensis*. From the initial discoveries at Hadar, the size variation in these hominids has been interpreted in different ways. Johanson and White (1979) proposed that this variation is a product of sexual dimorphism. Others have disagreed, proposing instead that these fossils actually represent two or more separate species (e.g., Olson 1985, Falk 1992). If so, then what would this do to our family tree? One suggestion, shown in Figure 10.17, is to show two separate evolutionary lines present in the fossils usually assigned to the single species of *A. afarensis*. One of these lines leads to the robust australopithecines, the other to the genus *Homo*.

Millions of years B.P.

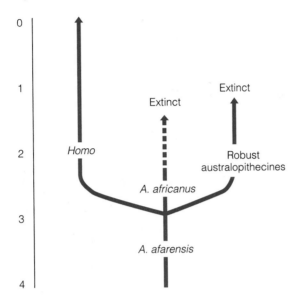

Figure 10.16

Alternative model of Plio-Pleistocene hominid. This is the same tree as shown in Figure 12.21 except that *A. afarensis* is the direct ancestor of *Homo*, not *A. africanus*.

Millions of years B.P.

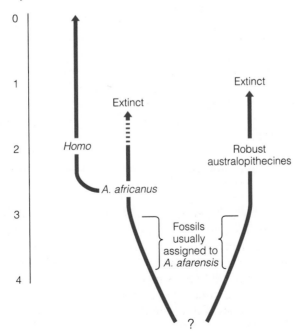

Figure 10.17

Alternative model of Plio-Pleistocene hominid whereby the fossils assigned to *A. afarensis* represent two separate evolutionary lines.

tool use model A model of hominid origins, no longer accepted, that stated that bipedalism, large brains, and small canines all evolved simultaneously during hominid evolution as a consequence of increased reliance on tool use.

Consensus? The three models shown here are not the only ones to be found in the anthropological literature. Many minor variants exist. Some trees, for example, show the robust australopithecines as two (or more) different species. Some split the fossils assigned to *H. habilis* into two or three species. Others lump traditional species together, such as combining *A. afarensis* and *A. africanus*. Given this range of ideas regarding the number of species and their evolutionary relationships, is there *any* agreement at all for this phase of human evolution? Fortunately, yes. All of the above debates and alternative trees are of course important but focus more on the *specific* aspects of Plio-Pleistocene hominid evolution. There is considerable consensus on the *general* findings.

Note that all of the trees discussed have several points in common. First, there is a split at, or prior to, 2.5 to 3.0 million years ago that gives rise to two different evolutionary paths. One path leads to the robust australopithecines, characterized by huge molar and premolar teeth and the cranial anatomy to support large jaws and large chewing muscles. This line ultimately died out roughly a million years ago. The other path ultimately led to the genus *Homo,* characterized by a large brain, smaller face and teeth, and an increasing reliance on cultural behaviors for survival. Regardless of the specific structure of any given family tree, there is much agreement among anthropologists about the basic general path of early hominid evolution.

Evolutionary Trends

The fossil hominid evidence is clear on *what* happened, at least in general terms. The final question we must address is *why* these patterns evolved. For the Plio-Pleistocene hominids, we must look at three evolutionary trends: (1) the origin of bipedalism; (2) the development of large back teeth, large facial structures, and powerful chewing muscles in the robust australopithecines; and (3) the increase in cranial capacity and the development of a stone tool culture in *H. habilis.*

The Origin of Bipedalism

The australopithecine fossils show us that of all the unique traits used to define hominids (Chapter 8), bipedalism is the oldest. Therefore, any model of hominid origins must consider the origin of bipedalism. The anatomical changes are known, and it would probably not take major genetic changes to bring about such changes. The critical question is *why* bipedalism would be selected for.

The tool use model. For many decades, the **tool use model,** which postulated that bipedalism and large brains were linked to the use of tools in adapting to the environment, was the accepted explanation for the origin of those characteristics. This idea was first suggested by Charles Darwin and was later expanded by a number of anthropologists such as Washburn (1960). The basis of the model is that **feedback** has occurred among the different hominid adaptations. In other words, one factor influences (and is influenced by) all other factors. This model views hominid characteristics as a complex of interrelated traits that evolved simultaneously.

The tool use model of hominid origins states that tool use shifted from being an optional strategy to an essential strategy, presumably as the environment changed. As tool use became more and more important, selection would take place for enhanced learning abilities, intelligence, and relatively larger brains. As larger brains evolved along with longer periods of infant dependency, tools would become even more important for survival. Thus, tool use affected brain size increase, which in turn affected tool use.

For much of the twentieth century, this model was supported by then-available fossil evidence. During the last two decades, however, newer evidence has led to the rejection of the tool use model as traditionally stated. As we saw earlier in this chapter, bipedalism evolved *before* the increase in brain size. Hominid evolution is mosaic, and we must separate the initial development of bipedalism from its ultimate function in later humans. Bipedalism allows tool use, but it did not evolve because of this characteristic.

Many other models have served to explain the origin of bipedalism. Some of the major ideas are outlined below.

Predator avoidance. Whenever hominids left the woodlands and moved on to the savanna, they were in danger of being hunted by larger carnivores. Four-legged mammals, such as the lion, can move faster than humans over short distances. Walking on two legs would seem to be a disadvantage. In terms of avoiding predators, however, the characteristic shows possible advantages. Some writers have suggested that standing on two legs would allow hominids to see over the savanna and spot potential predators. This is true, but it did not necessarily require the full bipedal adaptations seen in humans.

Reproductive success. One way of ensuring increased survival is to increase the number of children or increase the amount of care and protection given to each child. Bipedalism frees the hands, allowing more efficient transportation of babies and greater ease in transporting food.

Owen Lovejoy (1981) has expanded on the idea that bipedalism results in increased reproductive success. His basic premise is that bipedalism evolved as a means of having more offspring and providing better care for them. Lovejoy believes that overlapping births (a characteristic of modern humans) was made possible through bipedalism. When the hands are

feedback When one factor influences, and is influenced by, other factors in a system.

free to carry food and babies, more than one infant can be cared for at a time (assuming a sedentary population). Overlapping births would therefore result in greater fertility and population growth because a hominid mother would not have to wait until one infant was grown before having another.

Food acquisition. Along with avoiding predators and reproduction, the other major potential selective factor in survival is obtaining food. Having free hands allows a human to carry more food, which would be particularly advantageous in situations, such as an open woodland or savanna environment, where food was widely distributed. Also, bipedalism is more energy efficient in traveling long distances in search of food. Energy efficiency refers to the amount of energy expended relative to the task performed. In terms of movement, increased energy efficiency means using less energy to move about looking for and gathering food.

Though human bipedalism is less efficient than ape locomotion in the act of running, the opposite is true at normal walking speeds. Rodman and McHenry (1980) looked at the energy efficiency of bipedal humans and knuckle-walking chimpanzees at normal walking speeds. The results, shown in Table 10.1, indicate that bipedalism is more energy-efficient at speeds of both 2.9 km per hour (the normal speed of a chimpanzee) and 4.5 km per hour (the normal speed of a human). The results also show that not just walking upright is important but the specific striding bipedal movement of humans as well. Chimpanzees show the same energy efficiency regardless of whether they are knuckle walking or bipedal. Therefore, it is the specific type of bipedalism found in humans that is the most energy-efficient.

T A B L E   10.1
Energy Efficiency of Knuckle Walking and Bipedalism

Walking speed	Species	Energy cost	Energy cost compared to normal quadruped (percent)
2.9 km/hr	Chimpanzee	0.522	149
	Human	0.193	86
4.5 km/hr	Chimpanzee	0.426	148
	Human	0.170	94

At both normal walking speeds, bipedal humans are more energy-efficient than knuckle-walking chimpanzees and normal quadrupedal animals of the same size. The normal walking speed of a chimpanzee is 2.9 km/hr; the normal walking speed of a modern human is 4.5 km/hr. Energy cost is measured in milliliters of oxygen per gram per kilometer.

Source: Rodman and McHenry (1980).

In a changing environment such as that found at the end of the Miocene, food resources would be scattered. The ability to move long distances in search of food would be an advantageous trait, and the shift to a hominid form of bipedalism would provide this ability.

neoteny The retention of juvenile characteristics in adulthood.

Dietary Adaptation in the Robust Australopithecines

The large face, cheekbones, and back teeth of the robust australopithecines are all characteristics that support powerful chewing. The increased surface area of the back teeth of the robust australopithecines, especially *A. boisei,* indicates the ability to process large amounts of food. All these features have long been viewed as dietary adaptations. Over time, the robust australopithecines became more specialized to a diet that included a significant amount of hard-to-chew food, such as nuts, seeds, and hard fruits. This specialization allowed the robust australopithecines to make efficient use of environmental resources. As with any specialization, when environmental conditions change, a species may not be able to adjust. Many anthropologists feel this is what ultimately happened to the robust australopithecines, who became extinct roughly a million years ago.

Increased Brain Size in Homo Habilis

The robust australopithecines represent a branch in human evolution, but not our branch. The fossil record shows that *H. habilis* led to the later species *H. erectus* and *H. sapiens.* The major evolutionary changes along our branch of human evolution have been an increase in brain size, a reduction in the size of the face and teeth, and an increase in cultural adaptations. *H. habilis* shows the beginnings of both large brains and stone tool technology. Although it is reasonable to link larger brains with intelligence and cultural adaptations, the origin of larger brains is more difficult to explain. Any model requires explanation of a genetic mechanism for larger brains as well as the selective advantages of such larger brains.

The genetic basis for larger brains in *H. habilis* and later hominid species most likely lies in the regulation of prenatal and postnatal brain growth. Primates in general show rapid rates of prenatal brain growth. Because primates require larger brains early in life, such rapid rates are necessary. Following birth, the usual primate pattern is for the size of the brain to double during the growth process. Modern humans are different in having more rapid rates of postnatal brain growth, so that our adult brain size is roughly four times that at birth.

Neoteny. Our large brains can be explained by the process of **neoteny,** which is the retention of juvenile characteristics into adulthood (Gould 1977b). This process is best explained by looking at the difference between an infant chimpanzee and an adult chimpanzee, then comparing this difference to those found between infant and adult humans. Figure 10.18

Figure 10.18

An infant and adult chimpanzee.   (From *Human Antiquity: An Introduction to Physical Anthropology and Archaeology* 2d ed. by Kenneth Feder and Michael Park, Fig. 8.8. Copyright © 1993 by Mayfield Publishing Company)

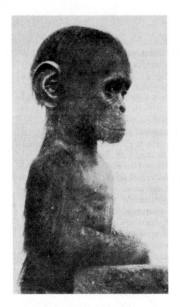

shows an infant and an adult chimpanzee. With its large rounded skull and relatively small face, the infant looks very similar to an infant human. The adult chimpanzee is different, with a relatively small brain and a large, protruding face. An adult human, however, looks very similar to an infant human. Infant apes have relatively large brains because of rapid rates of prenatal brain growth. After birth, however, the rate of brain growth slows down and the face continues to grow. The end result is an adult ape with a relatively small brain. In humans the rapid rate of prenatal brain growth is extended into infancy. Our brains continue to enlarge as our bodies grow. We retain the infant characteristic of a large, well-rounded skull.

The increase in cranial capacity of *H. habilis* could be a consequence of selection for some initial mutations leading to neoteny. This idea assumes that larger brains and greater intelligence are adaptive. Are they?

Advantages of larger brains. The benefits of larger brains and greater mental abilities are obvious. They allow greater behavioral flexibility in adaptation through cultural transmission from one generation to the next. Large brains also have a cost. The extension of fetal growth rates into infancy means that offspring will be born even more helpless and require greater parental care, which in turn requires greater reliability of food, more protection, and social structures capable of assisting others. Also, rapid fetal brain growth requires greater maternal energy, which in turn also requires adequate food and environmental stability. Martin (1981) has shown that a lack of adequate maternal energy limits fetal brain growth.

So that new mutations can be selected for, the advantages of larger brains must outweigh the disadvantages. In a population that does not have adequate maternal energy or postnatal parental care, such genes would be selected against. On the other hand, if conditions existed in which adequate maternal energy and postnatal care were available, then more helpless infants with greater rates of brain growth would be selected for. The increase in brain size, intelligence, and cultural adaptations would then provide the basis for additional selection for larger brains.

The radiator theory. If larger brains have an overall advantage, then why didn't they develop among the robust australopithecines? Dean Falk (1990, 1992) has proposed a model of brain evolution in hominids that focuses on heat stress as a constraint on the development of larger brains. Quite simply, large brains in large heads must shed quite a bit of heat. How does the brain cool itself? During heat stress, blood that is cooled by evaporation flows from the skin into the brain case. In modern humans, blood circulates through a network of veins that also allows blood to drain from the brain into the rest of the body. One of Falk's interesting findings was that although some early hominids had this type of drainage system, others had a different one, whereby blood circulated through enlarged sinuses in the occipital and mastoid regions of the skull. Falk suggests that this other drainage system is not as effective in cooling the brain.

It turns out that the robust australopithecines (and the *A. afarensis* fossils from Hadar) had the less efficient system. Skulls of *A. africanus* and *H. habilis* showed a higher frequency of specific foramina (openings in the skull) characteristic of the more effective system. Therefore, it seems that the robust australopithecines did not have a system that would allow a larger brain—they would not have been able to handle the heat stress.

Why didn't the robust australopithecines evolve such a system? Again, evolution works on what variation already exists. For whatever reason (it may have even been random, such as genetic drift), the robust australopithecines had a biological constraint that would have limited any increase in brain size. Their drainage system could only handle the heat stress of a smaller brain. Other hominids, such as *A. africanus,* had a system that *allowed* them to evolve larger brains.

SUMMARY

The first hominids belong to the genus *Australopithecus*. The earliest australopithecines, in the species *A. afarensis*, lived between 3 and 4 million years B.P. They were bipedal, but with many primitive features in the teeth, skull, and postcranial skeleton. Between 2.5 and 3 million years B.P., several evolutionary lines developed from *A. afarensis*. One or more lines led to the robust species *A. boisei* and *A. robustus*, and one line led to *Homo habilis*. The robust australopithecines had large back teeth, large faces and cheekbones, and a sagittal crest for anchoring jaw muscles. These characteristics represent specializations for chewing hard foods. The robust australopithecines became extinct by 1 million years B.P.

H. habilis existed in Africa between 1.5 and 2 million years B.P. The main characteristic of this species is its increased cranial capacity, roughly 50 percent larger on average than that of the australopithecines. Remains of *H. habilis* have been found in association with the earliest stone tools. The archaeological evidence suggests that *H. habilis* was a scavenger. The ability to manufacture and use stone tools, along with increased brain size, marks the beginnings of the evolution of the genus *Homo*. The continued evolution of the genus *Homo* is discussed in the next chapter.

Supplemental Readings

Falk, D. 1992. *Braindance*. New York: Henry Holt. This well-written and lively book provides an interesting discussion of several areas of current controversy in the evolution of hominid brains and also gives a general review of the "radiator theory."

Johanson, D., and M. Edey. 1981. *Lucy: The Beginnings of Humankind*. New York: Simon & Schuster. Tells the story of the senior author's discovery and interpretation of *Australopithecus afarensis*. Somewhat out of date but provides a lively historical review of Plio-Pleistocene hominids and is highly recommended.

Lewin, R. 1987. *Bones of Contention: Controversies in the Search for Human Origins*. New York: Simon & Schuster. An excellent account of the history of paleo-anthropology. Chapters 3, 4, and 7 to 12 focus on Plio-Pleistocene evolution.

Shipman, P. September 1986. Baffling limb on the family tree. *Discover* 7(9): 87–93. An article for a popular audience that looks at how a new discovery (WT 17000) has led to some reinterpretations of hominid evolution.

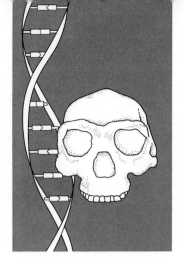

CHAPTER **11**

The Evolution of the Genus *Homo*

Three species are generally recognized in the genus *Homo: Homo habilis, Homo erectus,* and *Homo sapiens.* The evolution of the genus *Homo* involved an increase in brain size, a reduction in the size of the face and teeth, and increased sophistication of stone tool technologies and other cultural adaptations. This chapter looks at the major biological and cultural changes associated with the evolution of *Homo erectus* and *Homo sapiens.*

Homo Erectus

The species name ***Homo erectus*** literally means "upright walking human." This may sound odd, given the fact that five earlier species also walked upright. When the first specimens of *H. erectus* were found in the late nineteenth century, they were thought to represent the oldest evidence of bipedalism. Originally, the species was called "*Pithecanthropus erectus*" (upright walking ape-man). Later the genus name *Homo* was assigned because of the similar adaptations of this early hominid species with our species: larger brains and a reliance on culture.

Homo erectus A species of genus *homo* that lived between roughly 0.2 to 0.4 and 1.6 million years B.P., first appearing in Africa and later spreading to Asia (and possibly Europe).

Distribution in Time and Space

The oldest evidence of *H. erectus* comes from Lake Turkana, Kenya, in East Africa. Two skulls and a rather complete skeleton of a third indi-

265

vidual have been discovered there dating to 1.6 million years B.P. The most important aspect of the distribution of *H. erectus* is that it is the first hominid species found outside Africa. Asian remains of *H. erectus* have been found in India, China, and Java (Indonesia). Fossils and archaeological sites in Europe possibly provide further evidence of *H. erectus,* although there is a great deal of controversy over whether the European forms should be classified as *H. erectus,* archaic *H. sapiens,* or transitional forms. Figure 11.1 shows the location of all known and possible *H. erectus* sites.

Even if we exclude the European sites from consideration, the Asian material makes it clear that *H. erectus* was the first hominid to expand out from Africa. Because the earliest Asian forms are dated at roughly 1 million years B.P., and because the earliest African forms are older (1.6 million years B.P.), the interpretation that *H. erectus* originated in Africa seems reasonable. The most likely model is that some population(s) of *H. habilis*

Figure 11.1

Location of *Homo erectus* sites. It is still not definite if the sites in Europe represent *Homo erectus* or early *Homo sapiens* (see text).

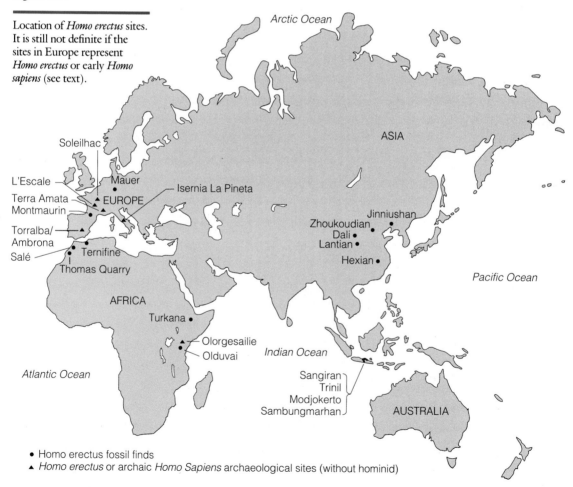

• Homo erectus fossil finds
▲ *Homo erectus* or archaic *Homo Sapiens* archaeological sites (without hominid)

evolved into *H. erectus* in East Africa in a short period of time. Because of biological and cultural adaptations such as hunting and the use of fire and shelter, *H. erectus* was able to move into new environments, and by 1 million years ago it had reached Southeast Asia.

The origin of *H. erectus* at roughly 1.6 million years B.P. seems reasonable because of the dramatic changes (see later) that took place from *H. habilis* in a relatively short period of time. Determining the most recent age of *H. erectus* is a more complicated process. The species does not exist today, having evolved into *H. sapiens* at some point in time. It is difficult, however, to establish the time of this change. By 200,000 years B.P., there is definite evidence of early forms of *H. sapiens* (not necessarily completely modern in appearance), and some *H. erectus* fossils may also date to the same time period (some of the dating is uncertain). Before 400,000 years B.P., the fossils are definitely *H. erectus*. In between those time periods, the fossil record is difficult to interpret. Many specimens have been found, but there is disagreement about whether they belong to *H. erectus* or *H. sapiens*. We therefore have an excellent record of evolutionary change but problems in assigning species names.

postorbital constriction The narrowness of the skull behind the eye orbits, a characteristic of early hominids.

General Physical Characteristics

The following section focuses on the physical characteristics of *Homo erectus,* specifically those of the skull, teeth, and postcranial skeleton.

Cranial and dental characteristics. The most obvious characteristic of *H. erectus,* compared to early forms such as *H. habilis,* is its larger brain size. The cranial capacity ranges from 727 to 1225 ml, with an average of 946 ml (Rightmire 1985). On average, the cranial capacity of *H. erectus* is 44 percent larger than *H. habilis* and 115 percent larger than *Australopithecus africanus*. The range in cranial capacity for *H. erectus* overlaps the high end of the range of *H. habilis* and the low end of the range in modern *H. sapiens*.

One of the earliest *H. erectus* skulls from Lake Turkana is shown in Figure 11.2, and a later skull from China is shown in Figure 11.3. The brain case is larger than that of *H. habilis,* but it is still smaller than that of modern *H. sapiens*. The skull is lower and the face still protrudes more than in modern humans. Neck muscles attach to a ridge of bone along the back side of the skull. The development of this bony ridge shows that *H. erectus* had powerful neck muscles.

Figure 11.4 shows a *H. erectus* skull and a *H. sapiens* skull from a top view. The frontal region of the skull is still rather narrow (**postorbital constriction**), suggesting lesser development in the frontal and temporal lobes of the brain relative to modern humans. This implies that the intellectual abilities of *H. erectus* were not as great as in modern humans. The best evidence for the mental aptitude of *H. erectus,* however, comes from

Figure 11.2

Homo erectus skull, specimen KNM-ER 3733, Lake Turkana, Kenya. Dated at 1.6 million years B.P., this is one of the oldest known specimens of *Homo erectus*. (© The National Museums of Kenya)

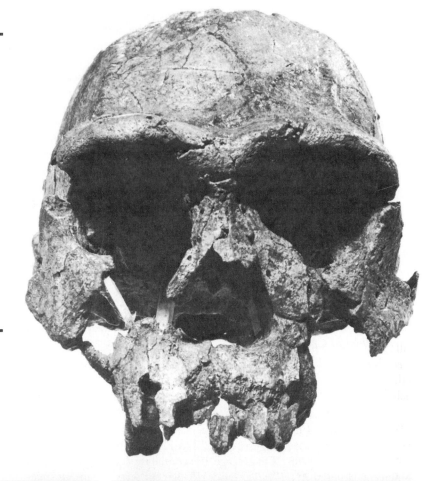

Figure 11.3

Frontal and side views of *Homo erectus* from the site of Zhoukoudian, China. The specimens from this site are sometimes referred to as "Peking Man" in older literature.   (Neg. No. 315446, 315447. Courtesy Department of Library Services, American Museum of Natural History)

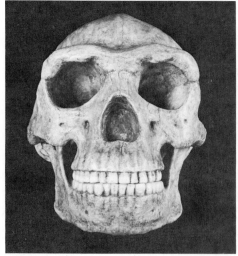

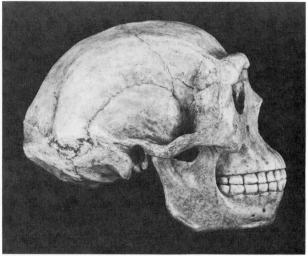

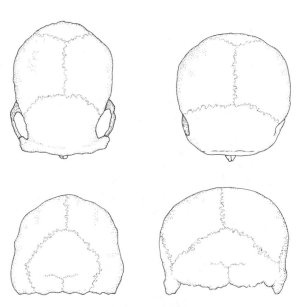

Figure 11.4

Top views of the skulls of *Homo erectus* (*left*) and modern *Homo sapiens* (*right*). Note the greater constriction behind the eyes in *Homo erectus*.

Figure 11.5

Rear views of the skulls of *Homo erectus* (*left*) and modern *Homo sapiens* (*right*). Note the broader brain case of *Homo sapiens*.

the archaeological record, discussed later. Figure 11.5 shows a *H. erectus* skull and a *H. sapiens* skull from the rear view. Note that the brain case of *H. erectus* is much broader toward the bottom of the skull. The jaws and teeth of *H. erectus* are still large compared to those of modern humans but smaller than those of earlier hominids.

    The face of *H. erectus* protrudes, but not as much as in earlier hominids. One noticeable characteristic of the *H. erectus* face is the development of large ridges of bone above the eye orbits (**brow ridges**). These brow ridges are not apparent in *H. habilis* and are much smaller in archaic and modern *H. sapiens*. The appearance and subsequent loss of large brow ridges in human evolution is an evolutionary reversal that makes sense in terms of the overall pattern of cranial and dental evolution. Changes in diet reduced the amount of force needed for the back teeth, and increased use of the incisors as tools led to an increase in the force exerted at the front of the jaw. Changes in overall brain and face size produced differences in the orientation of neck and chewing muscles. The crest at the back of the skull indicates the attachment of strong neck muscles. On the face the various forces exerted by chewing and neck muscles meet above the eyes. The brow ridges of *H. erectus* are a structural adaptation to strengthen the face at this critical juncture (Wolpoff 1980).

    The postcranial skeleton. The first specimen of *H. erectus* was discovered by Eugene Dubois in Java in 1891. This find consisted of the upper portion of a skull and a femur. Most scientists in the late nineteenth century would have been hesitant to include the skull cap in our genus, for the then-current view was that all human ancestors had large brains. The

brow ridges The large ridges of bone above the eye orbits, most noticeable in *Homo erectus* and archaic *Homo sapiens*.

Acheulian tradition The stone tool technology associated with some groups of *Homo erectus.*

biface Stone tool with both sides worked, producing greater symmetry and efficiency.

femur that Dubois found, however, was virtually the same as that of a modern human. Because the two bones were found together, Dubois reasoned that upright walking had developed before the completion of a modern human skull. Though this statement now seems perfectly reasonable, it was controversial at the time.

For many years the postcranial evidence for *H. erectus* was limited to portions of individuals—a femur here or a pelvic bone there. In 1984, this situation changed with the discovery of a nearly complete *H. erectus* skeleton at Lake Turkana dating back 1.6 million years (Brown et al. 1985). This skeleton (Figure 11.6) is that of a 12-year-old male; the age of the specimen is fixed by the differential eruption of the teeth. For the first time, the major parts of the postcranial skeleton were found for the same individual. The estimated adult height of this specimen is 160 cm, or roughly 5 ft 3 in (Feldesman and Lundy 1988).

Cultural Behavior

Given the change in brain size from *H. habilis* to *H. erectus*, it is no surprise that corresponding changes took place in cultural adaptations.

Stone tool technology. The stone tool technology used by *H. erectus* was more diverse than the simple Oldowan tools used by *H. habilis.* Some *H. erectus* sites contain more sophisticated versions of the Oldowan chopping tools; this variant is called Evolved Oldowan. The most common stone tool technology associated with *H. erectus,* however, is the **Acheulian tradition.** These tools have been found in Africa and Europe. Their first appearance is marked at roughly 1.5 million years ago. In some cases, they were still being used by early *H. sapiens* several hundred thousand years ago.

Acheulian tools are **bifaces;** the stone is worked on both sides. These tools are flatter and have straighter, sharper sides than Oldowan tools. The change in manufacture produced a more efficient tool. In the biface method, smaller flakes must be removed than in an Oldowan chopping tool, a process that requires greater skill. One method of flake removal involves the use of some softer material, such as wood or antler, instead of another stone. Softer materials absorb much of the shock in flake removal, allowing more precise control over flaking.

The basic Acheulian tool is the hand axe (Figure 11.7), which could be used for a variety of purposes, including meat preparation. Other tools were also made for different purposes. Scrapers were used for cleaning animal flesh, and cleavers were used for breaking animal bones during butchery (Figure 11.8).

The use of individual tools for different purposes marks an important step in the cultural evolution of hominids. The increased specialization allows more efficient tool use and also requires greater mental sophistication in tool design and manufacture.

Not all *H. erectus* populations made Acheulian tools. At sites in China the tools used by *H. erectus* are somewhat different. The Chinese sites contain many of the smaller tools characteristic of the Acheulian, but not hand axes. Instead, there are large chopping tools that were manufactured differently. Such regional variation in technology is to be expected. Adaptation to specific environments and their related materials requires different methods of manufacture.

Hunting and gathering. Recent evidence suggests that *H. habilis* was a scavenger instead of a hunter, but the fossil and archaeological records show that *H. erectus* was definitely a hunter of small and large game. The earliest evidence of hunting comes from Olduvai Gorge 1.5 million years ago. The bones of animals found at these sites differ in several ways from those at earlier *H. habilis* sites. All of the bones from larger animals are found, suggesting a single butchering site rather than fragmentary scavenging. The bones are also more fragmented, showing greater use of the animal carcass, including extraction of marrow from bones (Wolpoff 1980). The complete use of animal carcasses matches up with the pattern found in modern hunting and gathering groups and is different from that expected from scavenging. The increased variety of stone tools for butchering also supports the idea that *H. erectus* was a hunter, as does dental evidence, which shows a significant amount of meat in their diet.

One of the best known *H. erectus* sites with evidence of hunting is Zhoukoudian, China. Here *H. erectus* populations lived intermittently in caves between roughly 460,000 and 230,000 years B.P. The caves were used as living sites and are littered with animal bones, remnants of fire, tools and tool scraps, and fossilized hominid feces. In addition, parts of the remains of over 40 *H. erectus* individuals have been found at the Zhoukoudian caves. This site has long been known as the place of "Peking Man," named after the nearby city of Beijing (Peking), China.

The Zhoukoudian caves show evidence of two major cultural adaptations of *H. erectus*—fire and hunting. There are large hearths in the caves, some with ash as deep as 7 ft. Fire was important in the northern environments for warmth, light, and chasing off predators. Fire was also used to cook animal flesh. Charred bones found in the cave represent a number of animal species, such as wild pigs and water buffalo. Deer bones are the most numerous and represent the major prey for *H. erectus* in this region.

The bones and stones at different sites show that hunting was an important source of food. Was it the only source? Gathering of vegetables, fruits, nuts, and other foods was surely just as important to the survival of *H. erectus*. In modern hunting-gathering societies, up to 70 percent of the total caloric intake of a group comes from gathering. In the past, anthropologists have tended to focus more on hunting than on gathering. This focus was in part a consequence of the nature of the archaeological record (bones and stones preserve more easily than do vegetables or wooden containers).

Figure 11.6

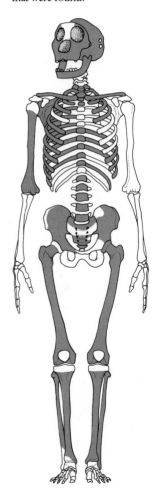

Homo erectus skeleton, specimen KNM-WT 15000, Lake Turkana, Kenya. This skeleton of a 12-year-old boy, dated to 1.6 million years B.P., is the most complete specimen of *Homo erectus* yet found. The shaded areas are the bones that were found.

Fire. The northward movement of *H. erectus* into Asia and (possibly) Europe shows the importance of cultural adaptations. Hominids are tropical primates, and expansion into colder climates required an appropriate level of technology. Fire was an important source of warmth, light, and cooking. In addition, fire can be used for tool manufacture. The tip of a wooden spear can be placed in a fire for a short period to harden the point. We can also speculate that fire allowed social interactions and teaching after dark.

Evidence for controlled fire comes from the cave hearths at Zhoukoudian and other *H. erectus* sites. The earliest known use of controlled fire is dated to almost 1 million years ago (Pfeiffer 1985), although recent evidence from South Africa suggests a *possible* earlier date of up to 1.5 million years B.P.). There are older sites with evidence of fire, but it is not clear whether these represent the controlled use of fire. Because fires occur in nature, we cannot merely look for ash and charcoal. We must look for small areas of ash, usually less than a meter in diameter, as evidence of campfires.

Although we know that *H. erectus* used fire, we do not know if they *made* it. The earliest evidence of manufactured fire, only 15,000 years old, consists of a ball of iron pyrites with deep grooves left by repeated striking. It is possible that *H. erectus* could not make fire and had to rely on nature

Figure 11.7

Making an Acheulian tool. Nicholas Toth uses a piece of antler to remove small flakes from both sides of the flint, producing a symmetric hand axe. Shown are flint hand axes and a cleaver.   (Courtesy of Nicholas Toth, Indiana University)

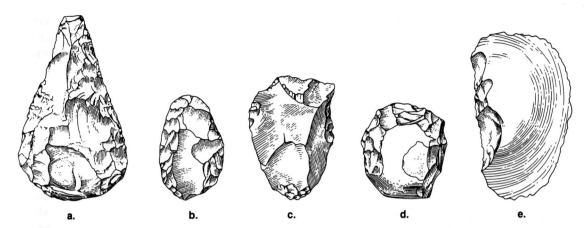

a. b. c. d. e.

Figure 11.8

Examples of Acheulian tools and other tools made by *Homo erectus:* (a) hand axe from Europe, (b) side scraper from Europe, (c) small chopping tool from China, (d) chopper from China, (e) cleaverlike tool from China. (From *The Old Stone Age* by F. Bordes, 1968. Reprinted with permission of the publisher, Wiedenfeld and Nicolson, Ltd.)

to produce fires. If so, then fires could be kept smoldering for long periods of time at camp sites.

Regardless of how *H. erectus* obtained fire, its use marks an important step in human cultural evolution. Making and using fire represents the controlled exploitation of an energy source. Because we rely on many other sources of controlled energy today, we tend to overlook the vital importance of fire as an energy source.

The Transition to Homo Sapiens

The oldest known specimens of *H. erectus* date to 1.6 million years ago in East Africa. It seems that *H. erectus* evolved from *H. habilis* quickly in this area, within 200,000 years or less. The archaeological record also implies a quick transition from scavenging to hunting.

The evolution of *H. erectus* into *H. sapiens* is less clear than the initial change from *H. habilis* to *H. erectus*. As mentioned earlier, fossils found between 200,000 and 400,000 years B.P. are often difficult to classify. An example is the skull from Petralona, Greece, shown in Figure 11.9. Dating between 200,000 and 300,000 years B.P., this skull has been variously classified as *H. erectus*, as early *H. sapiens*, and as a transitional form between the two species. Its cranial capacity is 1,200 ml, placing it at the upper end of *H. erectus* or the lower end of *H. sapiens*. Its cranial bones are thick, similar to those of *H. erectus*, but the skull is higher and shows the greater expansion more typical of early *H. sapiens*.

Another possible transitional form has been found at Steinheim, Germany (Figure 11.10). It has a small face and the rather well-rounded skull characteristic of *H. sapiens*, but its small cranial capacity (1,000 ml) is more typical of *H. erectus*. Like the Petralona skull, the Steinheim specimen has been classified in different ways. Recently, two skulls found in Yun County, China, dating to 350,000 years B.P., also show a mixture of *H. erectus* and early *H. sapiens* traits (Li and Etler 1992).

The general trends are apparent. Sometime between 200,000 and 400,000 years ago, some hominid populations began showing further increase in brain size along with a reduction of the face and changes in the shape of the skull. The fossil record shows that by 200,000 years B.P. such

Figure 11.9

The Petralona skull, Greece. Considered by many to be early *Homo sapiens,* the specimen has a small cranial capacity for that species, a low cranial vault, and thick cranial bones—all features suggestive of *Homo erectus.* This specimen provides a good example of a transitional form. (From Clark Spencer Larsen, Robert M. Matter, and Daniel L. Gebo, *Human Origins: The Fossil Record, Second Edition,* p. 112. Copyright © 1991, 1985 by Waveland Press, Inc., Prospect Heights, Illinois. Reprinted with permission from the publisher)

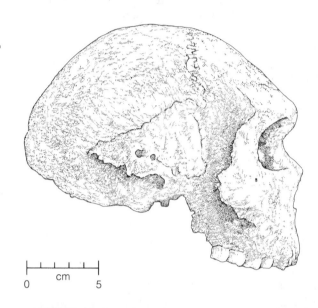

Figure 11.10

The Steinheim skull, West Germany. This specimen has a more well-rounded skull and a larger cranial capacity, on average, than *Homo erectus.* The face and brow ridges are still large, however, suggesting a transitional form. (State Museum for Nature, Stuttgart, Federal Republic of Germany)

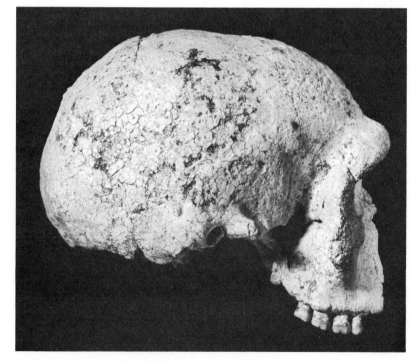

changes proceeded to lead to forms that can definitely be assigned to the species *H. sapiens*. The reasons for these changes are not known. One possibility is that changes in climate led to selection for hominids with larger brain size and other features. Another possibility is that the cultural adaptations of *H. erectus* allowed further evolutionary change when the appropriate mutations occurred for such changes (perhaps an increase in neoteny).

Archaic *Homo Sapiens*

The oldest specimens that can unambiguously be classified as *H. sapiens* are not identical with modern *H. sapiens*. There is considerable variation within our species past and present. Early twentieth-century scientists tended to assign forms to different species based on these variations, but today most (but not all) anthropologists agree that all hominids within the last 200,000 years or so can be placed within our species. The existing differences do not seem great enough to warrant classification as different species. If we call all these hominids by the same name, however, that implies they are all more similar than is actually the case. How do we name fossils that are not distinct enough to make up a separate species but are still not identical to modern humans? Though some scientists argue for the use of subspecies names, the present convention is to place all these hominids into one of two groups—**archaic *H. sapiens*** and **anatomically modern *H. sapiens*.**

Distribution in Time and Space

Archaic *H. sapiens* has been found at a number of sites in Africa, Europe, and Asia (Figure 11.11) dating between 32,000 and 200,000 years B.P. Given the large number of sites and specimens, it has become useful to look more closely at patterns of regional variation. Some of the better-known regions include Sub-Saharan Africa, North Asia, South Asia, and Southeast Asia and Australia (often lumped together as "Australasian").

Because of an early interest in European fossils, much emphasis in the past has been placed on a regional population known as the **Neandertals.** The word *Neandertal* is simply the German for "Neander Valley," the site where one of the first specimens was discovered. The Neandertals lived in the regions surrounding the Mediterranean, including Western Europe, Central and Eastern Europe, the Middle East, and North Africa. Neandertal remains have been found dating between roughly 32,000 to 125,000 years B.P. Earlier literature has often used the term *Neandertal* to refer to *all* archaic *H. sapiens* populations, but now we confine the term to a specific region and time period. The popular media have a tendency to portray

archaic *Homo sapiens* An earlier variant of *Homo sapiens*, found at dates ranging from 32,000 to roughly 200,000 years B.P.

anatomically modern *Homo sapiens* Modern *Homo sapiens*, dating to roughly the last 100,000 years.

Neandertals A regional population of archaic *Homo sapiens* found in the area around the Mediterranean, dating between roughly 32,000 to 125,000 years B.P.

Figure 11.11

Map of archaic *Homo sapiens* sites.

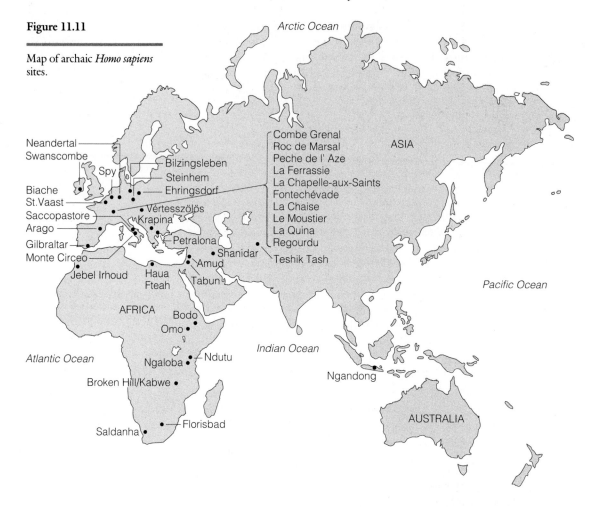

Neandertals as brutish half-humans, but in truth they were simply a regional population of archaic *H. sapiens* (Trinkaus and Shipman 1992).

Physical Characteristics

Both archaic and anatomically modern *H. sapiens* have large brain sizes and small faces relative to *H. erectus*. The average cranial capacity of modern *H. sapiens* is roughly 1,350 ml (Beals et al. 1984). The transitional forms discussed earlier and the earliest archaic *H. sapiens* have somewhat smaller cranial capacities, showing that an increase in brain size has taken place during the last 200,000 years. In fact, the rate of change between 200,000 years B.P. and 45,000 years B.P. was extremely rapid (Godfrey and Jacobs 1981). There has been no further increase in brain size during the last 45,000 years. In fact, a slight decrease in average brain size has occurred, reflecting a general decrease in skeletal size (Henneberg 1988).

Since both archaic and anatomically modern *H. sapiens* have large brains, brain size cannot be used to distinguish between the two groups. The morphology of the skulls of these two groups, however, is on average different. Archaic *H. sapiens* has a low skull with a sloping forehead, whereas anatomically modern *H. sapiens* has a high skull and a vertical forehead. The face and teeth of archaic *H. sapiens* are larger than those in modern *H. sapiens*. Specimens of archaic *H. sapiens* rarely have a chin, something found in modern *H. sapiens*. The postcranial skeleton of many (not all) archaic *H. sapiens* specimens is very similar to modern forms. In general, the bones of archaic *H. sapiens* are thicker and show greater musculature.

Regional variation. One early archaic *H. sapiens* skull (Figure 11.12) was discovered at the site of Broken Hill, Kabwe, Africa, dating to roughly 125,000 years B.P. The large brain size (1,280 ml) is readily apparent. The face is rather large and so are the brow ridges. The shape of the skull shows typical archaic features: a sloping forehead and a low skull.

Another example of an archaic *H. sapiens* skull (Figure 11.13) is from the site of Dali, China, and dates to between 150,000 and 200,000 years B.P. The cranial capacity is on the low end of the range for *H. sapiens* (1,120 ml) and the brow ridges are large. The skull is also low and has a sloping forehead, both typical archaic features. The Dali skull also illustrates regional variation. As in many archaic North Asian specimens, the face is smaller and flatter than in other regions of the world. These traits, among others, are also found in North Asian specimens earlier and later in time (Thorne and Wolpoff 1992).

The Neandertals. Of all the regional populations of archaic *H. sapiens,* the best known is the Neandertals. Also, some of the Neandertal samples appear to be the most different from other regional populations of archaic *H. sapiens,* although this point is still widely debated.

Figure 11.12

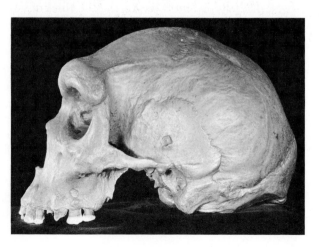

The Broken Hill skull, Kabwe, Zambia. An example of early archaic *Homo sapiens* from Africa.   (Neg. no. 410816. Courtesy Department of Library Services, American Museum of Natural History)

Figure 11.13

The Dali skull, Dali County, People's Republic of China. An example of archaic *Homo sapiens* from Asia. (From Clark Spencer Larsen, Robert M. Matter, and Daniel L. Gebo, *Human Origins: The Fossil Record, Second Edition*, p. 175. Copyright © 1991, 1985 by Waveland Press, Inc., Prospect Heights, Illinois. Reprinted with permission from the publisher)

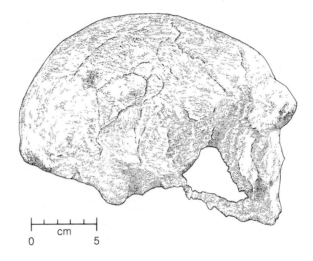

Würm glaciation One of the times of intense climatic cooling ("ice ages") during the Pleistocene epoch.

Many of the Neandertals lived during the time of the **Würm glaciation.** The Pleistocene epoch witnessed alternating periods of glaciation and interglacials as the earth's climate changed. In the Northern Hemisphere large sections of land were covered with advancing ice sheets during glaciations, which receded during interglacial periods. Earlier views on glaciation held that four major glaciations, or "ice ages," took place during the Pleistocene. It is now recognized that the climate changed much more frequently, perhaps as many as seventeen times, in this period. In any case, it is clear that the Neandertals lived during times when the climate was cooler in their habitat. The Neandertals did not live right on the ice, but the reduction in average temperature surely had an effect on their environments, especially Western Europe. The ability of the Neandertals to survive in these conditions is proof of their cultural adaptations, which included hunting, shelter, and use of fire.

Neandertals had the typical archaic features of sloping forehead, low skull, lack of chin, and large brow ridges. They also possessed several unique characteristics that tend not to be found in other regions (or at a much lower frequency).

The Neandertals had very large brains, averaging 1,485 ml. The males had larger average cranial capacities because of their larger body size. It seems likely that, relative to their body size, the Neandertals may have had slightly larger brain sizes than many modern human populations. According to a recent review by Holloway (1985), the structural organization of Neandertal brains, as assessed from endocasts, is no different from that of modern humans.

Neandertals differ from other archaic *H. sapiens* populations in several features. Figures 11.14 and 11.15 show two skulls of Western European Neandertals, both from sites in France between 40,000 and 55,000 years B.P.

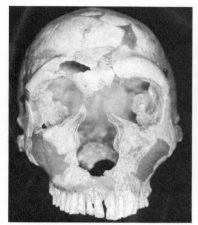

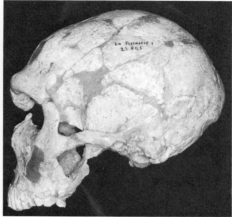

Figure 11.14

Frontal and side view of La Ferrassie skull, a Neandertal from France. (Courtesy of Milford Wolpoff, University of Michigan)

Figure 11.15

Two side views of La Chapelle skull, a Neandertal from France. (Courtesy of Milford Wolpoff, University of Michigan)

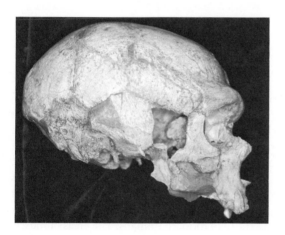

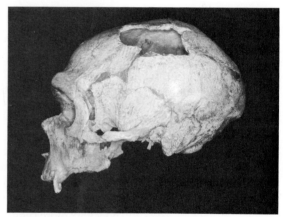

Neandertal faces are generally long and protrude more than in other archaic populations. The nasal region is large, suggesting large noses, and the sinus cavities to the side of the nose expand outward. The large nasal and midfacial areas on Neandertal skulls have often been interpreted as some type of adaptation to cold climate. However, Rak (1986) interprets the large faces of Neandertals in terms of the biomechanics of the skull. He suggests that the Neandertal face acted to withstand stresses brought about by the use of relatively large front teeth. The front teeth of Neandertals are large in relation to their back teeth and often show considerable wear, suggesting their use as tools.

Many Neandertal specimens have a large crest of bone running from behind the ear toward the back of the skull. The back of the skull is rather puffed out (a feature called an **occipital bun**). Though this feature is most common in Neandertals, it is also found in other archaic and modern *H. sapiens* populations.

occipital bun The protruding of the rear region of the skull, a feature often found in Neandertals.

Figure 11.16

Shanidar I skull, Iraq.
(From Clark Spencer Larsen,
Robert M. Matter, and Daniel L.
Gebo, *Human Origins: The Fossil
Record, Second Edition*, p. 128.
Copyright © 1991, 1985 by
Waveland Press, Inc., Prospect
Heights, Illinois. Reprinted with
permission from the publisher)

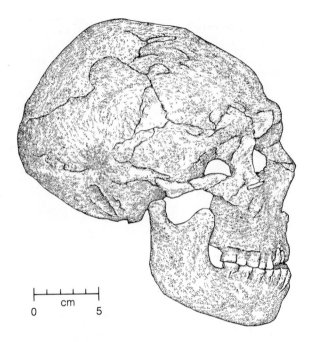

Mousterian tradition The
stone tool technology of the
Neandertals.

There is also variation within Neandertals. Figure 11.16 shows a skull
of a Middle Eastern Neandertal. The skull is a bit more well rounded than
most Western European Neandertal skulls.

Neandertal postcranial remains show essentially modern bipedalism,
out also a few differences compared with other *H. sapiens* populations.
Neandertals were relatively short and stocky. The limb bone segments
farthest from the body (lower arm and lower leg) are relatively short, most
likely reflecting cold adaptation (Trinkaus 1981). The limb and shoulder
bones are more rugged than those of modern humans. The areas of muscle
attachment show that the Neandertals were very strong.

Cultural Behavior

Archaic *H. sapiens* were hunters and gatherers, exploiting a wide
variety of natural resources. Remains of animal bones at their sites show
that they hunted both small game and large, including bears, mammoths,
and rhinoceroses. In some areas it appears that archaic *H. sapiens* hunted
year round; in others they appeared to have migrated along with animal
herds.

Stone tool technology. The stone tools of archaic *H. sapiens* represent
an advancement over the Acheulian and chopping tool traditions of *H.
erectus*. Much of the evidence for stone tool manufacture comes from
Neandertal sites, where the stone tool tradition is known as the **Mousterian.** Similar tools found in other regions of archaic *H. sapiens* are some-

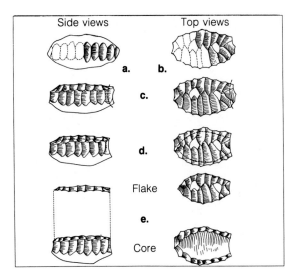

Figure 11.17

Manufacture of a Mousterian tool, using the prepared-core method. First, the core is shaped by removing small flakes from the sides and top (a–d). Then the finished tool is removed from the core (e). (From *Archaeology: Discovering Our Past,* 2d ed., by Robert Sharer and Wendy Ashmore, Fig. 10.3. Copyright © 1993 by Mayfield Publishing Company)

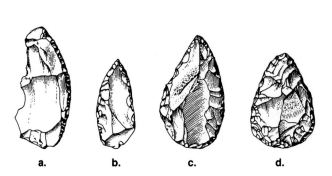

Figure 11.18

Examples of Mousterian tools: (a) scraper, (b) point, (c) scraper, (d) point, (e) hand axe. (From *The Old Stone Age* by F. Bordes, 1968. Reprinted with permission of the publisher, Weidenfeld and Nicolson, Ltd.)

times referred to as Mousterian or Mousterianlike, as well as by other names (for example, in Africa, the term *Middle Stone Age* is frequently used). In this chapter, the term *Mousterian* is used in a general sense to refer to the basic patterns of tool manufacture among archaic *H. sapiens.*

The key feature of the Mousterian tradition is the use of a prepared-core technique in tool manufacture. As Figure 11.17 shows, a flint nodule is first chipped around the edges. Small flakes are then removed from the top surface of the core. In the final step, the core is struck precisely at one end.

The use of the prepared-core technique, which produces sharp and symmetric tools (Figure 11.18), tells us two important things about archaic *H. sapiens.* First, they were capable of precise toolmaking, which implies an excellent knowledge of flaking methods and of the structural characteristics of stone. Second, they were able to visualize the final tool early in production. Not until the last step does the shape of the finished tool become apparent.

Symbolic behavior. Archaeological evidence suggests that archaic *H. sapiens* may have been capable of symbolic thought, perhaps even holding beliefs in the supernatural. Archaic *H. sapiens* (specifically, some Neandertals) were the first hominid to bury their dead deliberately. Evidence of burial comes from a number of European and Middle Eastern sites, where dead persons' bones have been arranged carefully in graves, often in association with tools, food, and flowers. At the Shanidar Cave site in Iraq, flowers had been placed all over the bodies, an event we can reconstruct from the presence of fossil pollen in the graves.

Such evidence suggests the evolution of symbolic expressions and the possibility of supernatural beliefs, because it seems doubtful anyone would go to all that trouble without a reason. This standard interpretation, however, is changing. Klein (1989) notes that burial need not have symbolic purpose; for archaic *H. sapiens* it may have been the easiest way to remove the dead from living space. In addition, although the Shanidar burial still stands as one of the best examples of symbolic behavior, it is possible the pollen was introduced by rodents burrowing into the grave *after* burial.

Language capability. Did archaic *H. sapiens* have language? Lieberman and Crelin (1971), who reconstructed the vocal anatomy of Neandertals, concluded they were incapable of vocalizing certain vowel sounds. The implication was that archaic *H. sapiens* did not possess as wide a range of sounds as modern humans and perhaps had limited language abilities. This hypothesis was criticized, however, because of differences of opinion on vocal anatomy reconstruction. The lack of direct fossil evidence at the heart of the debate was ultimately furnished with the discovery of the first hyoid bone for archaic *H. sapiens,* a bone lying in the neck that can be used to provide information on the structure of the respiratory tract. That this specimen is almost identical in size and shape to the hyoid bone of modern humans indicates that there were no differences in vocal ability between archaics and moderns (Arensberg et al. 1990).

Anatomically Modern *Homo Sapiens*

Human evolution did not end with the emergence of modern *H. sapiens.* By 30,000 years B.P., all fossil humans are anatomically modern in form. Though it is clear that archaic *H. sapiens* evolved into anatomically modern *H. sapiens,* the exact nature of this evolution is less certain.

Distribution in Time and Space

Anatomically modern *H. sapiens* are found in Pleistocene sites in Africa, Europe, and Asia. They are also found in areas previously unoccupied by hominids, such as Australia and the New World. Many anatomically modern *H. sapiens* sites date to the last 30,000 years. Recent evidence suggests that this form is actually much older than once thought. Cranial remains from the Border Cave site in southeast Africa are fragmentary but show typical anatomically modern features (Figure 11.19). The dating for this site is not definite but could range between 90,000 and 115,000 years B.P. Humans may have occupied the Klasies River Mouth, South Africa, at least as early as 90,000 years B.P. (Grün et al. 1990). Other African sites also provide evidence of an early appearance of anatomically modern *H. sapiens*: Omo, Ethiopia (roughly 130,000 years B.P.) and Laetoli (perhaps 120,000 years B.P.). There is also recent, controversial evidence of an early occurrence of anatomically modern *H. sapiens* in the Middle East, with both the Qafzeh and Tabun sites in Israel dating to perhaps 92,000 years B.P. (Grün et al. 1991). These early dates are still somewhat uncertain, and not all researchers accept them or the fossil evidence, but it is becoming increasingly certain that anatomically modern *H. sapiens* existed before the youngest known archaic forms.

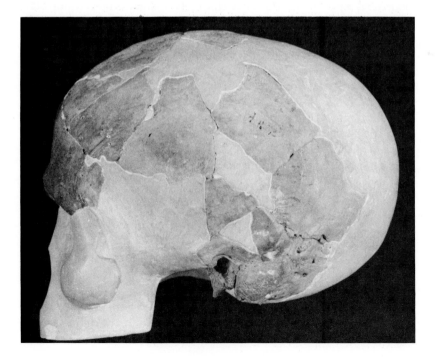

Figure 11.19

The Border Cave skull, South Africa. The fragmentary remains are clearly those of anatomically modern *Homo sapiens* (note the vertical forehead). Dating is not precise, but current estimates suggest an age of more than 100,000 years B.P. (Photo by Peter Faugust by permission of Phillip V. Tobias)

Figure 11.20

Frontal and side view of Cro-Magnon skull, France. This specimen is one of the best-known examples of anatomically modern *Homo sapiens*. (Neg. no. 109226, 109227. Courtesy Department of Library Services, American Museum of Natural History)

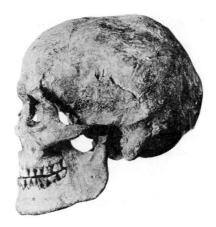
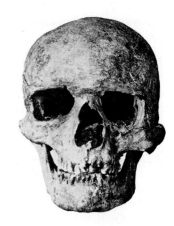

Physical Characteristics

Figure 11.20 shows a skull from one of the more famous anatomically modern sites—Cro-Magnon, France, dating between 23,000 and 27,000 years B.P. This skull shows many of the characteristics of anatomically modern *H. sapiens:* it is high and well rounded. There is no occipital bun; the back of the skull is rounded instead. The forehead rises vertically above the eye orbits and does not slope, as in archaic *H. sapiens*. The brow ridges are small, the face does not protrude very much, and a strong chin is evident.

Another example of anatomically modern *H. sapiens* is shown in Figure 11.21, a skull from the Skhul site at Mt. Carmel, Israel. This skull also has a high, well-rounded skull without an occipital bun and a small chin. Compared to the Cro-Magnon skull, the brow ridges are larger and the face protrudes slightly. The differences between the Skhul and Cro-Magnon skulls are typical of variation within a species, particularly when we consider that they existed at different times in separate places.

Cultural Behavior

Discussing the cultural adaptations of anatomically modern *H. sapiens* is difficult because they include prehistoric technologies as well as more recent developments, such as agriculture, generation of electricity, the internal combustion engine, and nuclear energy. So that we may provide a comparison with the culture of the archaic forms, this section is limited to prehistory before the development of agriculture (roughly 12,000 years B.P.).

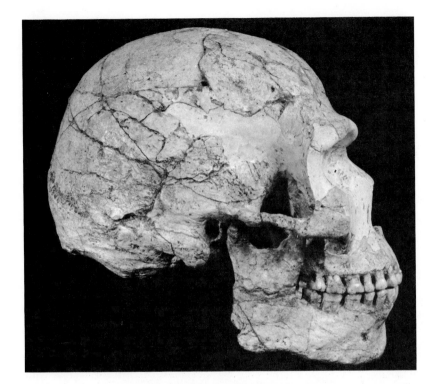

Figure 11.21

An early anatomically modern *Homo sapiens* skull from Skhul, Israel. (Peabody Museum, Harvard University, Photographed by Hillel Burger)

Tool technologies. There is so much variation in the stone tool technologies of anatomically modern *H. sapiens* that it is impossible to define a single tradition. For the sake of discussion, the types of stone tool industries are often lumped together under the term **Upper Paleolithic** (which means "Upper Old Stone Age"). **Lower Paleolithic** consists of the stone tool traditions of *H. habilis* and *H. erectus*, and **Middle Paleolithic** includes the stone tool traditions of archaic *H. sapiens*. Even though we use a single label to describe common features of Upper Paleolithic tool industries, do not be misled into thinking all traditions were the same. Variation, both within and among sites, is even greater in the Upper Paleolithic than in earlier cultures. This variation shows the increasing sophistication and specialization of stone tools.

Figure 11.22 shows some of the tools found at Upper Paleolithic sites. In general, these tools are more precisely made than earlier tools. Many smaller tools appear at this time, possible only through more sophisticated methods of manufacture. Materials other than stone were used, such as bone and antler. Another important feature of Upper Paleolithic culture is that tools were often used to make other tools. For example, small stone tools were made to carve other tools out of bone.

Upper Paleolithic The Upper Old Stone Age; also refers to the stone tool technologies of anatomically modern *Homo sapiens*.

Lower Paleolithic The Lower Old Stone Age; also refers to the stone tool technologies of *Homo habilis* and *Homo erectus*.

Middle Paleolithic The Middle Old Stone Age; also refers to the stone tool technologies of archaic *Homo sapiens*.

Figure 11.22

Examples of Upper Paleolithic stone tools: (a) knife, (b) scraper, (c) point, (d) scraper, (e) point. Tools *a*, *b*, and *c* are from the Perigordian culture; tool *d* is from the Aurignacian culture; tool *e* is from the Solutrean culture.   (From *The Old Stone Age* by F. Bordes, 1968. Reprinted with permission of the publisher, Weidenfeld and Nicolson, Ltd.)

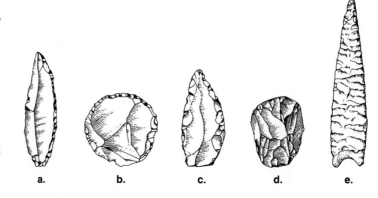

a.   b.   c.   d.   e.

Figure 11.23

Cave painting of a running horse from Lascaux Cave, France.   (Museum of Man, Paris; photographer F. Windels)

Cave art. Another form of symbolic behavior appears with anatomically modern *H. sapiens*—cave art. Many of these paintings are of large game animals and are anatomically correct and well executed (Figure 11.23). Painting is a form of human activity that is spiritually rewarding but has no apparent function in day-to-day existence. Why, then, did prehistoric humans paint images on the walls of caves? One possible interpretation involves sympathetic magic. By capturing the image of an animal on the wall, humans hoped to improve their chances at hunting.

    Geographic expansion. The archaeological evidence shows that humans became more and more successful in adapting to their environments, and consequently populations grew and expanded. By 50,000 years B.P., populations of anatomically modern *H. sapiens* had reached Australia (Roberts et al. 1990). During times of glaciation the sea levels drop, extending the land mass of the continents. The drop in sea level allowed earlier populations of hominids to reach Southeast Asia, but Australia was not then connected to the Asian continent. For humans to reach Australia, they had to cross many kilometers of sea. The only way they could do this was by some sort of raft or boat.

    Anatomically modern *H. sapiens* also moved into the New World. The number of such movements, and their dates, are a continuing source of controversy (Rogers et al., 1992). One fact all parties agree on is that humans were living in the New World by 12,000 years B.P. Some argue these dates are the earliest, whereas others cite newer evidence and reanalysis of previous finds indicating a much earlier initial occupation—perhaps 20,000 to 30,000 years ago.

    Archaeological evidence demonstrates an Asian origin for the first migrants to the New World. The most commonly suggested route is across the Bering land bridge. During periods of glaciation the sea levels fell, exposing a stretch of land connecting Asia and North America. This "land bridge" was almost 2,100 kilometers (roughly 1,300 miles) wide (Figure 11.24). It did not appear or disappear suddenly but instead developed over thousands of years as the sea levels dropped.

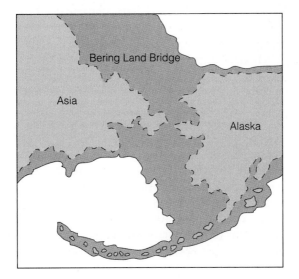

Figure 11.24

The Bering Land Bridge. Today the former Soviet Union and Alaska are separated by water. During the "Ice Ages," water was trapped in glaciers, producing a drop in the sea level that exposed the land area known as the Bering Land Bridge. This "bridge" connecting North America and Asia was actually 2,100 km wide!

recent African origin model A model of the evolution of *Homo sapiens* whereby archaic *Homo sapiens* evolved into anatomically modern *Homo sapiens* in Africa and then spread throughout the Old World, replacing archaic populations.

multiregional evolution model A model of the evolution of *Homo sapiens* whereby the change from archaic to modern forms took place in all regions of the Old World.

assimilation model A model of the evolution of modern *Homo sapiens* whereby the transition from archaic to modern *H. sapiens* occurred in a single region such as Africa, followed by assimilation into archaic *H. sapiens* populations elsewhere in the Old World.

The Origin of Anatomically Modern *Homo Sapiens*

When, where, and how did anatomically modern *H. sapiens* evolve from archaic *H. sapiens*?

Current Models and Debates

Three current models are considered here as hypotheses for the evolution of anatomically modern *H. sapiens*: the **recent African origin model,** the **multiregional evolution model,** and the **assimilation model.**

The recent African origin model. According to the recent African origin model, the transition from archaic to anatomically modern *H. sapiens* occurred in Africa roughly 200,000 years ago. The modern forms then expanded out from Africa, replacing earlier archaic populations throughout the Old World (Stringer and Andrews 1988; Wilson and Cann 1992). Little, if any, interbreeding took place with archaic populations outside of Africa. The replacement of archaic with modern forms may have resulted from an evolutionary advantage held by the latter, so that over time, moderns became more and more numerous and the populations of archaics declined and ultimately died out.

The multiregional evolution model. The multiregional evolution model states that archaic *H. sapiens* evolved into modern *H. sapiens* throughout the Old World. By 1 million years ago, *H. erectus* had moved out from Africa into different regions of the Old World. Over time, these populations differed from one another because of genetic drift and adaptation to local environments. Gene flow continued between regions, however, so that all regional populations remained part of a single species. As drift and selection acted to increase differences between regions, gene flow acted to reduce them. Through the *balance* of gene flow, drift, and natural selection, all regional populations changed from archaic to modern forms (though not necessarily at the same time), while also maintaining some regional differences (Wolpoff et al. 1984; Thorne and Wolpoff 1992).

The assimilation model. A variant of the multiregional model has been proposed by Fred Smith and colleagues (1989a) that also incorporates a feature of the recent African origin model. According to their model, the transition from archaic to modern *H. sapiens* occurred *first* in a single region such as Africa. Given the interconnections of populations over time, any advantageous genetic change then spread out into other archaic populations through gene flow (assimilation occurred, not replacement or invasion). Because gene flow takes time, moderns appeared first in one region, then later in others as gene flow caught up to them.

Fossil and Genetic Evidence

The three evolutionary models discussed above all make specific predictions that can be tested using the fossil record and evidence from patterns of genetic variation among living human populations.

The fossil evidence. Which model, or models, does the fossil evidence support? Although the comparison of archaic and modern *H. sapiens* fossils over time and space seems relatively clear-cut, in practice things are often more difficult. Differing interpretations of fossil morphology, disagreement about whether physical features are primitive or derived, and debates over dating of sites all complicate the process. In spite of these problems, there appears to be growing consensus on a number of points (although it is still by no means unanimous). First, modern forms appear to be older in Africa than in other regions (Smith et al. 1989a). While there is continuing debate over dating, this evidence suggests that modern forms arose *initially* in Africa and later in other regions. This finding supports both the recent African origin model and the assimilation model.

Second, there is strong evidence for regional continuity in several regions, particularly Asia and Australia (Wolpoff 1989; Kramer 1991), and evidence also exists for continuity in parts of Europe (Smith et al. 1989b; Thorne and Wolpoff 1992). That is, modern forms in a particular region tend to resemble archaics there. This finding supports both the strict multiregional evolution model and the assimilation model, although it is only fair to point out that some paleoanthropologists dispute the fossil evidence for regional continuity (e.g., Stringer and Andrews 1988).

The two lines of evidence together affirm the assimilation model. The evolution of *H. sapiens* appears multiregional, but with initial genetic change occurring in Africa and spreading to other connected populations by gene flow. (This is my interpretation of the current data, and it is by no means agreed on by all anthropologists!)

Indeed the assimilation model need not predict continuity in *every* region. At present, the evidence for regional continuity in Western Europe is not as strong as in Asia and Australia, and it is possible that the Neandertals remained relatively isolated from the rest of the species.

The genetic evidence. From a genetic standpoint, major support for the recent African origin model came initially from a new method of genetic analysis—the study of **mitochondrial DNA.** Most evolutionary analyses focus on the DNA within the nucleus of each cell. A small amount of DNA also exists within the mitochondria of the cells. Mitochondrial DNA (mtDNA) is different because it is only inherited through the mother. Eggs transmit mtDNA, but sperm usually do not (although recent data have shown that there is some paternal inheritance of mtDNA [Gyllensten et al. 1991]). As a result, there is no shuffling of genes during

mitochondrial DNA (mtDNA) DNA found in the mitochondria of the cells rather than the nucleus and inherited primarily through females.

reproduction as there is with nuclear DNA. If we assume that mtDNA is a neutral genetic trait (some evidence supports this), then the only factor affecting mtDNA evolution over long periods of time is mutation. Because of this characteristic, mtDNA can be used to trace ancestry through females back to an original source. By looking at different types of mtDNA, we can estimate the type and order of different mutations and come up with a genetic profile of a common ancestor.

Rebecca Cann and colleagues (1987) looked at the mtDNA of 147 placentas from women with ancestors from different parts of the world. Based on data suggesting a constant rate of mtDNA mutation, Cann and her colleagues estimated that the mtDNA of *all* modern humans stems from a single woman who lived in Africa between 140,000 and 290,000 years ago. The inference that all of humanity arose from a single female has led some to refer to this hypothetical ancestor as "Eve."

The mitochondrial DNA evidence suffered greatly in 1992 with the publication of two studies showing that the basic methodology for reconstructing family trees had been incorrectly used in the early studies (Hedges et al. 1992; Templeton 1992). Some newer reanalyses still support an African origin model, but others have suggested that non-Africans had more divergent mtDNA than Africans. These continuing problems, combined with evidence of paternal inheritance, suggest some problems in using mtDNA samples to pinpoint the time and place of modern human origins. Of course, these negative results do not rule out the possibility that mtDNA studies may someday be more useful in studying human origins—it is quite common in science for new methods to be revised after their initial application.

Summary. While all three models of the origin of modern humans remain viable to some extent, the combined fossil and genetic evidence to date may best support the assimilation variant of the multiregional model, this explains both the observed regional continuity in the fossil record and the possibility of initial modern origins in Africa.

Why Did Modern Humans Evolve?

The alternative models for the origin of modern humans are fascinating to debate, but we don't want to lose track of a basic fact that all agree on: only modern humans have been found in the last 30,000 years. In addition to explaining the timing and nature of the transition from archaics to moderns, we must also ask ourselves why this transition occurred in the first place. The available evidence suggests that anatomically modern *H. sapiens* had some evolutionary advantage over archaic *H. sapiens*. But what was this advantage?

Various biological and cultural explanations have been offered to account for this fact. The biological changes from archaic to modern are easy to describe, but they are much more difficult to explain. The change in cranial shape may suggest some associated change in patterns of brain growth and possible behavior. Language, for example, has been claimed as one such ability. According to this view, archaic *H. sapiens* lacked sophisticated speech. Evolutionary changes in anatomically modern *H. sapiens* may have led to advanced speech abilities that would certainly provide an evolutionary advantage. What we know about archaic and modern brain size and structure, however, does not support this model.

Technological changes have also been suggested as mechanisms for the change from archaic to modern forms. This view holds that many of the structural characteristics of archaic *H. sapiens* were the result of stresses generated by the use of their front teeth as tools. The large size and wear patterns of the incisor teeth of archaics (especially Neandertals) support the notion that these teeth were used for a variety of purposes. The stresses generated by heavy use of the front teeth can also be used to explain the large face, large neck muscles, and other features of archaic skulls. Once technological adaptations had developed sufficiently, these physical adaptations were no longer necessary and would not be selected for. Smaller teeth and faces might then be advantageous, because smaller structures require correspondingly less energy for growth and maintenance (Smith et al. 1989a). Similar arguments can be made to explain the reduction in body size and musculature (e.g., Frayer 1984). Once cultural behaviors took the place of larger teeth, faces, and bones, then smaller structures actually became more adaptive. Once again, evolution is best seen in terms of the overall balance between costs and benefits. In the past, as today, human culture can alter the nature of this relationship.

SUMMARY

Following the initial emergence of the genus *Homo,* the record of human evolution shows an increase in brain size and complexity, reduction in the face and teeth, and an increasing reliance on cultural adaptations. The basic sequence from *H. habilis* to *H. erectus* to archaic *H. sapiens* to anatomically modern *H. sapiens* is well documented, although the fine detail of this sequence is still under investigation.

The species *H. erectus* appears to have rapidly evolved from some populations of *H. habilis* in East Africa 1.6 million years B.P. *H. erectus* had an increased cranial capacity and exhibited a variety of cultural adaptations, including greater sophistication in stone tool technology, hunting and gathering, the use of fire, and the use and manufacture of shelter. These adaptations allowed hominids to expand out of Africa. By 1 million years ago, *H. erectus* had reached Asia. Later *H. erectus* or early *H. sapiens* populations inhabited the southern range of Europe by roughly 400,000 years B.P.

By 200,000 to 400,000 years B.P., archaic *H. sapiens* existed in the Old World. The major biological changes reflect a further increase in brain size, which continued until roughly 45,000 years ago. Archaic *H. sapiens* differs from anatomically modern *H. sapiens* in a number of ways, primarily in having a larger face and brow ridges, a sloping forehead, and a less well-rounded skull. Regional differences in archaic *H. sapiens* are apparent from the fossil record. The Neandertals from Western Europe and the Middle East make up the best-known regional population. Contrary to popular thought, the Neandertals were quite intelligent. They had a sophisticated stone tool technology, buried their dead, and adapted to harsh climates.

Anatomically modern *H. sapiens* is best known after 30,000 years B.P. There is growing evidence, however, that the first groups of anatomically modern *H. sapiens* emerged in Africa over 100,000 years ago. The transition from archaic to modern forms can be explained by three models. The recent African origin model states that modern humans arose first in Africa roughly 200,000 years ago and then spread out over the rest of the Old World, replacing archaic populations. According to this model, archaic populations outside of Africa did not contribute genetically to modern humans. The multiregional evolution model states that the transition from *H. erectus* to archaic *H. sapiens* to modern *H. sapiens* occurred throughout the Old World, with biological change reflecting both regional continuity and gene flow between regions that maintained a single species. A variant of this idea, the assimilation model, states that the *initial* change to moderns took place in Africa and then became incorporated into the rest of the species over time through gene flow resulting from migration between neighboring groups. Both fossil and genetic evidence have been used to test these models. While uncertainty and controversy remain, current data best support the assimilation model.

Regardless of which model is correct, the reasons behind the emergence of anatomically modern forms are not known with certainty. Possible factors include biological changes resulting from the increasing impact of cultural adaptations. Human evolution did not end with the emergence of anatomically modern *H. sapiens*. Our species continues to change.

Supplemental Readings

Klein, R. G. 1989. *The Human Career: Human Biological and Cultural Origins*. Chicago: University of Chicago Press. An excellent summary of the fossil and (particularly) archaeological records of human evolution. Considerable attention is given to *H. erectus* and *H. sapiens*.

Smith, F. H., A. B. Falsetti, and S. M. Donnelly. 1989. Modern human origins. *Yearbook of Physical Anthropology* 32:35–68. An excellent review of competing models of the origin of modern *H. sapiens*.

Thorne, A. G., and M. H. Wolpoff. April 1992. The multiregional evolution of humans. *Scientific American* 266(4):76–83. A nontechnical review of the multiregional evolution model and its supporting evidence.

Trinkaus, E., and P. Shipman. 1993. *The Neandertals: Changing the Image of Mankind*. New York: Knopf. An excellent and nontechnical review of the history of Neandertal discoveries and interpretations.

Wilson, A. C., and R. L. Cann. April 1992. The recent African genesis of humans. *Scientific American* 266(4):68–73. Appearing in the same issue as the Thorne and Wolpoff article, this paper provides a nontechnical review of the recent African origin model and its supporting evidence. Reading both papers together is recommended.

Wolpoff, M. H. 1980. *Paleoanthropology*. New York: Knopf. Although now out of date, this remains an excellent source for descriptions and discussions of variations in *H. erectus* and *H. sapiens* fossils.

Epilogue: The Future of Our Species

This book has focused on human biological variation and evolution, past and present. What about the future? Can biological anthropology, or indeed any science, make predictions about the future of our species? What possible directions will our biological and cultural evolution take?

One thing is for certain—we continue to evolve both biologically and culturally and will do so in the future. Human evolution is increasingly complex because of our biocultural nature. Much of our adaptive nature is culturally based. We can adapt to a situation more quickly through cultural evolution than through biological evolution. Theoretically, we can also direct our cultural evolution. We can focus our efforts on solutions to specific problems, such as finding a vaccine for AIDS or developing ways to further reduce dental decay. Biological evolution, on the other hand, has no inherent direction. Natural selection works on existing variation, not on what we might desire or need.

Our success with cultural adaptations should not lead us to conclude that we do not continue to evolve biologically. Regardless of our triumphs in the field of medicine, many incurable diseases still carry on the process of natural selection. Biological variation still takes place in potential and realized fertility. Perhaps as many as a third to half of all human conceptions fail to produce live births. We still live in a world in which up to 50 percent of the children have an inadequate diet. Even if all inhabitants of the world were raised to an adequate standard of living tomorrow, we would still be subject to natural selection and biological evolution. The fact that we are cultural organisms does not detract from the fact that we are also biological organisms. Scholars in various fields throughout history have argued about whether humans and human behavior should be studied biologically, as products of nature, or culturally, as products of nurture. Both sides were wrong. Humans must be studied as *both* biological and cultural organisms.

Given that we will continue to evolve, how will we evolve? This question cannot be answered. Evolution has many random elements that cannot be predicted. Also, the biocultural nature of humans makes prediction even harder. The incredible rate of cultural and technological change in the past century was not predicted. What kinds of cultural evolution are possible in the next hundred years? We may be able to forecast some short-term changes, but we know nothing about the cultural capabilities of our species hundreds or thousands of years in the future.

Another problem is that our own viewpoint can influence our predictions. An optimistic view might focus on the success of past cultural adaptations and the rate of acquisition of knowledge and then develop a scenario including increased standard of living for all, cheap energy sources, and an elevated life expectancy. A pessimistic view might consider all of the horrors of the past and present, and project a grim future. A pessimist might envisage widespread famine, overcrowding, pollution, disease, and warfare. Most likely, any possible future will be neither pie-in-the-sky nor doom, but a combination of positive and negative changes. If the study of evolution tells us one thing, it is that every change has potential costs and benefits. We need to temper our optimism and pessimism with a sense of balance.

In any consideration of the future, we must acknowledge change as basic to life. Many people find it tempting to suggest we would be better off living a "simpler" life. Others argue that we should stop trying to deal with our problems and let nature take its course or that we should trust in the acts of God. This is unacceptable—indeed our understanding of human evolution argues for the reverse. Our adaptive pattern has been one of learning and problem solving. More than that, these are our primate heritage. Our biology has allowed us to develop the basic mammalian patterns of learned behavior to a high degree. We have the capability for rational thought, for reason, and for learning. Even if many of our cultural inventions have led to suffering and pain, our *potential* for good is immense. In any case, we must continue along the path of learning and intelligence; it is our very nature. Good or bad, the capabilities of the human mind and spirit may be infinite.

Taxonomy of
Living Primates

The chart that begins on page 298 lists representatives of all living primate groups. The Anglicized, rather than Latin, names are used here for the taxonomic categories of suborder, infraorder, superfamily, family, and subfamily. Individual species were taken from Jolly (1985) but placed in a more traditional taxonomy following Hrdy (1981).

Order: Primates

Suborder: Prosimians

Infraorder	Superfamily	Family	Subfamily
Lemuriformes	Lemuroids	Lemurids	Lemurines
			Lepilemurines
			Cheirogaleines
		Indriids	
		Daubentoniids	
Lorisiformes		Lorisids	Lorisines
			Galagines

Order: Primates

Suborder: Prosimians

Genus	Species	Common name
Lemur	*L. catta*	Ring-tailed lemur
	L. fulvus	Brown lemur
	L. macaco	Black lemur
	L. mongoz	Mongoose lemur
	L. rubriventer	Red-bellied lemur
Hapalemur	*H. griseus*	Gray lemur
	H. simus	Simus lemur
Varecia	*V. variegata*	Ruffed lemur
Lepilemur	*L. dorsalis*	Nosy Be lepilemur
	L. edwardsii	Edward's lepilemur
	L. leucopus	White-footed lepilemur
	L. microdon	Microdon lepilemur
	L. mustelinus	Mustelinus lepilemur
	L. ruficaudatus	Red-tailed lepilemur
	L. septentrionalis	Montagne d'Ambre lepilemur
Microcebus	*M. murinus*	Western mouse lemur
	M. rufus	Eastern mouse lemur
	M. coquereli	Coquerel's mouse lemur
Cheirogaleuse	*C. medius*	Western dwarf lemur
	C. major	Eastern dwarf lemur
Allocebus	*A. trichotis*	Hairy-eared dwarf lemur
Phaner	*P. furcifer*	Forked lemur
Avahi	*A. laniger*	Woolley lemur
Propithecus	*P. diadema*	Diademed sifaka
	P. verreauxi	White sifaka
Indri	*I. indri*	Indri
Daubentonia	*D. madagascariensis*	Aye-aye
Loris	*L. tardigradus*	Slender loris
Nycticebus	*N. coucang*	Common slow loris
	N. pygmaeus	Pygmy slow loris
Arctocebus	*A. calabarensis*	Angwantibo
Perodicticus	*P. potto*	Potto
Galago	*G. alleni*	Allen's galago
	G. crassicaudatus	Thick-tailed galago
	G. demidovii	Demidoff's galago

Order: Primates

Suborder: Prosimians

Infraorder	Superfamily	Family	Subfamily
Tarsiiformes		Tarsiids	

Order: Primates

Suborder: Anthropoids

Infraorder	Superfamily	Family	Subfamily
	Ceboids	Callitrichids	Callitrichines
			Callimiconines
		Cebids	Cebinines
			Aotinines
			Callicebines

Order: Primates

Suborder: Prosimians

Genus	Species	Common name
	G. elegantulus	Needle-clawed galago
	G. inustus	Inustus galago
	G. senegalensis	Senegal galago
Tarsius	*T. bancanus*	Borneo tarsier
	T. spectrum	Spectral tarsier
	T. syrichta	Philippine tarsier

Order: Primates

Suborder: Anthropoids

Genus	Species	Common name
Callithrix	*C. argentata*	Silvery marmoset
	C. aurita	Buffy tufted-eared marmoset
	C. chrysoleuca	Goldern marmoset
	C. flaviceps	Buffy-headed marmoset
	C. geoffroyi	Geoffroy's marmoset
	C. humeralifer	Santarem marmoset
	C. jacchus	Common marmoset
	C. penecillata	Black tufted-eared marmoset
Cebuella	*C. pygmaea*	Pygmy marmoset
Saguinus	*S. bicolor*	Barefaced tamarin
	S. fuscicollis	Saddleback tamarin
	S. imperator	Emperor tamarin
	S. inustus	Inustus tamarin
	S. labiatus	White-lipped tamarin
	S. leucopus	White-footed tamarin
	S. midas	Red-handed tamarin
	S. mystax	Moustached tamarin
	S. nigricollis	Black-and-red tamarin
	S. oedipus	Cotton-top tamarin
Leontopithecus	*L. rosalia*	Lion tamarin
Callimico	*C. goeldii*	Goeldi's marmoset
Cebus	*C. albifrons*	White-fronted cebus
	C. apella	Tufted cebus
	C. capucinus	White-throated cebus
	C. nigrivittatus	Black-capped cebus
Aotus	*A. trivirgatus*	Night monkey
Callicebus	*C. personatus*	Masked titi monkey

Order: Primates

Suborder: Anthropoids

Infraorder	Superfamily	Family	Subfamily
			Saimirines
			Pithecines
			Alouattines
			Atelines
Cercopithecoids	Cercopithecids	Cercopithecines	

Order: Primates

Suborder: Anthropoids

Genus	Species	Common name
	C. moloch	Dusky titi monkey
	C. torquatus	Widow titi monkey
Saimiri	*S. oerstedi*	Red-backed squirrel monkey
	S. sciureus	Common squirrel monkey
Pithecia	*P. albicans*	White saki
	P. hirsuta	Hairy saki
	P. monachus	Monk saki
	P. pithecia	Pale-headed saki
Cacajao	*C. calvus*	Bald uakari
	C. melanocephalus	Black-headed uakari
	C. rubicundus	Red uakari
Chiropetes	*C. albinasus*	White-nosed bearded saki
	C. satanus	Black-bearded saki
Alouatta	*A. belzebul*	Black-and-red howler
	A. caraya	Black howler
	A. fusca	Brown howler
	A. palliata	Mantled howler
	A. seniculus	Red howler
	A. villosa	Guatemalan howler
Ateles	*A. belzebuth*	Long-haired spider monkey
	A. fusciceps	Brown-headed spider monkey
	A. geoffroyi	Black-handed spider monkey
	A. paniscus	Black spider monkey
Brachyteles	*B. arachnoides*	Woolly spider monkey
Lathothrix	*L. flavicauda*	Hendee's woolly monkey
	L. lagotricha	Humboldt's woolly monkey
Macaca	*M. arctoides*	Stump-tailed macaque
	M. assamensis	Assamese macaque
	M. cyclopis	Formosan rock macaque
	M. fascicularis	Crab-eating macaque
	M. fuscata	Japanese macaque
	M. maurus	Moor macaque
	M. mulatta	Rhesus macaque
	M. nemestrina	Pig-tailed macaque
	M. nigra	Celebes black macaque
	M. ochreata	Ochre macaque
	M. radiata	Bonnet macaque
	M. silenus	Lion-tailed macaque
	M. sinica	Toque macaque

Order: Primates

Suborder: Anthropoids

Infraorder	Superfamily	Family	Subfamily

Colobines

Order: Primates

Suborder: Anthropoids

Genus	Species	Common name
	M. sylvana	Barbary macaque
	M. thibetana	Thibetan macaque
	M. togeana	Togian macaque
Cerocebus	*C. albigena*	Gray-cheeked mangabey
	C. atterimus	Black mangabey
	C. galeritus	Agile mangabey
	C. torquatus	White-collared mangabey
Papio	*P. anubis*	Olive baboon
	P. cynocephalus	Yellow baboon
	P. hamdryas	Hamadryas baboon
	P. papio	Guinea baboon
	P. ursinus	Chacma baboon
Mandrillus	*M. leucophaeus*	Drill
	M. sphinx	Mandrill
Theropithecus	*T. gelada*	Gelada
Cercopithecus	*C. aethiops*	Vervet guenon
	C. ascanius	Red-tailed guenon
	C. cambelli	Campbell's guenon
	C. cephus	Moustached guenon
	C. denti	Dent's guenon
	C. diana	Diana guenon
	C. dryas	Dryas guenon
	C. erythogaster	Red-bellied guenon
	C. erythrotis	Red-eared guenon
	C. hamlyni	Hamlyn's guenon
	C. lhoesti	l'Hoest's guenon
	C. mitis	Blue guenon
	C. mona	Mona guenon
	C. neglectus	De Brazza's guenon
	C. nictitans	Spot-nosed guenon
	C. peraurista	Lesser spot-nosed guenon
	C. pogonias	Crowned guenon
	C. preussi	Preuss's guenon
	C. salongo	Salongo guenon
	C. wolfi	Wolf's guenon
Miopithecus	*M. talapoin*	Talapoin
Allenopithecus	*A. nirgoviridis*	Allen's swamp monkey
Erythrocebus	*E. patas*	Patas monkey
Presbytius	*P. aygula*	Sunda Island langur

Order: Primates

Suborder: Anthropoids

Infraorder	Superfamily	Family	Subfamily
	Hominoids	Hylobatids	
		Pongids	
		Hominids	

Order: Primates

Suborder: Anthropoids

Genus	Species	Common name
	P. cristata	Silvered langur
	P. entellus	Hanuman langur
	P. francoisi	Francois's langur
	P. frontata	White-fronted langur
	P. geei	Golden langur
	P. johnii	Nilgiri langur
	P. melalophos	Banded langur
	P. obscura	Dusky langur
	P. phayrei	Phayre's langur
	P. pileata	Capped langur
	P. potenziani	Mentawai langur
	P. rubicunda	Maroon langur
	P. senex	Purple-faced langur
Rhinopithecus	*R. avunculus*	Tonkin snubnosed langur
	R. brelichi	Brelichi snubnosed langur
	R. roxellanae	Golden snubnosed langur
Pygathrix	*P. nemaeus*	Douc langur
Nasalis	*N. larvatus*	Proboscis monkey
Simias	*S. concolor*	Pagai Island langur
Colobus	*C. angolensis*	Angola colobus
	C. badius	Red colobus
	C. guereza	Guereza colobus
	C. kirkii	Kirk's red colobus
	C. polykomos	King colobus
	C. satanas	Black colobus
Procolobus	*P. verus*	Olive colobus
Hylobates	*H. agilis*	Agile gibbon
	H. concolor	Black gibbon
	H. hoolock	Hoolock gibbon
	H. klossi	Kloss's gibbon
	H. lar	White-handed gibbon
	H. moloch	Silvery gibbon
	H. muelleri	Meuller's gibbon
	H. pileatus	Pileated gibbon
Symphalangus	*S. syndactylus*	Siamang
Pongo	*P. pygmaeus*	Orangutan
Pan	*P. troglodytes*	Common chimpanzee
	P. paniscus	Pygmy chimpanzee
Gorilla	*G. gorilla*	Gorilla
Homo	*H. sapiens*	Humans

Glossary

Acclimatization. Changes in organ or body structure that occur within an individual's lifetime in response to one or more stresses.

Acheulian tradition. The stone tool technology associated with some populations of *Homo erectus*. Many of these tools were constructed using a biface method.

Acquired characteristics. Lamarck's hypothesis that traits change in response to environmental demands and are passed on to offspring.

Adaptation. The process of successful interaction between a population and an environment. Cultural or biological traits that offer an advantage in a given environment are adaptations.

Adaptive radiation. The formation of many new species following the availability of new environments or the development of a new adaptation.

Admixture. The interbreeding of individuals from two or more initially distinct gene pools.

Adolescent growth spurt. The increase in rate of body growth during the adolescent years caused by hormonal changes.

Aegyptopithecus. A genus of fossil anthropoids found in Egypt dating to 33 million years B.P. It was a medium-sized, arboreal anthropoid, most likely representative of the common ancestor of later Old World monkeys and apes.

Afropithecus. An African Miocene ape that lived between 16 and 18 million years ago, and is perhaps a common ancestor of modern great apes and humans. This genus is similar in some ways to *Sivapithecus*.

Age at menarche. The age at which a human female experiences her first menstrual period.

Age-sex structure. A measure of the composition of a population in terms of the numbers of males and females at different ages.

Allele. The alternative forms of a gene that occur at a given locus. Some genes have only one allele, some have two, and some have many alternative forms. Alleles occur in pairs, one on each chromosome.

Allen's rule. States that mammals in cold climates tend to have shorter and bulkier limbs, allowing less loss of body heat, whereas mammals in hot climates tend to have long, slender limbs, allowing greater loss of body heat.

Allometry. The study of the change in proportion of various body parts as a consequence of their growth at different rates.

Anagenesis. The transformation of a single species over time.

Analogous trait. Physical trait that has a similar function in two species but a different structure. The wings of a bird and those of a flying insect are an example of an analogous trait; both perform the same function but have different structures.

Anatomically modern *Homo sapiens*. The modern form of the human species, which dates back 100,000 years or more.

Anthropoid. Member of the suborder of primates consisting of monkeys, apes, and humans.

Anthropological archaeology. The subfield of anthropology that focuses on cultural variation in prehistoric (and some historic) populations through an analysis of the culture's remains.

Anthropology. The science that investigates human biological and cultural variation and evolution.

Antibody. A substance that reacts to other substances invading the body (antigens).

Antigen. A substance invading the body that stimulates the production of antibodies.

Arboreal. Living in trees.

Archaic *Homo sapiens*. An earlier variant of *Homo sapiens,* found at dates ranging from 32,000 to at least 200,000 years B.P. Archaic forms had roughly the same brain size as modern humans but a different-shaped skull, including a sloping forehead and lower cranial height.

Archean era. The first geologic era, dating roughly between 2.5 and 4.6 billion years B.P. Life began during the Archean era.

Assimilation model. A model of the evolution of modern *Homo sapiens* whereby the transition from archaic to modern *H. sapiens* occurred in a single region such as Africa, followed by assimilation into archaic *H. sapiens* populations elsewhere in the Old World. This model is a variant of the multiregional evolution model of modern human origins.

Assortative mating. Mating between phenotypically similar individuals: for example, between two people with the same hair color.

Australopithecine. A general term used to refer to any species in the genus *Australopithecus.*

Australopithecus. A genus of fossil hominid that lived in Africa between 1 and 4 million years B.P., characterized by bipedal locomotion, small brain size, large face, and large teeth.

Australopithecus afarensis. The most primitive of the australopithecines, dating between 3 and 4 million years B.P. and found in East Africa. The teeth and postcranial skeleton show a number of primitive and apelike features.

Australopithecus africanus. A species of australopithecine dating between 2 and 3 million years B.P. and found in South Africa. The teeth and skull of this species are not as large as those of the robust australopithecines.

Australopithecus boisei. The most robust of the australopithecines, dating between 1 and 2.5 million years B.P. and found in East Africa. This species has extremely large back teeth and a large supporting facial and cranial structure, indicating large chewing muscles.

Australopithecus robustus. A robust species of australopithecine, dating between 1 and 2 million years B.P. and found in South Africa. This species has large back teeth, although not as large on average as *Australopithecus boisei.*

Balancing selection. Selection for the heterozygote and against the homozygotes (the heterozygote is most fit). Allele frequencies move toward an equilibrium defined by the fitness values of the two homozygotes.

Bases. Chemical units that make up part of the DNA molecule. There are four bases (adenine, thymine, guanine, cytosine). The sequence of bases in the DNA molecule specifies genetic instructions.

Bergmann's rule. States that (1) among mammals of similar shape, the larger mammal loses heat less rapidly than the smaller mammal, and (2) among mammals of similar size, the mammal with a linear shape will lose heat more rapidly than the mammal with a nonlinear shape.

Biface. Stone tool with both sides worked. The result is a more symmetric and efficient tool.

Bilateral symmetry. The right and left sides of the body are approximate mirror images, a characteristic of vertebrates.

Binocular stereoscopic vision. Overlapping fields of vision (binocular), with both sides of the brain receiving images from both eyes (stereoscopic). Binocular stereoscopic vision provides depth perception.

Biocultural approach. A method of studying humans that looks at the interaction between biology and culture in evolutionary adaptation.

Biological anthropology. The subfield of anthropology formerly referred to as physical anthropology that focuses on the biological evolution of humans and human ancestors, the relationship of humans to other organisms, and patterns of biological variation within and among human populations.

Bipedalism. Moving about on two legs. Unlike the movement of other bipedal animals such as kangaroos, human bipedalism is further characterized by a striding motion.

B.P. Abbreviation for Before Present, the internationally accepted form of designating past dates. The Present has been set arbitrarily at the year 1950. A date of 75,000 years B.P. thus means 75,000 years before the year 1950.

Brachiation. A method of movement that uses the arms to swing from branch to branch. Gibbons and siamangs are true brachiators.

Breeding population. A group of organisms that tend to choose mates from within the group.

Brow ridge. The large ridge of bone above the eye orbit. Brow ridges are most noticeable in *Homo erectus* and archaic *Homo sapiens*.

Canine. One of four types of teeth found in mammals. The canine teeth are located in the front of the jaw behind the incisors. Mammals normally use these teeth for puncturing and defense. Unlike most mammals, humans have small canine teeth that function like incisors.

Carbon-14 dating. A chronometric dating method based on the half-life of carbon-14. This method can be applied to organic remains such as charcoal over the past 50,000 years or so.

Carrying capacity. The maximum population size capable of being supported in a given environment.

Catastrophism. The hypothesis that patterns of evolutionary change observed in the fossil record can be explained by repeated catastrophes followed by repopulation from other areas by different organisms.

Catch-up growth. An increase in growth that can occur following the removal of a limiting factor to growth.

Cenozoic era. The fifth and most recent geologic era, dating roughly to the last 65 million years, also known as the "Age of Mammals." The first primates appeared during the Cenozoic era.

Cephalic index. A measure of cranial shape defined as the total length of a skull divided by the maximum width of the skull.

Cerebrum. The area of the forebrain that consists of the outermost layer of brain cells. The cerebrum is associated with memory, learning, and intelligence.

Chordata. A vertebrate phylum consisting of organisms that possess a notochord at some period during their life.

Chromosomal mutations. A type of mutation in which large sections of chromosomes are changed. These changes include rearrangements, deletions, additions, movements, and changes in chromosome numbers.

Chromosomes. Long strands of DNA sequences.

Chronometric dating. Method of dating fossils or sites that provides an estimate of the specific date (subject to probabilistic limits).

Cladogenesis. The formation of one or more new species from another over time.

Codominant. When both alleles affect the phenotype of a heterozygous genotype and neither is dominant over the other.

Comparative approach. A method used by anthropologists that compares populations to determine common and unique behaviors or biological traits.

Continental drift. The movement of continental land masses on top of a partially molten layer of the earth's mantle. Because of continental drift, the relative location of the continents has changed over time.

Cranial capacity. A measurement of the interior volume of the brain case, used as an approximate estimate of brain size.

Crossing over. Occurs when segments of DNA switch between pairs of chromosomes. Crossing over is an exception to linkage.

Cultural anthropology. The subfield of anthropology that focuses on variations in cultural behaviors among human populations.

Culture. Behavior that is learned and socially transmitted rather than instinctual and genetically transmitted.

Cusp. A raised area on the chewing surface of a tooth.

Demographic transition theory. A model of demographic change that states that as a population becomes economically developed, there will first be a reduction in death rates (leading to population growth), followed by a reduction in birth rates.

Demography. The study of the size, composition, and distribution of populations.

Dendrochronology. A chronometric dating method based on the fact that trees in dry climates tend to accumulate one growth ring per year. The width of the rings varies according to climate, and a sample can be compared with a master chart of tree rings over the past 10,000 years.

Derived trait. A trait that has changed from an ancestral state. For example, the large human brain is a derived trait relative to the common ancestor of humans and apes.

Development. The differentiation and specialization of cells making up different tissues and organs.

Developmental acclimatization. Changes in organ or body structure that occur during the physical growth of any organism.

Diastema. A gap next to the canine teeth that allows space for the canine on the opposing jaw.

Dietary hypothesis. A model first developed in the 1960s that states that two major evolutionary lines in hominid evolution took place during the Plio-Pleistocene. One line was characterized by adaptation to a vegetarian diet, the other by adaptations to an omnivorous diet (especially the development of a large brain).

Distance curve. A measure of size over time—as, for example, a person's height at different ages.

Diurnal. Active during the day.

Dizygotic twins. Twins who develop from two separate fertilized eggs (zygotes). Dizygotic twins are no more genetically similar than any two siblings.

DNA. Deoxyribonucleic acid. The molecule that provides the genetic code for biological structures and the means to translate this code.

DNA hybridization. A method of separating and recombining strands of DNA in different species that allows assessment of their genetic similarity.

Dominance hierarchy. The ranking system within a society that indicates those individuals who are dominant in social behaviors.

Dominant allele. An allele that masks the effect of the other allele (which is recessive) in a heterozygous genotype.

Electron spin resonance. A chronometric dating method that estimates dates from observation of radioactive atoms trapped in calcite crystals present in a number of materials, such as bones and shells. This method is useful for dating sites back to roughly one million years.

Embryo. The stage of prenatal life lasting from roughly two to eight weeks following conception, characterized by structural development.

Endemic. Pertaining to disease, when new cases occur at a relatively constant but low rate over time.

Endocast. A cast of the interior of the brain case, used in the analysis of brain size and structure.

Eocene epoch. The second epoch of the Cenozoic era, dating roughly between 38 and 55 million years B.P. The first true primates, early prosimians, appear during this epoch.

Epidemic. Pertaining to disease, when new cases spread rapidly through a population.

Epidemiologic transition. The change in disease patterns, seen in many developed regions of the world, in which there is a decline in infectious diseases and an increase in noninfectious diseases.

Epidemiology. The study of patterns of human disease and their causes.

Epoch. Subdivision of a geologic period.

Era. The major subdivision of geologic time. There are five eras in the earth's history: Archean, Proterozoic, Paleozoic, Mesozoic, and Cenozoic.

Estrus. A time during the month when females are sexually receptive (also known as "heat"). Among primates, human and orangutan females lack an estrus period.

Eurasia. The combined land masses of Europe and Asia.

Evolution. The transformation of species of organic life over long periods of time. Anthropologists study both the cultural and biological evolution of the human species.

Evolutionary forces. The mechanisms that can cause changes in allele frequencies from one generation to the next. The four evolutionary forces are: mutation, natural selection, genetic drift, and gene flow.

Exogamy. The tendency to choose mates from outside the local population.

Family group. A type of social structure in which the primary social group is made up of a single adult male, a single adult female, and their offspring.

Faunal correlation. A relative dating method in which sites can be assigned an approximate age based on the similarity of animal remains with other dated sites.

Fecundity. Potential reproduction, often defined as the number of people capable of having children.

Feedback. A situation in which one factor in a system influences, and is influenced by, other factors in the system.

Fertility. Actual reproduction—the number of births per individual.

Fetal Alcohol Syndrome. A group of birth defects resulting from major alcohol intake by the mother early in pregnancy.

Fetus. The stage of prenatal growth from roughly eight weeks following conception until birth, characterized by further development and rapid growth.

Fission-fusion. A form of population structure in which a group breaks into smaller populations (fission) and may then later combine with other populations to form a larger group (fusion).

Fission-track dating. A chronometric dating method based on the number of tracks made across volcanic rock as uranium decays into lead.

Fitness. The probability of survival and reproduction of an organism. Fitness is generally measured in terms of the different genotypes for a given locus.

Gene. A section of DNA that determines for a given biological function in an organism.

Gene flow. A mechanism for evolutionary change resulting from the movement of genes from one population to another. Gene flow introduces new genes in a population and also acts to make populations more similar genetically to one another.

Generalized structure. A biological structure adapted to a wide range of conditions and used in very general ways. For example, the grasping hands of humans are generalized structures allowing climbing, food gathering, toolmaking, and a variety of other functions.

Genetic distance. An average measure of relatedness between populations based on a number of traits. Genetic distances are used for understanding effects of genetic drift and gene flow, which should affect all loci to the same extent.

Genetic distance map. A picture that shows the genetic relationships between populations, based on genetic distance measures.

Genetic drift. A mechanism for evolutionary change resulting from the random fluctuations of gene frequencies from one generation to the next, or from any form of random sampling of a larger gene pool.

Genotype. For a given locus, the genetic endowment of an individual from the two alleles present.

Genus. A taxonomic category designating groups of species with similar adaptations.

Gigantopithecus. A genus of fossil ape found in Asia, dating between 0.5 and 9 million years B.P. Only teeth and jaw fragments have so far been discovered, but they indicate an ape with a massive jaw and huge back teeth.

Gradualism. A model of macroevolutionary change whereby evolutionary changes occur at a slow steady rate over time.

Grooming. The handling and cleaning of another individual's fur or hair. In primates, grooming serves as a form of communication that soothes and provides reassurance.

Growth. A change in the size of a living structure, most often caused by an increase in cell size or number.

Half-life. The average length of time it takes for half of a radioactive substance to decay into another form.

Hardy-Weinberg equilibrium. A mathematical model demonstrating that, in the absence of evolutionary forces, allele frequencies remain constant from one generation to the next.

Hemoglobin. The molecule in blood cells that transports oxygen.

Heterozygous. The two alleles at a given locus are different.

Holistic. Refers to the viewpoint that all aspects of existence are interrelated and important in understanding human variation and evolution.

Homeostasis. In a physiologic sense, the maintenance of normal limits of body functioning.

Hominid. Bipedal primates, including modern humans.

Hominoid. A group of anthropoids consisting of apes and humans. Hominoids have a shoulder structure adapted for climbing and hanging, lack a tail, are generally larger than monkeys, and have the largest brain size:body size ratio among primates.

Homo. A genus of hominid with three recognized species (*Homo erectus, Homo habilis,* and *Homo sapiens*), dating from 2.4 million years ago. The major characteristic of *Homo* is large brain size and dependence on culture as a means of adaptation.

Homo erectus. A species of the genus *Homo* that lived between roughly 0.2 to 0.4 and 1.6 million years B.P. *Homo erectus* first appeared in Africa and later spread to Asia (and possibly Europe). *Homo erectus* had a larger brain size than *Homo habilis* but not as large as *Homo sapiens*.

Homo habilis. The oldest known species in the genus *Homo,* dating between 1.5 and 2.4 million years B.P. and found in Africa. In overall appearance, this species is similar to the australopithecines but has a larger cranial capacity (an average of roughly 660 ml, with a range of 509 to 810 ml).

Homoiotherm. Organism capable of maintaining a constant body temperature under most circumstances. Mammals are homoiotherms.

Homologous trait. Physical trait in two species that has a similar structure but may or may not show a similar function. The arm bones in humans and whales are an example of homologous structure; the bones are the same, but they are used for different functions.

Homozygous. Both alleles at a given locus are identical.

Hormones. Chemicals released by endocrine glands that travel to body tissues and stimulate and regulate biological processes.

Horticulture. A form of farming in which only simple hand tools are used.

Hypothalamus. A structure of the brain that regulates the secretion of hormones.

Hypothesis. An explanation of observed facts. To be scientific, a hypothesis must be testable.

Hypoxia. Oxygen starvation. Hypoxia occurs frequently at high altitudes.

Inbreeding. Mating between biologically related individuals.

Inbreeding coefficient. The increase in the probability of homozygous offspring because of inbreeding. Inbreeding coefficients can be computed for individual matings; an average figure can be computed for an entire population.

Incidence rate. The rate of new cases of a disease developing in a population in a specified period of time.

Incisor. One of four types of teeth found in mammals. The incisors are the flat front teeth used for cutting, slicing, and gnawing food.

Infectious disease. A disease caused by the introduction of an organic foreign substance into the body. Such substances include viruses and parasites.

Insectivore. An order of mammals adapted to insect eating.

Kenyapithecus. An African Miocene ape, similar to *Sivapithecus* in some ways, but with relatively small canines. This genus dates to 14 to 17 million years B.P. It is a possible common ancestor of modern African apes and humans.

Knuckle walking. A form of movement used by chimpanzees and gorillas that is characterized by all four limbs touching the ground, with the weight of the arms resting on the knuckles of the hands.

K-selection. A reproductive pattern characterized by few offspring but extensive parental care.

Kuru. An infectious disease once found in areas of New Guinea that affected the central nervous system and was spread by coming into contact with the brain of an infected person.

Kwashiorkor. An extreme form of protein-calorie malnutrition, resulting from a severe deficiency in proteins but not calories.

Lactase deficiency. A condition in which an older child or adult lacks the ability to produce the lactase enzyme needed to digest milk sugar.

Lemur. A prosimian found today on the island of Madagascar. Lemurs include both nocturnal and diurnal species.

Life expectancy. A measure of the average length of life in a population.

Life table. A table that provides an estimate of the probability of an individual dying by a certain age. Life table analysis is used to estimate life expectancy.

Linguistic anthropology. The subfield of anthropology that focuses on the nature of human language, the relationship of language to culture, and the languages of nonliterate peoples.

Linkage. The situation in which alleles on the same chromosome are inherited together.

Locus. The specific location of a gene on a chromosome. (Plural *loci.*)

Loris. Nocturnal prosimian found today in Asia and Africa.

Lower Paleolithic. The Lower Old Stone Age. A general term used to refer collectively to the stone tool technologies of *Homo habilis* and *Homo erectus.*

Macroevolution. Long-term evolutionary change. The study of macroevolution focuses on biological evolution over many generations and on the origin of higher taxonomic categories, such as species.

Major genes. Genes that have the primary effect on the phenotypic distribution of a complex trait. Additional variation can be due to smaller effects from other loci and/or environmental influences.

Malnutrition. Poor nutrition, either from too much or too little nutrition, or the improper balance of nutrients.

Marasmus. An extreme form of protein-calorie malnutrition resulting from severe deficiencies in both proteins and calories.

Mass extinction. When many species become extinct at roughly the same time.

Meiosis. The creation of sex cells by replication of chromosomes followed by cell division. Each sex cell then contains 50 percent of an individual's chromosomes (one from each pair).

Mendelian genetics. The branch of genetics concerned with patterns and processes of inheritance. This field was named after Gregor Mendel, the first scientist to work out many of these principles.

Mendel's Law of Independent Assortment. The segregation of any pair of chromosomes does not affect the probability of segregation for other pairs of chromosomes.

Mendel's Law of Segregation. Sex cells contain one of each pair of alleles.

Mesozoic era. The fourth geologic era, dating roughly between 65 and 250 million years B.P., also known as the "Age of Reptiles." The first mammals and birds also appeared during the Mesozoic era.

Messenger RNA. The form of RNA that transports the genetic instructions from the DNA molecule to the site of protein synthesis.

Microevolution. Short-term evolutionary change. The study of microevolution focuses on changes in allele frequencies from one generation to the next.

Middle Paleolithic. The Middle Old Stone Age. A general term used to refer collectively to the stone tool technologies of archaic *Homo sapiens.*

Migration. The movement of individuals from one population to another. Migration may be short-term or long-term, and may or may not have genetic effects.

Miocene epoch. The fourth epoch of the Cenozoic era, dating roughly between 5 and 22 million years B.P. The first apes evolved during the Miocene.

Mitochondrial DNA. DNA that is found in the mitochondria of the cells rather than the nucleus. Mitochondrial DNA (mtDNA) is inherited primarily through females.

Mitosis. The process of replication of chromosomes in body cells. Each cell produces two identical copies.

Molar. One of four types of teeth found in mammals. The molars are back teeth used for crushing and grinding food.

Molecular dating. The application of methods of genetic analysis to estimate the sequence and timing of divergent evolutionary lines.

Monogamy. An exclusive sexual bond between an adult male and an adult female for a long period of time.

Monosymy. A condition in which only one chromosome rather than a pair is present in body cells.

Monozygotic twins. Twins who develop from a single fertilized egg (zygote); these are known as identical twins.

Morphology. The physical structure of organisms.

Mortality. Death. Mortality, fertility, and migration are the three prime determinants of population size.

Mosaic evolution. The concept that major evolutionary changes tend to take place in stages, not all at once. Human evolution shows a mosaic pattern in the fact that small canine teeth, large brains, and tool use did not all evolve at the same time.

Mother-infant group. A type of social structure in which the primary social group consists of a mother and her dependent offspring.

Mousterian tradition. The stone tool technology of the Neandertals, characterized by the careful preparation of a stone core from which finished flakes can be removed.

Multimale group. A type of social structure in which the primary social group is made up of several adult males, several adult females, and their offspring. This is the most common form of social structure found in nonhuman primates.

Multiregional evolution model. A model of the evolution of *Homo sapiens* that states that the change from archaic to modern forms took place in all regions of the Old World (although not necessarily at the same time).

Multivariate analysis. The analysis of human biological variation that takes into consideration the interrelationship of several traits at a time.

Mutation. A mechanism for evolutionary change resulting from a random change in the genetic code. Mutation is the ultimate source of all genetic variation. Mutations must occur in sex cells to cause evolutionary change.

Nasal index. A measure of the shape of the nasal opening, defined as the width of the nasal opening divided by the height.

Natural increase. The change in population size expected because of fertility and mortality but not migration. Natural increase is the number of births minus the number of deaths.

Natural selection. A mechanism for evolutionary change resulting from the differential survival and reproduction of organisms because of their biological characteristics.

Neandertal. Member of a regional population of archaic *Homo sapiens* found in the area around the Mediterranean, dating between roughly 32,000 to 125,000 years B.P. The relationship between Neandertals and later *Homo sapiens* populations in these regions is still being debated.

Negative assortative mating. Mates are chosen on the basis of having different phenotypic characteristics.

Neoteny. The retention of juvenile characteristics into adulthood. The rounded skull and large brain of humans are examples of neoteny.

New World Syndrome. A set of noninfectious diseases that appear in elevated frequencies in individuals with Native-American ancestry.

Nocturnal. Active during the night.

Noninfectious disease. A disease caused by factors other than the introduction of an organic foreign substance into the body (e.g., age, nutrition).

Nonrandom mating. Patterns of mate choice, other than total random mating, that influence the distributions of genotype and phenotype frequencies. Nonrandom mating does not lead to changes in allele frequencies.

Occipital bun. A slight protrusion of the rear region of the skull, a feature often found in Neandertals.

Oldowan tradition. The stone tool culture of *Homo habilis*. Oldowan tools are often simple tools made by removing several flakes from a stone. The flakes removed could also be used as cutting tools.

Oligocene epoch. The third epoch of the Cenozoic era, dating roughly between 22 and 38 million years B.P.

One-male group. A type of social structure in which the primary social group is made up of a single adult male, several adult females, and their offspring.

Orthogenesis. A discredited idea that evolution would continue in a given direction because of some vaguely defined nonphysical "force."

Paleocene epoch. The first epoch of the Cenozoic era, dating roughly between 55 and 65 million years B.P. The primatelike mammals lived during the Paleocene.

Paleoecology. The study of ancient environments.

Paleomagnetic reversal. The earth's magnetic pole has shifted back and forth from the north to the south in the past at irregular intervals. Use of this fact allows certain sites to be dated.

Paleopathology. The study of disease in prehistoric populations based on analysis of skeletal remains and archaeological evidence.

Paleospecies. Species identified from fossil remains based on their physical similarities and differences relative to other species.

Paleozoic era. The third geologic era, dating roughly between 250 and 550 million years B.P. The first vertebrates appeared during this era, including the reptiles and mammallike reptiles.

Palynology. The study of fossil pollen. Palynology allows prehistoric plant species to be identified.

Pandemic. An epidemic that occurs over a large geographic range.

Period. Subdivision of a geologic era.

Phenotype. The observable appearance of a given genotype in the organism. The phenotype is determined by the relationship of the two alleles at a given locus, the number of loci, and often environmental influences as well.

Physical anthropology. See Biological anthropology.

Piltdown Man. Name given to fossil specimens found in England that were once thought to be a "missing link" between apes and humans but were later exposed as a hoax.

Pituitary gland. A structure in the brain that secretes hormones that either act directly on body tissues or stimulate other endocrine glands to release hormones.

Placenta. An organ that develops inside a pregnant placental mammal. It provides the fetus with oxygen and food and helps filter out harmful substances.

Plasticity. The ability of an organism to respond physiologically or developmentally to environmental stress.

Pleiotropy. When a single allele can have multiple effects on an organism.

Pleistocene epoch. The sixth epoch of the Cenozoic era, dating from 0.01 to 1.8 million years B.P. The major event in human evolution was the continued development of the genus *Homo*.

Pliocene epoch. The fifth epoch of the Cenozoic era, dating from 1.8 to 5 million years B.P. The major event in human evolution was the origin of the hominid.

Plio-Pleistocene. A term used to describe the time of the australopithecines (from 1 to 4 million years B.P.).

Point mutation. A type of mutation in which the sequence of bases of DNA in a single gene are changed.

Polyandry. In humans, a form of marriage in which a wife has several husbands. In more general terms, it refers to an adult female having several mates.

Polygamy. In general terms, it refers to having more than one mate.

Polygenic. Refers to a trait that is affected by two or more loci. Complex traits, such as skin color and height, are polygenic.

Polygyny. In humans, a form of marriage in which a husband has several wives. In more general terms, it refers to an adult male having several mates.

Polymorphism. A discrete genetic trait, such as a blood group, in which there are at least two alleles at a locus having frequencies greater than 0.01.

Population pyramid. A graphic illustration of the age-sex structure of a population.

Positive assortative mating. Mates are chosen on the basis of their having similar phenotypic characteristics. An example is tall people choosing tall mates.

Postcranial. Referring to that part of the skeleton below the neck.

Postnatal. Referring to the period of life from birth until death.

Postorbital bar. The bony ring that separates the eye orbit from the back of the skull. The postorbital bar is a primate characteristic.

Postorbital constriction. The narrowness of the skull behind the eye orbits. Early hominids, such as *Homo habilis* and *Homo erectus,* show considerable postorbital constriction, particularly when compared to modern humans.

Potassium-argon dating. A chronometric dating method based on the half-life of radioactive potassium (which decays into argon gas). This method can be used to date volcanic rock older than 100,000 years.

Precambrian. That time in earth's history preceding the first major appearance of life. Precambrian times encompass the Archean and Proterozoic eras.

Prehensile. Capable of grasping. Primates have prehensile hands and feet, and some primates (certain New World monkeys) have prehensile tails.

Premolar. One of four types of teeth found in mammals. The premolars are back teeth used for crushing and grinding food.

Prenatal. Referring to the period of life from conception until birth.

Prevalence rate. The proportion of total cases of a disease, old and new, in a population during a specified period of time.

Primate. A member of an order of mammals that has a complex of characteristics related to an initial adaptation to life in the trees (even though many modern primates now live on the ground), including binocular stereoscopic vision and grasping hands. The primates are the prosimians, monkeys, apes, and humans.

Primitive trait. In biological terms, a trait that has not changed from an ancestral state. The five digits of the human hand and foot are primitive traits inherited from earlier vertebrate ancestors.

Proconsul. A genus of fossil apes that lived in Africa between 17 and 23 million years B.P. Though classified as apes, this genus also shows a number of monkey characteristics. It most probably represents one of the first forms to evolve following the divergence of the monkey and ape lines.

Prosimian. A suborder of primates. Prosimians are the most biologically primitive of all primates.

Protein-calorie malnutrition. A group of nutritional diseases resulting from inadequate amounts of protein and/or calories. Protein-calorie malnutrition is a severe problem in developing regions today.

Proterozoic era. The second geologic era, dating roughly between 550 million years B.P. and 2.5 billion years B.P. The first invertebrates appeared during the Proterozoic era.

Puberty. The time in the human life cycle when sexual and physical maturity is attained.

Punctuated equilibrium. A model of macroevolutionary change in which long periods of little evolutionary change (stasis) are followed by relatively short periods of rapid evolutionary change.

Quadrupedal. A form of movement in which all four limbs are of equal size and make contact with the ground, and the spine is roughly parallel to the ground. Monkeys are typical quadrupedal primates.

Race. In terms of biological variation, a group of populations sharing certain traits that make them distinct from other groups of populations. In practice, the concept of race is very difficult to apply to patterns of human variation.

Recent African origin model. A model of the evolution of modern *Homo sapiens* whereby archaic *H. sapiens* evolved into modern *H. sapiens* in Africa and then spread out through the rest of the Old World, replacing archaic populations. This model differs from the assimilation model in that it does not propose gene flow with non-African archaic populations.

Recessive allele. An allele whose effect is masked by the other allele (which is dominant) in a heterozygous genotype.

Regulatory gene. Gene that codes for the regulation of such biological processes as growth and development.

Relative dating. Comparative method of dating fossils and sites that provides an estimate of the older find but not a specific date.

Reproductive isolation. The genetic isolation of populations that can render them incapable of producing fertile offspring.

RNA. Ribonucleic acid. The molecule that functions to carry out the instructions for protein synthesis specified by the DNA molecule.

r-selection. A reproductive pattern characterized by large numbers of offspring and little parental care.

Sagittal crest. A ridge of bone running down the center of the top of the skull that serves to anchor chewing muscles. Sagittal crests are found in some australopithecines.

Savanna. An environment consisting of open grasslands. Food resources tend to be spread out over large areas.

Secular trend. A change in the average pattern of growth in a population over different generations.

Sensitive period of growth. Times during the life cycle when catch-up growth is not possible.

Sexual dimorphism. In terms of body size, the average difference in size between adult males and adult females. Primate species with sexual dimorphism in body size are characterized by adult males being, on average, larger than adult females.

Sickle cell allele. An allele of the hemoglobin locus. If two such alleles are present, the individual has sickle cell anemia.

Sickle cell anemia. A genetic disease that occurs in a person homozygous for the sickle cell allele; the altered structure of red blood cells leads to greatly reduced fitness.

Single-species hypothesis. A model of Plio-Pleistocene hominid evolution developed in the 1960s that stated that there was only one species of hominid in existence at any point in time. Later fossil discoveries led to the rejection of this model.

Sivapithecus. A genus of fossil ape found in Asia and Europe dating between 7 and 14 million years B.P. On the basis of cranial and dental remains, one of the Asian species of *Sivapithecus* appears to be an ancestor of the modern-day orangutan.

Social structure. The composition of a social group and the way it is organized, including size, age structure, and number of each sex in the group.

Specialized structure. A biological structure adapted to a narrow range of conditions and used in very specific ways. For example, the hooves of horses are specialized structures allowing movement over flat terrain.

Speciation. The origin of a new species.

Species. A taxonomic category designating a group of populations whose members can interbreed naturally and that produce fertile offspring.

Stasis. Little or no evolutionary change occurring over a long period of time.

Stratigraphy. A relative dating method based on the fact that older remains are found deeper in the earth (under the right conditions). This method makes use of the fact that a cumulative buildup of the earth's surface takes place over time.

Stress. Any factor that interferes with the normal limits of operation of an organism.

Structural gene. Gene that codes for the production of proteins.

Suspensory climbing and hanging. The ability to raise the arms above the head and hang on branches and to climb in this position. Hominoids are suspensory climbers and hangers.

Taphonomy. The study of what happens to plants and animals after they die. Taphonomy helps in determining reasons for the distribution and condition of fossils.

Tarsier. Nocturnal prosimian found today in Indonesia. Unlike other prosimians, tarsiers lack a moist nose.

Taxonomy. A formal classification of organisms. The term also applies to the science of classification.

Terrestrial. Living on the ground.

Theory. A set of hypotheses that have been tested repeatedly and that have not been rejected. This term is sometimes used in a different sense in social science literature.

Therapsid. An early group of reptiles also known as the mammallike reptiles. Therapsids were the ancestors of later mammals.

Thermoluminescence. A chronometric dating method that uses the fact that certain heated objects accumulate trapped electrons over time, which allows the date when the object was initially heated to be determined.

Tool use model. A now-rejected model of hominid origins that stated that bipedalism, large brains, and small canines all evolved simultaneously during hominid evolution as a consequence of increased reliance on tool use.

Transfer RNA. A free-floating molecule that is attracted to a strand of messenger RNA, resulting in the synthesis of a protein chain.

Trephination. Surgery involving the removal of a section of bone from the skull.

Trisomy. A condition in which three chromosomes rather than a pair occur. Down syndrome is often caused by trisomy by the addition of an extra chromosome to the 21st chromosome pair.

Typology. A set of discrete groupings in classification. Typologies emphasize average tendencies and ignore variation within groups. Racial classifications are a form of typology.

Univariate analysis. The analysis of human biological variation focusing on a single trait at a time.

Upper Paleolithic. The Upper Old Stone Age. A general term used to collectively refer to the stone tool technologies of anatomically modern *Homo sapiens.*

Variation. The differences that exist among individuals or populations. Anthropologists study both cultural and biological variation.

Vasoconstriction. The narrowing of blood vessels, which reduces blood flow and heat loss.

Vasodilation. The opening of the blood vessels, which increases blood flow and heat loss.

Velocity curves. A measure of the rates of change in growth over time.

Vertebrata. A subphylum of the phylum Chordata, defined by the presence of an internal, segmented spinal column and bilateral symmetry.

Würm glaciation. One of the times of glaciation ("ice ages") during the Pleistocene epoch.

Zoonose. Disease that is transmitted directly from animals to humans.

Zygomatic arch. The bone on the side of the skull which connects the zygomatic and temporal bones. This bone serves to anchor muscles used in chewing.

Zygote. A fertilized egg.

References

Abel, E. L. 1982. Consumption of alcohol during pregnancy: A review of effects on growth and development of offspring. *Human Biology* 54: 421–53.

Ackerman, S. 1987. American Scientist interviews: Peter Ellison. *American Scientist* 75:622–27.

Arensberg, B., L. A. Schepartz, A. M. Tillier, B. Vandermeersch, and Y. Rak. 1990. A reappraisal of the anatomical basis for speech in Middle Paleolithic hominids. *American Journal of Physical Anthropology* 83:137–46.

Armelagos, G. J., and J. R. Dewey. 1970. Evolutionary response to human infectious diseases. *BioScience* 157:638–44.

Armstrong, E. 1983. Relative brain size and metabolism in mammals. *Science* 220:1302–4.

Bakker, R. T. 1986. *The Dinosaur Heresies.* New York: William Morrow.

Beals, K. L., C. L. Smith, and S. M. Dodd. 1984. Brain size, cranial morphology, climate, and time machines. *Current Anthropology* 25:301–30.

Bittles, A. H., W. M. Mason, J. Greene, and N. A. Rao. 1991. Reproductive behavior and health in consanguineous marriages. *Science* 252:789–94.

Blum, H. F. 1961. Does the melanin pigment of human skin have adaptive value? *Quarterly Review of Biology* 36:50–63.

Blumenberg, B. 1985. Population characteristics of extinct hominid endocranial volume. *American Journal of Physical Anthropology* 68:269–79.

Bodmer, W. F., and L. L. Cavalli-Sforza. 1976. *Genetics, Evolution, and Man.* San Francisco: W. H. Freeman.

Bouchard, T. J., D. T. Lykken, M. McGue, N. L. Segal, and A. Tellegen. 1990. Sources of human psychological differences: The Minnesota study of twins reared apart. *Science* 250:223–28.

Bramblett, C. A. 1976. *Patterns of Primate Behavior.* Palo Alto, Calif.: Mayfield.

Brown, F., J. Harris, R. Leakey, and A. Walker. 1985. Early *Homo erectus* skeleton from west Lake Turkana, Kenya. *Nature* 316:788–92.

Brues, A. M. 1977. *People and Races.* New York: Macmillan.

Buss, D. M. 1985. Human mate selection. *American Scientist* 73:47–51.

Campbell, B. G. 1985. *Human Evolution.* 3d ed. New York: Aldine.

Cann, R. L., M. Stoneking, and A. C. Wilson. 1987. Mitochondrial DNA and human evolution. *Nature* 325:31–36.

Cartmill, M. 1974. Rethinking primate origins. *Science* 184:436–43.

Chakraborty, R. 1986. Gene admixture in human populations: Models and predictions. *Yearbook of Physical Anthropology* 29:1–43.

Ciochon, R. L. 1988. *Gigantopithecus:* The king of all apes. *Animal Kingdom* 91(2):32–39.

Clarke, R. J. 1985. *Australopithecus* and early *Homo* in Southern Africa. In *Ancestors: The Hard Evidence,* ed. E. Delson, pp. 171–77. New York: Alan R. Liss.

Conroy, G. C. 1990. *Primate Evolution.* New York: W. W. Norton.

Conroy, G. C., M. W. Vannier, and P. V. Tobias. 1990. Endocranial features of *Australopithecus africanus* revealed by 2- and 3-D computed tomography. *Science* 247:838–41.

Conroy, G. C., M. Pickford, B. Senut, J. Van Couvering, and P. Mein. 1992. *Otavipithecus namibiensis,* first Myocene Hominoid from southern Africa. *Nature* 356:144–48.

Cronin, J. E. 1983. Apes, humans and molecular clocks: A reappraisal. In *New Interpretations of Ape and Human Ancestry,* ed. R. L. Ciochon and R. S. Corruccini, pp. 115–36. New York: Plenum Press.

Damon, A. 1977. *Human Biology and Ecology.* New York: W. W. Norton.

Denham, W. W. 1971. Energy relations and some basic properties of primate social organization. *American Anthropologist* 73:77–95.

Dunn, F. L. 1968. Epidemiological factors: Health and disease among hunter-gatherers. In *Man the Hunter,* ed. R. B. Lee and I. DeVore, pp. 221–28. Chicago: Aldine.

Eaton, G. G. 1976. The social order of Japanese macaques. *Scientific American* 235(4):96–106.

Eldredge, N., and S. J. Gould. 1972. Punctuated equilibria: An alternative to phyletic gradualism. In *Models in Paleobiology,* ed. T. J. M. Schopf, pp. 82–115. San Francisco: Freeman, Cooper.

Encyclopaedia Britannica. 1988. *Encyclopaedia Britannica Book of the Year, 1988.* Encyclopaedia Britannica: Chicago.

Ereshefsky, M., ed. 1992. *The Units of Evolution: Essays on the Nature of Species.* Cambridge: MIT Press.

Falk, D. 1983. Cerebral cortices of East African early hominids. *Science* 221:1072–74.

———. 1990. Brain evolution in *Homo:* The radiator theory. *Behavioral and Brain Sciences* 13:333–81.

———. 1992. *Braindance.* New York: Henry Holt.

Fedigan, L. M. 1983. Dominance and reproductive success in primates. *Yearbook of Physical Anthropology* 26:91–129.

Feldesman, M. R., and J. K. Lundy. 1988. Stature estimates for some African Plio-Pleistocene fossil hominids. *Journal of Human Evolution* 17:583–96.

Fleagle, J. G. 1983. Locomotor adaptations of Oligocene and Miocene hominoids and their phyletic implications. In *New Interpretations of Ape and Human Ancestry,* ed. R. L. Ciochon and R. S. Corruccini, pp. 301–24. New York: Plenum Press.

———. 1988. *Primate Adaptation and Evolution.* San Diego: Academic Press.

Fleagle, J. G., T. M. Brown, J. D. Obradovich, and E. L. Simons. 1986. Age of the earliest African anthropoids. *Science* 234:1247–49.

Fleagle, J. G., D. T. Rasmussen, S. Yirga, T. M. Brown, and F. E. Grine. 1991. New hominid fossils from Fejej, Southern Ethiopia. *Journal of Human Evolution* 21:145–52.

Fossey, D. 1983. *Gorillas in the Mist.* Boston: Houghton Mifflin.

Frayer, D. W. 1984. Biological and cultural change in the European Late Pleistocene and Early Holocene. In *The Origins of Modern Humans: A World Survey of the Fossil Evidence,* ed. F. H. Smith and F. Spencer, pp. 211–50. New York: Alan R. Liss.

Frisancho, A. R. 1979. *Human Adaptation: A Functional Interpretation.* St. Louis: C. V. Mosby.

———. 1990. Introduction: Comparative high-altitude adaptation. *American Journal of Human Biology* 2:599–601.

Frisancho, A. R., and P. T. Baker. 1970. Altitude and growth: A study of the patterns of physical growth of a high altitude Peruvian Quechua population. *American Journal of Physical Anthropology* 32:279–92.

Fox, R. C., G. P. Youzwyshyn, and D. W. Krause. 1992. Post-Jurassic mammal-like reptile from the Paleocene. *Nature* 358:233–35.

Futuyma, D. J. 1983. *Science on Trial: The Case for Evolution.* New York: Pantheon Books.

———. 1986. *Evolutionary Biology.* 2d ed. Sunderland, Mass.: Sinauer.

———. 1988. *Sturm und Drang* and the evolutionary synthesis. *Evolution* 42:217–26.

Garn, S. M. 1985. Smoking and human biology. *Human Biology* 57:505–23.

Gingerich, P. D. 1985. Nonlinear molecular clocks and ape-human divergence times. In *Hominid Evolution: Past, Present and Future*, ed. P. V. Tobias, pp. 411–16. New York: Alan R. Liss.

Glass, H. B. 1953. The genetics of the Dunkers. *Scientific American* 189(2):76–81.

Godfrey, L., and K. H. Jacobs. 1981. Gradual, autocatalytic and punctuational models of hominid brain evolution: A cautionary tale. *Journal of Human Evolution* 10:255–72.

Goodall, J. 1986. *The Chimpanzees of Gombe: Patterns of Behavior*. Cambridge: Harvard University Press.

Gould, S. J. 1977a. *Ever Since Darwin*. New York: W. W. Norton.

———. 1977b. *Ontogeny and Phylogeny*. Cambridge: Harvard University Press.

———. 1981. *The Mismeasure of Man*. New York: W. W. Norton.

———. 1983. *Hen's Teeth and Horse's Toes*. New York: W. W. Norton.

———. 1991. *Bully for Brontosaurus*. New York: W. W. Norton.

Gould, S. J., and N. Eldredge. 1977. Punctuated equilibria: The tempo and mode of evolution reconsidered. *Paleobiology* 3:115–51.

Grant, V. 1985. *The Evolutionary Process: A Critical Review of Evolutionary Theory*. New York: Columbia University Press.

Greska, L. P. 1990. Developmental responses to high-altitude hypoxia in Bolivian children of European ancestry: A test of the developmental adaptation hypothesis. *American Journal of Human Biology* 2:603–12.

Grün, R., N. J. Shackleton, and H. J. Deacon. 1990. Electron-Spin-Resonance dating of tooth enamel from Klasies River Mouth Cave. *Current Anthropology* 31:427–32.

Grün, R., C. B. Stringer, and H. P. Schwartz. 1991. ESR dating of teeth from Garood's Tabun cave collection. *Journal of Human Evolution* 20:231–48.

Gyllensten, U., D. Wharton, A. Josefsson, and A. C. Wilson. 1991. Paternal inheritance of mitochondrial DNA in mice. *Nature* 352:255–57.

Harpending, H., and T. Jenkins. 1973. Genetic distance among southern African populations. In *Methods and Theories of Anthropological Genetics*, ed. M. H. Crawford and P. L. Workman, pp. 177–200. Albuquerque: University of New Mexico Press.

Harris, M. 1987. *Cultural Anthropology*, 2d ed. New York: Harper & Row.

Harrison, G. A., J. M. Tanner, D. R. Pilbeam, and P. T. Baker. 1988. *Human Biology: An Introduction to Human Evolution, Variation, Growth, and Adaptability*. 3d ed. Oxford: Oxford University Press.

Haub, C. V. 1992. Populations and population movements. *Encyclopaedia Britannica Book of the Year 1992*, pp. 250–52. Chicago: Encyclopaedia Britannica.

Hedges, S. B., S. Kumar, K. Tamura and M. Stoneking. 1992. Human origins and analysis of mitochondrial DNA sequences. *Science* 255:737–39.

Henneberg, M. 1988. Decrease of human skull size in the Holocene. *Human Biology* 60:395–405.

Hill, A., S. Ward, A. Deino, G. Curtis, and R. Drake. 1992. Earliest *Homo*. *Nature* 355:719–22.

Holick, M. F., J. A. MacLaughlin, and S. H. Doppelt. 1981. Regulation of cutaneous previtamin D_3 photosynthesis in man: Skin pigment is not an essential regulator. *Science* 211:590–93.

Horr, D. A. 1972. The Borneo orang-utan. *Borneo Research Bulletin* 4(2):46–50.

Johanson, D. C., F. T. Masau, G. G. Eck, T. D. White, R. C. Walter, W. H. Kimbel, B. Asfaw, P. Manega, P. Ndessokia, and G. Suwa. 1987. New partial skeleton of *Homo habilis* from Olduvai Gorge, Tanzania. *Nature* 327:205–9.

Johanson, D. C., and T. D. White. 1979. A systematic assessment of early African hominids. *Science* 203:321–30.

Johanson, D. C., T. D. White, and Y. Coppens. 1978. A new species of the genus *Australopithecus* (Primates: Hominidae) from the Pliocene of Eastern Africa. *Kirtlandia* 28:1–14.

Jolly, A. 1985. *The Evolution of Primate Behavior*. 2d ed. New York: Macmillan.

Kelly, J. 1988. A new large species of *Sivapithecus* from the Siwaliks of Pakistan. *Journal of Human Evolution* 17:305–24.

Kimbel, W. H., T. D. White, and D. C. Johanson. 1988. Implications of KNM-WT 17000 for the evolution of "robust" *Australopithecus*. In *Evolutionary History of the "Robust" Australopithecines*, ed. F. E. Grine, pp. 259–68. New York: Aldine de Gruyter.

King, M. C., and A. C. Wilson. 1975. Evolution at two levels: Molecular similarities and biological differences between humans and chimpanzees. *Science* 188:107–16.

Kitcher, P. 1982. *Abusing Science: The Case Against Creationism*. Cambridge: MIT Press.

Klein, R. G. 1989. *The Human Career: Human Biological and Cultural Origins*. Chicago: University of Chicago Press.

Kobyliansky, E., S. Micle, M. Goldschmidt-Nathan, B. Arensberg, and H. Nathan. 1982. Jewish populations of the world: Genetic likeness and differences. *Annals of Human Biology* 9:1–34.

Kramer, A. 1991. Modern human origins in Australasia: Replacement or evolution? *American Journal of Physical Anthropology* 86:455–73.

Leakey, L. S. B., P. V. Tobias, and J. R. Napier. 1964. A new species of the genus *Homo* from Olduvai Gorge. *Nature* 202:7–10.

Leakey, R. E. F., and M. Leakey. 1986a. A new Miocene hominoid from Kenya. *Nature* 324:143–46.

Leakey, R. E. F., and M. Leakey. 1986b. A second new Miocene hominoid from Kenya. *Nature* 324:146–48.

Leakey, R. E. F., and A. Walker. 1985. New higher primates from the early Miocene of Buluk, Kenya. *Nature* 318:173–75.

Leonard, W. H., T. L. Leatherman, J. W. Carey, and R. B. Thomas. 1990. Contributions of nutrition versus hypoxia to growth in rural Andean populations. *American Journal of Human Biology* 2:613–26.

Lerner, I. M., and W. J. Libby. 1976. *Heredity, Evolution, and Society*. San Francisco: W. H. Freeman.

Leutenegger, W. 1982. Sexual dimorphism in nonhuman primates. In *Sexual Dimorphism in Homo sapiens: A Question of Size*, ed. R. L. Hall, pp. 11–36. New York: Praeger.

Lewin, R. 1987. *Bones of Contention: Controversies in the Search for Human Origins*. New York: Simon & Schuster.

Lewontin, R. C. 1972. The apportionment of human diversity. In *Evolutionary Biology*. Vol. 6, ed. T. Dobzhansky, pp. 381–98. New York: Plenum Press.

Li, T., and D. A. Etler. 1992. New Middle Pleistocene hominid crania from Yunxian in China. *Nature* 357:404–7.

Lieberman, D., D. R. Pilbeam, and B. A. Wood. 1988. A probabilistic approach to the problem of sexual dimorphism in *Homo habilis*: A comparison of KNM-ER 1470 and KNM-ER 1813. *Journal of Human Evolution* 17:503–11.

Lieberman, P., and E. S. Crelin. 1971. On the speech of Neanderthal. *Linguistic Inquiry* 2:203–22.

Lilienfeld, A. M., and D. E. Lilienfeld. 1980. *Foundations of Epidemiology*. 2d ed. New York: Oxford University Press.

Linden, E. 1981. *Apes, Men, and Language*. Rev. ed. Middlesex, England: Penguin Books.

Livingstone, F. B. 1958. Anthropological implications of sickle cell gene distribution in West Africa. *American Anthropologist* 60:533–62.

Loehlin, J. C., G. Lindzey, and J. N. Spuhler. 1975. *Race Differences in Intelligence*. San Francisco: W. H. Freeman.

Loomis, W. F. 1967. Skin-pigment regulation of vitamin-D biosynthesis in man. *Science* 157:501–6.

Lovejoy, C. O. 1981. The origin of man. *Science* 211:341–50.

———. 1982. Models of human evolution. *Science* 217:304–6.

McElroy, A., and P. K. Townsend. 1989. *Medical Anthropology in Ecological Perspective*. 2d ed. Boulder, Colo.: Westview Press.

McEvedy, C. 1988. The bubonic plague. *Scientific American* 258(2):118–23.

McGrew, W. C. 1992. *Chimpanzee Material Culture*. Cambridge: Cambridge University Press.

McHenry, H. M. 1992. How big were the early hominids? *Evolutionary Anthropology* 1:15–20.

Malina, R. M. 1975. *Growth and Development: The First Twenty Years in Man*. Minneapolis, Minn.: Burgess.

———. 1979. Secular changes in size and maturity: Causes and effects. *Monograph for the Society of Research in Child Development* 44:59–102.

Markham, R., and C. P. Groves. 1990. Brief communication: Weights of wild orangutans. *American Journal of Physical Anthropology* 81:1–3.

Martin, R. D. 1981. Relative brain size and basal metabolic rate in terrestrial vertebrates. *Nature* 293:57–60.

Martorell, R. 1980. Interrelationships between diet, infectious disease, and nutritional status. In *Social and Biological Predictors of Nutritional Status, Physical Growth, and Neurological Development*, ed. L. S. Greene and F. E. Johnston, pp. 81–106. New York: Academic Press.

Mayr, E. 1982. *The Growth of Biological Thought*. Cambridge: Harvard University Press.

Meindl, R. S., and A. C. Swedlund. 1977. Secular

trends in mortality in the Connecticut River Valley, 1700–1850. *Human Biology* 49:389–414.

Molnar, S. 1992. *Human Variation: Races, Types, and Ethnic Groups.* 3d ed. Englewood Cliffs, N.J.: Prentice-Hall.

Montagu, A., ed. 1984. *Science and Creationism.* Oxford: Oxford University Press.

Moran, E. F. 1982. *Human Adaptability: An Introduction to Ecological Anthropology.* Boulder, Colo.: Westview Press.

Olson, T. R. 1985. Cranial morphology and systematics of the Hadar formation hominids and "*Australopithecus*" *africanus.* In *Ancestors: The Hard Evidence,* ed. E. Delson, pp. 102–19. New York: Alan R. Liss.

Omran, A. R. 1977. Epidemiologic transition in the United States: The health factor in population change. *Population Bulletin* 32:3–42.

Passingham, R. 1982. *The Human Primate.* San Francisco: W. H. Freeman.

Pfeiffer, J. E. 1985. *The Emergence of Humankind.* 4th ed. New York: Harper & Row.

Pilbeam, D. 1982. New hominoid skull material from the Miocene of Pakistan. *Nature* 295:232–34.

———. 1984. The descent of hominoids and hominids. *Scientific American* 250(3):84–96.

Pilbeam, D., G. E. Meyer, C. Badgley, M. D. Rose, M. H. L. Pickford, A. K. Behrensmeyer, and S. M. Ibrahim Shah. 1977. New hominoid primates from the Siwaliks of Pakistan and their bearing on hominoid evolution. *Nature* 270:689–95.

Post, P. W., F. Daniels, Jr., and R. T. Binford, Jr. 1975. Cold injury and the evolution of "white" skin. *Human Biology* 47:65–80.

Potts, M. 1988. Birth control. In *The New Encyclopaedia Britannica.* Vol. 15, pp. 113–20. Encyclopaedia Britannica: Chicago.

Potts, R. 1984. Home bases and early hominids. *American Scientist* 72:338–47.

Rak, Y. 1986. The Neanderthal: A new look at an old face. *Journal of Human Evolution* 15:151–64.

Reader, J. 1986. *The Rise of Life: The First 3.5 Billion Years.* New York: Knopf.

Richard, A. F. 1985. *Primates in Nature.* New York: W. H. Freeman.

Rightmire, G. P. 1985. The tempo of change in the evolution of Mid-Pleistocene *Homo.* In *Ancestors: The Hard Evidence,* ed. E. Delson, pp. 255–64. New York: Alan R. Liss.

Roberts, D. F. 1968. Genetic effects of population size reduction. *Nature* 220:1084–88.

———. 1978. *Climate and Human Variability.* 2d ed. Menlo Park, Calif.: Benjamin Cummings.

Roberts, R. G., R. Jones, and M. A. Smith. 1990. Thermoluminescence dating of a 50,000-year-old human occupation site in northern Australia. *Nature* 345:153–56.

Robins, A. H. 1991. *Biological Perspectives on Human Pigmentation.* Cambridge: Cambridge University Press.

Roche, A. 1979. Secular trends in stature, weight, and maturation. *Monograph for the Society of Research in Child Development* 44:3–27.

Rodman, P. S., and H. M. McHenry. 1980. Bioenergetics and the origin of human bipedalism. *American Journal of Physical Anthropology* 52:103–6.

Rogers, R. A., L. A. Rogers, and L. D. Martin. 1992. How the door opened: The peopling of the New World. *Human Biology* 64:281–302.

Rose, M. D. 1986. Further hominoid postcranial specimens from the Late Miocene Nagri formations of Pakistan. *Journal of Human Evolution* 15:333–67.

Rowell, T. E. 1966. Forest-living baboons in Uganda. *Journal of Zoology, London* 149:344–64.

Roychoudhury, A. K., and M. Nei. 1988. *Human Polymorphic Genes: World Distribution.* Oxford: Oxford University Press.

Schopf, J. W., ed. 1992. *Major Events in the History of Life.* Boston: Jones and Bartlett.

Schopf, J. W., and B. M. Packer. 1987. Early Archean (3.3-billion to 3.5-billion-year-old) microfossils from Warrawoona Group, Australia. *Science* 237:70–73.

Shea, B. T., and A. M. Gomez. 1988. Tooth scaling and evolutionary dwarfism: An investigation of allometry in human pygmies. *American Journal of Physical Anthropology* 77:117–32.

Sheehan, P. M., D. E. Fastovsky, R. G. Hoffman, C. B. Berghaus, and D. L. Gabriel. 1991. Sudden extinction of the dinosaurs: Latest Cretaceous, Upper Great Plains, U.S.A. *Science* 254:835–39.

Smith, F. H., A. B. Falsetti, and S. M. Donnelly. 1989. Modern human origins. *Yearbook of Physical Anthropology* 32:35–68.

Smith, F. H., J. F. Simek, and M. S. Harrill. 1989. Geographic variation in supraorbital torus reduction during the later Pleistocene (c. 80,000–15,000 B.P.). In *The Human Revolution,* ed. P. Mellars and C. Stringer, pp. 172–93. Princeton: Princeton University Press.

Smouse, P. E. 1982. Genetic architecture of swidden agricultural tribes from the lowland rain forests of South America. In *Current Developments in Anthropological Genetics*. Vol. 2, *Ecology and Population Structure*, ed. M. H. Crawford and J. H. Mielke, pp. 139–78. New York: Plenum Press.

Snowden, C. T. 1990. Language capacities of non-human animals. *Yearbook of Physical Anthropology* 33:215–43.

Stern, J. T., Jr., and R. L. Susman. 1983. The locomotor anatomy of *Australopithecus afarensis*. *American Journal of Physical Anthropology* 60:279–317.

Stringer, C. B. 1986. The credibility of *Homo habilis*. In *Major Topics in Primate and Human Evolution*, ed. B. Wood, L. Martin and P. Andrews, pp. 266–94. Cambridge: Cambridge University Press.

Stringer, C. B., and P. Andrews. 1988. Genetic and fossil evidence for the origin of modern humans. *Science* 239:1263–68.

Sutton, H. E., and R. P. Wagner. 1985. *Genetics: A Human Concern*. New York: Macmillan.

Swedlund, A. C., and G. J. Armelagos. 1976. *Demographic Anthropology*. Dubuque, Iowa: Wm. C. Brown.

Szabo, G. 1967. The regional anatomy of the human integument with special reference to the distribution of hair follicles, sweat glands and melanocytes. *Philosophical Transactions of the Royal Society of London* 252B:447–85.

Tanner, J. M. 1989. *Foetus into Man: Physical Growth from Conception to Maturity*. 2d ed., rev. and enl. Cambridge: Harvard University Press.

Templeton, A. R. 1992. Human origins and analysis of mitochondrial DNA sequences. *Science* 255:737.

Terrace, H. S. 1979. *Nim: A Chimpanzee Who Learned Sign Language*. New York: Knopf.

Thorne, A. G., and M. H. Wolpoff. 1992. The multiregional evolution of humans. *Scientific American* 266(4):76–83.

Tobias, P. V. 1971. *The Brain in Hominid Evolution*. New York: Columbia University Press.

Trinkaus, E. 1981. Neanderthal limb proportions and cold adaptation. In *Aspects of Human Evolution*, ed. C. B. Stringer, pp. 187–224. London: Taylor and Francis.

Trinkaus, E., and P. Shipman. 1992. *The Neandertals: Changing the Image of Mankind*. New York: Knopf.

Vrba, E. S. 1985. Ecological and adaptive changes associated with early hominid evolution. In *Ancestors: The Hard Evidence*, ed. E. Delson, pp. 63–71. New York: Alan R. Liss.

Walker, A., R. E. Leakey, J. M. Harris, and F. H. Brown. 1986. 2.5 Myr *Australopithecus boisei* from west of Lake Turkana, Kenya. *Nature* 322:517–22.

Walker, A., and M. Teaford. 1989. The hunt for *Proconsul*. *Scientific American* 260(1):76–82.

Washburn, S. L. 1960. Tools and human evolution. *Scientific American* 203:62–75.

Weeks, J. R. 1981. *Population: An Introduction to Concepts and Issues*. 2d ed. Belmont, Calif.: Wadsworth.

Weiss, K. M. 1973. *Demographic Models for Anthropology*. Memoirs of the Society for American Archaeology, no. 27. Washington, D.C.: Society for American Archaeology.

———. 1984. On the number of members of the genus *Homo* who have ever lived, and some evolutionary implications. *Human Biology* 56:637–49.

Wilford, J. N. 1985. *The Riddle of the Dinosaur*. New York: Knopf.

Willerman, L., R. Schultz, J. N. Rutledge, and E. D. Bigler. 1991. *In vivo* brain size and intelligence. *Intelligence* 15:223–28.

Williams-Blangero, S., and J. Blangero. 1992. Quantitative genetic analysis of skin reflectance: A multivariate approach. *Human Biology* 64:35–49.

Wilson, A. C., and R. L. Cann. 1992. The recent African genesis of humans. *Scientific American* 266(4):68–73.

Wolpoff, M. H. 1980. *Paleoanthropology*. New York: Knopf.

Wolpoff, M. H., W. X. Zhi, and A. G. Thorne. 1984. Modern *Homo sapiens* origins: A general theory of hominid evolution involving the fossil evidence from East Asia. In *The Origins of Modern Humans: A World Survey of the Fossil Evidence*, ed. F. H. Smith and F. Spencer, pp. 411–83. New York: Alan R. Liss.

Woodward, V. 1992. *Human Heredity and Society*. St. Paul, Minn.: West.

Index